His Practice in Modern and Elizabethan English

A Treatise on the Use of

the

Civilian Sword

By Henry Walker

His Practice in Modern and Elizabethan English:

A Treatise on the Use of the Civilian Sword

This edition first published 2022, by Sword and Book Enterprises
Brisbane, Qld, Australia
Copyright © Henry Walker, 2013
Foreword © Richard Cullinan, 2017
Author's Portrait © Julia Robertson, 2018

Neither the author nor the publisher of this text are responsible for any injuries or damage sustained that may occur as a result of using the information found herein. The reader should consult with a qualified physician before attempting any physical activity detailed in this text. Always use safety equipment in any form of weapon sparring.

The author and publisher claim copyright over material which is original and thus written or produced by the author and published by this publisher. All other material previously published not in the public domain is copyright to its original author and publisher. Images which appear in this publication have been taken from original sources, created originally or been given by the owners, and thus are either public domain, owned by the author or have been given permission for their use. All rights reserved. No part of this publication may be reproduced in any form without express permission from the author.

National Library of Australia Catalogue-in-Publication entry:

Walker, Henry Leigh, 1975– author.
His Practice in Modern and Elizabethan English: A Treatise on the Use of the Civilian Sword/ written by Henry Walker; foreword by Richard Cullinan.
Includes bibliographical references and glossary.
Cullinan, Richard, 1969– writer of added text.
290p. 29.7cm.

ISBN 978-0-9876447-2-5 (paperback)

ISBN 978-0-9876447-3-2 (eBook – Adobe PDF)

1.Swordplay; 2.Fencing – Historical; 3. Martial arts – Europe – Fencing
Dewey number: 796.86

Email: hlwalker1975@gmail.com
website: https://afencersramblings.blogspot.com/
website: https://oldewordes.blogspot.com/

DEDICATION

To my parents

who inspired my passion to write

and supported my love affair

with history and the sword,

and to my wife

who inspires me to continue it.

Contents

Acknowledgements	6
Foreword by Richard Cullinan	7
Introduction	10
Advice to Modern Reader	18
Of Language	21
His Practice (Abridged Modern English Version)	24
His Practice in Two Books	161
Afterword	281
Bibliography and Suggested Reading	283
About the Author	286

Acknowledgements

The acknowledgements and dedication written here are different to those written in the treatise to follow, but both apply just as much. I am really fortunate that I get to write two sets. Why two? One is required for the format of the Elizabethan version, and this one could not be missed.

This first set of acknowledgements allows me to thank people who have helped me with writing what you will find in this book, and who helped me develop the skills which are found in this book. The really interesting thing is that some will not even realise that they have done me this great service. I am going to start at the beginning, and this way, I hope not to miss anyone.

To my parents, who allowed me to fly and follow my dreams rather than clipping my wings. To my wife Casey, who keeps picking me up and keeping me going, and putting up with all of the "sword-talk" day-in and day-out. To Stephen Parsons, who put a foil in my hand, got my footwork going, and taught me how to lunge, this was the spark that started the fire; you always have something new for me to learn. To Paul Sawtell, who took a "poker" and helped turn me into a gentleman and a swordsman, I will always remember your lessons. To Richard Cullinan for his help in general, but more to the point with getting the language right, and the foreword. To my poor suffering editors, Chris Slee, Chris Godwin, Adam Kaye, Helen Gilbert, and Sam Baker, thanks for all the work. Also to Keith Farrell for his work and his faith in taking on this project and bringing it to a much-improved state. Thank you to Jen Fraser and Julia Robertson who assisted with bringing this book through to its final stages.

Finally, to all the other teachers who I have learnt from, students whom I have taught and from whom I have learnt, and fencers with whom I have crossed blades, each one of you taught me something about myself and what I was doing.

Last of all is Greg Lott. He gets to go last because this project is all *his* fault.

Foreword by Richard Cullinan

Welcome to the world of historical fencing, where we're all a little bit mad! There is something about the art of swordplay that stirs the soul and in some of us creates a deep lifelong passion. Who knows what it is that drives us to relearn this archaic art, which has little relevance to anything in today's world. Perhaps it's the romance of the sword that is deeply embedded in the core of our cultural psyche as the weapon of the noble and virtuous warrior, or perhaps it is the simultaneous mental and physical challenge it presents to us as individuals attempting to learn the art. All I know is that for some reason we just think swords are cool!

When it comes to the romantic ideal of fencing, the elaborately hilted rapiers of the late 16th century and into the 17th century epitomise the very concept. The sweeping flow of the delicately carved hilts and the fine delicate looking blades belie the deadly nature of this weapon. Here is a weapon intricately linked with the ongoing concepts of honour and justice, especially in the works of Shakespeare and Dumas. It is, however, a weapon of subtlety, that changed the face of fencing from a cut and thrust approach to one that is primarily thrust orientated. It became associated not with the warrior, but with the noble gentleman, which lies at the base of this romantic ideal. It also just happens to be the weapon being taught in this book, which has also received a resurgence in interest in its use for fencing over the last couple of decades. It is also one of the first weapons to benefit from the invention of the movable type printing press.

The fencing manual has a history going back to the late 13th century when a pair of bored clerics wrote about the use of sword and buckler in their spare time, probably pinching office resources to do so! This practice of writing and illustrating systematic fencing knowledge continued across Europe, but it was slow, cumbersome and few copies were made or written when reproduction relied upon handwritten letters and hand drawn illustrations. The 16th century saw this change with the ready access to the printing press which allowed for multiple copies to be quickly made and produced in quantity, fuelling the Renaissance with great works of thought, instruction and philosophy. The use of the sword was considered to be one of the accepted accomplishments for an educated gentleman, so fencing manuals were one of the benefits of this new technology.

We have a curious mix of manuals that have survived down to us today. I like to think that the ones that were written down were the ones from people who survived against real sharp swords and lived to write about it. The reality is probably more that those who could afford to publish were those who wrote the books, but for the Italian manuals it really seems to be the authors are those who were practising fencing masters, looking either for patrons or for students, so a kind of advertisement for their services. We do know there are exceptions to this such as Agrippa's treatise, but it is an exception. Out of all those manuals that survived until now, well, that is more a function of luck than success. Libraries were looted, burnt, bombed or plain out destroyed by the passage of time with no rhyme or reason for what manual survived. We also have the case of private libraries which have various manuals, but no public record catalogue, so we just don't know about them. Even so, we're lucky to have so many manuals to work from today, and we have to work from them on the assumption that what these authors wrote was what worked in real life with sharp swords.

The manuals that have survived have also left us with a researcher's dilemma. Like any human endeavour, fencing has developed its own rich technical language, and in many cases that language is specific to the author. Sometimes they tell us what they mean, and other times they use terms on the assumption that they are common knowledge. For a researcher, we must first understand what the author means by this technical language before we can even begin to interpret and understand the specific actions and sequences being described. Luckily, classical fencing theory allows us to develop some understanding of the purpose behind various actions, as well as how the concepts of time and distance can change the intent or application of these theoretical applications. A historical fencing researcher for needs both a good knowledge of language and fencing theory to make sense of some of these esoteric manuals. Fortunately, we have the likes of people such as Henry to help us in this process, so that we as a community can understand more deeply the treatises left behind by our ancestors. The dilemma then becomes, for us as researchers, how rigidly we must apply our modern fencing theory knowledge, and more specifically how we go about this interpretation process, so that we can develop a reasonable understanding of the material in question. Too rigid, and we miss the subtlety of some of these actions; too loose, and we have basically a back yard free for all that bears no resemblance to the material in question.

Pulling the various threads together to synthesise a viable fencing system is difficult and time consuming. There are many iterations of various actions, and sometimes we find that the actions described in the manuals are predicated on specific actions or responses from our opponents. Modern fencers (especially modern historical fencers) on the whole do not have the same reactions as our ancestors. Our swords are blunt, the risk of injury is low, and the consequences of failure are certainly not life threatening. Most of the manuals we work from are all written from the perspective that the sword is a weapon designed to inflict serious and mortal injury. This modern disconnect can really hinder the development of understanding, because of the lack of respect for the injury potential. The only real way we counter this is to approach the art with the mindset of "what if these swords were sharp?!" This small change in focus can really help eliminate the suicidal approach to the art that can develop due to the lack of fear of bodily harm. In turn, it allows us to be better fencers because we focus our energies on hitting without being hit. The material here certainly follows this precept, leaving you in good stead for becoming competent fencers.

The purists amongst the historical fencing circles are going to look at this material and disregard it because it is not pure to one author or to one group of related authors. This is a shame because the material here has one purpose, and that purpose is to provide a grounding for the beginner historical fencer, so that they can understand and pursue the aspects of the art they are interested in. It's really a grounding in generic Italian fencing theory that is being described here, the theory that laid the foundation for European fencing knowledge from the 17th century onwards. Even in history, we have the likes of Fiore, who tells us he trained with the best teachers across Italy and Germany, and Saviolo who is an amalgam of Italian and Spanish fencing knowledge from the end of the 16th century. Those authors were focused on their primary objective of teaching a fencing system to keep a man alive. Henry's approach reflects this old tradition, but the difference is to describe a system that will be effective in modern tournaments or friendly bouts, using the historical fencing weapons of today. After all, that really the main reason most of us pursue this art, to have some fun with swords with our friends.

Researching and interpreting historical fencing manuals is a long and lonely path to tread. It requires a keen analytical mind, a modicum of physical ability and a certain kind of craziness. It does, however, come with a collection of like-minded individuals, who over the years become firm friends, who provide the support you need to pursue what can at times can feel like a totally frivolous and futile pursuit. The friendships that develop are very long lasting, and over time we end up with connections across the globe. It's a small but passionate community that seem to be one of the last bastions of old-world civility. Maybe there is some truth to the old adage that fencing is the pursuit of gentlemen, because on the whole, I've met many gentlemen through my own passion for this art, from many places around the world. Henry just happens to be one of the original gentlemen I met when I started on my exploration of historical fencing.

So, for those of you reading this and who have reached this point, you may have started wondering why you are reading it! Don't worry - you're just a little bit mad, but it's a madness of a very cool variety, so relax, revel in your madness, and let your passion for swordplay take hold. It will reward you down the years in ways you could never imagine. Welcome to the fold!

Richard Cullinan,

Provost, Stoccata School of Defence

Instructor at Arms, SSU

Introduction

What we have received through the mists of time is but a mere fraction of the swordplay treatises that were written. Just as it is today, different people had their own opinions and concepts about how the sword should be used.

In the Elizabethan period in England, where public education, especially in the native English language, had increased due to the influence of the Tudors and the Reformation, more people began to put their thoughts down on paper and publish for all to read. Wordsmiths of all kinds and calibres published pamphlets and treatises with their various thoughts. The small selection that we have now is perhaps not reflective of the impact and number of the treatises on swordplay which may have existed in this period.

What is presented before you is a treatise written for the use of the civilian sword. The first part is written in Modern English, and the second part is written in Early Modern English, or to be more precise, the London dialect of Early Modern English, spanning a period of 1590 to 1600.[1]

The first part would seem to make sense for modern publication, as it discusses ideas about how the civilian sword of this period should be used in a way which is easy to read and learn. The second part would seem to confuse the issue, without even taking into account the trials of converting our modern language back into a previous version. The question should be asked: why might one consider doing this?

The challenge of language

One of the greatest challenges facing anyone interested in Historical European Martial Arts (HEMA), or indeed the study of anything which is based in a time previous to our own, is that of language. For many people, especially those who are new to studying documents from the past, this is a daunting prospect. Most of the significant rapier treatises were written in the 16th and 17th centuries. This makes the language in them difficult for the modern reader to read unless they have had practice or training. Even with practice reading the language, there is no guarantee that one person's reading will be the same as another's. Does this mean they are wrong? Or that they approached it from a different point of view? The translation effort often scares people off due to these questions, so as a result people often rely on secondary sources and the word of others, never taking that important step toward looking at primary sources and figuring things out for themselves.

The purpose of presenting a treatise in two different languages, one Modern and the other Elizabethan, and the origin being mostly the Modern, is designed to demonstrate that the

---

[1] My research process has been documented in blog format on "Olde Wordes: An Examination of Elizabethan English" (http://oldewordes.blogspot.com/), which describes my study of Early Modern English, and also the process of writing that part of this book. If you go back to the earliest posts, you will find my research into Early Modern English with an Elizabethan focus. A large part of this process was going through documents from the period 1590 to 1600 and extracting individual words (or lexemes) from them to form a lexicon for me to use; a kind of reverse dictionary. This was slow and frustrating work, but most interesting and helpful in the end.

differences in the language are not as stark as people might want to think. This way a passage can be read in a familiar language, and then be read again in something less familiar to see the similarities, thus developing the familiarity and turning it into a less daunting prospect to read. Even for those who have no interest in the operation of the civilian sword, but who are interested in texts where the source is written in Elizabethan English, this book can provide a stepping stone from the modern language to the older language, as every book has some technical language associated with it.

For the translation of further removed foreign languages, such as Renaissance Italian, these have been left to others. The enjoyment derived from merely dealing with the native tongue is sufficient, and the translation from another language and time is another step again. The focus chosen here is one which is closer to the English-speaking audience, as is appropriate to this English-speaking author.

One reason for the presence of two different languages is to familiarise the reader with an older language and make it a less frightening prospect to read other documents written in this language. This is not the only reason for including the two different versions of the treatise: each version has both a different language *and* a different approach to the subject.

The Modern and the Elizabethan

The Modern English version is mainly a theoretical and technical approach to the subject of using the single sword. This kind of approach can be found in many different translations and handbooks which have been produced over the past several years. It goes through all of the pertinent details to allow you to begin to understand how the weapon works. Each section is a building block that builds upon another. The theory lays the foundation, and the practical section based upon this foundation leads to the use of the weapon. The overall format is much the same as the Elizabethan English version, so that the reading of the one can be lined up with the reading of the other, for the study and understanding of the language.

The Elizabethan English version tackles the subject from a similar point of view, but it is not the same. There are different social aspects included in this version of the treatise, aspects that would have been pertinent to a reader in the Elizabethan period but that are less pertinent, in a sense, to the modern practitioner, and it is here that the two versions differ. The subjects of honour and nobility are present in various discussions throughout the treatise in this language version, as these subjects would have been of importance to a reader in the Elizabethan period.

Furthermore, there is an additional *Second Book* in the Elizabethan version, dealing with the subject of duelling and other such pertinent subjects. I decided to leave it out of the modern version as a social exploration of the feelings of the Elizabethan gentry and nobility from my own point of view, to help place this sort of manual within the time period to which it would have been native. For the modern reader, these discussions will most likely be sundry and unnecessary, but they are essential in this Elizabethan version to truly give it the flavour and information the swordsman of the period would have found necessary.

What's the point?

One question that an author needs to ask when writing any sort of book is that of the target audience. Who would be interested in reading the book? Who would gain benefit from the book? In the case of this book, the answer is that hopefully that there is a target audience spanning a reasonably broad set of people. There are some obvious readers who will be interested in reading this book, and there are some who may be less so.

Naturally, there are students of my own who will have been waiting for me to publish this book and wanting me to put something in print for them to read. There are also others out there who are interested in the use of the civilian sword and who, even though they may not use the same method is described in these pages, will gain some benefit from what is described here. Then there are those who have interest in the civilian sword but have just begun their own research, for whom this may be their springboard to go and look at Elizabethan treatises.

For others who have an interest in things Elizabethan, but who are stuck or intimidated looking at documents of the period, this may also provide a way to bridge the gap and enter a wider world. I hope that there may be others out there who would be interested in reading this merely for a different point of view either on the subject of the civilian sword or the social aspects of the Elizabethan period, or even merely for their own pleasure. Needless to say, there is a lot of hope in setting my target, but even if you, the reader, gain only a small amount from what you read, I will count it as a victory.

When writing, the author always has questions to answer. Indeed, the whole aspect of writing a book comes about due to a question. I have explained some of the reasons why I started writing this book, but there is one more reason, the trickiest of them all: one of the greatest challenges of this book was setting down onto paper my own collected knowledge of the single sword.

Previously, I have written textbooks for schools which I have run, along with lesson plans for my students to read. These were all based upon primary and secondary sources; the only way that I could call the work my own was that I collected the knowledge and then placed it in the format that I presented. This book is not to be that sort of thing at all. The information and ideas presented in this book are the techniques and theories which I have stored in my own mind.

What this means is that I sat down to write, I pushed all of the other sources aside, and used only my own memory and knowledge for my reference. This is the reason why you will find no bibliography or cited references of any kind whatsoever present in this book. For a university-trained individual such as myself, who relies on backing up significant points by referencing other sources, this was a hair-raising experience, I can tell you. People may well ask: "So where did it come from? You had to learn it somewhere." That is very true, but the same is the case of all of the masters that we follow all the way back to the beginning. The solution to this problem is having faith in what you know and what you have learnt through using the sword, just as they did. The knowledge presented in this book is knowledge that has stuck with me, not just what I have gained from being taught, but what has become *my* method.

What about the sources?

I do not claim that that what will be presented here will be entirely original as it is all based on my own learning and research. It is based on what has stuck with me and how I use the civilian sword; as such, this is the method that I use, hence the title of the book. What you read may be familiar and similar to other manuals, but the same can be said of many different manuals and masters. There are common elements to all forms of swordplay.

I have been fencing in some fashion now for more than two decades, and fencing with a rapier for almost that entire time.[2] During this time, I have been researching various methods for using the rapier, examining both primary and secondary sources. My own particular favourite period theorists are Vincentio Saviolo and Giacomo di Grassi – another reason for my pre-occupation with the Elizabethan period. Over the past several years, I have also been researching Elizabethan English, for the purpose of writing this book.[3]

In no way would I claim that this is "the one true way" for the use of the rapier. Nor would I claim that it is "the treatise" for learning how to use the rapier, or even for beginning your study of Elizabethan sources. I present "a" way, this one just happens to be mine. The method for using the rapier is the method that I use, or at least what I could remember of it when writing this treatise. I encourage you, dear reader, to ask questions. I encourage you to question my methods and find your own methods to suit yourself. No single method will suit everyone. I would not be surprised if, at a later date, there is a further work dealing with off-hand devices, or even further editions with addendums.

Speaking of editions and addendums, something of the layout and formatting must be noted. The first version of the treatise is written in Modern English, the second version is written in Elizabethan English, and not all of the same information is presented in both versions. For a complete understanding of what I have written, I encourage you to read both parts. The development of your thought processes by reading the Elizabethan English version can only do you good. With the foundation laid by the Modern English version, it should be relatively easy to read, as the two parts say much the same thing about technical issues. It is the issues not of a technical nature where much of the difference appears and much of the "flavour" of the weapon is found. If this "flavour" is not present then it might as well just be another sword.

The treatise

The treatise that I have written is about the use of the single sword, and more specifically, about the use of the rapier, a slender-bladed civilian weapon popular in 16th century English society. The most interesting thing about it is that this weapon has yet to be clearly

---

[2] I started fencing with foil, and practiced this for about six months or so until a relocation forced me away from it. It was about six months later that I found the rapier and began fencing with that, and discovered that I liked it a lot. Looking back, now I understand more of the nuances of the foil, I wish I could have done more, at least in the classical method.

[3] I have included many of the sources that I used for this research in the Bibliography and Suggested Reading. If you are interested in the subject, I would suggest having a look at my blog on the subject as well: http://oldewordes.blogspot.com/2012/05/

defined;[4] however, for the purposes of this book, I define it to be a long, slender-bladed sword, with a complex hilt, a sharp point, and sharp edges. For the most part, the same instruction could apply to any similarly designed weapon with equal effect.[5]

The first thing that you should note about the treatise is that it is a "treatise" rather than a "manual". These are actually two different things, although they are often taken to be the same thing. For the purpose of clarity, I define a "treatise" as giving an explanation of a system and its actions, which may demonstrate the elements of the system in some sort of practical fashion; a "manual" explains the system and also gives practical instruction about how each action should be learnt, and furthermore gives drills for their practice, these explanations and drills being essential parts of "manuals" but not necessarily "treatises". This treatise explains what is to be found in the art and method that I present before you, explains all of the key elements, and does go some way to explaining how techniques should be performed. Unlike a manual, however, it does not have drills and other training aids which would be expected from such a book or other "how to" guide. This is the reason for the method of organisation of the treatise explained below.

The treatise describes the aspects necessary for learning the single sword from the very beginning of the learning process. It starts with teaching the Theory behind the practice, so the student can understand what is going on, and then proceeds with basic descriptions. The Theory has been separated from the Practical so that the theory can be stated clearly rather than becoming disguised amongst practical aspects.

Next comes the Practical section. This gives a practical explanation of the skills based upon the theory presented previously. With the theory already in place, many of the questions a student might normally ask have been addressed already, or can be answered by going back to the Theory. The Practical part of the treatise gives the reader the tools, which are presented in very mechanical form that they can us against an opponent. These tools are reinforced by the Theory.

In the Application section, there are demonstrations of the Practical skills in action with application of the Theory which has been learnt. The result is that the two previous sections really come together in a demonstrative form, and the reader can then see the skills in action between two combatants, and can see how the Theory is applied. These Encounters, the fights between the two combatants, can easily be turned into drills that the reader can train with a partner to learn the system.

The final part present in both versions of the treatise is the Sundry Notes. This section consists of four articles of interest for the swordsman. These assist with using the skills which have been learnt previously, and applying them to different situations. The first

---

[4] There are curatorial discussions which focus on the hilt of the weapon rather than its use. Etymologically, the term "rapier" is only present in two countries for the middle decades of the 16th century. As such, the definition is somewhat confused, even if it is mostly considered general knowledge. See: Walker, 2019. Pages 394-398.

[5] You will note that if you read Giacomo di Grassi's *His True Arte of Defense* (1595) that the method can apply equally to both the rapier and the sword. The original 1570 version did use the word "spada", which means "sword" rather than "rapier" specifically. This treatise approaches the use of the sword with the same effect, with a slight bias toward the longer, slender type of weapon.

article highlights the usefulness of the indirect approach, compared to the direct approach to the opponent. The second discusses the use of a single weapon against various multiple weapons. The third discusses the ever-interesting left-handed opponent, and the final article addresses the true and false arts, which some call feints, but which encompass other elements as well. The Elizabethan version does not finish here, but continues with a *Second Book*, which will be discussed in some more detail shortly. The Modern version also contains a glossary of terms used within it, for the convenience of the reader.

The entire Theory section is based upon five principles. These principles are stated and then explained. What follows is then the various important aspects of fencing theory, both as they apply to fencing and as they will be used throughout the treatise which follows. If the principles are read properly and considered, each piece of theory discussed is either mentioned or implied by one of the principles.

The Practical section starts with the wards or guards, and there is a discussion about the difference between these two terms.

The Practical discussions are designed to build on one another. They start with easier discussions to form a foundation, and then move on to more and more complex subjects. Eventually, once the reader has read through the essential parts of the form, there are sections on the more advanced skills of blade engagement and also the use of time, as it was explained in the Theory previously. These elements are left to the end to ensure that the reader has a grasp of all of the essential skills before attempting the more complex and advanced matters.

The Elizabethan version

The Elizabethan version of the treatise is actually closer to the original manuscript that I first drafted. While the Modern version has been through various edits to make it sound better to our modern ears and to fit our modern grammar, the Elizabethan version has only really been edited for format and other such changes.

This methodology will be described in more detail in a later chapter about methodology and language. Due to the process, the Elizabethan version is actually closer to the spirit of what I wrote originally, and thus to my original treatise, meaning that all questions of the intent should be directed toward the Elizabethan version of the treatise.

Of course, the advantage is that both versions are written by the same author, so the meaning in both will be the same. For the most complete understanding of the text, it is best to read the Elizabethan, as is usually the case in reading historical treatises. The language, once you get used to its idiosyncrasies, is actually very elegant and quite easy both to read and to write. For the most part, the Elizabethan version was much easier to write than the Modern version, due to the lesser restrictions imposed upon the language.

The Elizabethan version uses the language of its day, thus addresses the reader with all the same attitudes and expectations. This also is part of the flavour of the language. There is a special discussion about language and remarks about it in a later chapter, since a separate discussion is required about the differences between Modern English and Elizabethan English and their resulting expression.

There is a contextual note that needs to be made. For the context and dating purposes of the treatise, because the treatise cannot be back-dated to a suitable date in the Elizabethan period, and a suitable individual cannot be chosen from history to whom to address the treatise in the fashion of the treatises of the Elizabethan period,[6] the date format and personas from the Society for Creative Anachronism (SCA) have been used to fill these gaps.[7] This is to allow the flavour of the language and address to be appropriate to the Elizabethan period. This use of personas and titles also allows appropriate Elizabethan naming conventions and other elements that would have been otherwise very difficult to incorporate if simple modern names were used.

The Second Book

The *Second Book* only appears in the Elizabethan version of the manual, along with a couple of other elements of the text and certain elements of the language. This is due to a simplification in the modern language and also a reduction, in some part, of the way that books are introduced in the modern age. The other reason is that the primary subject of the *Second Book* is only really applicable to an Elizabethan or Renaissance audience. These subjects, on the other hand, are timeless, and are as applicable now as they were then.

The *Second Book* discusses the subject of duelling, which was a topic of some prevalence in the Elizabethan period, and in which those who taught arms were considered to be somewhat of an authority. The other subjects are relevant to the subject of duelling, but were also an essential part of the knowledge of the gentleman at the time. While this part of the treatise is loosely based on Vincentio Saviolo's *Second Book* of 1594,[8] and even carries the same title, though the discussion is all made from my own point of view.

There are two subjects indicated by the title *Of Honor and Honorable Quarrels*, but there are actually four main subjects discussed. To address the matter of honour, it is important to include the dichotomous relationship that it carries with dishonour, thus it is important to discuss both honour and dishonour together. Returning to the honourable quarrel, there are all of the details as to how a duel, or honourable quarrel, should be conducted. Finally, there is the discussion of the "fairer sex" who were sometimes at the centre and cause of the duel,

---

[6] Fencing treatises in the Medieval and Renaissance periods were addressed to wealthy patrons, or to potential patrons to encourage them to become patrons. To maintain the feel and flavour of the way things were done in Elizabethan time, and since I felt it inappropriate to address this treatise to real people who have been dead for a few hundred years, I have chosen to use SCA personas as the individuals addressed as patrons or potential patrons, as a suitable workaround to achieve the desired flavour. It should be remembered that since a large part of this publication was inspired by my time in the SCA, and not just as part of the HEMA community, the work is intended to serve both communities.

[7] The dating format for the SCA is to count the years from Anno Societitas (Year of the Society, abbreviated to A.S.), from the beginnings of the Society in 1966 (A.S. I). The new year occurs on the 1st of May each year. Therefore, the year in which I wrote the treatise was 2018, or A.S. LIII. Further, being a Medieval and Renaissance recreation society, titles and such are bestowed upon its members for works and achievements in much the same way as they were during the period being recreated.

[8] If you look at an original or facsimile of Saviolo's work you will see that the *Second Book* is dated 1594, rather than 1595 like the *First Book*.

a subject that di Grassi tells his reader is the purpose of his treatise.[9] Each subject is, in and of itself, important, but together completes the landscape which is duelling.

A challenge

I would also lay a challenge to other experienced swordsmen out there, and I use the word in its most gender-neutral sense, is for you to do what I have done and write your own treatise. Put *your* method on paper for others to learn from.

Early in this introduction, I stated that we only have a fraction of the treatises from the periods which we study. It would be a great loss to lose the skills that we have developed and are developing. We should do our best to ensure that these skills are not lost to time as so many have been; we are only mortal but the words we pen can live on, as can the skills which the words contain.

It is true that we must preserve the skills of those who have come before us, but we must also preserve our own.

---

[9] Di Grassi (1594) explains in his section "To the Reader":

> Therefore it ought not to be exerciſed in Braules and Fraies, as men commonlie practiſe in euerie ſhire, but as honorable Knights, ought to referue themſelues, & exerciſe it for the aduantage of their Cuntry, the honour of women, and conqueringe of Hoſtes and armies.

Advice to the Modern Reader

Different fencing

When we use the term "fencing", the general idea is that of people dressed all in white, wearing masks. They move up and down a specified area at high speeds, striking at each other with bendy, light weapons, and when one or the other is hit a buzzer and light go off. This is not the sort of fencing that will be discussed in this book. What we shall discuss is an older form of fencing that could be considered the grandfather or even great-grandfather of the modern sport.

Fencing with a rapier was in its heyday in the 16th and 17th centuries.[10] This is when the use of the rapier was at its peak, and when it was at the height of fashion. The rapier was a weapon worn at the side as a piece of costume jewellery, but also to defend a person's life, or to settle matters of honour in duels. The combat with this weapon was not sport; it was a martial art. The method presented in this book is an attempt to recreate some of that martial art, admittedly with blunt weapons. This is not about points. This is about the examination of the skills of a contest that once decided life and death.

Not only is the context different, the weapons are different. While they can be as sublimely balanced as any of their modern counterparts in modern fencing, they tend to weigh somewhat more and be somewhat longer. This means that *some* actions possible in the modern art simply will not be found here, but many will appear. These ideas need to be accepted before proceeding further. It is true that some of the skills found in modern fencing are transferable; however, there are also differences which must be accepted.

Different thought

The treatise presented in this book is from no specific "school" of thought or practice. Unlike many of the modern schools of fencing, many of which have their origins in the 18th century, the rapier as a civilian sword was less confined to such "schools" of thought and practice. It is true that many extant treatises can be traced back to certain "traditions", as they could be called, but each author added their own thoughts as well. In this case, like some historical treatises, information has been adopted from multiple sources to form what is presented here, and this is also documented in Renaissance practice also.

The modern fencer will find that some terminology will be familiar. In some instances, it will even mean the same thing, but this must not be taken for granted, as it will not always be the case. There have been changes in the meanings of words in fencing terminology over time, and to assume that the words mean the same thing in all cases will leave the modern fencer and indeed the modern reader confused. Renaissance combat has a lexicon of its own and this must be learnt along with the physical actions to truly understand what is going on.

The theory which is found herein will also be familiar to anyone who has studied fencing, and will also be somewhat familiar to those who have studied other martial arts. This is

---

[10] This refers to when this weapon was most popular in Europe. The Spanish continued with it into the eighteenth-century at least.

because of a common foundation that they all share. Even with this familiarity, it is vital to pay attention to the theory. This forms the foundation of the art which is being expressed in the pages following. The theory explains how actions are possible and why the combatants would perform the actions in the way that they do rather than in a different manner.

Different organisation

Unlike the modern fencing book, which often includes theory, practice and application presented all together, the following treatise has these matters clearly divided into sections. This was a common practice especially in the later periods when the rapier was used. This will seem odd to some, and a little jarring at first, but suits the presentation of the material.

There is an advantage to this method of organisation, since the Theory, upon which all of the Practical is based, is presented first. This also establishes the fencing language which is used throughout the following parts, meaning that there is no need to stop and explain terminology in the middle of an explanation of an action. This allows for a better flow for the explanation of the actions during the Practical section. This same form of explanation is then established for the demonstrations of the actions found in the third part of the treatise, where it all comes together in the Application.

The Theory section will be the part which you will probably find the driest and the dullest in most cases, but it is also the most necessary. Without an understanding of how the theoretical elements are used and explained, and of course the terminology used to explain them, it will be very difficult to understand how the actions work in the following sections.

The second part is the Practical section, and for the most part this explains the practical skills that the fencer will use to perform the art which is described by the treatise. In some parts of this section, there is also a practical explanation of how the theory (which has been previously explained) works, but on a very practical level. This is where the book teaches the techniques that form the foundation of the system.

The third part is the Application section. This describes how both the theory and the techniques are applied against an opponent in various different scenarios or Encounters. These are representative combats between two fencers to demonstrate what has been presented in the two previous sections.

The fourth part is the Sundry Notes. These are short descriptions of elements that are important to the art and that assist in its application, but that did not fit into any of the previous sections. They cover important aspects of the use of this sword that usually do not come up until it has been used for a while, or at least learnt and then applied against an opponent. The subjects presented are: The Advantage of the Circle Over the Line, Single Against All, Of the Left-Handed Opponent, and Of the True and False Arts.

This is where the Modern version ends, the Elizabethan version continues with *Book II: Of Honour and Honourable Quarrels*. This is where the Elizabethan version delves into the mind and mentality of the swordsman and the reasons why one would use the sword. This is where the two versions are most starkly demonstrated to be different, but is not the only such place.

In this *Second Book*, the reader will find discussions on subjects of great importance to the (Elizabethan) swordsman. Subjects that will be found include such things as honour, dishonour, and the nobility of women. There is also a large section on the "honourable quarrel" that most would call a duel today. Many treatises of the period discussed duelling and posed questions about how a person should approach one; such subjects are quite foreign to the modern mind and also the modern fencing manual, making it an interesting topic to explore here from the Elizabethan point of view.

Different language

The Modern English version of the treatise is presented first, even though it was really written second. This is actually quite significant, especially if you want to understand the complete method in its raw form with all of its angles; you will need to read the Elizabethan version and understand all of it. While the Modern version is in essence the same, the Elizabethan version and the understanding of what it contains will help you to access other Elizabethan texts and thus gain a greater understanding of both the treatises and the minds of the period.

For a modern student delving into the past, especially if you have just begun your research into Renaissance treatises and the civilian sword, this is a great place to start. There is only the "noise" of the language itself between the original and the translation, as it is the same author who has written both versions. It is this "noise" which creates some of the greatest barriers to understanding what an author actually meant when their words were written down. Thus, without as much "noise", or in this case only the "noise" of the two languages themselves, there is a much clearer path to understanding the art which is presented.

Different uses

When a treatise presented in two languages, it offers different options, especially when the author is the same for both. This means that this treatise is also of use to those individuals who do not have an interest in swordplay but do have an interest in Elizabethan English. This widens the use of the treatise to include other people and other interest areas. As previously indicated, it can serve as a gateway to the reading of Elizabethan English and thus to manuals and other texts written in this language.

For those of a more sword-like nature, this fencing method may be different, but it still works. Indeed, if it did not, I would not have put it to print, nor continued to teach it or use it. The Encounters can be used, with the proper applied Theory and Practical as described, as drills to formalise the system which is presented here. Each one is a single Encounter with a single result making it easily repeatable, and thus perfect for a drill. Once a fencer gains the experience of what the Encounter is attempting to teach, then the fencer can substitute skills and change them to change the drill; but for this to make sense, the whole system must be understood properly.

Each one of the differences which have been pointed out in this chapter actually highlights a different use for the treatise. It is up to the reader to take advantage of these options and opportunities.

Of Language

There are some notes that must be made regarding the language in the treatises to follow. This is both to explain some of the choices that have been made and also to describe from where the language has originated.

Two versions

The two versions of the treatise are both are in English, but one is in Modern English and the other is in Elizabethan English. In other words, they are both in English, but in different types of English separated by a wide gulf of time, approximately 400 years. This time gap creates a meaningful difference for some very crucial elements in the language.

The Modern version is presented for ease of reading and for those who are primarily interested in the technical aspects of the art.

The Elizabethan version is for those who are interested in learning about the differences in language and social elements, which are introduced through the choice of language.

Research and translation

With regard to the language, for the convenience (and because it is more accurate) at least with the discussion of language, Modern English (or ME) will be referred to as Present Day English (or PDE), both of which are technical terms for the language,[11] and Elizabethan English, which is a sub-group of Early Modern English (EModE), will be referred to as Elizabethan English or EE. More precisely, the Elizabethan treatise uses the London Dialect, also known as the Southern Dialect. To be even more specific, the decade of the 1590s was chosen for the collection of words from Elizabethan texts. This is due to the dominant nature of the dialect in the period, and the location where a treatise (such as that found in this book) would have been most likely published, according to my own research into the rapier.

Before beginning to translate the treatise to EE, I already had a rough draft in PDE. I decided it would be advantageous to undertake a thorough research into the language that I was going to use. Thus, I conducted research beginning mostly quite humbly in 2011 with examining fencing texts,[12] and progressing to the examination of the language itself in a much more complex form.[13] It was through this process that I learned about the various dialects of Elizabethan English and developed a greater appreciation for writers such as Shakespeare (regardless if he be a single individual or many ghost writers was gained) and

---

[11] For brevity and comprehension, in other parts of this book I have referred to the modern language as Modern English rather than Present Day English, as the term may be more familiar to readers.

[12] My research into period manuals actually started sometime in the late 1990s, but this was for techniques rather than the language.

[13] I thought it was just going to be a matter of changing some spelling and formatting here and there. Well, it wasn't, and I am not one to do things by half.

others from the period. It was only after I completed this research that I translated the treatise to EE.[14]

My original draft of the treatise was written in PDE but in the format of EE, i.e. long paragraphs and a lack of sub-headings. I then translated this PDE into EE. From here, I separated the editing of the two versions.

The EE version was edited in elements to make the document more authentic to the language it portrays. The PDE version, on the other hand, was edited to suit modern conventions of language, to make it more readable for the modern reader.

Technical language

Fencing has its own terminology. Some of these words are in English, some are in Italian or French, and some are in other languages. In both versions of the treatise in this book, you will find both English words and Italian words, as both have been used where technical terminology has been required. This would seem relatively simple and straight forward, but some explanation is required.

Where possible, technical language has been presented in English. There is a simple understanding of intent with regard to the words used, and also some of the words are not used in their traditional forms as according to traditional fencing terminology. The different meanings need to be noted and applied where the word is used in the treatise. If these different understandings are not observed, then the system will not work.

Some Italian words have been used where there is no suitable translation into English to portray all of the subtlety and nuances required of the term. In the case where an Italian term is used, it maintains its original meaning according to fencing terminology.

Period-appropriate language

A special note needs to be made with regard to language with regard to gender: the language has been kept appropriate to its period.

What this means is that the PDE version has been written with a more considerate attitude with regard to gender, as will be noted in the introductory part of the treatise. The EE version has been written as it would have been in the 16th century, and therefore it includes the role of the female fencer in the introductory parts, but it is definitively more paternalistic and more male-centric as can be expected from a document in the language of that period.

I spent some amount of time considering this particular issue and how it could be resolved; but for the purposes intended by this book, the paternalistic tone of the EE version could not be changed, as this would greatly alter the feel of the overall document and negate the attempt to produce a document that had the sound and feel of a document from the Elizabethan period.

---

[14] If you are interested in my research of Elizabethan English, I wrote a blog about it with articles appropriate you can find it here: http://oldewordes.blogspot.com.au/

Nonetheless, I feel that it is important (if not imperative) to say that such pursuits of the blade should be encouraged for everyone. Every single person can gain from the great advantages given by learning the arts of the sword, regardless of gender or any other difference.

Personas and Place Names

There are names and referred to in the Elizabethan, I have used names and places from an SCA (Society for Creative Anachronisms) context. The result is that I have used my persona name, Henry Fox as the author's name and changed locations and the addressee of the dedication of the Elizabethan version to his persona name. I felt this was the best idea because there was no point in dedicating the treatise to some dead lord, rather to a friend who could actually use the knowledge herein. The use of such gives the completeness which is found in the Epistle Dedicatory, and other parts found in this part of the book.

Some would claim that such personas are unsuitable and fictional, however members of the SCA live these personas each time they participate in the events they go along to, develop stories to explain the lives of these individuals, and even have to describe them as aliases in a legal sense. The geographical groups are legal entities having legal requirements and so forth which affect the "real" world. Henry Fox, the name under which the Elizabethan part of this book is written under is as much a part of me as any nickname or pet name my relations might call me, or any ghost-writing name that any author might use.

Henry Walker: His Practice

(Abridged Modern English Version)

Sword and Book Enterprises,

Brisbane, 2022

Dedication

To Alex West,

You have demonstrated skill in arms and an interest in the knowledge which accompanies it as such I submit the following for your perusal and edification on the subjects presented. This is a collection of my own knowledge of the subjects elucidated. It is my hope that you will gain greater knowledge from the effort which has been put into this endeavour and see the knowledge profitable enough that you would pass such knowledge on to others.

Henry Walker

Introduction

Many treatises and manuals written extol the virtues of various different theories and the combative arts associated with them. For the most part, these result in approaches with disparate theories and ideas about how the sword should be used and often result in confusion how a weapon should be used. This is due to the different points of view taken by the different proponents of these theories. This treatise is written to collect and codify the collected knowledge of one swordsman in a single place.

Method and Theory

The method and theories presented are mine. This means it is new, but is based upon the collected knowledge of those theories assimilated from other theorists and learned while using the weapon against various opponents over an extended period of time. This treatise does not merely repeat the theories and principles of other masters, but is a collection of various elements from such masters collected and refined to a single method. While the method is new, it will also be familiar to those proponents of the arts of defence and their students.

Theory and Practice

From the various treatises and manuals written by various masters and theorists it can be noted that some will write their systems purely from theory, having no experience in the practice of the art. Some on the other hand, write purely from the use of the sword, and learning their art only from in the same fashion, denying the use of any particular theory, gaining their knowledge through experience with the weapon only.

Both of these "stand-alone" systems are flawed and need to be addressed. Those which learn only from theory have no practical experience. Thus, no knowledge of how the weapon actually moves in combat. They base their practice on mathematical and physical theory, but with no understanding of the pressures of combat and how they relate to its practice. Those who only learn from practical experience also have a flawed method. They do not understand why their method works or do not from a theoretical point of view. Thus, cannot explain why or how the system works adequately for another to learn it, save by practical demonstration.

What is missed in the pure theory is found in the practical, and what the practical is missing is found in the theory. Both approaches need to be combined to gain a complete understanding of a system. It is due to the flaws in both of these methods that this treatise will have practical elements of the sword based upon a theoretical basis, but applied to practical use of the weapon. The method presented provides both a theoretical and practical basis for the system.

There are many different paths to take to find the truth, but in the end a person will find that all paths will lead to the same truth, that the art is one which encompasses many different concepts and principles. The search which has resulted in the production of this treatise has resulted in one method developed from several different paths and views of the arts of the sword. Finding in the end, that while some theories and aspects of the art are different, in the end their commonalities are greater than their differences, and that such an approach can be applied to other discussions for a similar result and resulting in a greater expanse of knowledge than was first realised.

Organisation

For the presentation of the method described and such is the nature of the skills presented, that they are displayed in such a fashion that the foundations of the art are presented first in the theoretical elements. These theoretical elements are then supported by the practical elements, with sundry notes to follow which apply to their application in a practical sense. Foundations need to be laid first and the Theory presented so that the mind is in suitable condition to accept the Practical, and therefore resulting in a unification of mind and body to the purpose of the art presented here.

The theoretical elements presented, describe those parts which can only be seen with the knowledge of them, due to the speed of the techniques and the nature of the skills presented. Without the suitable explanation provided by the Theory the Practical cannot be understood properly and utilised in suitable fashion in a practical form. The Practical and Theory need to be presented and linked as such for the reader to gain the greatest benefit from both and to appreciate and attain the most from the system presented.

The Practical presented in these pages is based on a foundation which can be discovered in many other practices of the sword. Then taking such a foundation and practicing diligently to gain skill in the practice of the skills of the art. The skills expressed and described in this treatise are founded upon what has been discovered over an extended period of time of practicing with the sword, engaging with opponents, and in the research of various methods and theories of the use of the sword. This resulted in the discovery of the method presented gained through those methods which lead to the truth of the sword described and discarding only that which is not founded in true defence.

In Ferro Veritas (In Steel is Truth)

One of the virtues of the sword is that it reflects the nature of the individual who wields it. This treatise is designed to promote only those higher qualities and encourage the reader to engage only in those practices which will promote their renown through the use of the sword. The inner nature of the individual is reflected in their physical actions and those things which are quantifiable by presented actions. The nature of the sword is that in its speed, it does not allow sufficient time for an individual to carefully cover those negative aspects of their nature to be sufficiently hidden. Consequently, a system which is based on attributes of pure aggression and brute force will be exposed, as will a system which promotes the more noble qualities of the spirit and the intellectual facilities of the individual.

Mind and Body

The practice of arms has proven to be of great benefit to the person who would engage in it. Being that it is an exercise of both the mind and the body, it gives benefit to both in which other exercises may focus on either. From the more physical side, the practice of arms in a diligent fashion not only provides the fencer with the skills to defend themselves but also uses their muscles enhancing them physically in their pursuit. From the mental side of the person, the use of the knowledge of the art increases the thinking ability of the practitioner in that they gain the ability to solve problematic situations. The pure exercise of the mind to divine the best defence against the attack of an opponent increases the mental faculties of the practitioner; as a result, benefiting them in other situations.

The art of the sword is the definition of art and science combined into a single pursuit being that it is of both mind and body. The mind interprets and gains knowledge of the science while the body practices the art as defined by the science in a practical fashion. The lack of either the mind or the body in this will result in the lack of either art or science in the practice. Thus, it must be a combination of both body and mind to ensure that the skills are used in their correct fashion.

Benefits

Without doubt the practice of the art of the sword provides great benefit to the body of the practitioner and indeed it increases the longevity of the individual who chooses to practice it. The physical exercise of the art along with diligent practice in it provides such movement of the body and exercise of the limbs that assists the practitioner physically, leading to a healthier body overall.

Some of the benefits of the mind have already been expressed in that it increases the mental faculties of the practitioner and increases their ability to solve problems, but the practice of the art and science of the sword is also good for the temperament of the individual. The practice and learning as well as the exercise of arms teach patience and control over the emotions to have a greater advantage over the opponent. This ability to control that which is internal can then result, with the correct application, in the ability to gain advantage over the opponent and such abilities can be used in other situations for the same advantage.

To the Fencer

Any time a word is seen where the suffix or prefix "man" is used, you should realise that this comes from the Latin *manus* ("the hand", thus, "to operate"). In such meaning "swordsman" has the meaning of "hand that operates the sword". No further declaration of gender should be read into it. Further, you will note that the language in this text which follows occasionally uses a male pronoun to address the reader. This is a further extension of the same meaning and for simplification of the language.

The form of language in no way precludes a fencer of any gender from taking part or learning from the information which is presented before you. Indeed, it is established and recommended that all who take part in fencing can gain all of the physical and mental benefits which have been described herein. The pursuit and practice of arms is suitable for all who would choose to engage in it. Such pursuits of the blade should be encouraged in all.[15]

---

[15] For the left-handed fencer, as will be noted in the subject of Lines, it is merely a swapping of Lines which is necessary to accommodate the left-hander's learning. Most of the instruction that has been given has been without hand reference, so a left- or right-handed student can use them. When the

Individual Application

Of all the things that can be said about the arts of defence it is the individual's application of the skills which gains or reduces the benefit of the skills used. It is also the individual's application which results in whether or not those skills are practiced for noble or ignoble reasons and results. Should the individual choose the skills can be used for the greatest renown and honour, or the greatest notoriety and dishonour found. The skills found in this work are designed to be used in the most noble of situations and for the most noble of reasons found.

Theory

The Five Principles

The principles upon which something is based are the foundations which are laid. The other parts are those which are placed upon those foundations. It is therefore necessary that such principles are presented first so that you may understand upon what foundations the rest of the art being discussed is founded. An explanation of such principles is essential to comprehend what is meant by the principles being presented.

The principles are those elements which underlie all of the following theoretical and practical elements of this treatise. Knowledge of such principles is essential to understand the perspective from which the presented information which is presented. There are five principles which are the most important to the understanding of the material and instructions found in this treatise and they are found below.

1. Being the "Art of Defence", defence will always have priority over offence.
2. The straight line is the shortest distance between two points.
3. Every movement is accomplished in Time, and Time is used in every movement.
4. Practice is required for the fencer to improve and for the attainment of skill.
5. The fencer who dominates movement and action, dominates the combat.

These principles are the fundamental rules upon which my system of fencing is based. Each needs to be discussed in some detail so that they can be understood properly.

The First Principle

The first principle describes what the entire Art is based upon. Therefore, it is the most important. It is the "Art of Defence", and as such, the priority is that the fencer defends himself and keeps himself safe. Thoughts of offending the opponent are always secondary to a successful defence. However, the successful defence should always be followed by an offensive action against the opponent.

The Second Principle

The second principle is a simple statement of fact, but alludes to other elements which are important to the knowledge of the fencer. The straight line is the shortest distance between two points, which means that any offensive action which follows a straight line to the opponent is more effective and efficient than one that does not. Following this principle, the thrust has the advantage over the cut due to the straight line that is used by the point, though the edge should not be discarded as it has times of usefulness.

The Third Principle

Distance affects Time, and Time affects Distance, and these two elements are present in this principle in that it describes an element which involves both Time and Distance. Since the straight line is shorter in distance, it is also shorter in time taken. As such the combination of

Time and Distance is essential knowledge. The third principle describes the importance of Time.

As every movement is accomplished in Time, and every movement results in use of Time, the smaller amount of time that is used in an action, the more efficient it is. Extraneous movements in the performance of an action use and waste time, and also make it less efficient than it could be. This is discussed further in the fourth principle.

The Fourth Principle

Practice is required for the fencer to improve and for the attainment of skill. This improvement is the result of the refinement of the skills which he possesses and the introduction of new skills. The refinement of the skills reduces and removes extraneous movements in the performance of actions and makes the fencer more effective as a result. Practice is of great importance to the fencer if he wishes to improve and maintain his skills. A fencer can never do too much practice.

The Fifth Principle

Once a fencer has attained a level of skill, he can use this skill to manipulate encounters between himself and his opponents. The fencer can then apply the fifth principle and can dominate movement, and action dominates the interaction between him and his opponent. This is where the knowledge of Time and Distance becomes essential to know how it can be manipulated. Through this the opponent can manipulate the encounter to his advantage.

The principles which have been presented are those upon which the following discourse is based. These principles should be kept in mind both as this treatise is read and also as the fencer performs the actions of fencing. These principles will apply in both a theoretical and a practical sense. The following elements of theory will reinforce the ideas presented here and go into a more in-depth explanation of many of the principles presented here.

On Time

Time and Distance are the two primary principles upon which all fencing and indeed all martial combat is based. There are even places where it is impossible to separate Time from Distance and vice versa. If fencing is to be understood, then Time must first be understood, as it is a key concept.

The third principle, that "every movement is accomplished in Time, and Time is used in every movement", was described previously and alludes to the importance of Time. Time is related to all movement. Accordingly, Time is a part of every motion in fencing. The idea of the relationship between movement and Time is the key to understanding Time in fencing and those concepts which surround it.

Tempo

Time is often called *Tempo*, and this is related to actions. *Tempo* is used to describe actions rather than portions of Time, though sometimes they are the same. These portions are always associated with actions or inaction on the part of the fencer, both being necessary to one another. An example of a *Tempo* is a thrust or a step. *Tempo* is not used to describe

Cadence, or the flow of a combat. This is a different concept and will be described later. A *Tempo* is not concrete measure but is fluid and may be extended or shortened through manipulation. Put very simply, a *Tempo* is an action, or a period of action or inaction.

Timing

Time and Timing are two different things and it is possible to have one and not the other. It is the difference between what is found in treatises and what is seen in actual movement. This is a prime demonstration of the difference between the "art" and the "science" of fencing, the former, Time, being the "science" and the latter, Timing, being the "art". It is possible to understand Time but not have Timing. Timing is the practical application of the knowledge of Time, and comes about through the practical use of weapons and takes time to develop. Knowing Time means knowing when and how to deliver the blow; Timing is actually delivering the blow at the correct time. This is the difference between theoretical knowledge and practical knowledge of the same actions.

Wasting Time

Included within this concept of Time is also the proper performance of an action, so that it takes the proper amount of Time in delivery; so, arrives with the proper Timing. Thus, includes using and wasting time. Time is used when an action is performed properly, the *Tempi* are used properly and the blow is delivered with Timing. Wasting Time happens when an action is performed lazily or sloppily, and as a result, the action is larger and is performed without Timing.

To perform an action efficiently and hence, with Timing, it is important to practice. This reduces the amount of time taken in the performance of the action as the more practiced actions are more efficient in their movements. This applies to all the actions of fencing from the simplest to the most complex. The idea of a technique being performed with Timing is seen in the concept of an action performed "In Time", which is most often applied to an offensive action and will be discussed later.

Cadence

Cadence is the usual consideration of *Tempo* as the term is usually applied. This considers the flow of combat between two combatants and how this relates to the combatants. This is different to other concepts of Time found in fencing as it is not segmented but considers how fast actions are performed and the reactions from the combatants.

Cadence is determined by the performance of the actions and the gaps between them. Time in fencing is fluid and flows between the combatants and is not rigid, or like turns. Actions occur actively, as a result of another action, simultaneously or even independent of the action of the opponent. Cadence decides how fast the actions between the two combatants are performed. This is also determined by reaction time and skill.

Priority

Related to the concept of Cadence is the idea of Priority. This particular aspect of fencing is most important when in close but is also important at distance. When actions are being performed, if a fencer is not performing an offensive action, they do not have Priority and as such should be looking to their defence. The combatant with Priority is the one who is actively attacking. There are some ideas which will be discussed later on which will relate to this concept.

The most important part of Priority is that the fencer who does not have Priority should ensure that they are safe before any other action is performed. Breaking Priority is how to gain it, what needs to happen is that the defensive player needs to become the offensive player and in such gain Priority. This is also related to the idea of Breaking Time, which will be discussed under the Manipulation of Time.

Time of the Hand and Foot

In general, either the hand moves or the foot moves and the body will follow. This brings about consideration of what is called the Time of the Hand and the Time of the Foot. These two concepts discuss which should be moved first, the hand or the foot and their speed. It also considers how the body should follow.

The Time of the Hand discusses the movement of the hand and, as a result, the weapon attached to it. It also considers the movement of the arm, regardless of whether it holds a weapon or not. The Time of the Foot considers the movement of the foot and the leg, in other words footwork. There is a third time and that is the Time of the Body. This is where the body and head are moved.

The Time of the Hand is the fastest and for the most part will be moved first. The Time of the Foot is slower than the Time of the Hand and for the most part will be moved second. The Time of the Body is the slowest and will always be moved last. These are the true times of the hand, foot and body. There will be few exceptions to this rule.

True Times and False Times

A False Time is one that will lead the player into a dangerous situation.

Any movement of the body (regardless of torso or head) which happens before the Time of the Hand or the Foot, is a False Time.

In attack, the hand will be moved before the foot. This is a True Time. In attack, if the foot moves before the hand, this is a False Time. In attack if the body moves before the hand, this is a False Time.

In most cases in defence, it is the Time of the Hand that will be moved before the Time of the Foot. This is a True Time.

In movement across the ground, the foot will be moved before the body, and this is a True Time. In movement across the ground, if the body moves before the foot, this is a False Time.

A practical example of the Times is as follows: if a fencer moves his body into Distance of his opponent before his weapon there is a high chance that he will be struck. If the same fencer moves his weapon into Distance before his body, the opponent will have to react to the weapon before attacking the fencer. This demonstrates the importance of the use of the Time of the Hand before the Time of the Foot. This demonstrates the danger of the False Times and the advantage of True Times.

Fencing Time

Time has been discussed in some quite general terms. There are some more specific aspects of Time, and terms which accompany it, which are vital to understand Time and, as a consequence, fencing. These terms relate to specific instances in the flow of combat. These instances are usually used in response to the action of an opponent against the fencer. This would imply that they are mostly reactive, but this is not necessarily the case.

Double Time

For the beginner fencer, complex actions are broken down into simple actions, so the fencer can learn to perform these actions precisely. For example, in the defence and counter, these elements are separated into two actions, or *tempi*. This form of technique, where the defence and attack are made as two actions, is called Double Time. There is a single action for defence, often a parry, and a single action for the counter-attack, often a thrust. This enables the fencer to be sure in their defence as a focus, and then lead on to the attack as a following action.

As a fencer improves and the actions become more precise, these can be blended into a single *tempo*. It is more important that the fencer is sure of his defence. Thus, would be better for the fencer to stay with Double Time until his actions become precise in their movements. Even more advanced combatants will still use Double Time at least some of the time to ensure their defence. This follows the First Principle that defence has priority over offence.

Single Time

The Single Time response to an opponent's action is a more advanced technique than Double Time, and it takes a deal of precision to perform it properly. The Single Time action combines the defence and counter-attack into a single fluid action. The counter-attack is placed where it will both defend the fencer and offend the opponent in a single movement of the sword.

This requires the techniques to be performed with precision and so takes practice. It also requires knowledge of many of the aspects of fencing theory, especially Lines. If performed sloppily or inaccurately the fencer may end up struck in the process. It is imperative that the fencer ensures that his defence is in place so that he is not struck in the process of his action, as stated in the First Principle. The Single and Double Time responses are usually made in response to an opponent's action and defend as part of their process. There are other times which attack directly into the opponent's attack or interrupt it.

Counter-Time

Counter-Time is literally against the Time. It is against the flow of combat and also against Priority. What this means is that the action is performed as a response to the opponent's attack, but rather than defending, the fencer attacks into the opponent's attack.

This is an action which requires a lot of Timing and practice. As the fencer is attacking directly into the opponent's attack, another form of defence is often required to ensure that the fencer remains safe in his action. Disregarding the defence can result in the fencer being struck in the process of his action. Doing this correctly is one way for the fencer to break Priority.

Half-Time

Half-Time is actually not a measurement of Time at all it, but describes the Timing of the action in comparison to where an action would normally be performed. The Half-Time attack is a direct attack against the opponent's action and is designed to interrupt and arrest the opponent's attack before it is completed. It is called Half-Time because it happens in the middle of the opponent's *Tempo*, stopping it before it is completed.

An example of this is an attack by the fencer, to the hand of the opponent, as the opponent makes a cut or thrust against the fencer. The action of the fencer interrupts the action of the opponent so that he cannot complete it. There is no need for a defensive action as the attack is defeated before it is completed. However, it is better for the fencer to make some sort of defensive action to ensure his safety. This is an advanced technique requiring a great deal of precision and Timing on the part of the fencer. If the technique is not performed properly or accurately with the correct Timing, the fencer can be left in a lot of trouble.

In Time

An action performed "In Time" is an action performed at the correct Time resulting in the opponent being struck and the fencer remaining safe. It is also a situation manipulated to result like this. The fencer must have Timing to act In Time. In most instances, to act In Time, the fencer merely needs to deliver an attack when the opponent is most vulnerable and in such a way that he remains defended. This is entirely dependent on the technique being used and is used in regard to both simple and advanced techniques. It is the result of the opponent being struck and the fencer not, which is the key.

Relationships of Fencing Times

The relationships between the various times are important as it assists in the understanding of each one as they are all related. The longest time is obviously the Double Time as it takes two actions and so two *Tempi*. This being the case, it would suggest that the Half-Time is the shortest being the shortest number of *Tempi*, but this is not necessarily the case.

It is the length of the action which determines the length of the *Tempo*. What this means is that Single, Counter and Half-Time actually are all the same length as they all use a single action with the weapon. Other actions performed in the same *Tempo* do not lengthen the *Tempo*. Further relationships can be discovered.

There is a simple relationship between Single and Double Time, and indeed between Single and all the other times. Simply stated the Double Time action is the one used by beginners as it ensures that the defensive action can be the focus and then focus is shifted to the offensive. The other times, Single, Counter and Half all are times which blend a defensive action with an offensive action, and these must be done smoothly and precisely in order to succeed. This is the reason that Double Time is taught first and the others afterward.

Single Time, Counter-Time, and Half-Time are often confused with one another. Often this is because the theory is not clearly stated or the demonstrations of them do not adequately demonstrate the differences. All three are similar in that they use a single *Tempo* to achieve their goal. However, there are differences. Single Time uses the weapon in a defensive motion to defend while at the same time attacking. In Counter-Time the weapon is most often not used defensively and the fencer must use some other defence. It is the same with Half-Time; and this difference clearly proves that Single Time is different to both.

Counter-Time and Half-Time are also confused with each other, just as they are with Single Time. Both use a single *Tempo* to achieve their goals, and use another form of defence beside the weapon in defence. However, in Counter-Time the counter is made directly into the opponent's attack. Whereas, Half-Time, on the other hand, counters the opponent's attack before it is completed, interrupting it before it can become effective. Hence, in Counter-Time the attack of the opponent is made and completed, whereas in Half-Time the attack is stopped part way through the action.

Manipulation of Time

The manipulation of Time is something that the accomplished fencer will purposefully do and sometimes the novice fencer will achieve by accident. To manipulate Time, it is necessary to understand all of the theory with which it is associated. Consequently, to achieve it by design, it must be combined with precise movements of the weapon and body, and have good Timing. The fencer must know when and how Time can be manipulated in his actions against an opponent. The final element of manipulating Time is imposing the change on the opponent and this is the hardest part.

Both *Tempo* and Cadence can be increased and decreased. A fencer can simply take longer to perform an action or can speed up an action to manipulate the *Tempo*. The same can be said for Cadence.

If a fencer wants to increase the Cadence then he should move faster and perform more actions. If a fencer wants to decrease the Cadence, the fencer simply moves slower and performs fewer actions. Increasing the Cadence is more difficult than manipulating the *Tempo* as this requires the opponent to respond in kind. It is simpler to increase the Cadence than decrease it, but the decrease can be made by breaking from the encounter frequently to slow it down. This requires the effective use of footwork and Timing.

The times themselves can be used to manipulate the situation. Especially, they can be used to manipulate the Priority. A fencer can really only successfully manipulate the Time, if he has Priority and is dominating the encounter. If the fencer is not dominating it is much more difficult to manipulate the Time.

Changing from Single or Counter-Time responses to Double Time responses will slow the Cadence of the encounter because more *Tempi* are being used. Doing the reverse will increase the Cadence as the opponent will have to respond faster to the actions. Breaking the Priority and therefore dominance of the opponent is best achieved through the use of Half- and Counter-Time actions. This reverses the active and passive roles and forces the opponent to react to the fencer.

The Time must be chosen properly so that this can be achieved effectively. The same can be achieved any time the opponent breaks from the encounter or stops an action. This involves reading the opponent correctly and having good Timing.

Breaking Time

Breaking Time is an effective method of manipulating Time and manipulating the opponent into a worse situation. Breaking Time is simply achieved by lengthening the *Tempo*. This is easiest achieved by pausing during an action; as a result, pausing the *Tempo*. Breaking Time is a technique that must be performed unexpectedly to catch the opponent off-guard.

The technique is designed to force the opponent to move out of position and so, open a hole for the fencer to attack. An example of Breaking Time is to make a thrust but pause in the middle of it, and then complete the thrust. If the opponent reacts early to the thrust, he will be moved out of position and past where the blade will be by the time the action is completed. This technique takes an amount of skill and Timing to achieve its result.

Time is one of the keystones of fencing and any fencer who wants to achieve any real level of skill in fencing needs to understand it and be able to apply it practically. It is vital that the concepts which have been presented are understood to comprehend what will follow in the practical elements of this work. Any fencer who disregards the principles and theories presented here will have a difficult time in achieving their full potential.

Distance

Distance, also known as Measure, is another of the primary principles of fencing and is closely related to the concept of Time which was discussed previously. The principle of Distance in fencing is not discussing precise measurements, as some would think; instead is fluid in nature, much like Time. It is not concrete as it is based on elements which can change and some of them rapidly. Distance is often increasing or decreasing and is rarely static.

Foundation

In fencing it is primarily the distance between the fencer's point and the opponent; and also the opponent's point and the fencer. These are not set distances due to this being all dependent on the fencers. This is because Distance is not only based on the distance between the fencers, but also the length of the weapons being used, the length of the arm of each fencer, their bodies, and even their steps and the type of step used. These distances will change depending on factors including the weapons and the combatants themselves. All of these must be taken into account when judging Distance. It is footwork which changes Distance most drastically and most often.

There are several Measures or types of Measure that need to be taken into account in fencing. These Distances extend all the way from the fencers being too close, to the fencers being too far away from one another. There is also an additional distance, Just Distance, which is a concept not defined by a particular Distance, but rather, it is a concept which is nevertheless important.

In and Out of Distance

To begin with, there are two types of Distance which are the most general and need to be understood before any of the others can be discussed. One of these is being "In Distance", and the other is being "Out of Distance". The former will be divided into further pieces. The latter is much less complex. Being "In Distance" means that the fencer is within striking distance of the opponent or vice versa, this may not be an immediate attack, but it is in range to be threatening. Being Out of Distance simply means that neither of the combatants is within range to make any sort of meaningful threat. Being In or Out of Distance can change very quickly as Distance is most often increasing or decreasing.

It has previously been stated that Distance and Time have a very close relationship. This will be clearly demonstrated as the different elements of Distance are discussed. These Distances can actually be counted in measures of Time, or *Tempi*. This is important as it gives a level of measurement which is useful in this discussion for comparison.

Out of Distance is a Distance at which the combatants are not able to reach each other within a short period of time. This is the only Distance at which a combatant is safe, so long as the fencers do not close upon one another. At all of the other Distances the opponent may strike in some form or another. This Distance is usually two *Tempi* or more in measurement of Time. What this means is that either of the fencers will have to use some form of Time of the Foot, or maybe two, as well as Time of the Hand to reach the other. Next is to proceed to the measures which are found In Distance.

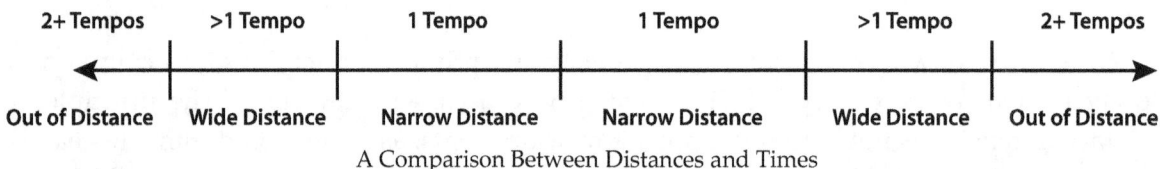

A Comparison Between Distances and Times

Fencing Measure

The two most common types of Distance, the ones that will be used the most in fencing, both in training and combat, are Narrow and Wide Distance. Neither combatant is safe at these Distances. Also, it is at these Distances that most of the combat will occur. They may also be called Close and Wide Distance.

Wide Distance

At this Distance the combatants will be more than a single *Tempo* away from one another, and in some instances may be two *Tempi* away from one another. This is essentially a Distance at which the fencers are a lunge or slightly further away from one another. To cross this Distance will require at least a Time of the Hand and a Time of the Foot, though these may be combined in a lunge. What this means is that the combatants are relatively safe from one another, though should never be too relaxed.

Narrow Distance

Narrow Distance is a Distance at which the fencers are a single *Tempo* away from one another. This means that a simple thrust or Time of the Hand can reach the other combatant. It is the optimum Distance for a thrust, but involves dangerously little time for the fencers. The combatants need to be extremely aware at this Distance and not linger here. This is the Distance where combat will be actively occurring between the two combatants.

Very Narrow Distance

There is a closer Distance than Narrow Distance. This is a Distance at which combatants will find themselves, usually by accident, but sometimes by design. The Measure is known as Very Narrow Distance. At this Distance when the bodies of the combatants are close it is usually awkward to move the tip of a sword to strike, as such it is most useful to use the edge. However, this Distance can also be measured where only a part of the combatants has come within this distance, usually the hand, arm or weapon. This is usually measured when a strike is made against an attacking hand in Half-Time.

The important relationship here is the closeness of the closest part of one combatant to the other. At this Distance there is only about half a *Tempo* and therefore there is really no Time. This makes this Distance the most dangerous. A combatant who is in Very Narrow Distance should be either acting against the opponent or doing his best to defend and clear himself from the engagement. It is at this Distance where the idea of Priority becomes most important.

Just Distance

There is one more type of Measure which does not actually have a measurement in Time or Distance as it is dependent on the situation in which the combatant finds himself. The Distance is known as "Just Distance" and is the Distance at which it is optimum for striking the opponent, without the opponent being able to do so against the fencer. This is actually a principle and not a Distance, believed to be at least two distances as for some it is at Narrow Distance and for others it is at Wide Distance. What this means is that it is actually very fluid. The most important thing about "Just Distance" is that the fencer is able to strike the opponent while not being struck and this is highly dependent on the situation.

Breaking and Closing Distance

Each one of the Distances is related to both the closer and further one. As such, the Wide Distance can become Narrow and vice versa, but can also become Very Narrow quite easily. This is the case because either fencer may increase or decrease the Distance. Increasing Distance is known as Breaking Distance and decreasing is known as Closing Distance. It is up to the fencer to be able to judge Distance and figure out whether it is Breaking or Closing.

To use measure and also manipulate Distance is an important skill. Between the options of Breaking or Closing Distance, Breaking is usually safer, but it is entirely up to the situation the fencer finds himself in. It is vital for the fencer to understand this particular relationship, and indeed all of the relationships between the different Distances. Knowing this will enable the fencer to arrive at Just Distance with the correct Timing. This involves the manipulation of Distance and requires the fencer to have an instinctive knowledge of Distance.

Manipulation of Distance

The first step in the manipulation of Distance is to know the Distances. This means to understand what it means to be at Wide Distance or Narrow Distance and so on. This must be known from practical perspective as well as an intellectual one. This will require time on the part of the fencer to develop an instinctive knowledge of Distance and to gauge Distance without thinking about it. All of the elements which make up Distance must be taken into account in this. Once the fencer can measure Distance instinctively, it will then be possible for him to manipulate it.

Distance is manipulated through the use of the feet, body and arms, though it is primarily controlled through using footwork. Small movements of the body and arms can make a difference, but primarily it is through the use of footwork that Distance is manipulated. The fencer must control their movements and use the appropriate footwork where it is required and this requires a lot of practice.

The judging of Distance must be done in *Tempo* and action, meaning the use of step, thrust and other actions needs to be performed without thinking, it must be a trained instinct. It requires a lot of time and paying attention to their movements to instinctively know their Distance. Fencing with different opponents will also give the fencer awareness of different movements on the part of other fencers that will affect Distance.

Once the fencer is instinctively aware of theirs and their opponent's Measure and how they both use them, then he can manipulate Distance. This is achieved by the different combinations of footwork to change the length of step. Circular actions are the most useful in this particular respect, but linear movements can also be used. Each fencer will discover particular methods of changing and manipulating Distance that suit them, but it is important that these movements are based in sound fencing theory.

Distance in Training and Combat

The last thing that needs to be discussed is the important difference between the Distance which is used in training and the Distance used in an encounter between different fencers. Much of the training that is performed will be at Narrow Distance. This is to enable the fencer to use the correct techniques in the prepared situation of drills. However, the Distance for combat will most commonly start at Wide Distance, preferably further away, to give the fencer time to react to the actions of the opponent. Contact between the two fencers which occurs at Narrow Distance will be very brief, and substantially shorter than in training.

The reason for this is to teach the student to understand what the correct Distance is. If parries, for example, were practiced at Wide Distance then the partner's thrust in the drill will not reach the student and this will teach them to parry much too early if only the arms are being used. Even where footwork is being used on both parts, the Distance will still be Narrow so that the distance between them is kept the same. Only when the fencers are using more footwork for parrying drills will the combatants start at Wide Distance. Obviously, were a combat to start at Narrow Distance it could be over very quickly. Hence, there must be a difference between the two. The Distance at which drills will start is dependent on the drill but a fencer should get used to using differing Distances in training.

Distance is an important part of fencing theory and the fencer who does not have at least a basic grasp of it will most likely be doomed to failure. It is important for the fencer to understand the different types of Distance and how they can change and quite quickly. The relationship between Time and Distance is also vital as the two principles intertwine in many parts of fencing theory. With this knowledge however the fencer is more likely to succeed.

Lines

The subject of Lines in fencing includes such things as the division of the combatant and the Guard or Ward. This portion of the theory is about how the combatant is divided and the associated theory with regard to how the fencer then defends these various divisions. While most of the theory with regard to Lines seems to be of a defensive nature it is also by connection offensive as the divisions also determine where attacks on the opponent will be made. The discussion of Lines also has strong connections to Engagement.

Division of the Combatant

The first part that will be examined to correctly introduce the subject of Lines is the division of the combatant. There are many different ways to divide the fencer into sections. The easiest way to divide the combatant, and most common, is to divide the combatant into four.

The combatant is divided once horizontally and once vertically and through the use of these two divisions four Lines can be named. To start with, the areas divided by each line will be described. The partition which divides the fencer horizontally results in a High Line, above the division, and a Low Line, below. This division is made at the height of the fencer's weapon, through the hilt of the weapon.

The vertical line divides the fencer also through the hilt of the combatant's weapon to create a left and right side, or Inside Line and Outside Line. This is dependent on which hand the fencer holds their weapon. For the right-handed fencer the Inside Line is on the left and for the left-handed fencer the Inside Line is on the right. The Inside Line is closest to the body, and the Outside Line is furthest.

The combination of these divisions results in four Lines, a High Inside, High Outside, Low Inside and Low Outside. The four Lines are closely related to the parries and attacks used. Parries close a Line so that it is defended, and it is vital that the parry does this to be effective.

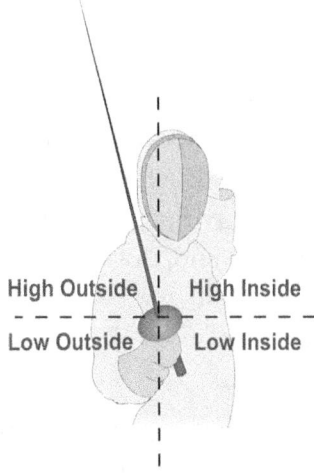

Lines for a Right-handed Fencer

Open and Closed Lines

Once the Lines are established it is possible to discuss how this theory relates to the defensive and offensive application of the weapon. In simple terms an "open" Line is vulnerable to attack and a "closed" Line is not. The parries and other options are used to close the Lines. Some of these options will be discussed here and some will be discussed later on.

It is difficult, but not impossible to close multiple Lines at the same time. It should be noted that closing the Line does not have to be an active movement, a simple positioning of the weapon and body may be sufficient. The idea of Lines is to open the opponent's Line to allow for an attack and at the same time close the fencer's own to be defended. The opponent's Line may be forced open using some sort of Blade Engagement or other physical method, or the fencer may convince the opponent to open the Line through some other method. The fencer may also open their own Line to invite an attack. This is performed through the use of feints and invitations.

Guard and Ward

There are two terms associated with the position from which a fencer starts, one is Guard and the other is Ward. Often these two are used as synonyms. This is not actually the case. A Guard is a position which closes a Line, a Ward is merely a position from which an attack or defence is launched. For the most part Wards are not defensive positions, though some do actually close Lines and can serve as such. When either term is used in this treatise it is actually a Ward, in the sense described above.

There are many different Guards which may be adopted. They are merely dependent on how the body and the weapon may be placed. Some of them are more useful than others as they place a weapon in a position of immediate readiness. There are four more common Wards which can be adopted, the most useful one being the Third Guard. There are three others which need due consideration, and they are quite important in the question of Lines as the Guard names also relate to hand positions.

The hand position is important, as it will be demonstrated later on, that this is vital to engagement. The three others are, with little surprise, First, Second, and Fourth. In discussing these particular Guards, it is important that the Guards are described by hand and some body in their description. While the First Guard is usually made with the weapon quite high, the same Guard can be called with the arm much lower, but the hand in the same position. There will be a more practical and closer discussion of this later in the Practical section.

Counter-Position

In the discussion of Lines, it is necessary to examine another theoretical element which is closely related to Engagement. It combines considerations of Guard, Lines, and Engagement, and this combination is Counter-Position. Counter-Position concerns positioning the fencer in a way that the fencer's Lines are closed while opening them on the opponent. It is vital that the fencer is positioned properly for this to work.

This particular technique, as the name implies, is designed to counter the opponent's Guard, or to oppose it. As such it is also called "Opposing Guard". The technique is intended so that there is an open, safe single attack from the current position against the opponent. It is of necessity that the fencer understands Lines and Engagement to use this technique properly. The key to this particular technique is for the fencer to position himself in such a way that the opponent is successfully opposed, his weapon kept against a closed Line, while the fencer's weapon is in an open Line. More of this will be discussed in the Practical when Guards are discussed, as will Lines.

Of Engagement

Engagement, or Blade Engagement, is an important concept and must be understood to fence properly. It is vital that while this particular explanation of Engagement will be from a theoretical basis, there are essential practical elements which are based upon this theory. Due to this there will be elements of theory which will re-appear in the Practical about Engagement. This is because the play between the weapons is part of fencing which the fencer must understand for success.

Definition

To properly understand Blade Engagement, it must first be defined. What should be noted is that there are two definitions, one which is commonly used, and one which will be used in this treatise. The common definition states that Engagement takes place in fencing where the two weapons of the fencers come into contact with one another. This is quite a narrow definition and takes away from some of the important parts of Blade Engagement which are essential for complete understanding.

For the purposes of this discourse Blade Engagement takes place where the fencer's blade is placed in a position near the opponent's weapon, where there is a tactical reason for doing so. This does not require contact between the weapons as it is the position of the weapon which is more important than actual contact between them. This definition takes into account more than is found in the common definition. Those elements where the weapons are not in contact are as important as those where the blades are in contact. Contact between the weapons in Blade Engagement will be referred to as Hard Engagement, while the mere positioning of the weapons will be called Soft Engagement.

Division of the Blade

The first part to understanding Blade Engagement is to examine the weapon. More specifically, it is looking at the blade of the weapon. For the most part, the handle and associated hilt is not involved. The blade is usually divided into halves. The first half starts at the hilt and goes to half way toward the point. The second part starts at half way and goes to the point. The first half is commonly called the *Forte* and the second half is called the *Debole*. The second half is also sometimes called the *Foible*.

The *Forte* is the strong part of the blade and this is because it is located close to the hilt. It is also the slower part of the weapon. The *Debole* is the weaker part of the weapon because it is located far from the hilt. It is also the faster part of the weapon. This being the case, the *Forte* is more likely to be used in defence, and the *Debole* more likely to be used for offence, as it also has the point.

There is a third part of the weapon which is the middle third of the blade. This part of the blade is half *Forte* and half *Debole*, as such it has some of the characteristics of both. This also means that it is not exceptionally strong at either. This part of the blade is called the *Mezzo*, being the Italian word for half or middle. Much of the action of the engagement of the blades will occur about this part of the blade.

The next parts of the blade that needs to be examined are the edges of which there are two. The edge which is most commonly pointed toward the opponent is the True Edge. The other edge which is closer to the fencer is known as the False Edge. Both edges of the weapon are necessary and need to be considered with regard to Blade Engagement and all other actions. There are some claims that the True Edge is stronger than the false, and it is for this reason that the False Edge is so infrequently used. This is actually not necessarily the case. There are instances where the False Edge will be stronger than the true.

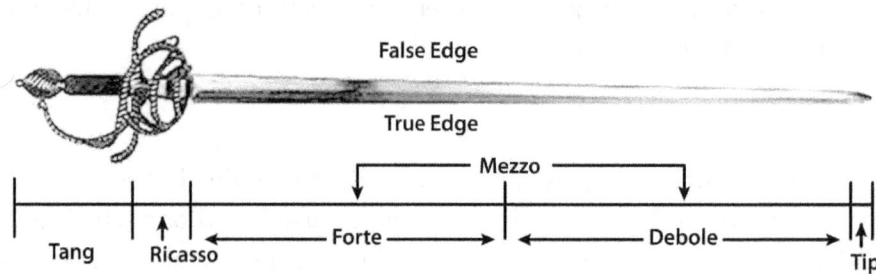

Hard Engagement

The most common conception of Blade Engagement is contact between the weapons as such this part will be discussed first. Contact between the weapons for Blade Engagement will be referred to as Hard Engagement, while the mere positioning of the weapons will be called Soft Engagement. This helps delineate between the two types of engagement. With regard to the contact between the weapons, this may be an instant, short or prolonged contact between them. All of these qualify as Hard Engagement.

During contact between the blades the fencer can, with enough practice feel through the blade. This is called *senso di ferro*, or sense through steel. It gives the fencer a kind of sixth sense of what the opponent will do as part of his next or even future moves. It is in no way mystical; it just requires the fencer to feel through the blade. This can only be achieved when the fencer sees the weapon as an extension of himself, rather than an object being used. More of this will be discussed in the Practical.

There are certain feelings that will be evident. An opponent may force their weapon against the fencer's, or the fencer may force against the opponent's weapon. This is called using the strong of the weapon against the other's weak. Yielding against the opponent's weapon is called using the weak against the opponent. Both of these are useful and can be used to great advantage, by the fencer who can feel properly and take advantage of the situation.

Soft Engagement

The second part of Blade Engagement is Soft Engagement, merely placing the weapon in the position to gain an advantage. This position may lead to Hard Engagement or it might not. A fencer can influence the actions of the opponent merely by the positioning of his weapon in comparison to the opponent's.

There is also a method which uses all Soft Engagement, which avoids Hard Engagement totally. This is called Absence of Blade. In this, the fencer avoids the opponent's weapon as much as possible, denying any information through Hard Engagement and *senso di ferro*. Both Hard and Soft Engagements can be used against the opponent with great success and this will be presented in the Practical.

Techniques

There are several techniques which are associated with Blade Engagement including Taking the Blade, Attacks on the Blade and other forms of Engagement. Each one of these has a time and place. These will be discussed along with their practical application, and with a practical discussion of Blade Engagement later in the treatise. Counter-Position relies on knowledge of Lines and Engagement, this is also an example of the use of Blade Engagement to achieve a goal; for the most part this will be Soft Engagement, but engagement nonetheless.

Understanding

The principles of Blade Engagement cover a great deal and it is vital that each element is understood to perform the Blade Engagements in an encounter with an opponent. To do this, the theory of Blade Engagement must be understood first. Understanding is the key to the application of the techniques which will be discussed in the Practical. Engagement is vital to understanding and performing fencing in a successful fashion and to understand this, the other elements contained within and without must also be understood.

Practice

Practice is essential for any skill if a person wants to improve their skill, or even maintain it. Practice is essential for fencing. There are many physical skills which need to be practiced so that a fencer can perform, and it is necessary that the fencer does this. Of course, practice needs to be coupled with learning to truly improve.

Learning and Practice

There are always new skills to be learnt, or different applications for the skills which have already been learnt, the learning never ends. In many schools there is much focus on the learning of the new rather than the maintaining of the current and old. Maintenance of old skills means that the new has a foundation to be built on, without this foundation, the new skills may not be learnt or established as part of the techniques that the fencer will use.

Learning and practice go together, one attains and the other maintains. Practice solidifies the learnt skills. The practice also encourages the new skills to be blended with the old so that they can all be performed smoothly.

Techniques of Practice

Practice is essential to improve and maintain skill. A student may learn something from his teacher. This skill may be learnt so that the skill is known. Without practice, this skill will not become a natural part of their skills, and he will never use it in an encounter because it is not natural. This requires practice of the skills which have been learnt. Further, only through the use of the skills of the art will the fencer improve.

Drilling is useful and allows the student to develop patterns to respond to. Only in an encounter can the fencer practice to find the correct cues from an opponent to use the skill when it is most useful. Bouting is ideal for this, especially where the bouting is controlled and both fencers know it. Both people involved in the bouting must use their skills as they would in a combative scenario in order for either of them to learn or practice completely. This is a requirement of the fencer and their partner.

Bouting as Practice

Bouting and practice should be with any partner who will accompany the fencer in this. Diverse opponents will assist the student to prepare for different situations as not every fencer will perform actions the same way, nor will they necessarily have the same answers to the same situations. This improves the experience of the fencer and makes them more complete in their approach. Fencing with different opponents will allow the fencer to prepare for unexpected situations, due to the differences in approach that the fencer may discover with different opponents. The more people the fencer plays with the more scenarios that he will run into, and the more he can prepare for.

Using Skill is Necessary

It is vital that both the student and their partner are committed to the practice and the processes involved. This means that they should both be putting their all into the situation. It is only through the full expenditure of skill that the fencer will improve and evaluate their skill against another. Should one of the fencers not perform with their complete ability, then one will be deceived as how skilled they are and how well they know their skills. The only time when there is an exception to this rule is when one is teaching the other, or where a particular technique is the focus of the bouting. The level of skill used against an opponent in bouting should allow the opponent to learn from the experience and not feel like they are a mere target. The result is that the more experienced fencer may not use all of their skill against a newer student, to test what they know and to hone areas of issue to assist in their training. In this scenario it is necessary to have the focus on the skill-set being practiced.

Regularity

Practice needs to be regular. If the fencer does not practice then his skills will degrade. This degradation is seen across all elements in fencing. Skills need to be practiced to a degree that the fencer does not have to think about what he is doing. This allows the fencer to act using trained instinct. What this means is that the skill is a part of the normal processes of fencing. These skills will last a longer period of time without practice, but they still need to be practiced to maintain a high level of proficiency. The hours put into practice over a week are more important than the time put into practice over a year. This is where skills become a normal process.

All aspects of fencing must be practiced. This includes the more theoretical elements of fencing such as Time and Distance. The fencer needs to practice these and be aware of them in action. This will enable the fencer to take them into account when fencing without having to actively think about them. Timing can only be practiced by actively fencing. It is only through use of the skills that the fencer will see the skills in action and be aware of their Timing. In this way, Timing is improved and maintained through practice in both drills and bouting.

Fatigue

Fatigue will increase over time if the skills are not used. The practice using drills and bouting also allows the fencer to maintain a level of fitness due to the active nature of the practice. This is not a purely physical concern for the fencer. The fitter he is the longer he will last when fencing. The less fatigue a fencer has, the more energy he will have to think about what technique is appropriate to the situation and to perform it with the correct Timing. Practice also maintains the muscles associated with the actions of fencing. Over time, without practice, they will degrade and the fencer will be less capable.

Finally, the fencer must practice in the gear and using the weapons that he will in an encounter. This is about being fighting fit. Gear is something that needs to be taken into account when practicing. A fencer can practice longer with lighter gear, but then this will be reduced in an actual encounter. The lighter gear will also not take into account the heat of the gear actually used and heat has a great effect on fatigue.

Essential to Fencing

Practice is essential. No fencer who is serious about what he is doing will neglect practice. Practice should be performed regularly to maintain skills. He should focus on what he is doing in the practice and use his skills completely without any reservations. This is the only way that he will improve or even maintain his skills. The fencer should seek out different partners to practice with as the experience of doing so will assist him greatly in the future. The fencer should seek partners with the same goals as him, and with the same thirst for real improvement.

Practical

Of Wards

Wards and Guards were discussed a little in the section on Lines, in the Theory. This current section will discuss similar subjects, but from a practical point of view. To do this, some of the previous theory will be discussed in a more practical sense. This is necessary as the theory which has been previously presented is the foundation for the practical elements which are demonstrated in this and following parts of this treatise. For convenience, the three of the wards will be depicted using images from Giacomo di Grassi of 1594.[16]

Gripping the Sword[17]

In regards to holding the sword, the sword should be held with a single finger over the forward quillon and around the ricasso. The thumb may be placed on the back of the ricasso, or placed on top of the index finger. Using a single finger rather than two allows easier control of the point through the fingers and wrist. However, should the fencer be more comfortable with two fingers over the forward quillon and around the ricasso this is also fine. The important thing here is comfort and control of the weapon.

The sword should be held as if holding on to a small bird, firm enough to stop the bird from flying away, but not so tight that the bird is crushed. Likewise, if the handle is grasped too tightly, there will be no movement in the fingers and it will be difficult to perform different actions, and to perform the actions with subtlety. Clearly if it is not held tightly enough it will to be controlled well and the fencer will be disarmed easily.

Four Guards

The Guards are numbered one to four. Each one of these represents a hand position and also an arm position. These positions originally represented the position of the fencer after he drew the weapon from the scabbard. First is a position in which the arm is held above the shoulder with the weapon pointed at the opponent, with the False Edge downward. This position is the first place where the weapon is pointed at the opponent after drawing the weapon from a scabbard. The First position of the hand is also found here in the hand with the knuckles upward. The following Guards represent the following positions as the sword is lowered into position.

Second is a position in which the arm is held outstretched from the shoulder, either toward the front or to the side. In any case the weapon remains pointed at the opponent and remains at shoulder-height. The Second position of the hand is found in this guard with the palm downward and the knuckles to the Outside.

---

[16] Di Grassi, Giacomo (1594). *DiGrassi his true Arte of Defence, plainlie teaching by infallable Demonstrations, apt Figures and Perfect Rules the manner forme how a man without other Teacher or Master may safelie handle all sortes of weapons aswell offensive as defensive; With a Treatise Of Deceit or Falsinge: And with a waie or meane by private Industrie to obtaine Strength, Judgement and Activitie.* I.G., London.

[17] This section does not appear in the Elizabethan version of this treatise but was added during the editing process after it was found that this information was useful and pertinent.

Third is a position in which the arm is down by the fencer's side, the weapon pointed toward the opponent. The Third hand position is with the knuckles toward the ground as in the Third Guard.

Fourth is a position with the hand across the body toward the inside, the point toward the opponent, with the palm upward. The Fourth position of the hand is also the same, knuckles to the Inside.

Some of these Guards will protect Lines, though in truth only the Third and the Fourth may do, depending on the position of the Guard. Neither First nor Second in their classic forms are in a position to protect any Line, though offence is much easier from these. These four are Wards in the truest sense of the word. It is important to delineate between hand and Guard position to reduce confusion.

Wards and Lines

The division of the fencer into Lines is the same as has been described previously, a horizontal and a vertical line both which pass through the hilt. Thus, as before, the areas above are High and those below Low; those areas toward the body are Inside and those away are Outside. For the right-handed fencer, this would mean that the Inside Line is on the left and the Outside Line is on the right. For the left-handed fencer the Lines are simply reversed.

Depending on which Ward the fencer is in, a Line may be open or closed. For example, a fencer in Third has a minimal Outside Line and a much larger Inside Line; conversely the reverse is the same for a fencer in Fourth, with a large Outside and small Inside Line. Should a fencer wish to close a Line, he must position himself in a Ward carefully and close the Line properly.

Ward and Guard

The discussion of what is a Ward and what is a Guard was made in the Theory section. As a tactical consideration, it is a serious one for the fencer. While the terms may be used one for the other and vice versa, the fencer must be sure of what he uses to be safe. A Ward may be named a Guard in this treatise, but they are all Wards nonetheless. Only if and when it is specifically stated will it actually be a Guard as defined previously. The discussion of the difference between a Ward and a Guard leads on to what can be considered to be a good Guard and so, one advantageous to the fencer.

A Good Guard

A good Guard is one which conforms to some basic principles. These are all based in fencing theory. To understand what a good Guard is, it is vital to understand the principles on which it is based. What the reader will find is that this list of principles will actually conform to more than one Ward, and this is advantageous.

Close a Line

The first thing that a good Guard will do is to begin to close at least one Line and do this properly. This being said, there is no way for the fencer to close all of the Lines. This Line, or Lines, should be closed enough that a direct attack from the Guard position of an opponent will not leave the fencer indefensible. Being aware of the open Lines, the fencer will be prepared to defend them, or deliberately leave them open to invite the opponent to attack there. This form of invitation could be seen as a feint as there is a deliberate opening left.

Offensive Potential

Following the Lines and their position, the fencer should consider how easy it is to launch an attack or defence from the position he is in. This is a consideration for a good Guard or Ward regardless of its position. There is little point for the fencer to be safe but unable to launch an attack. This requires the weapon to both be in a threatening position and yet to be in a position to defend as well. It is the ease of performance of these actions which is the key.

Balance

To launch an attack or defence, the fencer must be balanced. The fencer should have the body straight and supported. The feet should be about shoulder width apart for the maximum balance and potential movement. In combination with this, the knees should not be locked, but bent somewhat to assist balance and potential for movement. Balance allows for a good position and the ability to move.

Comfort

What will also be noticed is that a balanced position, as described will also be comfortable for the fencer. Comfort must be taken into account so that the fencer can maintain the position while preparing to act. If it is uncomfortable, the fencer will not maintain it. Consequently, may move out of position and leave himself open at the wrong time. To be comfortable the Guard should be as natural to the body as possible. This may take some practice for the Guard to become comfortable for the fencer. This will also assist to strengthen the muscles and prepare them for movement.

The Guard of Third

di Grassi's (1594) Low Ward

The Third Guard, or Low Ward, is the one used as the primary Guard throughout this treatise as such it will be described first. Some of the hand position needs to be taken into account when describing this Ward. This Ward is the primary one as it fulfils all of the requirements of a good Guard as described above. The typical Guard will be described along with some examples of its different versions. Unless otherwise it is noted, it will be the standard Guard that is being discussed, and any other will be a variation.

To establish the typical Guard of Third it is necessary to start from the ground and then work up as it is important to start with the foundation of the Ward. For the right-handed fencer, the right foot should be placed forward, the big toe pointed at the opponent and with the left foot to the rear. The feet should be shoulder width apart. The rear foot can be between ninety and forty-five degrees to the forward foot. The heels should not line up, but the left should be placed about the width of the foot, or wider depending on preference from the line of the front foot.

Foot position for Third Guard

The knees should be bent, so that the fencer is slightly sitting in the stance. The knees should line up with the feet, and hips. The weight of the body should be placed between the legs rather than biased to one or the other, and the fencer should have a straight back keeping the body upright. The head should be held erect.

The shoulders should be level with neither higher nor lower than the other. The right arm should be placed down by the fencer's side, not straight, but the arm should not be fully bent either. The bend in the arm should place the hand about a palm-width in front of the right thigh. The hand should be in Third position with the knuckles facing toward the ground.

The weapon should be pointed at the opponent and have the point raised enough that it lines up with the top of the shoulder. With the hand in Third position, the False Edge will be toward the fencer while the True Edge will be toward the opponent.

The left hand should be placed in front of the right breast with the elbow tucked into the body. The palm of this hand should not face the opponent, but be at a slight angle. Looking directly forward the fencer should see the point of their weapon directed at the opponent and the tips of the fingers of their left hand.

Variations

There are several variations which may be made to the Third Guard. All variations will be noted in the text where required. The hand positions may be changed. Either hand may be pushed forward. Usually one is placed more forward than the other, but in some instances, both may be pushed forward. It should also be noted that the hand may have a changed position, rather than being in Third, it may be changed to another position.

Just as the hand position may be changed, so too may the foot position also be changed. The feet may be swapped over, being the most obvious variation, or they may be placed further apart or closer together. The body may also be leaned either forward or backward, depending on the situation. This also alters the Guard. Each one of the variations in the Guard will be noted in the treatise to reduce confusion. Where no alteration is mentioned, it is to be assumed to be the Guard described in detail above. The same variations may be applied to all of the following Guards as well.

The Guard of Fourth

To establish the typical Guard of Fourth, the feet and body should be placed in the same position as found in the Guard of Third as described above. This remains the same to maintain the upright position of the body and the balanced nature of the guard established by the position of the feet. Where the Guard of Fourth differs is in the position of the hands. It must otherwise it will remain as in the Guard of Third.

The offhand comes over to the right and is placed in the middle of the chest, once again with the palm of the hand ready to deflect an incoming blade. The sword-hand is then turned so that the hand is in the Fourth position, with the palm up. The arm is then brought across the body at the height of the elbow in its usual position down beside the body. The point of the weapon should be toward the opponent at shoulder height.

The Guard of First

di Grassi's (1594) High Ward

The Guard of First, or High Ward, is one which is not often used, but it is still necessary for the fencer to understand its position, and be prepared for the opponent to take it, or take it himself, should the situation demand it. To establish the typical Guard of First, the feet and body should be placed in the same position as found in the Guard of Third and Fourth as described above. This remains the same to maintain the upright position of the body and the balanced nature of the guard established by the position of the feet. Where the guard of first differs from Third is in the position of the hands and arms. It must otherwise it will remain as in the Guard of Third.

It is the sword-arm and hand which is the primary difference. The off-hand remains in the same position as in Third. The sword-arm is extended directly upward from the shoulder. The hand is placed in First position with the knuckles upward, so, the False Edge will be downward. The point of the weapons should be threatening the opponent. The weapon should be almost horizontal in its position.

The Guard of Second

di Grassi's (1594) Broad Ward

The Guard of Second is similar to that of First as it is not used all that often. There are actually two different forms of Second and both will be described. As with Fourth and First, the feet and body remain in the same position to maintain balance and movement. As in the Guard of First, the off-hand remains in the same position as well.

In the first version of Second the sword-arm is placed directly forward of the shoulder with the point of the weapon threatening the opponent. The hand is in Second position with the knuckles outward and palm downward. In the other variation, sometimes known as Broad Ward, the hand remains in Second position, but the arm is directly outward to the side from the shoulder. The weapon is pointed toward the opponent as found in all of the other guards.

Third is the Primary Guard

While Third is the primary guard that the fencer will adopt when facing the opponent, knowing the others allows the fencer to be prepared to face them, or even utilise them. The other guards and variations of guards will be used as examples for different reasons in the text. These will mostly be a change in hand position rather than the adopting of the complete Guard as they have been described. However, the primary Guard that will be used in this treatise is Third as it presents more advantages for the fencer, both tactical and practical, than the other Guards.

Tactical Considerations

Once the principles have been established, and the typical Guards set, the Guards can then be examined from a tactical viewpoint. The focus is on how the Guards will operate in combat. The approach that will be taken is a much more interactive approach than what has been so far.

This will take into account those principles found in the Theory along with those found above to demonstrate how a Guard is or is not effective from the viewpoint of being one from which to defend the fencer and also strike against the opponent.

The first part of this is to refresh about the principles of the Counter Position or Opposing Guard which has been discussed in the Theory section. The tactical principle behind this particular approach is to close the fencer's Line and open a Line in the opponent. This is designed to give the fencer a direct safe attack against the opponent using only a single *Tempo* to achieve it. With this in mind, it is possible to look at the advantages of various guards and their tactical possibilities. This must take into account the principles of the good Guard.

First

From a purely tactical point of view, according to the principles presented, First is a horrible Guard. It is actually the worst. The first thing about this Guard is that it is uncomfortable, the sword arm is high in the air and a lot of strength is used to main this position. This is bad for the fencer, since if he relaxes, he comes out of Guard. The Guard is also not closed. It leaves all of the Lines open, with some very limited closure of the High Outside Line. This results in a very slow defence. There is only a single direct attack from the position all other attacks require additional movement. All of these factors determine that this is not a good Guard from a tactical point of view.

Second

Second is not much of an improvement, from the examination of Broad Ward. It is also uncomfortable due to its position and not particularly closed from a Lines viewpoint. There are few limited attacks as with First that do not require sundry movements. The other version is better.

The position can be comfortable if the fencer is trained in the position, it is a closed position due to the point being directed at the opponent. However, it is limited in attack due to the position of the arm. A thrust requires foot movement the only other motion is a cut.

Fourth

Fourth is an improvement in that it is more closed than the previous Guards, but it is also bound up due to the position of the arms. This binding along with the position of the arm results in limitation of the offensive options for the fencer. However, in comparison to First or Second, Fourth is a much more comfortable and defensible position.

Third

Third is the primary Ward of this treatise for many reasons, the tactical reasons are just another reason why it is as such. It is the most comfortable Guard of the four standard Wards due to its natural position. Due to its position it has wide options for attack and defence and it is definitively closed or closing on a single Line if formed properly, which can be defended with minimal movement. All of these factors result in Third being the most tactically advantageous ward.

Variations

There have been variations for each Guard noted. From a tactical point of view, the changes in the position of the Wards will change the tactical possibilities of each of the Guards. The fencer should be aware of the different variations of the Guards and how they affect them.

An example of a change in Guard resulting in a tactical change is extending the offhand forward in the Third Guard. This can nominally close another Line for the fencer, but can also draw them to attack straight down the centre Line between the hand and the sword. The fencer should be aware, and experiment with different variations to be prepared for the changes that result. What should be noted about the Guards presented is that they can close, or partially close the High Outside Line. Fourth is the exception in this case as it closes the High Inside Line.

Counter Guard

Once all the tactical questions of the Guard have been examined, next is to examine how to counter the opponent's Guard, therefore denying him the advantage of the position he has taken. The ideal is to deny the opponent an opening while creating an opening for the fencer to attack in complete safety. Should this not be possible, then the fencer should be focussed on denying the opponent his attack. This will be presented in the Counter Guards below.

The Guards can be countered by other Guards as presented, or with little modification. These counters are based upon the tactical principles presented and also the principles of the good Guard. It is of significance that the fencer must be aware of the position of the opponent in all aspects in his Guard. The various positions of the body, hands and sword can change things markedly as will be seen.

Against First

The Guard of First is countered by the Guard of Third due to the Opposing Positions. The high position of First is countered by the low position of Third. In this particular situation it will require movement on the part of the defensive fencer as this is not a direct counter without movement. The Guard of First is also countered by a Guard of Fourth where the hand and arm are raised to close the Inside Line completely. The Guard of First may also be countered by a Guard of Second in the first variation due to the increased distance of the second and the threat presented by the thrust which is closer to the opponent than his is against the fencer.

Some will claim that a Guard of First will counter a Guard of First, however, no Lines are closed and mere threats are made. This is simply copying the Guard to gain the same advantage. It is not an approach to countering an opponent's Guard that should be made unless the fencer knows the Guard particularly well and has additional movements in mind.

Against Second

The Guard of Second may be countered by another Guard of Second. This actually different to the example above, especially if the first variation Guard is taken. In this case the fencers will be in a neutral position because both are threatened and both are closed at the same time. This position requires one of the fencers to move to gain an advantage. The Broad

Ward may also be taken against another Broad Ward to threaten against the same Line which is taken. Once again, the fencer must be careful in using this counter as there are really no Lines closed unless the off-hand can close a Line.

The most effective counter to a Guard of Second, in Broad Ward, is a Guard of Fourth. The position of the Guard of Fourth will close the Inside Line to the opponent, especially effectively where the fencer is able to close and physically close the Line. Even where contact is not possible the Guard of Fourth will effectively counter that of Second. For the first version, a similar Guard can be used, as described above, or a first version Guard of Second with the hand in Fourth can be used against the opponent's Inside Line to close the fencer's Inside Line. This is more effective than just copying the Guard. This Guard can also be countered with effective footwork due to the Guard relying on footwork or cut for effect as such a Guard of Third can be taken also.

Against Third

The Guard of Third can countered by a Guard of Fourth with the fencer's blade to the opponent's Inside, closing the Inside Line completely. This can be executed with or without Blade Engagement. Interestingly, the Guard of Third may also be countered by a Guard of Third to the Outside, the hand is turned to Second to close the Outside Line, or with a Guard of Third to the Inside with the hand in Fourth. This is dependent on where the fencer seeks to strike the opponent, and also the position of the Guard relative to the opponent. In this particular case it is the hand which assists in closing the Line and moving the opponent out of Line.

Against Fourth

The Guard of Fourth may be countered with a Guard of Third to the Inside. This is designed to close the Outside Line. The hand is turned in Second to reinforce the position. A Guard of Second, in the Broad Ward could also be used so long as the weapons are placed together and the Second is to the inside of the Fourth. This requires positioning on the part of the fencer in Second. It is ironic that the Guard of Fourth has so few counters but can counter several other guards. This should be taken into account both when using and against a Guard of Fourth.

Use the Wards

The best way to understand and use the Guards and their counters is to use them. A fencer should practice these with another fencer to become proficient in them. They should also use some of the variations to be aware and more comfortable with them as well.

The instructions for the four primary Guards should be read carefully and the position of the fencer considered carefully, especially in reference to the opponent's Guard. Further thought should be given as to how the variation may change the Guard and the effect this change will have on the fencer's position. It is the Guard of Third that should have most attention paid to it as it is the primary Ward that will be used throughout this discourse.

Of the Feet

Footwork is an essential element in fencing. It is footwork that determines Distance. The ability to use footwork properly is the ability to move across the field in a comfortable and efficient manner. With this in mind it is vital that the fencer understand footwork and its terminology. The fencer should, after training in footwork, use the footwork found in fencing as normally as he would walking. Footwork should never be glossed over in training.

Footwork Terms

Before any practical matters can be addressed with regard to footwork, it is important that the terminology is discussed. These terms must be understood so that the fencer can use the terms and the appropriate footwork associated with these terms. Using these terms will make it simple to describe any footwork motion that a fencer wishes to perform.

There are four prime terms which the fencer needs to understand; Step, Pace, Pass and Half. These four terms can be used to describe any footwork action which the fencer may wish to perform. A Step is any single motion of footwork this includes all Paces and Passes. This requires the movement of both feet. A Pace is footwork where the fencer's feet do not cross over one another. A Pass is footwork where the fencer's feet do cross over one another, like motion of walking normally. Half is used to describe the movement of a single foot. Both Paces and Passes require the movement of both feet, as such there can be Half-Steps, Half-Paces and Half-Passes. These terms will be the standard ones used in reference to footwork throughout this treatise.

One of the essential things about footwork is that it needs to be performed without thinking about it. This means that it needs to be comfortable, like walking. What footwork requires is practice. If the fencer is concerned about his footwork he will be occupied with this thought and will not be thinking about the other necessary aspects of fencing. Hence, the footwork must be natural to the fencer. To achieve this state of normality in motion, the fencer needs a lot of practice so the instant response to a stimulus is the correct motion with footwork. The fencer should take any opportunity that he can to practice his footwork and so, enable it to become as natural in motion as possible.

Footwork Rules

There are certain rules, if the fencer follows them, he should not have any problems with his footwork. These rules describe the essential parts of footwork and its efficient motion. For the most part the rules will remain in place, but there are exceptions to these rules and the fencer should be aware of them. Some of the exceptions will be described in this discourse and those rules which rules are most likely to have exceptions to them will be noted.

First Rule: Balance

The first rule of footwork is: always remain balanced. The fencer in his motion should do his best to remain balanced and upright. This is achieved by maintaining an even amount of weight between the feet and not leaning in any direction. Balance is essential to perform any action in fencing efficiently and effectively. Maintaining balance will also prevent the fencer from falling over. An action which undermines balance should be strongly assessed before it is used, and if it is, the fencer should always regain his balance immediately after the action is performed.

Second Rule: Both Feet

Every complete step in fencing requires the movement of both feet to complete it. This being said, each foot should be moved once only, any extraneous shuffling of the feet afterward wastes time and energy. There are rare times where a Half-Step will be taken and the fencer will remain at the Half-Step. The Step should always be completed in some fashion even if it is to return to the original position.

Third Rule: Knees

The knees should always be bent when in Guard. Bending the knees is the first part to making a Step, with this completed the stepping is more efficient. Bending the knees also assists with the maintenance of balance and the efficient movement of the fencer across the ground.

Fourth Rule: Movement

The method of movement is important. It should be clean and efficient. The fencer should not shuffle his feet in the Step. The fencer should not drag his feet in the Step. The fencer should not skip in the Step. The fencer should not bounce when making a Step. Each one of these is deleterious to the efficiency and effective movement of the feet and therefore footwork. Each foot should be picked up and placed. Each foot should glide just above the ground.

Fifth Rule: Length

The fencer should never stretch nor shrink his Step to maintain length with his opponent. This will deceive the fencer as to his correct Distance. The length of the Step should always be maintained at the natural level that the fencer is always at.

Sixth Rule: Facing

The fencer should remain facing the opponent. There are very rare occasions where this manual will instruct the fencer to have his back to the opponent. There are a few exceptions to this rule, but this will be performed with purpose, and the purpose described. In general, however, the fencer should remain facing the opponent. This gives the fencer access to all means of offence and defence.

Seventh Rule: Crossing

Finally, with regard to the general rules of fencing, the fencer should not cross his feet in the movement in fencing. Obviously, there is an exception to this rule when performing a Pass. There are also other exceptions to this rule, but in general the fencer should not cross his feet as this will affect his balance and his efficient motion.

Key Steps

Footwork is based around two, Key Steps. The action of these two steps describes the actions of all of the other basic footwork motions that will be found in this manual. There are exceptions, but the motions described in these two Steps will be found in all but a few of the Steps. One Step is the Forward Pace, or Advance as it will be referred to in this treatise. The other is the Pass Forward. Both of these Steps present the action that will be found in the following Steps.

Advance

For the Advance, taken from a Guard of Third, the toe of the front foot is lifted the heel is then pushed forward just skimming the ground, the front foot is moved forward about the length of the foot. The rear foot is then moved forward the length of the foot. This completes the Step.

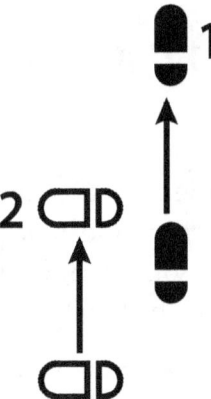

Pass Forward

The Pass Forward is much like taking a normal walking step. Taken from the Guard of Third, the rear foot moves forward passing the front foot to land equal with the big toe of the front foot or a small distance ahead of it, the front foot then passes the rear foot to regain its original position ahead of the rear foot. The actions found as described in these two Steps will be found in the other Steps which will be presented.

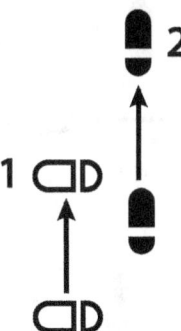

Forward and Backward

To start with two simple Paces, one which has been described already, and the other which is the reverse of one already described will be the beginning. These two Paces are the Advance and the Retreat. This enables the fencer to move forwards and backwards. The Advance is the forward Step and has been described as one of the Key Steps above.

Retreat

The Retreat is the exact reverse of the Advance and allows the fencer to move directly backward. For the Retreat, the back foot is moved backward the length of the foot, and the front foot follows. The feet should just skim the ground. The Retreat is the exact reverse of the action described for the Advance, and it is a controlled moving backward. The fencer should end up back in his Guard as he started. The same can be said for most of the Steps which are described.

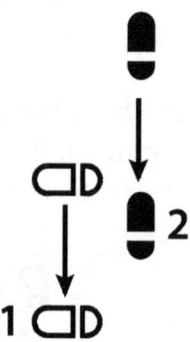

Traverse

The Traverse is a Pace which allows the fencer to move directly right or left of his current position. Regardless of the Ward taken or the foot position, it is always the foot in the direction which is required that is moved first. Indeed, the same thing can be said for most of the Paces. There are some exceptions which will be noted further along.

To perform a Traverse Right, the right foot is moved sideways about the length of the foot, the left foot is then also moved right the length of the foot. The Traverse Left is the same process except the left foot moves first followed by the right. If the opposite foot is moved first the fencer may change his facing and the feet will cross. This will adversely affect the fencer's balance. In no part during the performance of a Pace should the fencer's feet cross. What will be noted is that the Traverses are using the Advance as a Key Step in simply making the movement to the sides rather than forwards.

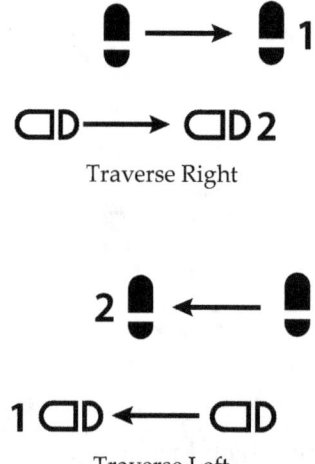

Traverse Right

Traverse Left

Diagonal

Steps may be taken in a diagonal direction to change the angle that the fencer is approaching the opponent. These must be executed with some care. There are two directions which are simple and follow the standard rules, and there are two directions which are a little different. For the right-handed fencer in a Guard of Third, it is the forward and right, and the backward and left which are the simple ones. The forward and left, and backward and right are the more confusing ones. The simple rule in this particular scenario is Footwork Rule 6: Facing.

Simple

For the right-handed fencer in Third, to move forward and right the fencer moves his right foot first diagonally forward on foot-length and follows it with the left foot. This is simply an Advance in a diagonal direction to the right. To move backward and left, the left foot is moved first a foot-length followed by the right foot. This is a Retreat in a diagonal direction to the left.

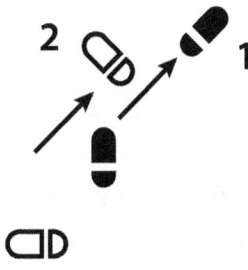

Forward and Right

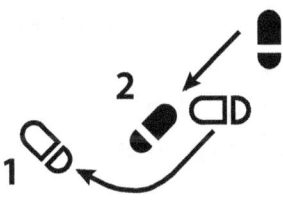

Backward and Left

More Complex

The other two directions, forward and left, and backward and right are a little more complex, but not too much. To move forward and left, using the same fencer in the same Guard, the left foot is moved first followed by the right foot. Now this will briefly cross the feet, but it will maintain the facing of the fencer. Thus, he will remain defensible. To move backward and right, it will be the right foot that moves first followed by the left.

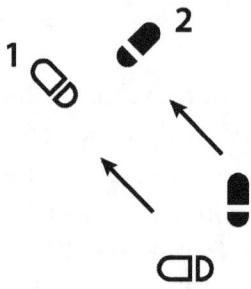

Forward and Left

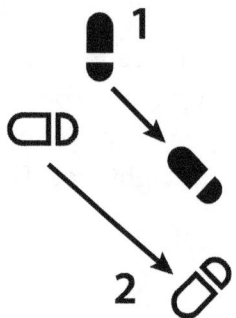

Backward and Right

What should be noted for memory is that it is the direction, left or right, which determines the foot that will be moved first. In all diagonal movements, as in all of the previous, the foot should only be moved the length of a foot or thereabouts, further than this will over-extend and unbalance the fencer. As before, the fencer will end up in the same Guard with the same foot placement as before. Diagonal steps are also known as Slopes.

Pass

The Pass is different from the Pace in that the feet intentionally cross over, this makes it a slower Step, but it makes up for this with the distance covered by each Step which is larger than found in the Pace. Due to the nature of the Pass, the fencer should be wary of the time it is used due to the middle part of the Step where the fencer is a little vulnerable due to the feet being crossed.

Pass Backward

The Key Pass which has been described before is the Pass Forward. The Pass Backward is the exact reverse of the Pass Forward in much the same way that in Paces the retreat is the exact reverse of the Advance. The Pass Backward is executed as such, the front foot is drawn back past the rear foot until the toe lines up with the heel or a little past it, the rear foot then simply regains its position in the Guard.

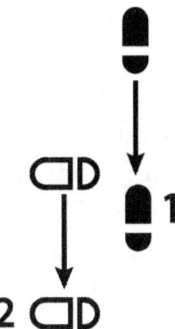

Traverses may also be performed using the Pass rather than the Pace as described above. In this particular case, to move right, the left foot moves first until it is past the right foot, and then the right foot regains its position in Guard. To move left, the right foot moves first until it is past the left foot and then the left foot regains its position in Guard. As stated, the Passes result in an increase in distance made by the fencer, but care should be taken in their use due to their vulnerability. The Pass in a diagonal direction may be performed, but will not be described here as the Step is difficult and leaves the fencer exceptionally vulnerable. The fencer should feel free to experiment with this Step, but great care will be required for its use.

Half Step

What have been described so far are complete Steps where both feet are moved and the fencer ends up back in his Guard. There are Half-Steps where only one foot will move, and these Steps can be useful to the fencer. What the fencer should note is that either the foot will then have to return to its original position or the other foot will also have to move for the fencer to regain his Guard.

Gather and Slip

The first of the Half-Steps that will be described are the Gather and the Slip. These two Steps are designed to close the feet of the Guard. These are often made as a prelude to a following action, or to withdraw the fencer slightly. The Gather moves the rear foot forward up to the position of the front foot. This moves the body slightly forward this is often used as a preparation Step. The Slip moves the front foot backward to the rear foot. This moves the body slightly backward and is often used as a simple limited defence or a preparation as with the Gather. It will be noted that both of these movements are Half-Paces.

The Lunge

The obvious Half-Pace that is made as part of an action is the Step used in the Lunge. This is a large Half-Step moving the front foot forward a distance usually to extend the distance of an attack. The execution of this Step is important, the power and speed of the lunging Step is derived from the explosive use of the rear leg pushing the body forward. The front foot is merely lifted slightly to release the pressure which has built up and to stop the Lunge at its other end. Many will attempt to throw themselves forward using the body or simply falling over and using gravity. This is an inefficient method. More of this Step will be said in accompaniment to the thrusting action it is most often associated.

Other Steps

There are other Half-Paces and indeed Half-Passes. The fencer should be aware that any movement of a single foot is a Half movement. The fencer should feel free to experiment with these. The greatest use of the Half-Step is to change the Step part way through it. Through these, the fencer can change direction and indeed even change the Step being made. There are many different footwork actions which may be made. Some of these will be described later on due to their association with other actions.

Footwork is a skill which the fencer must experiment and practice to perform the actions without thinking. The fencer should react with his feet against the action of an opponent without having to think about it. More footwork actions will be found throughout this manual. What has been presented are the essential Steps which are the keys to movement.

Of Voids

To defend the fencer against the attack of the opponent, there are two defensive actions which will be described, the Void and the Parry. These skills are vital and must be learnt properly for the fencer to avoid being struck. It is these defensive elements that must be discussed and learnt first as they comprise the foundation of the First Principle, being that defence is more important than offence.

The first defensive action that will be discussed is the Void. It is a very simple action, for the most part, and based on a very simple principle. There are some complex elements that need to be noted and taken into account. This is the easiest follow on from footwork as it uses the feet in most parts of it, and is another movement of the core part of the body.

Defence by Absence

The Void is based on the simple principle of moving the target of the opponent's attack away from the attack, or in other terms, not being where the opponent's attack is. There are some different ways to do this, but all are based on removing the target from the Line of Attack. The Voids can be broken up into three types, using the feet, using the body, and using the feet and the body together. A Void is most effective where it moves the fencer away from the attack in the most efficient method.

Footwork Void

For the most part, the Voids using the feet have already been presented. These are all footwork actions which have been discussed previously. This section discusses using them more directly for a defensive purpose. The simplest action in this case is the Retreat. It is a basic Step which increases the Distance between the opponent and the fencer, aiming at having the opponent's attack fall short. Most of the actions described using footwork aim at doing similar things.

The Diagonal Steps backward to the left and right can be used in the same way as the retreat to avoid an attack. These are very simple actions but can be very effective. The Traverse can also be used, but some care needs to be taken in its use defensively as this requires some Timing so that the fencer moves at the correct time and in the correct direction. This is because the direction away from the attack is not directly away, but to the side. The increase in Distance from the opponent's attack is less than in withdrawing directly away. The Slip can also be used in a similar way to the Retreat as it moves the body away from the attack, but the fencer must be well aware of their Distance as it does not move as far as the Retreat. Ironically, this is also its greatest advantage as it keeps the fencer close to the opponent, allowing for a quick counter if the fencer chooses.

Body Void

The body may be moved without the movement of the feet to avoid an opponent's attack. These are, for the most part, simple actions. In most cases, the body is simply leant one direction or another to avoid the attack. The important thing is that the fencer maintains his balance while performing these actions and does not over-balance. The leaning action should be centred round a combination of bending and twisting at the hips and shoulders, meanwhile remaining as upright as possible. The body may be bent in any direction he chooses so long as it follows the principles presented above. Further to this, a single piece of the body may be removed from the attack also. This is most useful and effective when an attack is made against a limb as it is quite simple to move the body part out of the way to keep it safe.

Combination

Of the three types of Void, the movement of the body with the feet is the most effective as it combines the advantages of the other two techniques. This may simply be a step added to the movement of the body, or it may be a purposeful technique such as what is known as the *Inquartata* and *Half-Inquartata*. These two techniques need care in their performance, to miss-time them could result in the fencer being struck, as such it is vital that they are performed with precision.

Half-Inquartata

It will be noted that the techniques are related and that the one is half the motion of the other. The *Half-Inquartata* is half the *Inquartata* as the name would suggest, and indeed it is also half the movement. To perform the *Half-Inquartata*, the rear foot is moved behind the front foot, so that the toe lines up with the heel of the front foot. From a position of the Guard of Third, this is effective in defending the High Inside Line.

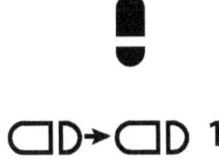

Inquartata

The *Inquartata* is a larger movement as the back foot moves further across to increase the angle. The back foot can go far enough that it is almost parallel with the front foot. For comfort's sake, it is enough that the foot is placed one foot-length across from the front foot. As with the *Half-Inquartata* this action protects the High Inside Line, in this particular case it can go some way to also protecting the Low Inside Line as well. Both of these actions can also be performed using the front foot to come behind the rear in order to defend the other side. Care should be taken in the use of these techniques and they should be practiced before executing them in an encounter.

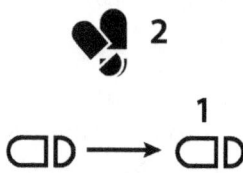

Usage

Voids are an effective form of defence and can be spectacularly so when performed. The position of the technique can also allow the fencer to set up for a counter-attack. While Voids are effective against thrusts, it should not be forgotten that they are effective against a cut. The Void is a better defensive action against the Cut than a Parry of any kind. The Cut which is parried is stopped and then the fencer acts from a position where the opponent can still be effective. A Cut that is voided will pass by the fencer, and must complete due to the nature of the Cut, which unbalances the opponent and leaves a larger opening for the fencer against him.

Voids need to be practiced, and they must be practiced against valid attacks in a safe environment. The fencer who can effectively learn how to Void can defend himself using simply this technique. However, it is advised that further defensive techniques are taken into account and learnt so that the fencer will be truly effective.

The Parry

The Parry is another defensive option, enhanced when combined with the Void; this increases the effectiveness of both the Parry and the Void, making a more effective defence as a result. The Parry may be used on its own effectively however a defence of two actions is better, as will be demonstrated later. There are two types of Parry that can be utilised when using the single sword, one with the sword and the other with the off-hand. The former is the more obvious of the two being performed with the weapon. The latter one is not used as often and needs to be considered as it can be very effective, especially when combined with other forms of defence or offence. Before either is discussed, the principles upon which they are both based will be discussed.

Waiting for the Attack

The first principle of the Parry applies to all forms of defensive actions and it is through this principle that a fencer's defensive actions and actions in general become more effective. The principle which is being discussed is to wait for the opponent's attack to arrive before performing a defensive action. This involves patience and confidence in skill.

The newer fencer will parry much earlier than the more experienced one because the more experienced has more confidence in his skill. This is based on what will be referred to as a "panic space". The "panic space" is the closest a fencer will allow an opponent's attack to come before reacting to the attack. In more experienced fencers, this will be much closer than in less experienced. This is due to the practice and confidence in the skill being used.

If the fencer chases the opponent's weapon, the Parry will be made much closer to the *Debole* on the fencer's weapon than if he waits. If the opponent's weapon is chased too much, this can reduce the effectiveness of the Parry markedly. The more the fencer waits the closer to the hilt and, as a result, further down the *Forte* the opponent's attack will be received. This makes for a more effective Parry. Of course, if the fencer waits too long he will be struck. This means that this particular action requires Timing, just as with all actions. The Voids described previously will also be substantially more effective if the fencer waits for the opponent's attack.

Two Types of Parry

There are two types of Parry, the Beat Parry and the Parry with Opposition. It is important to understand the difference between the two types of Parry and the effect of each and how effective they can be. Both apply to both sword and hand. It is easier to perform both with the sword, as the Beat Parry performed incorrectly can be painful on the hand, but both can be effectively used by the hand.

Beat Parry

The Beat Parry uses the impact of the weapon or hand to force the opponent's weapon off-line and therefore out of danger. The Parry with Opposition guides the opponent's weapon away after gaining contact and maintains it. The Beat Parry is much simpler to use as it simply involves striking the weapon away from the fencer.

The same technique used can be modified for offensive purposes in the Beat Attack, discussed further along. The experienced fencer may even use the Beat Parry against the opponent's *Debole* before the attack arrives, but this involves very accurate Timing on the part of the fencer. The disadvantage of the Beat Parry is that it loses engagement once the opponent's blade has been struck and therefore the opponent's weapon cannot be felt through contact, and so the location by feeling is lost.

Parry with Opposition

The Parry with Opposition, like all techniques, is most effective when it is executed properly. It is a slower Parry than the Beat Parry, but it maintains contact with the opponent's weapon and therefore can feel where the opponent's weapon is. There are also more options open to the fencer who uses the Parry with Opposition due to the maintenance of contact. Through this contact a fencer can gain an extended period of Hard Engagement where several Blade Engagement options are possible.

Due to its advantages, it will be the Parry with Opposition that will be the primary Parry used in this treatise. The Beat Parry should, however be kept as an option for the fencer for those times where it is advantageous. Both types of Parry have their place in the use of the sword, and not just the rapier.

The Off-Hand Parry

The off-hand as a parrying option, and indeed a defensive option, is often forgotten in favour of the sword. The fencer who does this reduces his defensive options. Of course, the usual argument against the use of the hand as a defensive option is that the hand may be struck or hurt in the process of being used to Parry. The fencer should consider whether it would be better to possibly hazard a little damage to the hand or possibly a greater damage to something more vital. There are gauntlets which are designed for the purpose of using the hand in defence, but the off-hand should still be considered a viable option even without this option.

Palm

It is the palm that should be used to Parry the opponent's weapon. This is more padded than the fingers and as such will be less painful, likewise using the palm rather than the back of the hand. To this point if a Parry is made and it is missed with the hand, the forearm is viable in defence so long as the arm is kept straight when the Parry is made. Also, when the palm is used, there is more control possible over the opponent's weapon.

Smooth

The action of the Hand Parry should be smooth. This will result in a much more effective Parry than if it is jerky. The fencer will also maintain greater control of the opponent's weapon if the Parry is smooth. The opponent's weapon should be moved away from the body and never across it. The shortest distance away from the body should be chosen, even if this means moving the hand across the body.

Not Too Low

In using the hand, the fencer should never attempt to Parry too low. To measure this, the fencer should put his arm by his side and never Parry anything lower than the position of his wrist. If the fencer parries any lower, he will have to lean and this will make him closer to the opponent's weapon and this is dangerous. As described before, the fencer should not reach for the opponent's weapon but allow it to come and then Parry.

Move the Sword

The Hand Parry may be effectively used against attacks on all Lines. The simple thing for the fencer not to get tangled is to move the sword out of the way of the hand. Hence, from the Guard of Third, a Hand Parry to cover the High Inside Line is simple. The parry for the High Outside Line involves the moving of the sword point downward so that the fencer's weapon is not impeded. Similarly, for the Low Outside Line, the sword should be lifted away from the Hand Parry. The other two Lines simply follow the rules as they have been described.

Beat Parry

The action described above is the parry with opposition using the hand. The Beat Parry is more than merely slapping the sword away. The same rules apply, the action should be smooth, the shortest distance away from the body, not parrying too low, not reaching, and moving the weapon away from the Parry to avoid becoming tangled. It is the impact which makes the Beat effective, so the impact must be sharp but controlled, and must use the palm.

Flat Not Edge

In both cases the fencer should attempt to come in contact with the flat of the opponent's weapon rather than the edge. This makes the parry more effective and means less chance for damage to the hand. The Hand Parry should not be used against a cutting attack due to the increased potential for damage to the hand. There are techniques where the off-hand can be used defensively against the cut, but these are an advanced technique which will not be described in this treatise.

The Sword Parry

The Sword Parry is a more natural defensive action than that of the Hand Parry, but it is more complex and must be executed properly to retain its maximum effectiveness.

Lines

The purpose of the Sword Parry is to defend the fencer using the sword against an attack of the opponent. The fencer creates walls against the attacks of the opponent. When all of the Parries are put together, this creates a defensive box with the sword and Parries as the sides of the box. With this in mind, it is possible to use a single Parry to close any one Line. This is the primary purpose of the Parry. This relates back directly to the subject of Lines discussed in the Theory.

Forte to Debole

Some of the *Forte* and *Debole* has been discussed previously with regard to waiting for the opponent's attack to arrive, it is important for the fencer that he catches the opponent's *Debole* on his *Forte* so that the Parry is effective, essentially using the strength of his sword against the weak of the opponent's.

Edge Not Flat

Using the same principle, the edge of the sword should be put against the opponent's weapon, being that the edge is stronger than the flat. The fencer should not use the flat of his weapon against that of the opponent's due to the same reasoning, the opponent's point may also roll around the fencer's blade if the flat of the blade is used to Parry. The Lateral Parry, simply moving the weapon from one side to the other without turning the edge, is simply less effective than turning the edge to the opponent's weapon.

Point Position

The point position of the weapon in the Guard which the fencer takes can also affect the effectiveness of the Parry and the ease of its performance. In the Guards of Third and Fourth, the point of the weapon should be as high as the fencer's shoulder. The angle of the sword which is created by the position of the weapon covers more than if it is lower. It is simple that the higher position of the point increases the defence, but a lower point is faster for the counter-attack. Being that defence is primary, it is important that the point is kept up.

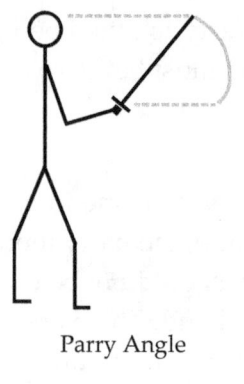

Parry Angle

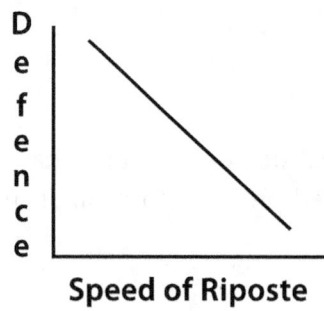

Defence versus Riposte

Edges

There are two edges on a sword, regardless of whether both are sharp or not, and as such two Parries for each position, one with the True Edge and one with the False Edge. It is the True Edge Parries which will be used. Some of the False Edge Parries will be mentioned, but not as primary Parries.

Four Parries

The four Parries which are demonstrated here are those designed to cover the four Lines. There are other Parries, some of which will be mentioned later on. What should be noted is that while the Parry with Opposition is the primary, and that the Beat is secondary, the easiest way to consider the Parries is to perform them as Cuts. This will assist with the delivery of the Parry.

Parry of First

The Parry of First is the Parry which covers the Low Inside Line. From the Guard of Third it is made as a sweeping action diagonally across the body and down low. The Parry should be delivered as though the fencer has the intention of delivering a Cut to the opponent's sword. The point of the weapon should not drag on the ground, and as such may be angled slightly forward to avoid this.

Parry of Second

The Parry of Second is the Parry which covers the Low Outside Line. From the Guard of Third, the point is dropped and the hand turned outward so the edge comes in contact with the opponent's weapon. Once again, this should be delivered in the manner of a Cut against the opponent's weapon sweeping downward and outward. Again, the point may be lifted slightly to avoid coming in contact with the ground.

Parry of Third

The Parry of Third covers the High Outside Line. From the Guard of Third it can be as simple as merely turning the hand to Second position so that the edge of the weapon meets the opponent's weapon. This can also be delivered in the manner of a Cut should the fencer inscribe a "C" in the air when performing the Parry.

Parry of Fourth

The Parry of Fourth covers the High Inside Line. From a Guard of Third, the hand is turned to the Fourth position; the weapon is then pushed directly across the body leading with the knuckles so that the edge comes in contact with the opponent's weapon. Once again, this Parry can, and should, be delivered in the manner of a Cut.

These are the four True Edge Parries designed to cover the four Lines. These Parries will be effective if performed as described against both Thrust and Cut attacks, however as has been mentioned previously, avoiding a Cut can be more effective than parrying it.

Other Parries

False Edge

There are other Parries, as mentioned before which can be utilised by the fencer. For example, False Edge Parries can be used for Third and Second. In this particular case for Third, the hand is turned to Fourth position and pushed outward so that the False Edge comes into contact with the opponent's weapon rather than the True Edge. The same process is used to use the False Edge rather than the true for the Parry of Second. The hand is turned to Fourth position and the point is dropped so the False Edge comes into contact with the opponent's weapon. These are optional Parries and will require practice to be effective. The True Edge Parries are the ones which will be the focus here.

Window Parry

The Parries of First and Second can also be lifted in order to protect the High Line, but these are not standard Parries and as with the False Edge Parries, will require a lot of practice. There are also Parries called Window Parries. In these, from a Guard of Third, the point is dropped downward. The hand is then lifted with the palm toward the opponent with the knuckles toward the Inside Line parrying with the True Edge. This parry is designed to cover the High Inside Line. The position which results is an effective position from which to deliver a vertical Cut known as a *Fendente*. Another interesting, and final note is that the Parries of Third and Fourth can actually be used to change the guard from Third to Fourth and vice versa.

Ceding Parry

There is also the Ceding Parry which is made in response to the Riposte of an opponent, once the opponent has made his Parry and begins to Riposte, the sword is drawn back toward the fencer while remaining engaged with the opponent's weapon into the most appropriate Parry. This is the most useful response to a Riposte as it is effective and simple and may be used in conjunction with other defensive techniques. Parries can be extremely effective when used properly and following the directions described.

Defensive Combination

The effectiveness in defence is improved by using more than one action against an opponent's attack. While it is true that an effective defence may be mounted by the use of only one action with the right Timing, the use of additional actions is more effective and gives assurance that the fencer is defended. It is better that the newer fencer uses more than one defence to be sure of his defence. The principle upon which this idea of defensive combination is founded is redundancy.

Layers of Defence

The concept of using more than one defensive action, for the purpose of this manual, is called Layers of Defence. This principle is based on the idea of redundancy and that the defence provided by any one action is improved by the use of second or further actions.[18] An attack may be defended using a single action when it is performed properly and with the correct Timing, but it is more effective when multiple actions are used.

A single Parry of sword or hand may be used to defend against a Thrust, but the same Parry will be increased in effectiveness through the use of another defensive action. If the Parry fails to stop the attack, and it is the fencer's only defence, the fencer will more than likely be struck. If there is an additional defensive option, then the attack has to pass through two defences to strike the fencer rather than only one. Further, if a third defensive option is used, then the defence increases further.

A Thrust made against the High Inside Line against a fencer in a Guard of Third may be parried by a Parry of Fourth. Executed with the correct Timing and performed accurately, this will be an effective defence. If the fencer miss-times the Parry he will be struck by the Thrust. If, however, the fencer combined the Parry of Fourth with a Void of his body, then he has increased his chances of remaining safe from the attack. This is because the Thrust now has to defeat two defences to succeed. The scenario presented demonstrates how the use of a second action can improve defence of the fencer.

Against a Thrust against the High Outside Line a fencer may Parry Third, or he may Parry Third and use a Void, he may also use his off-hand to support the Sword Parry. Added to this he may also use footwork to draw himself away from the opponent's attack. Each one of the sundry actions mentioned for defence will increase the defensive potential of the whole.

Training Asset

The principle of Layers of Defence is primarily designed to increase the defensive potential of the fencer against an attack. However, the use of this principle in using multiple actions against a single attack at once increases the mobility of the fencer and increases the familiarity of the fencer with the movements of his own body.

---

[18] A similar principle is seen in risk management, the military, and security.

The ability to use multiple actions against an opponent can only be an asset to the fencer. This ability will allow the fencer to perform more and more complex actions. Such training is not only building physical body motion, but is also mental as it allows the fencer to develop the mental ability to perform multiple actions at the same time. The ability to perform multiple actions at the same time will result in a great asset as the fencer progresses.

The defensive combinations which have been presented here are only a small portion of those possible against an attack. What the fencer should be considering is how another action can be used against the attack made by the opponent. Practice should be taken considering various attacks, and then multiple defences against it, using multiple actions to find the most effective combination for each type of attack. This way the fencer will also have opened his mind to different options that are available against different attacks.

Of the Thrust

The Thrust is an attack delivered with the point of the weapon against an opponent with the intent on causing damage through penetration. The point is projected primarily through the use of the muscles of the shoulder and arm to a point in space. When used offensively against an opponent, this space will be occupied, but the delivery is the same as it would be delivered against any target, including when there is a lack of target. This is a technique-focussed action.

The Thrust is the primary offensive action in this form of fencing. For most, the Thrust would seem a simple action which would need little instruction and they would marvel at the amount which has been written about it. However, there are certain details which need to be emphasised so that the Thrust can be delivered properly and so maximise the offensive potential of this particular action, merely haphazardly throwing the point at the opponent is not sufficient.

Primary Offensive Action

The Thrust is the primary offensive action in fencing due to several reasons, which will be explained. Firstly, it is the most efficient method of delivering an attack. The Thrust is quicker than a cut due to the Second Principle, that of the straight line and it also uses less muscle power to cause damage.

Secondly, the weapon itself biases fencing toward the Thrust. The weapon has a small cross-section, and is long and pointed. The small cross-section reduces its effectiveness in cutting, but the Cut should in no way be neglected as it is also a useful offensive tool. The length of the weapon also increases the advantage toward the Thrust due to the reach of the weapon.

Accuracy and Efficiency

Much has been said about the importance of speed, but accuracy is more important. There is little use having a Thrust which is faster, if that Thrust cannot arrive at its intended target. It would be better for the fencer to have a slower Thrust that can be delivered to the target of his choice; rather than having a fast Thrust which he has little or no control over. This is a technique-focussed action rather than one which merely uses muscle power to deliver it. If the power used is not focussed in the correct direction it will be of little use to the fencer.

The concept of speed in the Thrust is a fallacy. There are those who will claim that some experienced swordsman has a fast Thrust and this is due to the speed and power at which he delivers his Thrust; this is inaccurate. The speed of the Thrust is not due to simple muscle power but due to the efficiency of motion which the fencer uses to deliver the Thrust. There is some muscle power used to move the weapon, but the primary reason that an accurate Thrust is fast, when delivered by an experienced fencer, is due to the precision in the method of delivery. This can be related to all the actions of fencing.

The actions of the experienced fencer are faster due to efficiency. The fencer will attempt to use as little energy as possible in an action and as such it needs to be executed in the most efficient manner possible. The less extraneous actions which are used in an action, the more efficient it will be, and as a result, will seem to be quicker, even if this is not the fencer's intention. This efficiency is a result of practice and also experience, the more comfortable a fencer with a set of actions, the easier it will be for the fencer to perform these actions and so they will seem faster. The important thing is that it is technique which is important not the brute power of the fencer.

Types of Thrust

There are different types of Thrust all of which rely primarily on the same technique. What differentiates them is the direction in which they are delivered. A Thrust is named for the method and direction from which it is delivered and not in which it lands. This is because the same Line can be targeted by different Thrusts rather than just a single one. It also due to this method of delivery and naming that the Thrusts are named for the direction in which they are delivered rather than the Line which they target.

Similar to the Lines, there are four directions which will define the type of Thrust being delivered. They are from below, from above, from the right and from the left. Of course, depending on the situation, these names can be combined to give a horizontal and vertical direction. The horizontal is given before the vertical for both cuts and thrusts. In the same way, a thrust delivered purely from a single direction will have only one name.

Stoccata

The primary Thrust is the thrust that comes from below meaning that the hand of the fencer has to rise to deliver the Thrust. This is called a *Stoccata*. It is a Thrust which could also be referred to as a "normal" Thrust as it is the most commonly delivered.

Imbroccata

The Thrust delivered from above meaning that the hand of the fencer has to descend to deliver the Thrust is called an *Imbroccata*. The simplest and most obvious position from which this is delivered is from the Guard of First. However, this is not the only position from which it can be delivered. For example, an *Imbroccata* can be delivered from a Guard of Third against the foot or leg of the opponent.

Mandritta and Riversa

The two terms for Thrusts which come from the left and right apply to both Cuts and Thrusts. For the right hander, a Thrust or Cut delivered from the right side of the fencer against the opponent is called a *Mandritta*. Once again for the right-hander, a Thrust or Cut delivered from the left side of the fencer against the opponent is called a *Riversa*. This is sometimes called a Cross-Blow because the arm has to cross the body. More will be said of the description of the Cut in a section further on in this treatise.

Naming

Usually, to delineate between a Cut and a Thrust, in the left and right blows, the word *Punta*[19] or *Botta*[20] would be added to those which are thrusts. The *Stoccata* and *Imbroccata* only refer to Thrusts. There are further names for the Cuts. For the left-handed fencer the left and right blows will be reversed due to the changed position of the sword. So, for a left-hander a cut from the left is a *Mandritta* and a cut from the right is a *Riversa*.

Execution

The Thrust, for the most part, is a simple action, but mistakes are often made in its execution. Care needs to be taken so the Thrust is executed properly and effectively. There are some common mistakes often made in the execution of the Thrust and they will be noted in the examination of this technique. The first is that power is not required in the execution of the Thrust. The design of the weapon and the Thrust itself means that only a small amount of pressure is required to do damage to the opponent. The execution of the thrust along with the weapon's own weight is sufficient.

Shoulder Use

The shoulder is the prime mover in this action. The elbow, wrist and hand merely guide the point to its target. This enables a larger muscle group to perform the major action and uses less energy. It is the shoulder that should move first, if one of the other joints or parts of the arm moves first then the point could be thrown off target and will reduce the effectiveness of the technique as a whole. Though the shoulder must move first, it is not merely that the arm will swing forward and backward; there needs to be purpose in the action. Each Thrust needs to be performed as a single, purposeful action.

Velocity

While the action has some velocity, in no way is the arm thrown. Each part of the arm activates singly and performs its purpose in the action. This is controlled by the joints and the muscles. While it is the shoulder that activates the Thrust, it should not move forward before or after the Thrust is made unless another action is made after the Thrust. If the shoulder moves forward before the Thrust is made, the opponent will use this as a cue when the fencer will Thrust and avoid or counter it. If the shoulder moves forward after the Thrust, the fencer may force the point off target and will alter the distance to the target. This is especially important in practice so the fencer does not deceive himself as regard to his own Distance.

---

[19] Italian for "tip," thus meaning a Thrust.

[20] Italian for "blow," thus meaning either a Thrust or a Cut, though often referring to a Thrust.

Targeting

Just as the front foot and toe is used to point the body toward the opponent, so too should the hand and fingers point at the target when the Thrust is made. The front foot and toe should also point at your target as biomechanically this will assist with your accuracy. This simple concept and action will assist in the accuracy of the Thrust.

The shortest distance between two points is a straight line (Second Principle), as such the shortest distance between the point of the weapon and its target is also a straight line. This is the line that the point should follow when the Thrust is made. The point should neither move upward nor dip in its action. The point should move directly from its current position to the target. Any deviation from this will affect the Timing of the Thrust and its accuracy.

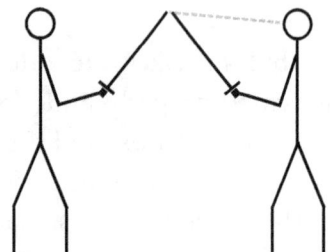
Correct Line for Thrust to the Head

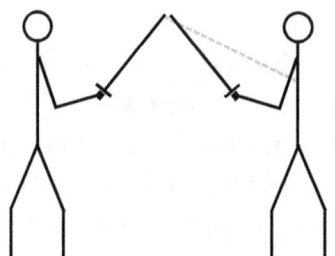
Correct Line for Thrust to the Body

Hand Position

The position of the hand needs to be considered with regard to the Thrust, this applies both before, during and after the Thrust. The hand itself, for the most part should not change position in the process of delivering the point to its target. Changes in hand position will affect the direction of the point and may move it off target.

Some will argue that the hand should be turned to Fourth or Second position in the Thrust when it is completed, or even during the Thrust. The only reason for this is to turn the edge toward the opponent's weapon. Otherwise, the hand should remain in the same position as it was at the beginning of the Thrust throughout the action so that the point remains on target.

Some will claim that twisting the hand and the arm during the Thrust will increase velocity and make for a more effective Thrust. It *may* indeed increase velocity, but the deviation in the hand can result in a deviation from the intended target. The simplest action in the Thrust is the most efficient and is the most effective. This is simply because any extraneous movement of the hand or arm has the potential to deviate the point and also will use extra energy. These two factors will result in the Thrust being less effective. The fencer should keep his Thrust as simple as possible.

The Lunge

The Lunge is simply a Thrust with footwork.[21] The Thrust itself has a limited range, limited to the length of the sword and the length of the arm. The Lunge is designed to extend the range of the Thrust by adding a Half-Pace to it. The footwork attached to the Lunge can also change the direction of the attack. This relates to a modification of the normal Lunge.

The standard Lunge projects the fencer straight forward, the modified versions use other footwork to change the direction of the attack. These will be examined after the details of the standard Lunge have been presented.

Principles

First of all, and most importantly, the Lunge is one of the techniques where the importance of moving the hand before the foot is demonstrated. In the Lunge a Thrust is made and then the Step follows, hence hand before foot. This is a very simple view of the Lunge however, if the foot moves first, it is most likely that the fencer will be struck before the attack is completed.

Secondly, the speed and power of the Lunge in its movement comes from the power generated by the legs. This is important if it is to be performed properly. Many will attempt to throw themselves forward at the ground using their forward foot to stop them as the action of the Lunge. This is an inefficient method and is flawed. The power must be generated by the legs to project the fencer forward in the Lunge.

Footwork

When the Lunge is thought of, it is a large Step which is made to dramatically increase the range of the Lunge however a simple Half-Pace is sufficient for the action to be called a Lunge. Both of these actions relate to the same actions and the same principles. The action of the arm is simply the Thrust, which has already been discussed. The same action is used in this situation. The footwork action has already been discussed somewhat in the section on footwork, but more detail is required. These two actions need to be combined to complete the Lunge.

Execution

This is a Half-Pace as has been described. The same principles follow. The front foot needs to be picked up and placed, gliding above the ground not dragging. The speed of the Lunge is made through the efficient use of the muscles of the legs and nothing more. The power of the Lunge is generated from the rear leg, more specifically the muscles of the upper leg. The action of the leg is to straighten the rear leg and move the fencer forward. It is vital that the fencer understands that the energy generated by the rear leg needs to be directed forward and not upward as some will do. This needs to be executed explosively. The fencer's rear foot should also remain anchored and should not drag in any way.

---

[21] Knowledge evolves with time. Since the original writing of this treatise, my understanding of the lunge has developed to realise that the thrust is not the only attack that can be made with the lunge. The result is that the lunge is not merely defined by the thrust. It is defined as a forward action of the feet and the body which is carried by them. It is added to the attack to make it more effective.

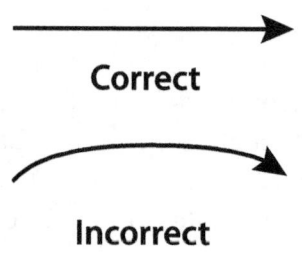

Power Direction for the Lunge

The Thrust is started first and the described footwork motion follows. The Thrust should be made as has already been described, and should be almost complete before the foot movement begins. However, the action of the Thrust should not drag the fencer forward in the action of the Lunge; the forward motion must be generated by the legs. The Lunge will require much practice to perfect and become the most efficient that it can be.

Change of Direction

Something has already been said of Thrusting actions which can be made against the opponent using different angles to achieve a greater result. Each one of these actions can be further enhanced through the use of footwork. In most cases, a simple Pace will increase the effect of the attack.

The Lunge action described above can be projected in different directions, including to the rear. This is a difficult action and the fencer should consider carefully how to achieve this. However, the Lunging actions forward and off at an angle will increase the effect of a thrusting attack.

For the right hander, the *Punta Mandritta* can be enhanced through the use of a Lunge in a forward and right direction. This will increase the angle of attack and make it more difficult to defend. The *Punta Riversa* is a Thrusting action which breaks one of the rules of footwork. In this the right foot crosses over the left, moving left and forward, to project the attack in the correct direction. The attack is directed around the opponent's defence. For the left hander the directions are simply reversed. Executed correctly, the fencer should be in little danger due the attack being made against the opponent and the necessity of defence on his part. One of the things that make the Lunge a successful action, which is often forgotten, is the Recovery.

Recovery

The Recovery is an important part as it moves the fencer out of the position found at the end of the Lunge and back into a more defensible position. In most cases, this merely involves the completion of the Pace which was started. This recovery may be made forward or backward.

In the Forward Recovery, the fencer merely completes the Forward Pace which was started. In the Backward Recovery, returns to his original starting position. For the *Punta Mandritta* and *Punta Riversa* it is better for the fencer to complete the Step moving forward than it is to return to the original position.

The Recovery breaks the rules with regard to Timing. In this particular instance, the foot will move before the hand. The fencer should return to a normal Guard position with his feet before returning the weapon to his Guard. Proceeding in this manner means that the fencer will remain with his weapon pointed at the opponent until he has returned to a Ward. Thus, the opponent remains under threat.

The Recover Backward is useful to move the fencer away from the opponent after the attack. The Recover Forward is useful to follow the opponent and keep him on the defensive. If another opening is found during the Recover Forward, once the feet have been returned to position, the Lunge may be repeated, especially as the arm is already in position. A tactical consideration is that a fencer on the defensive, against an opponent lunging, should not use a simple Retreat Step in defence but move off-line in defence this reduces the chance of the opponent following his Lunge with another after the Recovery.

Summary

The Thrust is the primary attack found in fencing due to the shape and nature of the weapon. It does not require any of the force of the Cut, and is much quicker due to the direct lines that it takes. However, the Thrusting actions need to be executed correctly to be most effective.

The Lunge is a simple extension of the Thrust adding a footwork motion on to the Thrusting action to increase its range. The Timing of this action must be performed properly to be effective and any dereliction in this particular action will result in the Lunge being less effective and the fencer potentially being in danger. The Lunge is only really successfully completed with the addition of the Recovery, which also must have attention paid to it many a fencer has neglected his Recovery to his demise.

Of the Edge

The Cut is an attack delivered with the edge of the weapon. This can be performed with either edge in at least two different methods. While the Cut is a secondary attack to the thrust, it is still necessary for the fencer to know this attack and understand how to perform the Cut properly. Merely smashing the edge of the weapon into the opponent will be ineffective. There is technique involved which is essential in the proper delivery of the Cut.

Opportunities for the Cut

With regard to the rapier, the Cut is a secondary method of attacking the opponent, but it is still a useful one to know. It has the disadvantage that it is slower than the Thrust, but it has the advantage of being more useful at closer ranges where it is difficult to get the point to the target. This being said, it is also possible to successfully deliver a Cut and be effective at some distance. Accordingly, it is not necessary to be close for the Cut to be effective. Effectiveness is a matter of technique rather than the range at which it is delivered.

In fencing with the rapier there will be opportunities to use the Cut and the fencer should always attempt to take advantage of these opportunities. One clear opportunity for a Cut is when a Thrust has missed the opponent, with the point past the opponent with the edge close to the opponent, and this is only one example. There are several other times where the similar opportunities will be present. To take advantage of these opportunities, the fencer has to be aware of them and not be too focussed on delivering the Thrust.

Two Edges

The rapier has two edges. So, both edges can be used to cut. Often the Cut is focussed on the True Edge, with the False Edge all but ignored. The Cut with the False Edge can be just as effective, and indeed more effective in some instances; just as the Cut with the True Edge can be delivered from a multitude of different directions, so too can the False Edge. In some instances, the name of the direction will be changed to suit the False Edge rather than the True Edge. This is simply because the blow is easier to deliver with the False Edge than with the True Edge.

Divisions of the Cut

In examining the directions of the Cut, it must be remembered that each may be delivered with both the True Edge and False Edge. Two of these directions have already been discussed under the Thrust, the *Mandritta* and the *Riversa* each being a description for a Cut which comes from a particular side of the fencer against the opponent. The *Mandritta* is sometimes called the "right blow" or forehand being a normal fashioned blow, and the *Riversa* called a backhand or "cross-blow" in that it comes across the fencer. These are used to describe all of the blows which come from one side or the other. Please note, that the diagram below is orientated for the right-handed fencer facing his opponent.

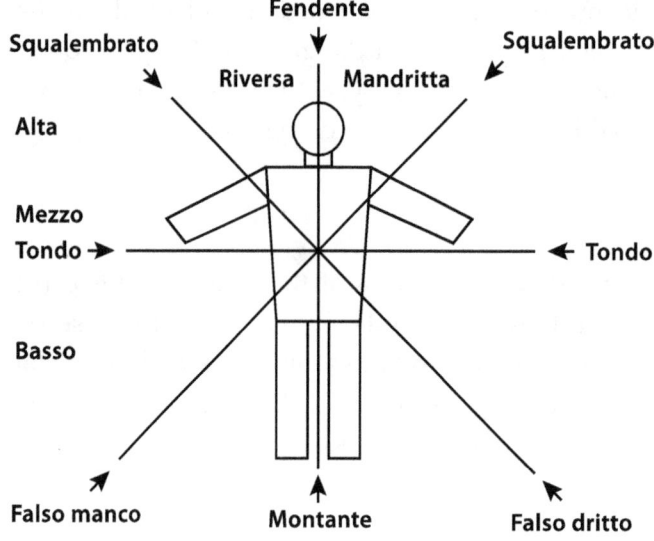

Facing the opponent

Horizontal

The simplest and most commonly thrown Cut is the *Tondo*. This is a horizontal Cut delivered parallel to the ground. They may be delivered to the upper part of the body, middle or lower. Each one of these has a name, from the upper to lower they are, *Alto*, *Mezzo*, and *Basso*. Thus, for a right-handed fencer, a horizontal blow thrown from the right at the middle of the opponent is called a *Mandritta Mezzo Tondo*. Most often the height of the Cut is not named.

Vertical

A vertical Cut delivered downward against an opponent is called a *Fendente*. If it is to one side or the other the right or left delineation may be used as it is for all Cuts. Any exceptions to this will be noted. A vertical cut delivered upward against an opponent, following the same line as the *Fendente* is the *Montante*. This may be delivered with either the True or the False Edge, though most commonly it is delivered with the False.

Diagonal

The last direction for the Cuts that needs to be discussed is the diagonal line. A downward cut on a diagonal is called a *Squalembrato*. The cuts travelling upward are called a different name for each. For the *Mandritta* side the Cut on the diagonal upward is called a *Falso Dritto*, for the *Riverso* side, it is called a *Falso Manco*. Upward Cuts may be delivered with the False Edge or True Edge along the diagonal line depending on which is most comfortable. Upward Cuts may be also delivered with the reverse, but they may not be as comfortable. Experimentation with the Cuts is useful to discover which cuts are easier with which edge.

Blade Location

Distance is an important factor when considering the Cut. There are two optimum places on the blade for cutting. One is located on the *Forte* and the other is located on the *Debole*. In both cases, they are located approximately one hand span from the hilt and point respectively. In a purely cutting weapon these may be referred to as the Inner and Outer Percussion Points. It is at these points which the fencer will gain the greatest amount of impact and the cleanest blow when using the weapon to cut.

Should a fencer wish to cut properly, it is these parts that the fencer should focus on and it is these parts which will determine the best distance. Of course, the entire edge and point may be used to cut, but these specific spots will gain the fencer the most leverage and advantage. The Cut with the tip of the sword, or *Stramazone* is a technique which has not been addressed, will be addressed separately as while the technique is much the same as the other Cuts, it is a different sort of blow.

Distance

The Outer Percussion Point, that which is located on the *Debole* can be used at some range against the opponent. This is because it is simple enough to extend the arm and use the outer part of the weapon against the opponent. This will most often result in the cleanest and safest cut. However, the same part of the weapon can be used in close, should the fencer require.

The Cut at close is often facilitated through the use of the Inner Percussion Point that located on the *Forte* this is usually a rough and tumble affair called Closes and Grips; a subject which will have some attention paid to it in a later part of this treatise. The use of these specified spots on the weapon in cutting will reduce the potential for the weapon bouncing off the opponent and the Cut being ineffective. In the case of the rapier, it is the technique used in the Cut which results in it being effective, not any brute force applied by the fencer.

Techniques

There are two methods of causing damage with a sword against an opponent, one which is focussed on the impact and the other which is focussed on placement and slicing. While many will separate these two and say that they are distinctive. Even when a fencer is using an Impact Cut with the rapier it is necessary to involve some of the technique involved in the Slicing Cut, simply due to the profile of the rapier's blade.

The shape of the weapon will determine the most successful method for cutting. The angle of the edge is an important factor, it a primarily cutting weapon the blade will be wide and the angle of the edge will be low. This is not the situation in the case of the rapier; it has a narrow blade and sharper angle on the blade. This makes the profile of the weapon determine that it is not suited to the style of cleaving blow that is found in weapons such as the longsword. It is due to this angle of the blade that the slicing action becomes vastly more important than any sort of impact or cleaving action. This changes the method in which the cutting attack with a rapier is delivered.

Slicing Cut

To start with the purely Slicing Cut will be examined. In this case, the weapon is placed against the target, pressure is applied and the weapon is pushed or drawn along the target. It is important that the pressure of the blade against the target is maintained while the action is performed. This action has much in common with how a knife is used to cut bread.

An important note should be made at this point in time that the weapon may be pushed or drawn by the fencer; both of these actions are equally valid. The pushing action will force the hilt closer to the opponent, and the drawing will pull it away from the opponent. Each has its particular use in its particular situation, and the same actions can be used in both the Slicing Cut and the Impact Cut. The Slicing Cut will most likely be used in the close, but does not prevent it from being used at range.

This technique is good practice for the Impact Cut technique which follows. The purely Slicing Cut does have its limitations; it tends to be slower, and also tends to be most effective against exposed flesh. It also seems, in some cases, to be lacking in some cutting ability against some targets.

Impact Cut

The Impact Cut is delivered in a much more flamboyant fashion. It is delivered much as a cleaving cut would be, but it is not the impact which is the primary aim. If the blow is delivered too hard the weapon will simply bounce off and the Cut will be ineffective. This is due to the shape of the weapon. The impacting portion of this Cut is merely to allow the blade to bite into the target to allow the slicing action to cause more damage. The slicing action is the same as described previously except that the blade has already been put into position for the Cut.

The impact and slicing action are not separate; they need to be performed as one smooth action to be effective. This means that the weapon should flow, lead to the target, bite and cut all in one smooth action. Any slowing or stopping will destroy the momentum of the Cut and reduce the effectiveness of it. Slowing in any form during any Cut will allow the opponent time to mount a defence or perform some other action to counter the Cut being performed. The Impact Cut will most likely be used at some distance due to the preparation required, however this does not preclude it from being used closer.

Stramazone

The *Stramazone* is a different style of Cut to those which have been described even though it uses many of the same principles which have been described for the other Cuts. It is different in that this Cut only uses the very tip of the weapon to cut. This is the reason why it is sometimes called a "tip cut". What should be noted here is that it is still using the edge of the weapon to do damage, it is merely that it is the very tip of the weapon that is being used.

This is a scratching cut which results in small cuts, however, these Cuts can be just as debilitating, if not more so in some instances, as those performed by other forms of Cut. The *Stramazone* is usually delivered against those targets which will cause the most problems for, or damage to the opponent. In this particular instance the primary targets are those exposed vital areas such as the throat, or against simply debilitating targets such as the forehead to blind the opponent with blood in his eyes. This Cut should not be aimed at the chest due to the protection of the rib cage. Hence, this Cut should be aimed at softer, fleshier targets.

Two Methods

There are claims that there are two methods in which the *Stramazone* may be delivered. One version of this is very vigorous and the other which is somewhat less so. One method is to deliver the Cut in much the same way as found in the Impact Cut above, and the other is to place the point on the target and then draw it across. The second method described will not be used in this treatise as if the fencer can place the point in this manner, a Thrust may much more easily be delivered and will cause more damage; as a consequence, the effectiveness of this method is clearly disputed.

Distance

It is of vital importance that the fencer has his distance correct for the delivery of the *Stramazone*. If he is too far away, he will simply miss the target, if he is too close the tip of the weapon may simply impact on the opponent and bounce off or the Cut will simply be ineffective. The fencer must be at a distance where just the tip of the weapon will reach the target; and thus, only this part will come in contact with the target. This should be practiced so that the fencer is able to do this before attempting this cut in an encounter.

Delivery

The delivery of the Cut itself is much the same as the Impact Cut described above, with only the tip coming in contact with the target. It should be one smooth action which delivers the point to the target passes it across the target without any slowing. The tip should literally scratch the target, a small, short, sharp cut. This is a very vigorous style of Cut. Its true effect relies on the speed at which the Cut is delivered rather than any real impact of the weapon on target; there is very little if any power in this Cut, it is the slicing action of the tip which does the damage.

Of the Delivery

To attack an opponent is an action which uses the techniques which have been previously described. This is an introduction to the concept of the attack and some of the elements which are involved in performing a successful attack. This will focus mainly on those practical elements, some of which have been previously described in the techniques of the offensive actions above, but more on the application of these techniques. It will describe the other elements which must be taken into account and lead on to other parts of the treatise which will follow and improve the ability of the fencer to deliver a successful attack.

Active Rather than Reactive

There is much said about defensive and counter-offensive actions in many different works, but very little about actual offensive actions against an opponent. Offensive actions are described, but very little is described about their simple application without some sort of offensive action from the opponent. This puts the fencer on a very reactive rather than active footing in his fencing, waiting for the opponent to act rather than taking the initiative where an opportunity is present.

It should be noted, however that this treatise would not, and does not, claim that the attack is an action that should be taken lightly, or seen as a simple matter of delivering the attack, quite the contrary. There are many elements which must be discussed so that the fencer understands how a successful offensive action using either the point or edge is delivered. This is an introduction to some of those considerations which must be made by the combatant.

Technical Aspects

The first thing that must be addressed is the technical aspects of the attack itself. These are details which are vital for a successful attack. The attack must be executed properly. There is little use for an attack which is performed without thought or which is lax in its execution. Such an attack has a high chance of being ineffective against even the simplest target. Thus, the attack must be performed using the correct technique.

Following this, the theoretical principles which underpin the attack need to be taken into account, Time and Distance being two of the most vital. Without these principles the attack may fail due to many reasons including such simple things as being Out of Distance or lacking the *Tempo* to complete the action successfully. All of the principles must be taken into account so that the attack is successful.

Accuracy

In some instances, a fencer will simply throw out an attack attempting to utilise as much muscle power to make an attack fast. This often results in an attack which is wild and inaccurate. Such an attack is in many instances worse than making no attack at all. It is the accuracy of an attack which is the essential element of the attack. This accuracy is part and parcel of the technique and the performance of the action as well as striking the intended target.

The accuracy of an attack in its delivery is vital; it is more important to hit any target that the fencer requires or chooses to than delivering a blow with great velocity. The technical aspects of any attack need to be considered seriously for the attack to be successful.

Optimum Time and Place

Once the technical aspects are dealt with some of the tactical considerations can be examined. These are considerations of when the blow is delivered and where the blow is delivered. The optimum Time to deliver an attack against an opponent is when he is the most vulnerable. The optimum place to deliver an attack against an opponent is where he is most vulnerable. Recognising the Time and place for an attack comes with being able to read an opponent, this is an aspect which will be discussed in some detail in a later part of this treatise.

Open and Closed Lines

What any fencer, even a new fencer, should recognise is when a Line is open or closed. An attack made against a closed Line for the beginning fencer is a waste of Time as the opponent can easily defend against it. The techniques for opening Lines are something which will be discussed later in the treatise. For the fencer at this point in time, it is better that the fencer only attacks an open Line. This is a place where the opponent is vulnerable to attack.

The attack to an open Line, even if the opponent defends against it, is much more useful than an attack against an already closed Line. This is simply due to the opponent having to use Time and energy to close the open Line, whereas a closed Line is already defended and therefore needs no attention paid to it.

Defensive Considerations

The fencer needs to consider his own defence against the offensive or even counter-offensive actions of the opponent. The fencer should close the Line in which the opponent's weapon is found. This is achieved through the use of footwork or Blade Engagement, the second of which will be found in a later part of this treatise, the first of which is found under the description of defensive actions previously described.

Attack with the Edge

Should the fencer choose that an attack with the edge is the most successful way to approach an opponent, he should consider how he will close with and recover from the opponent. These sorts of considerations will be discussed in the portion of the manual about Closes and Grips, the close-quarter element of rapier combat. In general, however, a Cut should not be a fencer's opening attack with the rapier as it will be slower and more easily defended than the Thrust.

Timing

Much has been discussed so far about the optimum place for an attack to be delivered; little has been said about the optimum Time in which the attack should be delivered. Time can be manipulated in order to suit the actions of the fencer. This is a concept and a skill-set which will require a great deal of practice on the part of the fencer. The theoretical concepts have already been discussed previously with other elements of theory, but it is the application of these concepts which the fencer needs and these too will be described in a later part of this treatise.

Important Considerations

With these considerations in mind, both technical and tactical, there is a lot that needs to be considered so that the fencer can deliver a successful attack against an opponent. Each one of these needs to be considered and the relevant skills practiced for the fencer to deliver a successful attack.

In any place where something is lacking the fencer can find himself in a great deal of trouble. Simply delivering the blow of point or edge against an opponent is not enough. There are things which the fencer needs to consider so that the attack is successful and that the fencer is not also struck in the process of making the attack against the opponent.

Blade Engagement

Blade Engagement is one part of fencing which the fencer will, in some way, have to participate in when engaged with an opponent. This is one of the most important interactions between the fencer and the opponent and it is all performed through the weapons and their position.

Blade Engagement is an important concept and involves a set of specific techniques which the fencer will find useful in his engagement with opponents. Used correctly, these can be used to defeat an opponent's attack by a mere positioning or re-positioning of the weapon. Used incorrectly, it can leave a fencer exposed and at the mercy of the opponent. These techniques can also allow a fencer to dominate an opponent in his engagement with the blade.

Blade Division

There is a third part of the blade which has been indicated, but not discussed particularly much this is called the *Mezzo*, which is the middle part of the blade. This part of the blade comprises half *Forte* and half *Debole*. It is about this part of the weapon that much of the Blade Engagement techniques will be made. This part of the blade has the advantages and disadvantages of both parts of the weapon. These advantages and disadvantages need to be understood for it to be utilised properly.

The other two parts of the blade which are useful for Blade Engagement are the Inner and Outer Percussion Points which were discussed previously. Each part of the weapon has its own purpose, advantages and disadvantages, and for the fencer to perform the actions of Blade Engagement successfully each part of the weapon must be familiar to him, without this understanding, the fencer will have trouble performing the actions.

Absence of Blade

The concept of Absence of Blade is to come into contact with the opponent's weapons as little as possible, and not at all if possible. It means that the fencer using this technique will use a lot of Voids in defence and very little Parries. The idea behind this technique is to deny the opponent the information that he would have gained through contact between the blades. This can be used by the fencer very effectively but he has to be aware of his own positioning and that of the opponent.

The influence of Absence of Blade over the opponent is achieved merely through the position of the weapon and the body in comparison to the opponent. This can be clearly related to Counter-Position as in both situations an advantage is gained through positioning the weapon and primarily without coming into contact with the opponent's weapon. This technique is sometimes used, in the most rudimentary fashion, by novice fencers who are unsure about Blade Engagement. Will accordingly, stay at distance from their opponent.

There has to be a reason to use Absence of Blade against an opponent. One reason would be where the opponent is stronger than the fencer, or where the opponent clearly has a more dominant position when the blades are engaged, or where the opponent clearly knows more about Blade Engagement with contact than he does without contact.

The fencer needs to be sure of his Distance with regard to Absence of Blade and also his own positioning as it is these two elements which comprise the primary elements in his defence. The hand or weapon can be used to parry, but when the weapon is used, it results in blade contact; and consequently, loss of Absence of Blade.

In some instances, Absence of Blade will be used with engagement of the opponent's weapon, but this engagement will only be at the choice of the fencer. This takes the advantage of both forms of Blade Engagement. The advantage of Absence of Blade when combined with direct contact in this fashion is that the opponent has a much shorter time in which to react to the actions of the fencer due to the shortened period of contact between the weapons. The position of advantage is already gained and the contact happens as a part and parcel of the offensive action as a result of the advantage gained through the position established by the fencer.

Blade Engagement

Blade Engagement, involving contact between the weapons, is complex and involves many different elements that need to be taken into account. Much of the information found here is also important for the fencer using Absence of Blade as some of the techniques may be used through this method.

Blade Engagement with contact is the most commonly thought of method of Blade Engagement when thoughts of Blade Engagement are present. As such, to simplify things, Blade Engagement using Absence of Blade will be referred to as Absence of Blade and that using more contact between the weapons will be called Blade Engagement. This being the case, it must be remembered that both are methods of Blade Engagement and are just as relevant to the use of the rapier as one another.

Feeling Through the Blade

In Blade Engagement, the most important thing is the contact between the weapons, it is therefore vital that the fencer can feel through the weapon to find out what the opponent is doing and thinking. This feeling through the blade is referred to as *Senso di Ferro* in Italian.

This idea relates to an almost sixth sense where the fencer can feel through the blade of his weapon as if it were an extension of him. The ability to do this allows the fencer to feel what the opponent is doing before he actually moves and supplies a sort of precognition of what the opponent plans to do, but this is only if the fencer is practiced in this.

Strong and Weak

Along with this feeling through the blades, the fencer should also be aware of the degree of pressure exerted by the opponent upon his weapon. The fencer will be able to feel a strong pressure or a weak pressure. This can be related purely to strength, but also to other aspects such as the position of the blade. What must be clear to the fencer is that there is advantage in both.

Clearly the strong may push away the weak, and in some instances the strong may resist the strong. The former will result in advantage, the latter in a neutral position where neither weapon will move. But the weak used against the strong can also be used as an advantage. If the fencer yields to the opponent's strength, this can result in the opponent being moved out of position and out of Line; thus leaving the fencer a Line through which to attack. The use of weak against weak will result in the same situation as that found with the strong against the strong. This is something which the fencer should be aware of.

The tactical games that can result between the fencers as a result of the simple use of the strong and the weak are most interesting. What should be noted however is that the strong and weak principle is principally applied when the blades are in contact at the *Mezzo* or *Debole*. But the same above can result where the weapons are in contact *Forte* to *Forte*. A weapon is always strong regardless of the strength applied at the *Forte* where the opponent's *Debole* is against the fencer's *Forte* at which the fencer has the advantage.

Gaining Position

Gaining advantage when combating with a rapier concerns being in a dominant position, it involves the fencer being in a position where he has an advantage over the opponent. For the most part, this involves the fencer having his weapon in an open Line where an attack can be made against the opponent. For the fencer using Absence of Blade, this is achieved by simple positioning the weapon in an open Line. Once achieved the fencer should attack immediately along that Line.

Stringere

For the fencer using Blade Engagement, gaining position involves the use of *Stringere* to open a Line. *Stringere* is the application of a small amount of force against the opponent's weapon to force it out of Line while the fencer's weapon is moved in Line. It is important to note that the fencer's weapon does not smack into the opponent's weapon it is placed there and then pressure is applied to it. The fencer should use the edge of the weapon to get the best feeling through the weapon and the best pressure for the action.

Depending on the side the pressure is applied will determine whether the Inside or Outside Line is opened. The position of the weapon in either the High or Low Line will determine whether it is the High or Low Line which is opened. The second advantage of the use of *Stringere* is that the location of the opponent's weapon is known when this technique is applied. This will also shut the opponent's weapon out of Line; as a result, it will not be threatening the fencer.

Once *Stringere* is applied, and the advantage is gained, the fencer should attack immediately. There are other techniques which can be used to open a Line on the opponent, and just as with the *Stringere* once this is achieved a straight attack should be made along the Line which has been opened as soon as it is opened.

Stringere is also applied where the blade is merely placed into a position where it dominates a position where it can attack i.e. into an open Line. It does not necessarily have to move the opponent's blade. To achieve this, the fencer needs to angle their blade properly in the correct angle, possibly along with their body position to achieve the same result as with the Hard Engagement option expressed previously. As with the Hard Engagement option, once this Soft Engagement option has been achieved an attack should be made into the open Line created by the position.

The important thing with regard to *Stringere*, Blade Engagement and indeed all fencing techniques, there must be purpose behind the technique. A technique should not be performed without reason a fencer must have a clear reason for performing a technique against an opponent, and the primary reasons should be that it either defends the fencer or gains an advantage over the opponent. An action performed without a purpose wastes time and energy and can also leave the fencer vulnerable to an attack by the opponent.

Stringere is used to open a Line. This is done to attack, should the fencer not respond to this particular action he will be struck, as has been described above. Regardless of the choice of technique used the optimum response to having a Line opened and the opponent's weapon in place to attack is to close the Line again. This may be achieved through several different techniques including the use of footwork.

What will be presented below is some of the options using Blade Engagement. The counter to *Stringere* when using Blade Engagement is to perform a Disengage. This may be performed under or over the opponent's blade, but its purpose is to close the Line which the action of *Stringere* has opened.

Disengage

The Disengage called *Cavatione* in the Italian, is an action to change the Line of engagement, from Inside to Outside or vice versa, and also counter *Stringere* by closing the Line as a result. This action is performed by shifting the point of the weapon under and around the opponent's weapon to move to the other side of the weapon, or by shifting the point over the opponent's weapon for the same result.

It is encouraged that the Disengage under is performed more often as the Disengage over, or Cut Over, can leave the fencer exposed for a short amount of time while the point is not in Line. It is true that the Disengage under, called for the purposes of this manual, the Disengage, leaves the fencer exposed also in the middle of its performance, but this is a shorter period of time as compared to the Cut Over. The action of the Disengage, either over or under changes the Line of engagement and opens the opponent to attack. This advantage should be taken advantage of immediately, attacking as a result. There is also a counter to this action.

Counter-Disengage

The action to counter the Disengage is called the Counter-Disengage, or *Contra-Cavatione* in the Italian. It is performed to change the engagement back to where it was when the *Stringere* was performed. The action of the Counter-Disengage is to perform a Disengage around the opponent's Disengage, or indeed in response to the Disengage of the opponent.

Double Disengage

There is also a counter to the Counter-Disengage. With little surprise, this is a second Disengage performed to counter the Counter-Disengage. Unsurprisingly, this is called a Double Disengage. This is a second disengage performed to counter the Counter-Disengage. The action itself is actually the same as the Disengage. In Italian this is called a *Ricavatione*.

String of Engagements

From the performance of *Stringere* to the performance of the Double Disengage is what could be called a String of Engagements. Each action which follows is designed to counter the previous action. The important things to note here are that at each completion of an action there is the opportunity for an attack made by the person who has completed their action, and this should be the focus rather than a simple battle of changing engagements.

Also, each action is performed in response to the previous action. There is little point to performing a Counter-Disengage if the opponent has not performed a Disengage and so forth. This comes to purpose and the purpose of each of these actions must be understood in order that they can be used effectively.

There are two further actions which change the engagement and are designed to do this. One is the Half-Disengage, and the other is the Time Disengage. Each of these is a Disengage and therefore is the start of the responsive actions. Each can be countered by a Counter-Disengage performed effectively in response to the action.

Half-Disengage

The first action is the Half-Disengage, or *Mezzo Cavatione* in the Italian. This is a Disengage which changes the engagement from a High Line engagement to a Low Line engagement or vice versa. It will also change the engagement from Inside to Outside or vice versa as the normal Disengage does. The action itself is exactly as it is described a half a Disengage. Therefore, the action of the Disengage is stopped half way through to change the Line along the vertical engagement. The point is therefore placed above or below the opponent's weapon to change the Line along the vertical Line of engagement.

Time Disengage

The Time Disengage, or *Cavatione di Tempo* as it is called in the Italian, is an action while simple is sometimes difficult to grasp due to the fact that it is different from the other forms which have been presented so far. Each of the actions which have been described above work around the physical placement of the opponent's weapon, the Time Disengage does not.

The Time Disengage works around the position of the opponent's blade in Time; thus, in motion, rather than being static. In the Time Disengage, the Disengage is performed around the position where the opponent's blade will be rather than where it is. This action is used against an action in motion. For example, a Time Disengage can be used in response to the performance of *Stringere* before the *Stringere* comes into contact with the fencer's weapon.

This particular action utilises much of the theory of Absence of Blade in that the weapon does not come in contact with the opponent's weapon before the action is performed, but only may once it is completed. This is an action which should be performed in concert with an attacking action, most simply a thrust, to be effective.

The action itself is the same as a normal Disengage, the point is moved under the opponent's weapon to change the engagement. The difference is that the weapon is always in motion and does not come into contact with the opponent's weapon before or during the action. The other difference is that it can be performed while the fencer is preparing to Thrust. Accordingly, change the Line of the attack as the action of the opponent is performed. This is one of the few times when the point of the weapon may deviate from its target in the performance of the Thrust.

Attack on the Blade

Attacks on the Blade are actions in which the fencer uses their weapon to open a Line in the opponent to attack it. Some of these are simple actions of force, others are much more subtle. Each one, regardless of the method, has technique behind it. None of the actions merely bash the opponent's weapon out of the way.

Beat

The Beat is one of the simplest actions used to displace the opponent's weapon. It is also one where many people will make mistakes. The Beat is an Attack of Force and it uses percussive power to move the opponent's blade out of Line. This action was briefly mentioned in the discussion of the Parry. This is the action in its offensive mode. The novice fencer will often, by instinct, attempt to swat their opponent's weapon out of the way to deliver an attack. This is the rudimentary beginnings of the Beat. The Beat, however, utilises this action and adds certain points to be more effective.

Firstly, fencer should aim to use the Percussion Point against the opponent's Percussion Point. These Points were discussed when addressing the Cut. Secondly, the fencer should be using the edge of his weapon against the opponent's. The flat will be substantially less effective and will often lead to the point being out of Line. Thirdly, the fencer should be using his wrist and fingers to generate the power for the Beat, the arm should not withdraw to generate power. The simple action of the wrist directing the action against the opponent's weapon combined with a vigorous closing of the hand is all the power that the fencer will require to deliver this action.

Using these three points, from a Guard of Third, the hand is turned to Fourth if the fencer is on the Inside of the opponent's weapon or Second if he is on the Outside of the opponent's weapon. This should be combined with the vigorous actions of the wrist and fingers to complete the action. The correct performance of this action will be sufficient to Beat the opponent's weapon out of Line and leave an opportunity for an attack. The Thrust which follows should be a simple extension of the point from the position the fencer finds himself in. If too much power is used the point of the fencer's weapon will also be out of Line. The Beat is about the correct delivery and amount of force in the correct place.

The Beat is useful against opponents who leave their point out far, especially if they are holding their weapon too loose or too tight. In the Beat, the place is as important as the time of the delivery. The best defence against a Beat is to Disengage as the Beat is delivered, another defence is to use the power of the Beat to move the point of the weapon back into Line, or simply not place the weapon in a position where it can be beaten.

Press

While the Beat uses percussive force against the opponent's blade, the Press and related actions use an increase in pressure against the opponent's blade to open a Line through which the fencer can attack. The Beat uses impact to displace the opponent's weapon, the Press and associated actions do not. In fact, impact when using these techniques reduces the effectiveness of their delivery.

The key piece of theory which is required for the use of these techniques the weak and strong parts of the blade. Essentially the Press places a strong fencer's weapon against a weak opponent's weapon and forces it out of the way by increasing pressure.

The Press is the simplest form of this kind of attack on the blade. The *Mezzo* of the blade is used against the *Debole* of the opponent's and the weapon is forced away by pressure of one on the other. The same can be used where the fencer places the *Forte* of his blade against the *Mezzo* or *Debole* of the opponent's. The opponent's weapon needs only to be moved enough so it is out of Line of the fencer.

The fencer must use the edge of the weapon against the opponents. The flat is useless for this technique. The weapon should strike the opponent's weapon, but be placed there. The increasing pressure should be made as the fencer moves his weapon into Line at which time an attack should be made. This is the principle of all of the Pressures.

Pressure Glide

The Pressure Glide takes the concept of the Press a little further as it uses the increase in pressure not only to displace the opponent's weapon, but also to place the fencer's weapon into Line and even start the delivery of the attack. The point of the weapon will move closer to the opponent as the pressure against the weapon increases. All the fencer has to do is to continue extending his arm to deliver the attack at the end.

The blades will come into contact with the fencer's *Mezzo* on the opponent's *Debole*, the fencer will move his weapon forward increasing the pressure on the opponent's weapon forcing it out of Line. The point of the fencer's weapon will gradually be further and further into Line. At the final point of extension, the fencer's *Forte* will be against the opponent's *Mezzo*.

With the angulation of the blade the fencer's *Debole* will not come into contact with the opponent's weapon due to the resultant position at the completion of the action. In this way, the fencer will always be in the stronger Blade Engagement position. If the fencer's point is not forced closer and closer to the opponent while the opponent's is forced further and further out of Line, then the action is being performed incorrectly.

The best defence against this attack is to catch the opponent's blade by performing a Parry against the increasing pressure. This can be enhanced by retreating to change the Blade Engagement. Changing the Blade Engagement is the key to defeating the Press and related actions, making the fencer's weapon strong against the opponent's sword.

Flowing Attack

The Flowing Attack is unlike the Beat or Pressure in that it uses very little contact between the weapons. In some instances, it may not even come into contact with the opponent's weapon at all. This Attack on the Blade is concerned with the placement of the weapon rather than forcing the opponent's weapon out of the way. It is a very subtle but very fast attack resulting in a simple thrusting attack at the end.

It could be mistaken for a simple extension of the arm into a Thrust against the opponent. This action controls the Line by the mere presence of the weapon against the opponent's sword. There should be no pressure against the opponent's weapon during this action and there should be no impact against the opponent's weapon either.

The Flowing Attack is performed by the placement of the weapon in Line against the opponent's sword. The mere position of the weapon makes the opponent's weapon out of Line. The attack itself is performed very close to either edge of the opponent's weapon. The edge of the fencer's weapon should be turned toward the opponent's weapon to close it out of Line.

From this position, the fencer extends the weapon toward the opponent using the position of the weapon close to the opponent's sword to open the Line and attack in a single flowing action. The position of the weapon prevents the opponent from replying down the same Line. This is a fast action and should be performed vigorously. The defence against the Flowing Attack is to Parry in the direction of the weapon to close the Line. A Retreat Step in this instance is advantageous.

Taking the Blade

Controlling the opponent's weapon is one of the keys to being victorious in a combat with an opponent there are Blade Engagement actions which assist in this. They are often referred to as a group of actions called Taking the Blade. This essentially describes the action of taking the control of the weapon away from the opponent and placing it somewhere it is of more use to the fencer. Using these actions, a fencer can change the Line of engagement or even regain control of the encounter through a change of engagement. These actions are all very similar in their performance and also purpose.

Bind

For those actions where the Line of engagement is changed by the action, called Binds, the fencer should always engage the opponent's blade with his *Mezzo* or *Forte* depending on where the blades sit. Should the fencer attempt this with the *Debole* he will not gain a sufficient mechanical advantage or control over the opponent.

To move the opponent's weapon, the fencer will need to turn his hand. The direction is determined by where the fencer wishes to direct the opponent's weapon to. The hand may be turned either clockwise or anti-clockwise depending on the desire of the fencer, but special note and attention should be paid where the point of the opponent's weapon crosses over the body of the fencer. The hand should be turned about the wrist. There should, for the most part, be very little movement in the rest of the arm. The fencer should use a circular action in the turn to turn the opponent's weapon to the location required, and not further.

Each direction that the blade can be moved, vertically, horizontally and diagonally can have its own name, but the principle of the action and its performance is much the same. The only difference really is the direction in which the opponent's weapon is moved.

Should the principles of the actions presented above be followed, the fencer should have little difficulty figuring out how to move the opponent's weapon in any direction he may choose, for the purposes of referring to these actions later, the term Bind will be used to describe the action, and a direction indicator will be used.

Envelopment

There is an action, as indicated previously, that enables a fencer to regain control over the weapons during a combat. This is called an Envelopment. Externally it looks like a much the same as the action of the Bind which has been described previously except that in this action the blade completes the circle and looks like it has come back to where it started, this is not actually the case as a change of Blade Engagement has also occurred during the performance of this action.

The purpose of this action is to regain control the blade and this is achieved through this change of Blade Engagement. A fencer's weapon has the advantage where the *Debole* of the opponent's weapon is placed on his weapon near the *Forte* of the weapon. Should the reverse be the case then the fencer is not in control. The Envelopment is used to gain this control.

To perform the Envelopment, the fencer should lift their point so that their *Debole* is about the opponent's *Mezzo*. This will gain the fencer a measure of strength on the weapon and also some control as well. Should the fencer's weapon be on the Outside of the opponent's weapon, the weapon should be turned to the Inside. Should the fencer's weapon be on the Inside of the opponent's weapon it should be turned to the Outside.

The important thing about this turning, and indeed with all actions of Taking the Blade, is that contact must be maintained throughout the entire process. Otherwise the fencer will lose control of the opponent's weapon. The circular motion of the hand should be a complete circle, but not more than a complete circle the weapon should end up on Line when it is completed.

The circular action with the hand should shift the engagement so that the opponent's *Forte* will end up on the fencer's *Debole*. If it does not, then more angulation of the blade is required in the turning. It should be noted that this will be in the same Line as when the action started. The fencer should give some consideration to covering that Line as soon as the action is completed.

Counters

In the case of both the Bind and the Envelopment, they are actions which can be countered. The countering is achieved by the application of force at the correct time to stop the turning motion of the actions. In the actions described, there is a spot in all of them where the engagement is not so solid between the blades. This may be accompanied by a slipping feeling between the blades. Should a fencer wish to stop the action which is being performed, all he has to do is to turn his weapon's edge toward the opponent's weapon at this point and hold firm with his weapon. In most instances it will result in both weapons meeting at the *Mezzo* of each, which is a neutral position.

The force needs to be applied at the correct time in the action. Against some actions allowing the action's motion to carry the sword and then continuing with the velocity of the weapon can also be effective, but the fencer needs to be aware of the consequences of following the action and the potential harm involved.

As in all actions which involve Blade Engagement, information is passed between the two combatants during the contact between the weapons, and care needs to be taken in their performance. Should the applicable theory be followed and note taken of the engagement, then the fencer should be able to apply actions of Blade Engagement successfully against the opponent.

In and Out of Time

A fencing action can be described as being "In" or "Out" of Time. This is usually determined by whether the action is made at the correct moment and is suited to the situation. An action which is performed "In Time" is one which is performed at the most suitable instance for that action. An example of an action performed In Time is a Thrust which is directed against an open Line on the opponent where the position of the Thrust prevents an immediate counter-attack from the opponent. The attack is also made where the opponent is stationary and not attacking himself. This is because the fencer is making his attack while the opponent is stationary, thus not acting against the fencer, and against an open target. This concept has already been discussed in the Theory; here it is the practical application which is important.

Time Available

Another important element of determining whether an action is performed In Time is whether there is the correct number of *Tempi* available for the action to be performed, the expression could also be termed as "in *Tempo*". Of course, for a simple Thrust only a single *Tempo* is required, but for a more complex action, more *Tempi* will be required.

Using the previous example, if the two combatants are at Narrow Distance, a simple extension and so a single *Tempo* will be required. Should the combatants be at Wide Distance, the fencer may have to close on his opponent, and this may require the expenditure of an extra *Tempo* to advance, if this is the case, the fencer may find himself "Out of Time" for his action, where both combatants' movements have to be taken into account that things get more complex. Should the fencer in the example use a Lunge, and as such, a single *Tempo*, the same situation as described above will still result and so he will be

In Time, so long as the Distance is correct. This also gives a practical example of the influence of Distance on Time.

Dependent on Situation

Whether an action performed is In or Out of Time is dependent on the situation more than the action performed. The same Thrust made by the fencer in the original example would be Out of Time if the opponent was thrusting at the same time, and of course the result would be likely worse for both. The same Thrust would also be Out of Time if the fencer was not in position, or if the opponent had the intended Line covered, as this would require additional *Tempi* to open or change Lines.

Should the opponent be attacking first, a correct action In Time would be a defence of some kind, a defence against the in-bound attack. Hence, the fencer must be aware of the situation to determine the correct response and remain In Time. For the most part, where the opponent attacks first, the action In Time will be a defensive action of some kind. This follows the First Principle. Where the situation is correct and the fencer attacks first, it is the attack which will be In Time.

Use of Time

There are those situations where the fencer will deliberately move Out of Time to achieve his goal. It is useful to determine which of the other Times which are used are In or Out of Time. This is both for demonstration purposes and also for theoretical application of these times.

Double Time is a use of Time in fencing which clearly falls within the idea of In Time. The opponent attacks, the fencer responds with defence first, reacting to the Time presented, and then follows with his counter-attack, using two *Tempi*.

Single Time works in much the same fashion as Double Time except the two actions are blended into a single action. The defensive action is combined with the offensive action in a single *Tempo* in response to the attack of the opponent, the fact that the fencer responds with the defence against the attack means that it follows the Time present. Consequently, it also falls within the idea of In Time.

The remaining two times which are used in fencing, Counter-Time and Half-Time do not really follow this format and are as such not so easy to deal with. The action in Half-Time is one which is both offensive and defensive in the same instant, but without the deliberately defensive action of Single or Double Time. The action in Half-Time attacks the opponent's attack before it is completed, intercepting it before it strikes. This is an offensive action in a situation where the fencer should be defending himself and so is Out of Time, yet is also a defensive action in that it is countering the opponent's attack, and as such is In Time. This makes Half-Time truly "half"; half In Time and half Out of Time.

The action of a Counter-Time response is one which is an offensive action directed against the opponent while he is attacking, an attack launched to counter an attack, of course, this results in an attack where a defensive action should really be made, thus making the action of Counter-Time one of Out of Time. There could be some argument that this action also counters the opponent's offensive action. This would make it In Time, but the very name of the action, Counter-Time, demonstrates evidence to the contrary as it is literally against Time.

Effect of Distance

The actions which are In or Out of Time are dependent on the situation in which the fencer finds himself. In a normal situation at Narrow Distance the difference between an action In or Out of Time can make a big difference, at Wide Distance it is less important, but still needs to be considered. Thus, Time and Distance are related once again.

Should the fencers come within Narrow Distance and engage in Closes and Grips, the difference between being In or Out of Time can decide the outcome of the encounter. The concept of Priority in this situation is most useful and is related very much to being In and Out of Time. The In Time action at this Measure is determined by Priority. If the fencer is acting, he acts offensively, if reacting, defensively. The only way to break this pattern is to use an action Out of Time, but this must be done at the correct Time or the fencer will find himself struck. More will follow about actions at this Very Narrow Distance, and the elements which surround it.

Priority

The theoretical elements in regard to Priority have already been discussed. This is practical discussion of how it operates in combat. Priority is primarily related to close combat, or Closes and Grips, however the same principles can be applied at Narrow and even Wide Distance. There will be a further discussion of Closes and Grips later in which the concept of Priority will be demonstrated to be significant and, as a result, requires special attention. For the purposes of the current discussion it is the application of Priority in general. This is a discussion on the Active and the Reactive, the attacker and defender.

The fencer wants to gain Priority to act against the opponent. The opponent also wants to gain Priority to act against the fencer. Priority describes the condition of the required action of the fencer or the opponent. If the opponent attacks first, the Priority, and indeed the In Time response is to mount a defence against the attack. Accordingly, in this instance the opponent has Priority and the fencer does not.

Active and Reactive

Actions performed following Priority also follow Time and are performed In Time. Another way to describe this is to say that the combatant who attacks first is the Active and the other is the Reactive. In Priority the fencer must respond to the action of the opponent if they are the Reactive.

A simple example follows as such: two fencers, Arthur and Bartolomeo, meet one another on guard and Arthur makes a thrusting attack against Bartolomeo, so gaining Priority. Bartolomeo must respond to the action and as such parries the thrusting attack. One acts, the other reacts. Once the parry is made Bartolomeo may then counter-attack Arthur. Thus, gaining Priority, to which Arthur must respond. This simple example describes how Priority is gained and changes in a simple fashion, obviously things can be much more complex.

Effect of Distance on Time

Where one attacks before the other, the other must follow or immediately counter the attack. One fencer may remain on the Active and the other may remain on the Reactive if the situation plays out that way. This is something which can happen at close quarters due to the minimal Distance and minimal Time.

However, when combatants are further away from one another, where the Distance is longer and so is the Time, the Priority can change, though it may not always work out as such. In general, the longer the Distance and Time, the more chances the Reactive fencer will have to change to being the Active. Obviously, the shorter the Time and Distance the less chances the fencer will have to change the Priority. This demonstrates a relationship between Time, Distance and Priority.

Close Combat

The main application of this concept is in close combat, or Closes and Grips. In this situation the fencers need to be aware of what is going on to act efficiently and to their own benefit. Should Arthur and Bartolomeo find themselves at the close the importance of Priority increases greatly, should Arthur cut at Bartolomeo in the close, Bartolomeo will have little time to react and will, as a result, use a *Tempo* to defend, at which time Arthur may spend another to attack again. This situation will leave Bartolomeo on the defensive as if he does not defend, he will be struck by Arthur. This is what Priority revolves around, the action a fencer must take to survive the encounter with the opponent. The only way for Bartolomeo to survive is to continue to defend while trying to either leave from the encounter or find a place in which he can change the Priority.

Gaining Priority

The fencer should do his best to get on the Active or offensive, remembering to ensure his defence in the process. To stay there, following Priority and remaining In Time, the Reactive can only defend. If the Reactive one is to change this situation, he must either disengage from the encounter and start again, or go Out of Time. The fencer needs to make Time to make a change to the situation and then force that change on the situation and the opponent.

Manipulating the Time is one way to achieve this end, as is changing the Distance or the Blade Engagement. An example of changing Priority would be if Arthur makes his Cut *Mandritta Squalembrato* against Bartolomeo, and instead of simply Parrying to block Arthur's weapon, Bartolomeo uses an angled Parry of Fourth to deflect the Cut and have it slide toward the hilt stopping it, he changes the Blade Engagement and gives himself Time to respond with a *Riversa Tondo*, so, changing the Priority. Indeed, the action of the Parry and Cut can be performed as one single fluid motion, giving him even more Time. This is only one example of how the change can be made.

Counting *Tempi*

One way of thinking about Priority is: what can the fencer do in a single *Tempo* or action in response to the current action? In this way each action is measured against that of an opponent. One attacks, the other parries. One action each at a time, this takes into account the action of an opponent as well as the action of the fencer. The fencer needs to be thinking about Priority in this manner to use it properly.

The *Tempi* have nothing to do with the speed of the actions, merely the actions themselves. Each action needs to be taken into account. An attack is made, one action. The weapon is withdrawn after the attack, one action, and so forth. Every action of fencer and opponent needs to be taken into account in this particular process.

Each time that the Active fencer is not attacking the defensive fencer, there is an action which can be performed to change the Priority. In this way, more actions can be found to change the Priority. The difference between Very Narrow, Narrow and Wide Distances should be taken into account through this particular process. At wider Distance there will be more opportunity for actions which need to be taken into account.

Necessary Action

Priority is designed to have the fencer think about what he needs to do at that particular time and how he can go about gaining the advantage in the current situation. In some instances, there will be a very simple response to the current situation and in others it may be much more complex. The necessary thing for the fencer is to ensure that the action which is performed ensures that the fencer remains guarded against the attack of the opponent.

The idea of Priority delineates between the attacker and defender, Active and Reactive fencers. The actions and descriptions of changing the Priority are not necessary as there are many and varied methods of achieving the result which is required. Priority is a concept which can be applied to all situations in fencing and one which the fencer should consider at all times.

Double Time

Double Time is the first form of Time that the fencer will be introduced to when they start to fence in this method. This form of Fencing Time separates the defence and the counter-attack into two actions. It means that the actions can be separated for practice and so that the fencer can be sure of their defence before launching a counter-attack. This type of Time has already been described in the Theory.

Defensive Play

Should the opponent launch a thrusting attack against the fencer, several responses could be made. One response to the attack would be to Parry the opponent's attack and then launch an attack in reply. This is the definition of the Double Time response to an opponent's attack. The advantage of this is that the fencer can make sure that the Parry has been effective against the attack before the counter-attack is launched. This is the definition of the defensive play, being that the defence is primary and the counter-offensive action is secondary to ensuring that the defence is effective.

This form of response will be slower than other responses which will be described later on in this treatise, but the advantage is that the defence can be ensured before the counter-attack is launched. The other advantage is that this type of fencing also follows the First Principle.

Example

The fencers, Arthur and Bartolomeo, start in a Guard of Third, Bartolomeo makes a *Stoccata* to the High Outside Line of Arthur. In response, Arthur performs a Parry of Third with Opposition to cover the Line, and also performs a Slip to increase the Distance. The defensive action here described uses two actions in a single *Tempo* to ensure that the fencer is safe then he moves to his counter-attack.

Using the engagement made through the Parry, Arthur Thrusts along the Inside Line of Bartolomeo's sword and strikes him in the chest using a *Stoccata* and placing him back in Distance by the return of the foot used in the Slip. The counter-offensive action against the opponent uses a second *Tempo*. Completing the action described in two *Tempi*, being a perfect example of a Double Time response to a thrusting attack against the High Outside Line.

The action described separates the defensive action, in this case a Parry of Third, from the offensive action, in this case a Thrust *Stoccata* using the already engaged blades. This is the definition of a Double Time action. The advantage of performing the actions in this manner is that the defence can be ensured before the counter-attack is launched to keep the fencer safe from the initial attack. This is a form of Fencing Time, and a method of defence that the fencer should familiarise himself with. This type of attack and counter-attack conforms to both the concepts of In Time actions and also Priority. Any action where the defence and counter-attack are separated as such is a Double Time response.

Single Time

Single Time is the next logical step in discussion from Double Time. The difference between Single and Double Time is that while in Double Time the actions of defence and attack are separated, whereas in Single Time the defence and counter-attack are blended into a single action, as a result, using a single *Tempo*. It is often seen that in a Single Time action there is a simple blur of motion as the fencer attacks into the opponent's attack, but this is not actually the case. The reason why it may appear as though the fencer has merely attacked into the opponent's attack is that the actions of defence and counter have been combined into a single action. There is a defensive action performed in the Single Time response, but it is combined with the counter-attack, making it difficult to notice.

Accurate Blending of Motions

The opponent attacks the fencer and the fencer launches out of his Guard performing a response which both closes the Line, to defend him, and attacks the opponent all in a single action. This is the essence of the Single Time response. It is much faster than the Double Time response as it combines what is done in two *Tempi* into a single *Tempo*.

It is essential that the fencer is accurate in his defence otherwise he can find himself impaled upon the opponent's weapon. The Single Time response relies upon the fencer being accurate in his defence and his attack. He combines the simple actions of Parry and Thrust into a single action which defends and offends in a single *Tempo*.

Example

In the demonstration of the Double Time response the fencers started in Guard, one attacked the other defended, using two actions and then counter-attacked, using the same demonstration the single time response can also be demonstrated. The fencers, Arthur and Bartolomeo start in a Guard of Third. Bartolomeo makes a *Stoccata* to the High Outside Line of Arthur. In response, Arthur closes the Line by turning his hand into the Second position to engage Bartolomeo's blade with the True Edge, and in the same motion thrusts forward with a *Stoccata*, striking the Bartolomeo in the chest. Footwork motions may be used to ensure the safety of the defence and the success of the attack, most likely they will be of a forward nature.

Succinct Action

The defence and counter are both present as they were in the Double Time response to the same action, however in this instance the defence is to merely close the Line by the turning of the hand. What should be noted is that this is the start of a Parry. The turning of the hand closes the Line and also prepares for the Thrust with Opposition which is performed once the hand is put into position. The Thrust is then made from this position as a completion of the action rather than as a separate action as in the Double Time response.

The Single Time response is faster than that of the Double Time response but the fencer must be sure that his defence is sufficient to defend him against the attack of the opponent. Consequently, the fencer must be familiar with the action. Without the defence, the fencer may strike the opponent, but is likely to be struck. The fencer should be sure of his actions before attempting to perform the Single Time response to the attack of an opponent.

Based on Double Time Actions

The Single Time response to the opponent's action can be extremely effective as the action gives the opponent very little time to respond to the counter-offensive action. The fencer should practice the simple actions of defence and attack before attempting this form of response. The relationship between Single and Double Time is close as the actions of one can prepare the fencer for the actions of the other.

To perform a Single Time response properly, the fencer needs to perform the actions of defence and counter-attack in a single *Tempo*, but close the Line of the incoming attack of the opponent properly. Defence is still a vital part of the action in Single Time, without it both the fencer and the opponent are likely to be struck. While it would seem that Single Time responses go against both Priority and Time, it is not actually the case as a defence is being mounted against the opponent's attack before the counter is made.

Counter-Time

The action in Counter-Time is directed against the opponent when they attack. This is an action which is performed against Time, where Double Time, defence then attack, is seen as the normal response to an opponent's attack. This is literally against Time.

Attacking into an Attack

When the opponent attacks, the usual response is for the fencer to make a defence of some kind and then a counter. In the case of Counter-Time the attack and defence are performed in a single motion, but unlike Single Time no specific thought is really made about the defence. The fencer considers defence, but this is a consequence of, or adjunct to, the attack made against the opponent. The defence is usually covered by some other aspect such as the position of the weapon in comparison to the opponent's, footwork or void. This is not a clear defence as is found in Single or Double Time.

Examples

Some examples of Counter-Time need to be made so that the fencer understands exactly how this method operates; using the common example presented in both Single and Double Time, the differences will be demonstrated as to how Counter-Time differs.

Arthur and Bartolomeo start in a Guard of Third. Bartolomeo makes a *Stoccata* to Arthur's High Outside Line.

In response, Arthur launches a *Stoccata* against the Bartolomeo closing the Line with his weapon preventing the Bartolomeo's weapon from coming back in and striking him. This defence can be enhanced by a diagonal Step to the forward and toward the Outside Line. The weapon should strike Bartolomeo in the chest. This is a Counter-Time response to an attack with a *Stoccata* to the High Outside Line. Arthur's position needs to be exact for him to remain untouched. This is a very precipitous response to the attack of his opponent.

An example needs to be made of a response to a cut. Should the Bartolomeo deliver a Cut *Riverso Mezzo Tondo* against Arthur, the same response can be made, catching the Cut with the *Forte* of the weapon in the Thrust. What should be noted is that it is the position of the weapon along with the footwork which both defends the Arthur and enhances his attack against Bartolomeo. Using these responses, the response may be made against either a Thrust or a Cut. Indeed, using the correct position and the correct response the fencer may also deliver either a Cut or a Thrust in response to the attack of the opponent. The Thrust is used as the primary example as this is the most advantageous attack in most instances.

Effective Counter

The Counter-Time response is effective due to the speed of the response to the opponent's attack. This speed of the response leaves little time for the opponent to respond. Indeed, it leaves even less due to the commitment to the attack made by the opponent. The Counter-Time response is also effective due being against Time and is the unexpected response to an attack. The normal response is to make a defence first and then counter-attack, the Counter-Time action puts the counter-attack first and the defence is a consequence of position.

With regard to the speed, the Counter-Time response is quicker than the Single Time response. For Single Time to occur the opponent's attack has to be completed, whereas in Counter-Time the opponent's attack is not completed. However, even with all the advantages of this particular response noted, care needs to be taken in its use as it is risky unless the defensive options are covered properly. If the fencer is out of position by very little then he can be struck by the attack of the opponent.

Against Time

This is a precise response and not merely throwing an attack against the opponent's action. The Counter-Time response being against Time is Out of Time in that it does not defend before an attack is made. It is also against Priority in that the fencer should be defensive and is not, but also should be noted that it is one of the ways to change Priority, forcing the opponent to defend against the attack of the fencer rather than completing his own, thus forcing him on the defensive. The Counter-Time response is very effective but needs to be practiced and used properly to be effective.

Half-Time

For some, the concept of Half-Time is difficult as it is thought that it involves dividing a *Tempo*, and in a way it does. The *Tempo* that is divided is the opponent's *Tempo* rather than the fencer's *Tempo*. The action in Half-Time is designed to interrupt the action of the opponent and prevent him from completing it, in this manner, cutting the *Tempo*. Rather than allowing the action to be completed as it is in the other times described, Half-Time interrupts the action of the opponent and prevents it from being completed. The fencer makes an action against the attack itself.

Attack Interrupted

The action in Half-Time should stop the opponent's attack from being completed. However, other defensive actions should be taken so that the fencer is not struck. This may be in the form of the position of the body or weapon, footwork or a Void. The thing that differentiates Half-Time from the other Times is that rather than deliberately attacking the opponent, it attacks the opponent's offensive action, consequently, interrupting it in the middle of the *Tempo* hence the name Half-Time. This action against the opponent's attack is effectively an attack and defence in the same action. The counter by the fencer attacks the opponent but this is executed so that the attack of the opponent is defeated, and as a result, the fencer is defended from the attack.

Example

An example of the action follows as such; Arthur and Bartolomeo start in a Guard of Third, Bartolomeo starts to make a *Stoccata* to the High Outside Line of Arthur. In response, Arthur performs a Slope forward to the Inside and Thrusts *Stoccata* to Bartolomeo's forearm before the Thrust is completed. Another response to the same attack involves Arthur Traversing to the Inside and performing a *Falso Dritto* to the wrist or forearm of the attacking arm of the opponent. In all instances, the opponent's attack is interrupted before it is completed and Arthur performs a footwork action so that he is not struck by some action of the opponent.

Effective Response

The action in Half-Time is effective due to the speed and Timing of the response. The opponent has really no time to response in that the fencer interrupts his action before it is allowed to complete. Even from a purely theoretical point of view the opponent has no Time as it is caught in the middle of the action and therefore in the middle of the *Tempo*. The other aspect which makes the Half-Time response effective is that the counter is against the opponent's attack. Thus, the fencer does not have to close particularly far to reach the opponent, using the Very Narrow Distance of the opponent's weapon, arm and hand. The risk of the use of the Half-Time is if the counter-attack is not accurate in the attack and the opponent's attack is allowed to be completed. Accordingly, care needs to be taken in the use of this form of Time.

For and Against

The action of the Half-Time response to the opponent's action is both In and Out of Time, just as it is both for and against Priority, and indeed it is for the same reason. The action is In

Time and for Priority as the action defends against the opponents attack; but it is also Out of Time and against Priority as rather than some purely defensive action used against the opponent, he is using an offensive one, as a consequence, attacking where the fencer should be defending. The action in Half-Time is very effective if used and executed properly, just as with the other Times, it does stand out in that it catches the opponent in a half *Tempo* rather than allowing him to complete his action and responding to this.

Closes and Grips

Closes and Grips is the part of combat where two fencers come into close contact with one another. This form of combat with an opponent may or may not occur during an encounter, however it is important to understand the reasons for it happening and how to deal with the situation regardless. The elements presented here are all based upon the theoretical elements previously discussed.

Close work is usually the result of the fencers entering Very Narrow Distance. This is the Distance at which close work happens and where the principles presented will apply. Some of them may apply at wider Distances also, but their primary effect is in the close.

Reasons

Closes and Gripes, close quarter combat, or close work happens for two real reasons. Either the situation was intended by one of the fencers, or one, or both, of the fencers have failed to control Distance. The second option usually happens when two overtly aggressive fencers come into contact with one another. It can also happen with one more aggressive fencer, and one who loses control of the Distance between the fencers. A fencer may also design to close with the opponent and this also needs to be considered as there are those reasons where a fencer may choose to close with the opponent to affect contact in close contact.

Choices

A fencer may choose to engage in Closes and Gripes where he is the stronger of the two fencers. This may enable him to have more control over the situation. A fencer who can move quickly may also choose close contact due to his speed. This brings into account another reason for choosing close contact. Weapon length may dictate that the fencer may have the advantage in the close. A fencer may also choose to engage in the close where his skill level is clearly above the opponent's and he believes that he can gain an advantage over the opponent in the close.

Obviously, a fencer in all of the opposite situations will decide that action at the close is not advantageous to him and will mostly choose to avoid it. A simply weaker or slower fencer will choose not to put himself in a situation where those attributes he does not have are the primary. Clearly a fencer with a longer weapon will want to stay more at range to take advantage of the length of the weapon. Also, it is unlikely that a fencer with less skill in the close will choose to put himself in such a situation where he has little or no advantage.

General Rules

The action of the Closes and Gripes can be very confusing, and is very quick due to the closeness of the combatants. Many scenarios could be described and presented here and still elements would be missed in the description. The action at the close is quite varied and many different things can affect the outcome of the encounter.

Rather than giving precise description of every encounter possible, some general rules will be presented. Much of what happens at the close happens often by instinct rather than design. The fencer needs to act and react to the situation he is placed in rather than attempting to find the perfect answer to the situation.

This is the first element that must be understood, the fencer should follow his instincts rather than fighting them. This primeval instinct is useful to the fencer and should be harnessed. With the general description presented, it is then possible to examine the important elements present to maximise the advantage for the fencer and to keep intact.

Priority

The concept of Priority as presented is vital to the fencer for him to survive the close. If the fencer is attacking, he has Priority; if he is not, he is defending and does not. In this situation an offensive action of any kind qualifies as an attack; be it an actual attack or the controlling of the opponent's weapon. Priority is important as if the fencer is not defending when he does not have Priority there is a highly likely chance that he will find himself struck.

Priority can change, and this is something that the fencer will want to do if he does not have Priority. This can be achieved through the use of Counter and Half-Time actions. These are particularly effective as their speed reduces the chances of the opponent to respond to the action of the fencer. The fencer should apply the appropriate answer to the problem presented. If the opponent is beginning his attack then the fencer can use Half-Time to stop it. If the attack is in motion then the fencer will more likely have more success using a Counter-Time action. Care needs to be taken in the application of these times to ensure that the fencer is guarded during the action.

Once Priority and the advantage have been gained, it is vital that the fencer control the situation and remain in the advantage. This is most easily achieved through staying on the offensive and keeping the opponent defensive, in this way, the Priority is maintained. The opponent needs to be kept off balance so that he is unable to regain or gain Priority.

The Cut

In the close, cutting actions tend to be the primary form of attack. This is because the point is often too awkward to bring on target due to weapon length. While the point is the prime method of striking the opponent and the other Distances, in the Very Narrow Distance the edge is usually most convenient.

Cutting must be performed efficiently and with the motion of the combat, a Cut is much easier to deliver when the body is moving in the direction of the Cut than when it is moving away. The fencer should be aware of this. It is also easier to deliver a Cut when in the correct position and in the correct motion, for this reason accurate and efficient footwork in the close is vital. For the most part the lower parts of the edge will be used. This also results in more leverage for the fencer in delivering the Cut, so the cut will be more effective when it is delivered.

Using Cuts rather than the point may require a change in focus, as the delivery of a Thrust is more efficient than the Cut and targets which are easily vulnerable to a Thrust may not be so with the Cut. While the Cut is primary, there may be opportunities for a Thrust to be used and so it should not be ignored.

The Off-Hand

The off-hand is a most useful tool in the close. This is the case whether it holds an item or not. In some instances, it is actually more advantageous for the fencer to be not carrying something in his off-hand, as the off-hand can be more effectively used to manipulate the opponent's weapon than an item in the off-hand.

The first thing that should be noted about the use of the off-hand in the close is that it should be used against the opponent's weapon and not their person. This is the case for two reasons which are interrelated. Firstly, controlling the weapon prevents the weapon from being moved or moving around into a position where it may strike the opponent by design or by accident. Secondly, if the fencer fastens on to the opponent rather than their weapon, the opponent may use their other hand to take the weapon and strike the fencer with it.

Weapon Control

When the weapon is controlled, the fencer controls the offensive potential of that weapon and can move it in such a way that it will not strike the fencer during the action. In controlling the weapon, there are things which need to be considered. The first is the location of the hand on the weapon.

It is optimum for the off-hand to be placed on the hilt of the opponent's weapon as this is where the fencer will gain the most control over the weapon. Should the fencer not be able to place their hand on the hilt of the weapon then the fencer should place his hand as close to the hilt of the weapon as possible. If the fencer should place and keep his hand higher on the weapon, he will have less control over it. This can result in the opponent being still able to utilise the weapon either defensively or even offensively.

Open or Closed

The next consideration is whether the fencer should close his hand or leave it open when it is placed on the opponent's weapon. There are advantaged in both methods of control just as there are also disadvantages to both methods. The closed hand would seem to gain the fencer the most control over the opponent's weapon, but also gives the potential that the fencer's hand may be cut if the sword is withdrawn from the grasp. The solid grasp on the weapon allows no movement, and as a result, can be both an advantage and also detrimental.

The open hand has no solid contact with the opponent's weapon so is easily able to move up and down the weapon depending on the desire of the fencer, and would seem to give less control. Should the opponent attempt to cut the fencer's hand, it can easily be removed or moved. The open hand also does not supply an instinctual response from the opponent to want to draw the weapon away as grasping the weapon often does.

With these considerations in mind it would seem more advantageous to have the hand more open than closed, though a gentle closing of the hand rather than a hard grasp could also be seen as useful. Regardless, the off-hand placed on the opponent's weapon needs to flow with the combat to stay attached to the weapon. Through this harmony with the combat the fencer can enable the off-hand to place the weapon in a more advantageous position for the fencer allowing both offensive and defensive potential.

Entry, Action and Exit

Close work is divided into three sections, the Entry, the Action and the Exit. Each one of these parts is important to the fencer and he needs to understand how each can affect the outcome of the contact between him and his opponent. The Entry is the initial part of close combat where the two combatants close on one another or one fencer closes on the other. The Action is the attacks, defences and movements made while the two fencers are in contact at close range, and the Exit is where the fencers break off from one another or one fencer breaks off from the other fencer.

Each part needs to be considered from a defensive and an offensive point of view. It is the defensive which should be foremost in the fencer's mind to ensure that he can survive the encounter unscathed. At no time should the fencer sacrifice his defence to strike the opponent. It is true that some of the defence will have to be reduced so that an attack against the opponent can be made, but this should not be made by leaving his defence fatally flawed. All parts of the action in the close are important and none should be neglected.

Entry

Where the Entry is made against an opponent it needs to be performed so that the fencer ends up engaged with the opponent in an advantageous position. This means that the fencer needs to have Priority at the end of the Entry. Where the Entry is made against the fencer, he should do his best to ensure that he has at least evened the position with the opponent by the time the Action has started, even if this simply means ensuring his defences against the action of the opponent.

Where the Entry is attempted against an opponent and the advantage is not gained or maintained, the fencer should move immediately to the Exit and attempt to enter again when the advantage is present. This Exit may be as simple as withdrawing from the engagement, ensuring that his defence is active. In all parts, the fencer should be prepared to mount some sort of defence against the opponent. Should the Entry be successful and the fencer has Priority, he should do everything to maintain the advantage against the opponent.

Action

The Action is the part where most of the action will take place and is where Priority is the most important. Should the fencer find himself in a position where he does not have Priority, he should be doing everything to make his defence and Exit. Success at this can leave the fencer in a position where he can make another Entry. Forcing a bad situation in any part of the action of the close can leave the fencer wounded or worse.

Exit

A voluntary Exit is usually made after a successful attack against the opponent, even in this situation, the fencer should make sure that his defences are up and that he returns to an on guard position. Where the Exit fails a fencer may be drawn back into the Action and this is the reason why it is important that he remain on the defence and come out on Guard. Should the fencer simply Exit at any time with no consideration of defence, he can still be struck by the opponent.

An involuntary Exit is where the fencer has lost the Priority and is on the defensive; in this situation he is forced out of the Action to increase his defensive potential. Where the opponent has made the Entry, the fencer wants to gain Priority to at least force the opponent to Exit.

Forcing an Exit on the opponent puts them on the defensive and gives the fencer the advantage. This is the best result where the Entry was forced by the opponent. In all instances the fencer should see to his defences to ensure that he is not struck in any part of the process.

Reading the Opponent

Reading the opponent is a useful and indeed essential skill. For many fencers it will be automatic, something activated in the subconscious to prepare a response to the opponent's attack. It can also be an active skill which makes it much more useful to the fencer so he can begin to know things about the opponent before he even comes on Guard.

Everything that the opponent does gives a clue as to the calibre of the opponent and how he will fence against you. Some of these details are small and seem insignificant, but every piece of information can be used. This is more than observation: it is intelligence gathering. Through the information discovered about the opponent, theories may be made about how the opponent will act and respond to actions against him in fencing. No piece of information about the opponent should be discarded out of hand.

Off the Field

Even before the opponent picks up a weapon, things can be observed about him. Watch the way he moves off the field and information can be gained as to how he will move in combat. Simple things as the way he moves across the ground and how he reacts to the actions of others will tell you something about the opponent. His interactions with others, even in a social situation, can tell you something about him.

Being calm or agitated in conversation or in a social situation can give you some idea about the way he will act on the field. His conversations and the way that he makes them can also tell you about how he will act with a weapon in his hand. Is he arrogant and overbearing? Or is he calm, respectful and collected in his conversations with others? Each one of these allows you to see a little below what he projects to others around him and alludes somewhat to his thought processes. These underlying processes most often determine how a fencer will act against an opponent.

Engagement with Others

In this particular part of the observation, the most useful information comes from how the fencer acts against another. Especially in tournament, special attention should be paid to how fencers act and fight one another. See whether the tactics change dependent on the opponent or whether they stay the same against all opponents.

What sort of thought processes are happening? Are they actively thought or more based on instinct and subconscious thought? Do the fencers think about what they are doing, or are they just reacting to the circumstances presented to them? Each one of the answers to these queries will give a small clue about how the fencer will act against us. Reading the encounters between other fencers is a useful skill and can say a lot about other fencers and can give clues about how they will act against others. This is one of the most useful reasons to watch encounters between other fencers.

Equipment

Fit

While some of the information gained about a fencer's equipment can sometimes be misleading, this information can also be used to tell something useful about a fencer. The first thing that should be noted is how well fitting the equipment is. Does the fencer seem comfortable in the gear? The level of comfort will affect how the fencer moves and plays against an opponent. Could the equipment be borrowed? Unfamiliar equipment will not move as well as that which the fencer knows well, this is especially the case for weapons.

Condition

Next thing that should be noted, especially if the equipment fits well and therefore is most likely not borrowed, is the condition of the equipment. This can describe how much care is taken of the equipment and this can tell how much respect the fencer has for what he is doing. It can also describe whether the fencer practices often or not.

Age

The age of equipment can even give some impression of how long the fencer has been fencing, especially if the fencer seems to be very comfortable with it. A fencer who has been fencing for an extended period of time with the same equipment will get comfortable with it. Brand new equipment can indicate a less experienced fencer, while older equipment can indicate a more experienced one.

The Weapon

With more focus on the weapon, a hilt which is clean and untouched can indicate a weapon which has not been used before and may be unfamiliar, or a new weapon which may indicate a newer fencer. Should the weapon have wear-marks and evidence of use, this can indicate that the fencer is comfortable with the weapon and has used it frequently; this can also indicate a more veteran combatant as it is often the weapon which is changed the least. The experience of the combatant is often written in the condition of the weapon where this is obviously due to combative contacts.

On Guard

Once the gear has been examined, next look at the combatant himself. Clues will be present in how he presents himself. Simple things such as how he stands on guard are important. It is useful to start from the bottom and work upward and then outward.

Feet

The way that the opponent stands is important and this begins with the feet. Are either of them pointed at the opponent? This can indicate some idea of the direction that the combatant is moving or may move. The weight distribution between the feet can also give some indication as to which way the fencer may move from the position he has taken. The spread between the feet can also tell something about how the fencer may move as this spread moves the centre of balance up or down.

Legs

The position of the feet is directly related to the position of the legs. Bent knees indicate a fencer who is willing to move and with some velocity. A fencer with straight knees will find it more difficult to move as quickly as one whose knees are bent. The feet and legs are connected and so must be read apart but also as a whole. This information will describe how the fencer will move about the field and what sort of ease this may be done with along with some indication of speed.

Body

The body is the largest mass of the fencer and it is that to which all of the peripheral parts of the body are joined, due to this, the position and carriage of the body can tell a lot about the opponent. The position of the body can also reveal things about the opponent, for example a bending of the body along with the cramping of the extremities might reveal fear in the opponent.

The position of the body is important, especially whether it is upright or crouched and how comfortable the opponent feels in this position. An upright position of the body keeping the body straight and tall can convey confidence; it also releases the muscles and relaxes the fencer. This fencer is ready for action and is no doubt confident in his position.

A crouched position which is obviously shrinking and tense reveals that the fencer's muscles are already active and the fencer will react slower, this may be due to fear. A special note should be made. A crouched position which is designed that way for the Guard will be notes as the opponent will be comfortable and not tense, his limbs will be at ease and ready for action. Careful note should be made of the difference between the two.

Head

The head is the next largest mass and the position of which can give some indication of the direction the fencer may move. More detail can also be revealed where the fencer can see the opponent's face. Facial expressions can reveal what the opponent is thinking and also their state of mind. It can also reveal what sort of condition they are in, most of these things are obvious, but can also be forgotten.

Attention should be paid to all of the head. A fencer whose head is leant forward may indicate that they are trying to shrink and therefore are fearful. A head which is upright betrays confidence in what the fencer is doing and also enables the fencer to move with less restriction than if the head was tilted to one direction or another. This is due to the skeletal alignment of the spine and head. A tilting of the head can indicate a direction to which the fencer may go; this is especially the case where the body is also tilted in the same direction.

The combination of the body and head account for the largest mass of the individual and gives a great deal of detail where the fencer will go. While the extremities may be moved in different places, the body must move as one and must follow together. There is no separation possible.

Arms and Hands

The arms and hands must be examined together. While a small movement of the hand can make a lot of difference, gross movements must come from the movement of both hand and arm. It is best to look at the bigger and then examine the smaller. In the current position whether the arm is straight or bent can make a lot of difference.

The relaxed arm which is easy to move will be more straight than bent. A bent arm uses muscles and this burns energy. The movements will also be slower due to having to release tension and then re-tense the muscles. Consider the position of the arm first and then examine the hands.

Examine the position of the hand, this will give an indication of the direction that the weapon will go, this is determined by the hand position. In closer detail, the grip on the weapon should be noted. Determine whether the hand is relaxed or tense. Examine the position of the hand and fingers within the hilt. This information can say something about how the weapon will move and the condition and attitude of the fencer. It is to the arms and hands that the fencer should look as to where the weapon moves or may move. The weapon itself can also give clues about the opponent.

Weapon

The next thing that needs to be examined is the weapon. The position of the weapon is of great importance as it will determine where the next attack from the opponent will come and also any parts of the opponent that he has covered due to the position of his weapon. With regard to the position of the weapon, it is important to examine all aspects of it.

While the position of the blade and the point are the most important the position of the hilt can also be. It is more significant to examine the weapon as a whole rather than in parts as the position of the weapon in entirety is more important. The weapon should be pictured as a line and the position of this line is important as it will determine those things which have been expressed already.

The Thrust, being a straight line attack, will flow easiest along the line created by the weapon. A Cut may originate from this line but will be a much broader on being the width of the weapon as it sweeps through the air. Knowing these lines enables the fencer to counter the actions associated with them.

If a line is drawn from the tip of the weapon horizontally backward toward the fencer, and then another is dropped perpendicularly from this to the hilt, this can be seen as a wall, and it determines which line is covered by the position of the weapon. The movement of the weapon is also important and will be discussed later.

Guard Position

With the entire position of the opponent discovered, it is possible to look at their Guard. The Guard will determine what defensive and offensive actions can be most easily made, and this will enable the fencer to prepare defences and counters to those actions. This was discussed in the sections on Counter-Position. A true Ward is a position from which an attack or defence can be made, any position that the fencer stops in which cannot do either with ease is a vulnerable position and is one that can be taken advantage of.

Movement

With the pieces of the opponent examined and then as a whole while static, it is now possible to examine the movements of the opponent. The movements of the opponent are important as it is through these movements that offensive gestures will be made against the fencer and also defensive gestures to defend against those offensive actions of the fencer. Whether the actions performed are smooth or jerky is an important consideration, as those actions which are performed easily are smooth and those which are jerky are probably not as practiced. This can also reveal a level of confidence in the action.

The difference between a smooth and a jerky action is often determined by whether the combatant is relaxed or tense. Relaxed muscles are easier to move, while tense ones are harder to move, this relaxation or tension may come from apprehension about the situation or the actions being performed and this dichotomy is useful to determine things about the opponent.

The next question of movement that follows is whether the actions are done with energy, this can determine whether the opponent is energetic or tired. Should the opponent have energy, the fencer will need to conserve his energy to last against the opponent, making the opponent move will gradually reduce his energy; should the opponent be tired, the fencer can use this to his advantage, as the actions will most likely not be as sharp as they would be while he had energy.

Time and Speed

Speed is a consideration which needs to be made. While speed is important, Time is more significant. A fast opponent can be slowed and a slow opponent can be defeated with speed. Manipulating the *Tempi* is more significant. An opponent who uses actions of short *Tempo* may seem faster than one who extends the *Tempo*. It has already been demonstrated that *Tempi* can be extended and shortened. Thus, the Cadence of the bout can be increased or decreased, so long as the fencer has the correct information.

True speed in fencing comes from the practice of actions and in consequence, the development of efficiency, an opponent with fast actions is one who has practiced them, or who is using a lot of muscle energy to perform them. The former is much more dangerous and harder to deal with than the latter. Fatigue will affect both, but more the latter than the former.

Footwork

The opponent's footwork determines how well he moves across the ground, if it is sloppy this is an advantage which the fencer can use against him. So too is the absence of much footwork. This is most easily read by making the opponent move and seeing how well he achieves this.

Weapon Movement

The blade actions are the final movement which the fencer needs to pay attention to. These determine how effective their offensive and defensive actions are. This is less about power and more about precision. The lack of precision in blade movement, footwork, or indeed any action leaves gaps in the opponent's defence which can be exploited.

Actions Made

Movement is an important part of the examination of the opponent, how they move is important, but what they do in the movements is also of importance. In the question of what actions the opponent makes, there are further details which can be found.

Repetition

If the opponent repeats a certain action either deliberately or not, they can be patterned and as a result, a response can be forced. The repetitions do not necessarily have to repeat one action after another, as repetitive patterns can also be found over series of actions. Knowing this can be very useful in planning a counter to the actions of the opponent.

Mistakes

Mistakes are made by all fencers, catching an opponent in one of these mistakes is useful; realising that they make the same mistake repeatedly in an action is a boon. This is especially the case if the same mistake appears in multiple actions. A mistake in an action which is repeated over and over again leaves a gap for the fencer to strike through; this especially the case where the mistake is made in a defensive action.

Peculiar Delivery

A combatant may develop a peculiar method of delivery for an action. This may be an offensive action or a defensive action. This is something that the fencer should be aware of as it may change how the action is delivered and the position from which it can strike to and from.

On a more offensive note, the peculiar delivery may be correct in a sense, but may also result in leaving a gap in their defence elsewhere. There are many things which need to be taken into account when examining the actions of an opponent. Each point gives something for the fencer to think about and possibly even use against the opponent. The observation of movement is difficult and will require practice, but the advantage it results in is worth a much to the fencer.

Reason for Movement

The final element is to examine the reasons behind the movement of the opponent. This delves into the movement of the opponent and the reasons for the movements. This is the final key to correctly reading the opponent, and thus of taking advantage of this movement.

Active or Reactive

The easiest way to examine the reason is through a series of dichotomies. The first is the Active or Reactive. If the combatant is Active, he will make the action and make the opponent respond. This sort of combatant always attempts to seize Priority. On the other side is the Reactive combatant, the one who waits for the action of their opponent and then moves to counter the action before making an action against the opponent. The way to defeat each of these is to counter them.

The Active fencer should be forced to react rather than be active, achieved by taking Priority. The Reactive fencer should be forced to act against the fencer. In both instances it is to move the opponent out of his comfort zone. This is the key in all instances.

Another way to look at this dichotomy is to see whether the fencer is one which takes the offensive or who uses counter-offensive actions. The former will wait for a hole to appear in the other opponent and strike, the latter will wait for the opponent to strike and then counter them, this fencer may even use provoking actions to force the opponent to strike first.

Purpose, Reaction or Instinct

The next thing is to examine the reasons for the movement of the fencer. The actions can be purposeful and, as such, part of a plan used against an opponent, or they may be simply reacting to what the opponent does to counter them, or fencer may be moving on pure instinct. Each one of the three portrays a level of training.

The instinctive has the least training and he will react as does instinctually with no purpose to the action, simply defending or attacking as the situation requires. This is often how the beginning fencer will fence. The next level of training is the Reactive fencer who reacts with purpose; this fencer can plan a response to the opponent's action, but will only be responsive to the actions; the actions are more complex but only controlling the encounter at the simplest level. The purposeful fencer has the greatest amount of training and every action that they perform has purpose behind it; this fencer can actively provoke, lure and use advanced techniques in series to force the opponent to move where he wishes.

The only way to determine one from the other is to examine the actions and the possible thought processes behind them. The difficulty in countering an opponent will increase the more experience and training that the fencer gains, this is an aspect which must be taken into account, especially as they will be using the same investigations to see what you do and how you do it.

Application – Encounters

The application of the Theory and Practical elements are how a set of proposed theories and techniques are proven to be valid. While the best way for this to happen is in actual crossing of blades, some presentations can be made to demonstrate the application of such information. What is presented here is based upon the theories and skills presented in this treatise. These Encounters are merely a beginning to the sequence of techniques which are possible using the system which has been described through this treatise.

For every technique there is a counter and for every counter there is a counter to that and so forth. In some instances, the counter can be very simple, and most often against the complex actions of an opponent. The fencer should be aware that any counter which achieves his goal of not being struck is an effective counter. The ability to strike the opponent while performing this counter should always be a secondary consideration, as is determined by the First Principle.

Foundation Notes

Some notes must be made before the applications are read and used. Firstly, the Guard of Third is used throughout the demonstrations as it is the primary Ward used in this treatise. It should be noted however, that this does not preclude the techniques which have been described being performed from some other Ward. The same Guard in the demonstrations supplies a simple base from which all of the applications may be made.

Secondly, on a similar subject, the initial attacks are primarily made to the High Inside Line, as this is the Line which is most open and vulnerable in Guard of Third. The Outside Line in the Guard of Third is easily closed and attacks to the Low Line are hazardous without some sort of preparation made to occupy the opponent's weapon. Leaving the attacker exposed to simple counters.

Thirdly, the initial attacks are all primarily made with a *Stoccata* as the low position of the Third Guard makes this the optimal and simplest attack from this position. Both the *Imbroccata* and cutting attacks use more *Tempi* than the *Stoccata* and as such, are subject to counter-attack much more easily.

Fourthly, all of the techniques which are demonstrated below will result in the conclusions presented as a consequence of correct reading of the opponent and correct performance of the technique with the optimum Timing in the encounter. Any deviation from the technique described or the requirements here laid out may result in an outcome other than that presented in the demonstration.

Lastly, in all instances presented here the combats are between two individuals using the rapier alone and dressed in civilian dress. The off-hand may be assumed to have a leather glove to protect it during those actions against the opponent's weapon. Any addition of supplementary weapons or armours could affect the result of the encounters described due to these additions. The techniques and theory described and used in these combats will be the ones which have been described previously.

Organization of Combats

The combats presented are intended to demonstrate the essential techniques and principles which have been presented thus far in this treatise. The combats themselves will be divided into sections so that the various elements presented in the treatise can be presented in a logical fashion.

Each one of the demonstrations in these sections will start with an action which is similar to all the other others in the section. Each section will have a descriptive section at the beginning to describe the techniques presented and the reason that they have been grouped together. An explanation of the individual application may be present to better describe the actions and the reasons for the actions which have been presented in the demonstration. For ease of language the same characters used previously in demonstrations, Arthur and Bartolomeo will stand for the fencer and the opponent.

Attack to an Open Line

The attack to an open Line is one of the simplest methods of approach. For the purposes of the following demonstrations, the combatants have closed to Narrow Distance and the encounter follows this closing. The attack is made when the Line is open and the opponent will have a hard time stopping the attack. The following demonstrations will begin with a simple attack to an open Line where the opponent is most vulnerable.

First Encounter

Both combatants come to face one another in the Third Guard in the Narrow Distance. Bartolomeo makes a move to change his Guard to gain an advantage over his opponent. Arthur performs a simple *Stoccata* to the Inside Line which was open due to the original Guard, made possible in *Tempo* by the movement in changing Guard striking his opponent in the Line which has been made open due to the movement.

There are two lessons to be learnt from this combat, one defensive and one offensive. The first is that the fencer should ensure that he is Out of Distance before changing Guard, and the second is that an attack should be launched where and when an opponent is most vulnerable for the attack to have the highest chance of success. In the action the attacking fencer may choose to turn his True Edge toward his opponent's weapon to guard any chance of a response.

Second Encounter

The second encounter places both combatants in the Third Guard as before and at Narrow Distance. Bartolomeo makes a *Stoccata* toward the Inside Line of the Arthur, a Line not covered by the Guard of Third. Prepared, Arthur responds to the attack by making a Parry of Fourth and once he has ensured his safety, maintaining his blade in opposition, he then proceeds to make a counter, thrusting against his opponent, striking his Inside Line.

This is a simple attack, defence and counter in Double Time. Arthur could have Beat Parried the opponent, and while effective it would not have maintained the Engagement of the blades, and thus provided him with a guide for his attack.

Third Encounter

The third encounter proceeds the same way as the second in the beginning with both combatants on Guard in Third at the Narrow Distance with the same attack being made. Rather than defending with the weapon in this instance Arthur chooses instead to Parry with his off-hand while making a Traverse to the right, assured of his safety he then performs a *Stoccata* to the Outside Line of Bartolomeo to the armpit.

The same elements are present as in the first encounter, an attack, defence and counter; the defensive option was simply changed and combined with footwork to enhance the defence. In this particular instance a Beat Parry with the off-hand would make not much difference to the encounter as it is combined with footwork to ensure the safety of the fencer. The off-hand and the foot should be made in the same *Tempo* with the counter-offensive action following.

Fourth Encounter

In the fourth the beginning is the same with the same Third Guard for both and the same attack as the previous, however Arthur chooses to make a different response to the attack. In this instance a Void by the use of a simple Retreat is made, followed by the counter of thrusting *Stoccata* to the Inside Line while making a Slope forward and to the left of Bartolomeo.

The counter works because the simple Retreat will force the opponent to extend too far forward, while he is here the Step and counter-attack is made. The opponent does not have the Time to withdraw his attack and counter the fencer at the same time as he cannot be going forward and backward in the same action. Care should be taken in this to ensure that the rearward action is sufficient to clear from the opponent's attack.

Fifth Encounter

The fifth counter to the attack to the Open Line is much like the fourth, using the body and feet to Void the opponent's attack while keeping both the sword and the off-hand free. The beginning is the same in position, Distance and action. When Bartolomeo makes his *Stoccata* to the Inside Line, Arthur performs a Void in the form of the *Half-Inquartata* moving the target out of the way of his opponent's attack. The weapon is turned toward the opponent and a simple extension will result in the opponent being struck in the Inside Line, mostly by his own forward motion. Should the fencer be a little unsure of his defence, he can use his off-hand to enhance the effect of the Void. The same action can be performed in Counter-Time with the Void and the counter-attack being made as a simultaneous action.

Sixth Encounter

The sixth encounter increases the complexity of the actions which have been described and demonstrates the importance of the simple fact that there is always a counter to every action. For this action it is best return to the motions described in the second encounter. The attack and countering Thrust are made as the same, rather than simply being struck by the Thrust Bartolomeo performs a Ceding Parry of Fourth, defeating the countering Thrust and presenting the opportunity for a *Stoccata* made from the Parry.

This action presents an attack, defence, counter, and a counter to the counter, of course should Arthur be prepared another Ceding Parry to Fourth could be made against this. With this Blade Engagement being present in this action, other Blade Engagement techniques become possible such as a Disengage to counter the Ceding Parry and to give another opportunity to attack.

Cut Consideration

The opening attacks which have been described so far have all been thrusting attacks. The Cut to an Open Line will result in much the same result as has been described, except where the Cut is made too slow, which is usually the result of inefficient or lax technique on the part of the attacker. What should be noted is that the Cut is slower than the Thrust as such the simplest response is to Void the Cut and make a counter against the opponent. The attack can be delivered into the Open Line the delivery of the Cut has made in the opponent. The opponent does not have the time to redirect the Cut once it is too far completed as the Cut must complete its fall, and is also difficult to pull back, consequently, the response with the Cut is slower. It is simply due to the speed of the Cut that the primary opening attack against an opponent should be the Thrust. Opening with a cutting attack also leaves the fencer far more exposed to attacks in Half-Time.

Opening a Line

The encounters which have been described have been those in which an attack is made to an open Line, where this opportunity is present the fencer should take the advantage given. However, an open Line is not always present in the opponent, and for the most part often it is not. This means that the fencer needs to open a Line to attack the opponent. This can be achieved through several different methods.

Just as in all the cases previously the combatants started in the Narrow Distance so too will the combatants all be assumed to begin at the Wide Distance and in the Third Guard. These demonstrations will present how to open a Line in an opponent and use this to achieve an attack.

First Encounter

In the first, the combatants stand opposite one another in the Guard of Third and at Wide Distance. Arthur gains Bartolomeo's sword by turning his hand in Fourth and using *Stringere* to further open the Inside Line against the opponent. Once the Line is open, Arthur steps forward continuing the action of his *Stringere* into a *Stoccata* into the open Line of the opponent. The opponent's weapon must be forced off-line enough and only enough for the fencer to pass by in with safety.

Second Encounter

In the second, the combatants stand opposite one another in the Guard of Third and at Wide Distance. Arthur makes a Beat to the Inside of the Bartolomeo's weapon to open the Inside Line further, using the momentum of the Beat, he extends his arm in a *Stoccata* against the opponent with his hand in Fourth, stepping forward striking the opponent in the chest. The weapon is held in Fourth to guard against the opponent's weapon returning. The Beat must be made and performed properly for the attack to succeed and without the fencer being struck in the process.

Third Encounter

In the third as in the previous two, the combatants stand in Wide Distance on the Third Guard, as in the second, an attack on the blade is used. A Pressure is exerted against Bartolomeo's weapon by Arthur with his hand in Second to open the Outside Line. Once the point is off-line the Glide is executed in the form of a *Stoccata* with the hand still in Second to further open the Line and strike Bartolomeo in his Outside Line.

Both this and the Beat used in the second can be used to open the Outside Line in a Guard of Third due to the force applied to the opponent's weapon, however in both cases the attack which follows the blade action must be made with velocity to prevent the opponent from closing his Line again. The hand should remain in position, Fourth for the inside, and Second for the outside, to defend against the opponent's weapon returning to Line.

Fourth Encounter

Attacks of subtlety can also be used to open a Line to attack the opponent, such an example is the use of the Flowing Attack in the fourth encounter. The combatants stand as previously described in a Third Guard and at Wide Distance. Arthur, making sure to be aware of Bartolomeo's movement and with velocity, makes a Slope forward and left, performing a Flowing Attack to the Outside Line of the opponent, striking him with a *Stoccata*.

In the Flowing Attack the hand needs to remain for the most part in Third to achieve the best muscular action. The hand can be turned to Second at the completion of the attack to guard against the action of the opponent, but it is unnecessary. The same attack can be made by shifting or leaning a little to the left of the opponent however the Step described is a surer defence against a response of the opponent. In this particular instance it is less the action of the blade which opens the Line and more the movement of the fencer.

Fifth Encounter

In the fifth, the action begins as described in the previous actions with the combatants in Third Guard at Wide Distance. For Arthur to make his attack he must close with Bartolomeo to the Narrow Distance, this is achieved using a simple Advance ensuring that his opponent's weapon is covered and observing the movement of his opponent. Once in the Narrow, Arthur strikes the opponent's weapon with his off-hand to the outside and strikes in a *Stoccata* to the Inside Line. The off-hand may also simply engage the opponent's weapon and move it rather than Beating it, the same result will eventuate and the fencer will retain control over the opponent's weapon.

Sixth Encounter

The action of the sixth bears resemblance to that of the fifth in that Arthur must close the Distance to Narrow Distance from Wide Distance. This can be achieved by the use of a simple Advance, but he must be aware of the movement of Bartolomeo and ensure that his opponent's weapon is covered. With this Advance from the Third Guard from Wide to

Narrow Distance, Arthur then Binds the opponent's weapon to the Outside and strikes with a Cut *Riversa* to the now open Line.

In this action the fencer must ensure that he has control over the opponent's weapon before attempting to strike the opponent. Should the fencer Bind the opponent's weapon to the Inside, the attack will be a *Mandritta Falso Tondo*. In this particular instance the Cut is an easier attack due to the position of the weapon at the end of the Bind. A further action on the Bind will result in the point of the weapon being in a position to strike the opponent.

Seventh Encounter

The action of the seventh uses an action to provoke the opponent into action at which the fencer can move to strike the opened Line. The provoking action must be one which the opponent believes for the action to work. Starting at Wide Distance and in the Third Guard, Arthur approaches Bartolomeo using an Advance extending a Thrust or attempting *Stringere* against his weapon. As Bartolomeo moves to counter the action with his weapon, Arthur uses a Time Disengage to avoid the action of his opponent then Thrusts *Stoccata* to the open Line created by the action of his opponent.

In this action Bartolomeo opens the line for Arthur in response to the provoking action made initially. The forward motion needs to be made at the same time as the initial action to bring it into a Distance where the opponent will respond to it. In this action the fencer should be aware of any counter-offensive action of the opponent which may be performed in not against the threat presented.

Eighth Encounter

In the eighth, the fencers start as in previous actions in the Guard of Third and in the Wide Distance. Arthur extends his weapon toward the open Line of Bartolomeo as he moves to counter the action a Cut Over is performed and simple Thrust with an Advance will follow against the open Line of the opponent. The Advance to Distance should be made with the second part of the action of the Cut Over; movement earlier will leave the fencer exposed to a counter attack. Should the opponent not respond to the initial action of the fencer he must not close to perform the second as the opponent will be prepared to counter him.

Efficiency in Motion

In the previous section actions are used to open the opponent's Line so that the fencer can strike against the opponent. These actions to open the opponent's Line vary in complexity as appropriate to the actions used. The action that involves the least action of the fencer and the least action of the opponent is the better action performed. Every time the fencer has to use an additional movement to perform the opening or attack, and for each action the opponent must perform for the Line to be open there is a chance for failure of the action and the potential for the fencer to be struck. The offensive actions against an opponent should only be as complex as they need to be and no more.

Closing a Line

The next section describes counters to the actions which have been previously described. These actions will describe how, once a Line is opened, it is possible to close that Line and use the action of the closing to put the fencer in a position to counter-attack against the opponent.

This will begin with basic counters and then move on to more complex sequences as the counters are countered. These actions all begin in the Wide Distance as to engage in such techniques in the Narrow Distance are possible but it is much more dangerous due to the shortened *Tempo* due to the Distance. As in all the previous encounters, and to preserve some continuity, the combatants will engage from the Guard of Third.

First Encounter

In the first, Bartolomeo uses *Stringere* to open the Inside Line on Arthur, this is countered by him performing a Disengage to the Outside Line on an Advance and a simple *Stoccata* performed to the opponent's now open Outside Line. As in true *Tempi*, the Disengage must be begun before the footwork movement, ensuring his defence the completion at the same time results in the action being performed in a single *Tempo*. The *Stoccata* follows once the fencer is opponent's weapon has been put aside and the Line to the fencer is closed. Arthur is in a position to attack, and should at his soonest opportunity once the Line is closed.

Second Encounter

In the instance of the second engagement, Arthur performs *Stringere* to open the Inside Line of Bartolomeo, in response he performs a Disengage to the Outside Line as before. Instead of being struck in the counter however, Arthur performs a Counter-Disengage in response, and then Advances with a *Stoccata* to the Inside Line of his opponent. Once again, the offensive technique must only follow once the fencer is safe from the threat. Even in the offensive technique, the *Stoccata* should be extended before the foot moves so that the foot and hand are completed at once. This is a counter to a counter.

Third Encounter

The third follows in similarity to the second so that the last counter performed is countered by another. In this instance Bartolomeo uses *Stringere* to open the Inside Line, Arthur counters with a Disengage. Then Bartolomeo counters with a Counter-Disengage, finally Arthur counters with a Double Disengage. The encounter is finally settled with an Advance and a *Stoccata* to Bartolomeo's Outside Line.

One action follows the other as a result of the other's action, there is no reason to concern the use of a Double Disengage if no Counter-Disengage is made. These actions are connected to one another and must be used as such, the process must be followed. Should a combatant perform a technique against one that was not used, the combatant will find himself out of Line and vulnerable.

Fourth Encounter

The fourth proceed with Bartolomeo using *Stringere* to open the High Inside Line. Rather than countering as above, Arthur performs a Half-Disengage, a Slope forward left and a simple *Stoccata* to the forward leg of his opponent. The strike to the leg will stop the opponent from moving toward the fencer. So, the action is effective.

The fencer must also ensure his safety through the use of some defensive action, in this case a diagonal Step removes the intended target; this can be supplemented by a Void or Hand Parry. The defensive action is vital otherwise the fencer will be struck as soon as the Half-Disengage is made. The Half-Disengage itself can be countered by a similar action. Care should be taken in the use of the Half-Disengage.

Fifth Encounter

Just as the Cut Over can be used to open a Line so too can it be used to close a Line and open another, the fifth demonstration presents as such. Bartolomeo uses *Stringere* to open the Outside Line of Arthur, in response he uses a Cut Over to change the Line and close his own and Advances with a simple *Stoccata* to the Inside Line of Bartolomeo. It must be remembered that just as in a previous section, the Advance should accompany the second part of the Cut Over along with the resulting *Stoccata*.

Care should still be taken as to the location of the opponent's weapon in this action. All the usual counters to the Disengage can be applied to the Cut Over. Simplest response is in that the Cut Over is vulnerable to simple Thrust part way through as the point is lifted over the sword. So, the technique used in the demonstration must be applied carefully, the point following the demonstration describing the counter to a Cut Over used against the fencer.

Sixth Encounter

In the sixth, Bartolomeo uses a Pressure to open the Outside Line of Arthur, in response as soon as the Pressure is felt exerted against his weapon, a Disengage is made to the Inside Line of the opponent and a counter attack is made with an Advance and a *Stoccata*. This technique requires the fencer to have good *Senso di Ferro* and to be sure that it is a pressure being used and is committed to.

The Disengage from the Pressure is the simplest response as it uses some of the force applied by the opponent to start the action of the Disengage. A simple counter is much more effective than something which may take additional time.

Seventh Encounter

The seventh involves the opponent using the technique described previously for opening the Line and striking using the Flowing Attack. Bartolomeo advances to Narrow Distance using a Slope forward and left, and makes a Flowing Attack toward the Outside Line of Arthur. Arthur counters by turning his hand to Second, placing the edge against the attack, a simple *Stoccata* with the hand in Second may now be made against the opponent.

This counter works against the Flowing Attack as the change of the hand from Third to Second position changes the angle of the weapon and in this manner, redirects the attack of the opponent out and away from the fencer through simple deflection. This technique should be examined and practiced before it is used in an encounter against an opponent.

Eighth Encounter

The eighth involves the counter to the use of the action of the Beat with the off-hand and the impact of it against the beater. Bartolomeo Advances and Beats Arthur's weapon to the Outside, opening the Inside Line, this is countered by a Disengage using the force of the Beat to turn and strike to the open Line while the using the off-hand against the opponent's weapon to defend against the attack following the Beat. This can be further enhanced by the use of a Slope Pace forward and left. This is a technique which can be applied to any technique which removes the weapon by force.

The Disengage works simply using the power of the opponent's action against them, care should be taken in the turning of the point to ensure that it takes the shortest path to come back on Line. The next easiest is to remove the weapon from where it can be beaten this is most easily achieved through the use of a passive Time Disengage, disengaging the opponent's weapon or hand before it arrives, consequently leaving the opponent out of position and vulnerable.

Ninth Encounter

Just as the previous was designed to counter the Beat, so too is the ninth designed to present how to counter the use of the Bind. Bartolomeo advances to Narrow Distance and attempts to Bind Arthur's weapon, in response he should stop the Bind as it loses engagement on his weapon by strengthening against the Bind most easily achieved by turning the True Edge of the weapon against the opponent's. This technique can be used when the Bind begins also to prevent the movement of the fencer's weapon. This is a technique which requires practice and feeling through the blade to use accurately.

Tenth Encounter

In the tenth, Bartolomeo advances to Narrow Distance extending a thrust or attempting *Stringere*, as Arthur attempts to Parry the action Bartolomeo Time Disengages. Arthur increases his Distance by a Retreat, thus making the following attack fall short. The other technique to counter the Time Disengage is to only move against the second action of the opponent.

The movement of the footwork is the easier option of the two but the waiting for the second action places the fencer in a much better position to respond to the opponent. The fencer should practice both techniques to become proficient at both and as a result have more options available.

A Counter to Every Action

The techniques in this section were designed to counter those actions which are designed to open a Line in the fencer's defences. Each one has a counter which can be used against the attempt. The Blade Engagement techniques which have been presented demonstrate how to every action there is a counter it is more a matter of finding the counter to the action. To this the fencer should also note that even these counters can be countered and so forth. This is the tactical aspect of fencing which becomes apparent once these techniques are understood.

Closes and Grips

There are many techniques which can be used in Closes and Grips; it is the application of such techniques which is important. The fencer needs to think about the three parts to a close engagement, the Entry, Action and Exit. Each one of these is essential and each needs to have serious consideration made. This needs to be done before and during the actual contact. There being so many ways that a close contact encounter can happen, a single demonstration of such an encounter will be presented.

A Close Encounter

With both fencers starting in the Third Guard and at Wide Distance Bartolomeo steps and makes a *Stoccata* toward Arthur's Inside Line. Arthur Beat Parries in Fourth to cover himself, allowing the point of the weapon to roll over a little and then makes a Slope forward and right dropping his point under the Bartolomeo's weapon delivering a *Riverso Mezzo Tondo* to his body. Should the Arthur require he can also use his off-hand to prevent the opponent's weapon from returning by simple placement of the hand toward the opponent's weapon, Arthur then makes a Pass Forward to Exit from the encounter turning once it is completed to face the opponent in Guard.

The second *Tempo* for the fencer is possible due to the recovery time taken for the opponent. The key to a successful close and attack is speed and efficiency; the simpler the attack the better. In this case the fencer takes the Priority with the Parry and then maintains it through his attack. The Entry is actually assisted by the opponent's attack and is completed with the Slope Step; the Action is the Cut against the body with or without the off-hand placement; and the Exit is the Passing Step and returning on Guard.

Efficiency in Motion

The key to successful and safe close contact encounters is to have a clean, Entry, Action and Exit. Where the two combatants come into closer contact and more prolonged contact is where issues can happen. The key to surviving such an encounter is to ensure that the defences are maintained and that the fencer gains Priority over the important part of the encounter; this gives him all of the options. The fencer needs to at least gain the Priority on the Exit to ensure that he can do so safely and also so that he can successfully Exit without the opponent attempting to continue the Action.

In most instances, it is the Entry and Exit where the fencer will find himself most vulnerable to counter-attack from the opponent at these times the fencer needs to be sure of his defences and be sure of the actions of the opponent. There are many different attacks, defences, and approaches to Closes and Grips this is a single demonstration to present the principles behind the actions.

Use of Time

The actions presented so far have primarily used Double Time, there are some instances of other Times, but for the most part it has been Double Time. Each combatant uses a single action followed by the action of the other combatant in response or as a counter. It is also important to examine the other forms of Time, Single, Counter- and Half-Time in a more practical setting to see how they operate and differ from one another. This set of encounters is designed to do just that. It is the different use of Time which is important rather than the actions used in the encounters. Each demonstration will begin with the same set of actions from the same Guard; to present the examples of the different Times in the responses to the same action clearly.

First Encounter

The first encounter will demonstrate Single Time. The combatants stand across from one another in Wide Distance. Bartolomeo makes a *Stoccata* with an Advance to Arthur's Inside Line. In response Arthur turns his hand in Fourth to collect the blade of Bartolomeo and extends in a *Stoccata* to his Inside Line. Bartolomeo's weapon is deflected out of Line by the turning of the hand and the forward action of the Thrust.

The combination of the defensive and offensive techniques in a single *Tempo*, the counter to the opponent's attack is performed in Single Time. In this instance it would also pay for the fencer to move his hand a little toward the opponent's attack as he extends the Thrust to ensure contact between the weapons and as a consequence gain safety in the technique. This form of technique and use of Time takes a great deal of precision in the action, a simple error in placement could see the fencer struck during his action.

Second Encounter

The second encounter is used to demonstrate Counter-Time. The combatants face one another as before, in the Wide Distance at the Guard of Third. Bartolomeo thrusts a *Stoccata* to the Inside Line on an Advance. In response Arthur makes a Slope forward and right while striking a *Stoccata* to Bartolomeo's Inside Line with the hand in Fourth. The counter-attack made against the opponent is made in response to the attack made by the opponent, so against Time, so in Counter-Time.

The counter is not merely launching an attack into the opponent's, there is consideration for where the opponent's attack is coming from, going to and also there is an aspect of defence made in the Slope made. Should the fencer merely launch an attack against the opponent without these considerations he will most likely find himself struck.

Third Encounter

The third and final encounter to be described is one which demonstrates the use of Half-Time against the opponent. The beginning and initial attack proceeds as has been described previously with both combatants on Guard of Third and at Wide Distance. Bartolomeo makes a *Stoccata* to the Inside Line on an Advance. In response to the offence of his opponent, Arthur withdraws his Inside Line through the use of a simple Void and strikes against Bartolomeo's forearm with a *Stoccata* before his offensive action is completed. Bartolomeo's *Stoccata* is interrupted before it can be completed, and so the action of Arthur is made in Half-Time.

A cutting attack against the opponent's arm in this instance would result in the same conclusion. The essential part is that the action of the fencer is made against the attack of the opponent. The action may arrest the action of the opponent but the fencer should still make some other defensive action to be safe, in the demonstration, a void was used.

Simple Example Demonstrations

Each of the three previous demonstrations has highlighted the use of techniques associated with a particular form of Time. Each one is different and the differences are important. There is much confusion made when using such advanced techniques in combat, and much misinterpretation when they are seen. The explanation presented is designed to present the differences so that the different Times may be understood better.

The demonstrations presented are only a small proportion of the techniques that could be used in the same situation. This is not designed to cover all options, merely to give a presentation of some of the options the fencer may have at his disposal. These practical demonstrations are designed to present the theory and practical elements together in a situation where responses are being made by two combatants who are in the encounter. The encounters presented in the demonstration of the application above will only work as described so long as the correct Timing and techniques are used. This will require that the fencer make sure that he has had sufficient practice before attempting any in an encounter with an opponent.

Sundry Notes

Advantage of the Circle Over the Line

There is an advantage in fencing for taking the circle over the line. This aspect is directed at the approach to engaging an opponent in combat. To understand this advantage, some things need to be made clear. The usual approach is that the line will always have the advantage over the circle, but through the aspects described and principles presented, it will be revealed that this is not always the case. This is a relatively old thought process as the Spanish use the principles of the circle and movement to gain advantage in their methodology. The principles described here will be similar to these, but also different in the approach due to the nature of the system of fence employed.

On-Line and Off-Line

The first thing that needs to be made clear is what is considered to be on-line and off-line in regard to the opponent. This is different to the Lines described previously in the section on Theory. There is a line which can be drawn between the two combatants. This is a direct line which is drawn from the middle of one combatant to the other when they are standing across from one another. A similar line can be drawn connecting the shoulders of the combatants.

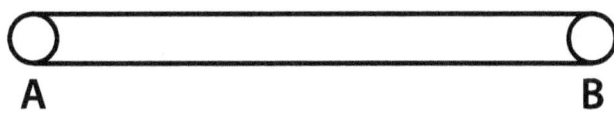

A is Online to B and vice versa

This creates a clear line between the two combatants and it is this which determines whether the combatants are on-line to one another. A fencer who steps off this particular line is off-line from the opponent's perspective. It should be noted that the lines extend from the natural direction of the facing of the combatants. It is here where the circle can dominate the line.

Movement Creates Advantage

The advantage of the circle over the line is based on movement, and more to the point fluid and active movement. The advantage is lost at any time where the fencer uses a static approach to the encounter. Circular movement refers to any action which deviates off-line as previously described. This movement moves the fencer out of the opponent's direct facing and therefore off-line to the opponent and gains him advantage.

Movement off-line is found in Voids, especially the *Inquartata*, and also in footwork actions such as Slopes and Traverses. These actions all change the angle to the opponent, as a result, gain advantage over the opponent, so the circular movement of the fencer gains the advantage over linear movements of the opponent. Movement off the line is used to disrupt the actions of the opponent; in the offensive case this can change position and point of attack, change the Line of engagement and change Distance; in the defensive similar changes are appropriate, but also the movement can limit the attack of the opponent or even simply defeat the attack of the opponent through simple movement.

Size of Movement

The movement off-line does not have to be gross, indeed it can be fine and in some instances the size of the movement is inversely proportional to the effect that it can have on the combat. Gross movements have their place and can be very effective, but the finer movement can also make it easier for the fencer to keep his weapon in on-line, threatening the opponent. The weapon in presence, directed at the opponent, is always more effective than the weapon that is not.

Movement in Defence

In defence, the change of direction can be used to defeat a straight-line attack, especially one at the limit of the opponent's reach, and one dependent on the velocity of the attack. A simple movement out of line is sufficient. The circular motion defeats the straight by deviation off the line and taking the targeted fencer out of presence through a simple action. The Cut is especially effectively defeated by the movement off-line or movement out of Distance. The Cut is slower than the Thrust and its path can be more easily predicted due to its nature. A vertical Cut is voided by movement to the side; other Cuts can be similarly defeated.

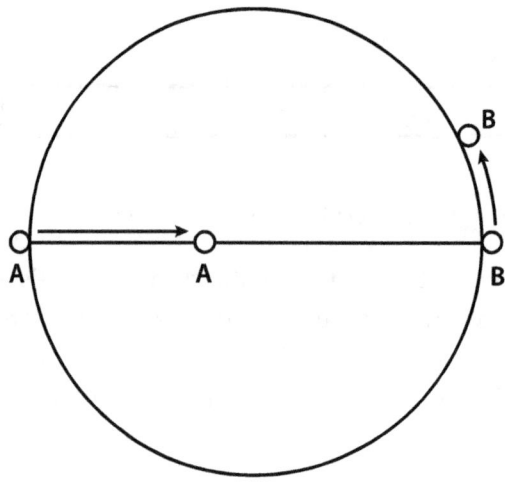

B moves off-line to A

In the movement off-line, the angle of attack is changed and the straight-line attack is easily avoided through the same movement. This movement off-line should not prevent the fencer from keeping his weapon in presence and accordingly, on-line to the opponent. This allows for simple attack against the opponent or counter-attack against the opponent depending on the situation presented.

Movement in Attack

The attack is still based on the line due to the speed of the attack; the Thrust is faster than the Cut due to the use of the straight line approach. However, the circular movement gives more options for the direction of the attack. The angles of attack can be changed due to the movement on the circle.

The attack along the Line is designed on the basis of speed and the advantage taken by having the opponent out of position, consequently, vulnerable. This is a direct attack against an exposed Line of the opponent. The attack using circular motion can be moved about the opponent's defences, by-passing and avoiding the defences presented to strike areas where the opponent is not covered. Depending on the circular movement of the fencer a Line can be further opened, discovered or closed.

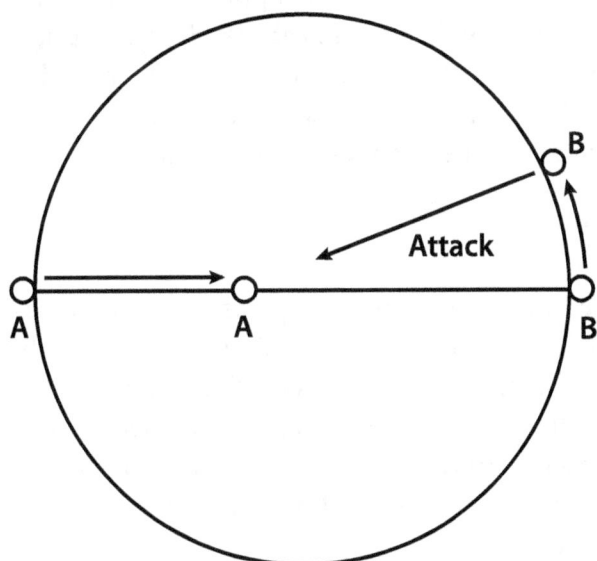

B moves off-line and attacks against A's on-line movement.

The fencer should examine which direction he intends to move and what effect this will happen on the Lines of the opponent. For the most part it is better to move where the opponent will be more exposed than to move where he is more closed, however, if the fencer has something more complex planned such as an approach consisting of several movements designed to open the Line, then movement to the more defended may be more appropriate in that situation.

Fluid Motion

Regardless of the movement the fencer uses to change his attack against the opponent, this movement must be fluid in nature and the movement of the hand must accompany the movement of the feet. If the fencer moves his feet and then as separate movement moves his hands, the opponent can simply turn and negate the effect of the movement of the feet. If, however the movement of the hand accompanies the movement of the feet then the advantage gained is preserved by the delivery of the attack during the movement off-line.

In the use of the movement off-line in defence and followed by a counter-attack or accompanied by a counter-attack, the advantage is preserved due to the action of attack against the fencer by the opponent. In the *Tempo* of the attack of the opponent, the fencer moves off-line in his defence, gaining the advantage. The attack must be completed or withdrawn, either way the fencer has this *Tempo* to strike against the opponent.

Change of Circumstance

The idea that the circle can defeat the line will seem somewhat foreign to some as it has been demonstrated that the Cut is slower by the nature that it uses the circle for motion and the

Thrust is faster by the nature that it uses the line. This remains true however the movement off-line while slower in some aspects gives the fencer advantages in changing the situation between him and his opponent.

The engagement can be changed, Distance can be changed and indeed the position is changed by the nature of the movement. The opponent has to react to these changes that the fencer makes and so remains unsettled in his approach to the fencer. In this manner, the fencer gains an advantage. Where the fencer is attacked by the opponent and he responds by movement off-line, he changes the situation and gains the advantage in time for his response. It is through these aspects and also those which have been described that it is demonstrated that the circle has the advantage over the line.

Single Against All

The instruction presented in this text previously has been on the basis of the fencer using a single sword against an opponent who is also similarly armed. This is because the single sword is the foundation weapon of the system. Other items may accompany the single sword but it is primarily the sword that will be accompanied by another item. However, an opponent may not always be carrying a single sword, or indeed matching implements to an encounter. To this point the fencer needs to know how to deal with an opponent who has a companion when the fencer does not.

The descriptions given below will be general in their approach. In all instances the fencer should study their opponent carefully before making any sort of action against them. The actions presented below are designed to present some solutions to some problems presented by the opponent. They are guidelines how to approach an opponent. In all instances the fencer should consider what the opponent is doing and act accordingly to the situation presented.

Foundation Theory

In approaching the situation where the fencer has a single sword and the opponent has a sword accompanied by another device, either offensive or defensive, there are certain things that the fencer should keep in mind. Firstly, there are some things that cannot change regardless of the items which are in use. The prime one being that you both have two hands. Secondly, all of the same principles which have been previously presented apply just as much as they would when only a single sword is being used, and with little modification. Thirdly, a fencer will have spent more time with a single weapon than with any other combination of weapons and this is an advantage which can be used by the fencer against the opponent.

In certain circumstances the second implement can actually hamper the opponent rather than aiding them and this needs to be used to the fencer's advantage. If the fencer can learn to dominate and defeat a combination before learning how to use that combination it will gain the fencer an advantage and this can be used in future studies of the weapon and its combinations. Companion weapons will be addressed in a future book. The only real other change to an encounter besides the addition of items to the encounter is where the opponent is fighting left-handed against the fencer. This issue will be addressed in the next section of this treatise.

Advantages and Disadvantages

There are inherent advantages and disadvantages in each weapon combination. The fencer needs to discover these, preferably before the encounter ensues. Dealing with other combinations is based upon the advantages and disadvantages of the forms being used. The advantages of the opponent's form need to be neutralised while the disadvantages need to be accentuated so that the fencer can gain dominance. The fencer needs to work tactically in his encounter with the opponent to succeed in the situation. As has been stated, each form has advantages and disadvantages.

The Empty Hand

The universal advantage of the single over a two-hand combination is that the use of an extra item or weapon does not leave the opponent with an empty hand, except in the case of the gauntlet, and that is still not the same as an empty hand. The empty hand is easier to use to control an opponent's item regardless of what it is. The other advantage is that the empty hand is a natural thing and is not added to the fencer and, as such, the fencer has to spend less thought on its correct application. This small amount of time taken in thought, or lack thereof, is an advantage which can be used. In all cases the fencer should be considering what the opponent will attempt to do to gain the advantage. Accordingly, attempt to negate this advantage or the chances to gain this advantage.

Case of Rapiers

The case of rapiers is the most intimidating weapon form for the fencer with a single rapier to face due it being two long weapons against a single one. This makes it a good place to start to see that it can be defeated by a single weapon. It is also the primarily offensive combination that a fencer can arm himself. The fencer should not simply throw himself into the fray as this will result in him being struck. Time should be taken to study the form for its advantages and disadvantages.

Length

The first thing that will be noted is that in the use of two long weapons the opponent will have the advantage at longer range, while at the closer range to the opponent he will lose this advantage due to the length of the weapons. If the fencer can get inside the range of the opponent's weapons, his advantage will increase markedly.

Offensive

It will be noted that in the use of two weapons and two long ones at that, the form is more offensive than defensive. This presents one of the keys to defeating the opponent with case of rapiers. If the opponent is kept on the back foot, thus on the defensive, it will make it difficult for him to make an offensive action against the fencer. In this method, the fencer takes Priority and keeps it from the opponent. The fencer must make the opponent use both weapons defensively and not allow him offensive actions.

Spoil

Remembering the two-hand principle described previously, the fencer should apply his weapon to one weapon and his hand on the other weapon. The fencer does not even need to attack, merely to spoil the opponent's chance to attack. Simple contact against the opponent's weapons will often achieve this. Through this spoiling the opponent can be frustrated into a mistake or even entanglement, this is obviously an advantage which the fencer can use to his advantage.

Movement

The fencer should also move to a position where one weapon is closer than the other. Once this is achieved then the fencer can use single sword techniques against single weapons. The engagements will work the same as they would with a single weapon, but the fencer should always be aware of the other weapon. The fencer can also, with a great deal of care, work between the weapons as the Inside Lines are often forgotten. Remember with two weapons there are double the Lines, two Inside Lines and two Outside Lines. Both sets can be attacked and if the opponent is not careful, he can actually leave Lines open where he did not realise. Even though the case of rapiers has lots of advantages and offensive potential, it also does have disadvantages. The studious and careful fencer can find situations where he can have the advantage even in this situation.

Rapier and Dagger

The other common combination, and indeed more common than the case of rapiers, that two offensive items are carried is rapier and dagger. This is more common as the gentleman would more likely carry a dagger rather than another rapier in his everyday dress. It would seem that this form is less intimidating than the case of rapiers as it has a short weapon and a long one, but this also gives the advantage that the fencer has an advantage both at long and short ranges. Even with this increased advantage the fencer with the single sword can still prevail.

Dagger

The dagger cannot strike at longer ranges, so it should simply be avoided. The fencer should do his best to avoid contact with the dagger at all, and while staying at range, this will do a lot to neutralise its advantage. Against the single long weapon single sword techniques can be used against the opponent while staying out of contact with the dagger. The fencer should move to a position where the sword is on the dominant side to neutralise the use of the dagger. The shorter reach of the dagger will make it difficult to bring it into play.

Lines

To further gain advantage the primary attack of the fencer should be to the Outside Line where the dagger has difficulty reaching; or to the Inside Line close to the opponent's sword where the dagger will have difficulty being used without entangling the sword. If the fencer can force the opponent to self-entangle, this will give him a great advantage and, no doubt, an opportunity to strike in safety. This approach, it will be noted, will be the standard approach to most of the combinations which the fencer will face.

Rapier and Buckler

The buckler is a defensive item which is used with the rapier. In general, it is not used to strike the fencer, accordingly, as a direct threat it is absent. From this point of view, it can be ignored. Avoidance is the best option in the fight against the buckler where the fencer only has a single weapon. Where the buckler is likely to be used to strike with, avoidance of the buckler becomes even more important.

Movement

The fencer should move to the Outside Line to neutralise the effect of the buckler as much as possible. Once this is achieved, the fencer can then use single sword techniques. To bring it back into use, the opponent will have to shift their position, and may foul their own weapon in this shift of position. However, another approach can be used against the buckler which works due to the nature of the item.

Buckler

The point of the fencer's weapon can be hidden behind the buckler and so, out of view of the opponent, thus using the buckler against them. From here the fencer can make actions and initialise movements which the opponent cannot see. The covering aspect of the buckler is used against the opponent. The same effect can be used if the fencer makes attacks which move close to the position of the buckler, so using the buckler against the opponent.

Anytime that the opponent blocks his vision with the buckler the fencer will have a chance to make an action and has an advantage, the fencer should use these opportunities as much as possible. Some of these positions can be forced by the fencer. The same can be said for anytime that the buckler is moved into a position where it will foul the movement of the sword. Once again, many of the approaches when the opponent is using a dagger can work where he is using a buckler. Movement to the sword-side and attacks close to the sword can work effectively.

Withdrawal

Anytime the buckler comes into contact with the fencer's weapon, the fencer should disengage and re-position his weapon to neutralise the effect of the buckler. It is often a good idea to withdraw, if possible, at least to Wide Distance, to increase the Distance and the immediacy of the possible following attack of the opponent, and should it be the case, the threat of the buckler itself. This applies to the use of any off-hand item, Disengage, and withdraw from the encounter to counter the effect of the item.

Rapier and Cloak

Rapier and cloak is another defensive combination that the fencer may be faced with an opponent carrying. The purpose of the cloak is to block sight, and to bind and entangle the weapon. In some instances, it may be thrown to achieve its goal, but still it is a defensive item so from the point of being struck to be killed, it can be ignored.

Avoidance

The prime mode of dealing with an opponent's cloak is to avoid it as much as possible. If the opponent cannot come into contact with your weapon, then it is difficult for them to perform most of the effect of the item. As with the other combinations, the fencer should move to the Outside Line to neutralise the effect of the cloak in the off-hand. To use the cloak effectively the sword will have to be moved and this can result in the opponent becoming entangled in his own cloak.

In the case of the cloak, it is effective at defending against Cuts, but not so much against Thrusts, so the off-hand can be attacked with a Thrust to harm the hand or arm. Care should be taken in this attack not to become entangled in the cloak in the process. With the change in position and the opponent's weapon being primary, and the cloak being neutralised, simple single sword techniques can then be used against the opponent.

Cloak

In general, contact with the cloak should be avoided to avoid any chance of deflection or entanglement. However, the position of the cloak as placed by the opponent can be used by the fencer to obscure the position of his weapon and indeed in cases even his entire body. This is using the cloak's ability to block sight lines against the person who is using the cloak. This can be achieved in a similar manner to that described in the use against an opponent using a buckler. Once again, it should be emphasised that should the opponent's cloak come into contact with the fencer's weapon and start to become entangled he should withdraw into a secure Guard.

Rapier and Gauntlet

The final combination that the fencer is likely to encounter in the company of gentlemen is the sword and gauntlet. This form is actually very similar to that of the single sword except that the gauntlet is invulnerable to Cuts made against the armoured part of the hand. The gauntlet should be avoided at all costs as the opponent may grasp the fencer's weapon and gain control over it. This can be achieved through the simple technique of the Disengage. Further, just as with the other forms described, the fencer should place himself more on the Outside Line to make it more difficult for the opponent to fasten upon the weapon.

The gauntlet makes the opponent's hand invulnerable to Cuts, but this same protection does not apply to Thrusts and as such these can still be targeted against the gauntleted hand of the opponent. For the most part however, once the fencer has positioned himself correctly more to the sword-side of the opponent simple single sword techniques can be used just as if the opponent were armed only with a sword.

Differing Combinations

In coming to an encounter with an opponent, unless the terms of the encounter and the weapons were agreed beforehand, he may find himself facing an opponent with many different combinations of weapons and other off-hand devices. These descriptions have given some ways in which a selection of these devices can be dealt with even though the fencer may only be armed with a single rapier.

The principles of these are very similar and should be taken note of so that devices which have not been mentioned may also be dealt with in an efficient and safe manner by the fencer. It should be noted that armed with such information a fencer places him in a much better position to learn how other devices of an offensive and defensive nature work due to knowing what their limitations are before starting with them. The more common and natural devices of the gentleman shall be addressed in a future exploration designed for the purpose.

Approach

In all instances where a fencer faces an opponent with unmatched weapons, whether he is armed with an item in his off-hand or not, the fencer should survey the opponent and discover what the opponent can do with their combination and how they would go about this. Once this is gained the fencer can then go about thinking about ways in which these uncovered objectives can be undone by the fencer so that the fencer can be victorious. This process is the same as that which was described in the section on Reading the Opponent earlier in this treatise. All of the same principles elucidated there apply to the current described situations. There is a solution and a way around any combination of items that an opponent may carry with a single sword or any combination that the fencer may carry; this above all else the fencer should remember in his encounters.

Of the Left-Handed Opponent

For some fencers, the left-handed opponent will cause a deal of consternation. For the teacher, the left-handed student also presents some unique problems. Just as with dealing with a left-handed opponent, teaching a left-handed fencer involves an examination of the situation and in part an examination from their point of view. The talented teacher will find no difficulty in teaching the left-handed student so long as what he is teaching is based on sound fencing theory and applied to the peculiarities of the left-handed fencer.

With regard to the left-hander, and as the title of this section implies, it is the left-handed opponent being discussed here and not the left-handed student, though many of the same principles still apply. What should also be noted is that it is the right-handed fencer facing a left-handed opponent. Should the fencer and the opponent be both left-handed, then the fence applies just as it would for a right against a right the Lines are simply reversed, as will be explained below, and all applies as previously described in the previous instruction.

Same Theory

Regardless of what hand the sword is held in, the same basic principles of sword operation apply. The left-handed fencer is still bound by the primary principles of Time and Distance and these are applied in the same way as they would be to the right-handed fencer. This is because these principles do not change, regardless of the weapon and regardless of the hand the particular weapon is being held. There are, however, some principles which are modified by the position of the weapon and the hand in which the weapon is held.

Lines

The principle which is primarily affected by the change in hand from right to left is that of Lines. Due to this, there is some modification to the principle of Engagement. Even so, the changes for Engagement are only on the basis of the side on which the opponent's side lies rather than the position of the weapons against one another. The *Forte* remains dominant over the *Debole* in strength and dominance of Engagement. What do change are the Lines.

The Lines are swapped over due to the sword position as they are always relative to the position of the weapon, and this is also the reason why two swords result in two sets of Lines, though the reference to a Line in this particular situation is usually referred to basis of the dominant hand or weapon engaged at the time. The names of the Lines remain it is just the sides which are swapped; the principles of their naming remains.

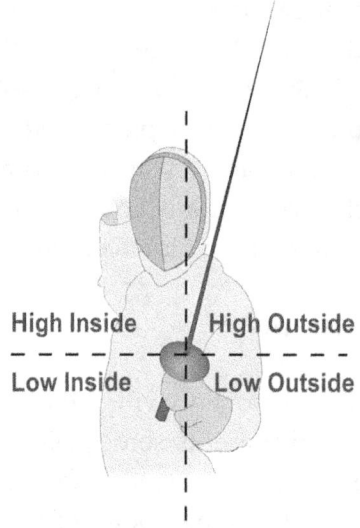

Lines for the left-hander

Even for the left-hander, the Outside Line is to the Outside of the weapon and closest to the Outside of the fencer and the Inside Line is obviously the reverse of this being to the Inside of the weapon and closest to the Inside of the fencer. However, the Outside Line will be on the left and the Inside Line to the right rather than the reverse as it is with the right-handed fencer. In the discussion of fencing against the left-handed opponent, the Lines will be described from both the position of the fencer and their opponent.

Changing Hands

The first mistake which is often made by a fencer facing a left-handed opponent is that the fencer will change to his left hand so that the principles will right themselves and that the Lines will be the same for both. This is a fool-hardy mistake as the fencer should only change hands where he is required to by injury or by honour. The fencer will have less skill in his off-hand as compared to his dominant hand this goes whether the fencer is left or right-handed to begin with.

Changing hands takes away any advantage of skill that the fencer may have had in using his right hand in the encounter. It is sure in this situation that the left-handed fencer will still have the advantage as it is more likely that he has faced more right-handed opponents than he has left-handed opponents, but it is due to the skill of the fencer, rather than the opponent that the hand should not be changed.

Line of Attack

In attacking and making actions against the left-handed fencer, and indeed for the left against the right-handed fencer, it is the Outside Line which is often the target for attacks and actions, and often advised as such by many theorists. This makes a great deal of sense in that the Outside Line is closer for both combatants in the particular situation, so it makes sense from the point of view of the Measure between the fencers. However, the Inside Line of the left-handed fencer should not be disregarded out of hand.

From the simple point of view that the Outside Line may be choked in an engagement due to both fencers attacking down a similar Line, the possibility of another option for the fencer should be appealing. In engaging along the Outside Line, and if the opponent's weapon is pushed to the Outside, the Inside Line is left open to attack. Even where the fencer moves the opponent's weapon further out to use the Outside Line and remain covered, there is still the threat of the Inside should the opponent disengage and change Lines to the Inside Line. Here it is demonstrated that the Line is choked by the actions of both fencers using the Outside Line, and indeed the fencer is threatened to the Inside Line.

Inside Line

Would it not be easier to work to the left-hander's Inside Line as the sword is in position already to defend against attack? In saying this, it is the shallow Inside Line that should be examined to maintain a correct position with the opponent, to stretch deeper into the Inside Line threatens the fencer with extended Times and Distance. In this working the fencer should aim to angle his weapon to cover the Outside Line with position of the weapon, covering the opponent's weapon with his *Forte*, and thus, attacking the Inside Line in safety.

To attack the Inside Line, the fencer needs to clear the opponent's weapon and ensure that he has Distance and Time to achieve his end. This will involve the use of footwork and clever engagement of the weapon against the opponent's sword to remain guarded. The opponent will clearly not give up his Line voluntarily as this will place him in a position under threat, so the fencer must use his skill to open the Line for an attack.

With engagement on the opponent's blade the fencer can open the opponent's Inside Line by stepping toward the opponent's Outside Line and pressing. The same can be achieved through an attack made to the Outside which is changed to the Inside while stepping to the Outside. If the fencer should still wish to attack the Outside Line, a similar approach, reversed to reflect the change in Line, can be made to move against the Outside Line. The fencer can engage the opponent's weapon and step, pressing to the Inside to open the Outside Line, or as described previously an attack changed from Inside to Outside while making the same movement of the feet can also be used.

Tactical Approach

The left-handed fencer presents many different problems for the fencer, but they are problems which, with intelligence and a careful approach, can have a solution found for them. In engaging the left-handed fencer, the fencer should remember that all the same principles and theories which have been presented for the right-handed fencer also apply just as much to the left-handed fencer and it is within these principles and theoretical elements that the solution lays.

The correct application and use of skill needs to be applied to the situation. The solutions which have been presented here rely upon the fencer applying his skill in the correct manner and using the correct techniques, Times and Distances to achieve the desired result. The fencer should always be aware of his opponent and any changes regardless of whether he is right or left-handed.

Of the True and False Arts

The True and False Arts are concepts which have come into debate by various masters and theorists over many years. Some find the use of the so-called False Arts to be base and dishonourable, others find them to be the skills of the gifted combatant, and others again merely see them as a set of skills which the combatant may or may not use depending on the situation. There are questions that arise and points of view that are expressed; those found here are mine and mine only.

To delve into this most perplexing question, some foundations need to be laid. From these foundations a discussion will emerge about this particular subject rather than instruction on how each operates. True, there will be some principles on their use presented, and also ways to counter these actions presented, but these will be in a more general than specific approach. This will educate both those who are interested in their use and also those who would wish to know how to defend against their use. Thus, this discussion and instruction is useful to both.

Division of the Art

The True Art is considered to contain those actions which are direct attacks upon the opponent with no deviation in their delivery. The False Arts are those which use deception and do not deliver a direct attack to achieve their final goal. According to this definition any action which is performed to provoke action from the opponent is part of the False Art, whereas any action which has the intention of striking the opponent directly is part of the True Art. Of course, this would bring into question such things as simple defence, but these actions are excluded from the argument.

The question of the True and False Arts discuss the attack rather than any other action. A direct attack is considered to be True and an action that provokes the opponent to action so that the fencer can then respond is False. The result of this is that an action in some instances can be part of both the True and False Arts simultaneously. A thrust which is directed against the opponent with the intent to strike the opponent is part of the True Art, whereas a thrust which is directed against the opponent with the intent to draw some action from the opponent against the action would be part of the False Art. The important thing with regard to definition into the True or False Art is the intent of the action performed rather than the action itself.

Questions of Use

For some, the definition of the True and False Arts is something which is to be held strictly; and never the twain shall meet, regardless of the usefulness of the skills involved. These individuals would have the fencer only perform actions against the opponent which are direct attacks against him. To this particular point they would also bring into question honour with regard to the technique performed stating that the actions of the False are base and dishonourable and to be avoided at all costs.

In this particular discussion you will see none of these arguments being presented. Neither Art will be presented as anything more than a set of skills to be used or discarded should that be the choice. Instead, the arguments that will be presented will be based on those aspects of the fencing theory upon which all fencing is based. Questions of honour should never be about a particular skill or set of skills, but about the application of the skills of the Art.

The only reason that the skills of deception will be called the False Art is that it is most commonly they are called such in the fencing vernacular which is present in treatises upon the subject. For the present it will be a discussion of the application of a certain skill set against an opponent and the advantages, disadvantages and correct application of these skills.

Argument Based in Theory

To begin with arguments for and against the use of the False Art will be presented. The arguments are founded in fencing theory and its application which has already been presented in previous sections of this treatise. The prime argument against the use of the False Art is that which is based on Time.

Against

The argument based on *Tempo* is founded on the idea that *Tempo* is expended in the use of each action in fencing. Thus, the *Tempo* used in the action to draw the action of the opponent is one which is lost to the opponent and gives them a chance to act. Accordingly, the action using the False Art uses two *Tempi* whereas the action only uses a single *Tempo* in that it is a direct attack performed. The use of the False Art according to this theory expends more *Tempo* than it is worth, using two *Tempi* where a single *Tempo* can be used by the opponent in response, consequently leaving the fencer in a deficit.

For

The argument *for* the use of the False Art in an encounter is also based upon *Tempo*. In this argument the fencer gains *Tempo* through the action performed. The fencer performs an attack not intending to strike. The opponent responds to the action of the fencer not knowing that the attack is false, during this time, the fencer, breaking from his previous action, re-directs his attack to another Line which has been uncovered by the movement performed by the opponent.

The fencer gains *Tempo* by making the opponent use *Tempo* to cover a Line which is not under threat. This is the argument for the use of the False Art and in this case is that it can cause the opponent to perform actions which are reactions to the false action. So spend *Tempo*, giving the fencer *Tempo* in which to act. It is the reaction which is the key to the success of the false action.

Reaction and Intent

There is one simple key that sees the success of the action in the False Art regardless of how simple or complex it may be, that is the reaction of the opponent. The only way to draw the reaction of the opponent is for the action performed to have intent, a lack of intent will lead to the opponent not reacting to the action and so the action failing. These requirements, intent and reaction are the keys for the action using the False Art to succeed.

If there is no intent behind the action, then the opponent will not react to the action and the fencer will lose the Time and give the opponent a chance to react in some other manner, indeed even to strike the fencer. The reaction must be present to draw the opponent's attention to some other place than where the fencer intends to strike.

Techniques

With regard to the False Arts, there are several different methods which can be used; this is not an exhaustive list but shows a selection of actions which may be performed.

Breaking Time

Breaking Time is a technique in which the fencer pauses part-way through his action and then completes the action. Breaking Time is intended that the fencer will move against the action, but move past where the fencer's weapon is, allowing him to strike behind the opponent's weapon.

Change of Line

A simple change of Line using a Disengage is also possible, most likely a Time Disengage. The fencer makes an attack along a certain Line encouraging the opponent to react. As the attack proceeds, the fencer changes the Line and strikes somewhere else.

Patterns

Patterns can be also used against the opponent. The fencer makes repeated attacks against the same place, and then changes the attack striking somewhere the pattern has not been established.

Distraction

Simple distractions such as a movement of the hand or foot can also cause the opponent to be unaware of an attack which follows.

Blade Engagement

Many of the Blade Engagement sequences can also be used to place the opponent into a position where the fencer wants them. This works especially well where the opponent has been trained to merely respond to stimulus rather than think the engagement through. Each one of these techniques, and several others can be successful should they be performed correctly and illicit the correct responses from the opponent.

Defence Against

With the ability to correctly use the skills of the False Art, a fencer will also more ably defend against the same when they are performed against them. The keys to the success of a technique using the False Art also happen to be the key to not being struck by the same. The first thing that is necessary is to understand how the actions of the False Arts work. Thus, an education in the False Art, even if the fencer has no intentions of ever using them in an encounter, is useful to the fencer.

The fencer using a feint of some kind, regardless of its type, is attempting to draw a response from the fencer to move him out of place. The reaction is the key to the action. In defence against the action, the fencer should do all he can not to react to the feint and only against a true attack. The fencer will learn as he gains more proficiency with the sword what attacks will strike and which ones will not, and it is through this knowledge that the fencer will gain the ability to determine the True from the False. Some of this is found in training and other parts are found in simple experience in fencing with different opponents.

A fencer who has knowledge of a thing can learn to defend against that same thing. A fencer who has no knowledge of a thing will find much more difficulty in defending against it.

A Skill-Set

A skill-set is merely that, a skill-set. Any accruing of feeling with regard to the honourable state or lack thereof is a personal attribution by the person regarding it. The techniques themselves can be useful should they be used in the correct circumstances and in the correct manner; if they should be used otherwise then the fencer could easily find himself imperilled by the use of the action.

For the most part, the skills take ability to use correctly. Consequently, training is necessary, as in all skills. Due to this, worth can be found in the skills which are presented. The skills presented are skills, and any attributing should be directed to the fencer who uses them and the manner, in which he performs them, rather than for or against the skills.

Glossary

Notes

The glossary which follows, like the treatise which has preceded it, has been created and written from my own knowledge. Accordingly, all the definitions are given as according to the understanding as laid out in the treatise above. This glossary needs to be used in accompaniment with the treatise and not separate from it.

A

Absence of Blade

> A method using Soft Engagement against the opponent, if any Blade Engagement at all, and avoiding any sort of Hard Engagement with the opponent's weapon; this denies the opponent information gained through *Senso di Ferro*.

Action

> The attacks, defences and movements made while the two fencers are in contact at Closes and Grips.

Active

> A concept related to the concept of Priority; the combatant who is performing an action, the offensive role.

Advance

> The toe of the front foot is lifted the heel is then pushed forward just skimming the ground as such the front foot is moved forward about the length of the foot; the rear foot is then moved forward the length of the foot; also known as a Pace Forward.

Attack of Force

> An Attack on the Blade in which the opponent's weapon is removed by some forceful action of the fencer and includes the Beat, Pressure and Pressure Glide.

Attacks on the Blade

> Actions in which the fencer uses their weapon on the opponent's weapon to open a Line in the opponent to attack it, some of these are simple Attacks of Force where others are much more subtle.

B

Back Edge

> See False Edge.

Beat
: Also known as a Beat Attack; an Attack of Force and it uses impact power to move the opponent's blade out of Line, most useful against opponents who leave their point out far, especially if they are holding their weapon too loose or too tight; See also Attacks on the Blade.

Beat Parry
: Uses the impact of the weapon or hand in order to force the opponent's weapon Off-Line and therefore out of danger.

Bind
: An action performed upon the opponent's blade designed to gain control of it and to place it where it can be of more use to the fencer, resulting in a change of Line.

Blade Engagement
: Where the fencer's blade is placed in a position near that of the opponent's, where there is a tactical reason for doing so; doesn't require contact between the weapons as it is the position of the weapon which is more important than actual contact; See also Absence of Blade.

Body Void
: Moving the body, or part of the body, to avoid an attack of the opponent.

Botta
: See Thrust.

Breaking Distance
: To increase Distance away from fencer and the opponent.

Breaking Priority
: Relates to Priority and determines how a fencer swaps from the Reactive role to the Active role; also relates to Breaking Time.

Breaking Time
: Relates to Manipulating Time; an unexpected lengthening of the *Tempo* of the fencer to create an opportunity for an attack, usually achieved by pausing or slowing down during an action; a technique in which the fencer pauses part of the way through his action and then completes the action.

Broad Ward
: See Guard of Second.

Buckler
: Small round shield with a handle on the back.

C

Cadence
> Considers the flow of combat between two combatants and how this relates between the combatants; determined by the actual performance of the actions and the gaps between them.

Case of Rapiers
> A pair of rapiers, used together one in each hand, originally matched, originally designed to be placed in a case together hence the name of the form.

Cavatione
> See Disengage.

Cavatione di Tempo
> See Time Disengage.

Ceding Parry
> Primarily used as a defence against a Riposte, but can be used in other instances; once the opponent has made his Parry and begins to Riposte, the sword is drawn back toward the fencer while remaining engaged with the opponent's weapon into the most appropriate Parry.

Closed Line
> A Line which is defended in some sort of manner.

Close-Quarters Combat
> See Closes and Grips.

Closes and Grips
> Also known as Close-Quarters Combat, or Close Work; is the part of combat where the two combatants come within easy thrusting range of one another, and usually to a single *Tempo* or less of one another; the rough and tumble part of sword combat; where the utility of the concept of Priority is demonstrated.

Close Work
> See Closes and Grips.

Closing Distance
> To decrease Distance between the opponent and the fencer.

Combat Distance
> The Distance at which a bout or actual match is started, this will be much wider than Training Distance, and most likely Out of Distance.

Contra-Cavatione
> See Counter-Disengage.

Counter-Disengage
> Known as a *Contra-Cavatione* in Italian; action to counter the Disengage, is performed to change the engagement back to where it was when the *Stringere* was performed; to Disengage around the opponent's Disengage.

Counter Guard
> See Counter-Position.

Counter-Position
> Also known as Opposing Guard or Counter Guard, about positioning in a way that the fencer closes Lines of attack while opening them on the opponent.

Counter-Time
> Literally against Time, and against the flow of combat, thus against Priority, an action which is Out of Time; an attack made directly against the opponent's attack, some sort of other defensive measure is made other than using the weapon.

Cross-Blow
> See *Riversa*.

Cut
> An offensive action delivered primarily with the edge of the weapon with the intent to do damage through cleaving in some form; with a civilian sword some sort of slicing action is necessary to do damage.

Cut Over
> A Disengage in which the point of the weapon passes over the opponent's weapon rather than beneath it.

D

Dagger
> A short, Two-edged blade with a sharp point, some examples have had blade lengths up to 40cm (16") and longer, hilt with quillons and often more.

Debole
> Upper half of the blade from the mid-point to the Point and includes it; faster but weaker part of the blade; primarily used for offence; also known as the *Foible*.

Demi-Volte
> See *Half-Inquartata*.

Diagonal Step
> See Slopes.

Disengage

> Called *Cavatione* in Italian; an action to change the Line of engagement and also counter *Stringere* by closing the Line as a result; performed by shifting the point of the weapon under and around the opponent's weapon to move to the other side of the weapon, or by shifting the point over the opponent's weapon for the same result, the action over is known as a Cut Over.

Distance

> Also known as Measure; one of the primary principles of fencing and is closely related to the concept of Time, like Time it is fluid in nature and not concrete; primarily concerned with the distance between the two combatants, and also their weapons.

Double Disengage

> Known as a *Ricavatione* in Italian; counter to the Counter-Disengage, a second Disengage performed to counter the Counter-Disengage.

Double Time

> An action where the defence and counter-attack are two separate actions, hence, a Parry and a Riposte.

E

Engagement

> See Blade Engagement.

Entry

> The part of Closes and Grips where one combatant closes on the other, or the two combatants close on one another.

Envelopment

> A circular action the purpose of which is to regain control over the engagement and this is achieved through this change of Blade Engagement.

Exit

> The part of Closes and Grips where the fencers break off from one another or one fencer breaks off from the other fencer.

F

False Art

> Considered to be those actions which use deception and do not deliver a direct attack but use other means to achieve their final goal, therefore, any action which is performed in order to merely provoke action out of the opponent.

False Edge

> Sometimes known as the Back Edge, faces toward the fencer.

False Edge Parry

> Where the False Edge is used to Parry rather than the True Edge; there are at least four of these which correspond to the four True Edge Parries which have been presented, but these have not been presented here.

False Time

> Any action which will lead the fencer into a potentially dangerous situation. An action which breaks the Time of the Hand and Foot.

Falso Dritto

> A diagonal Cut delivered upward on the *Mandritta*.

Falso Manco

> A diagonal Cut delivered upward on the *Riversa*.

Feeling Through the Blade

> See *Senso di Ferro*.

Fendente

> A vertical Cut delivered downward.

First (hand) Position

> With the knuckles upward and palm outward.

Flowing Attack

> Uses very little contact between the weapons, all about the placement of the weapon rather than forcing the opponent's weapon out of the way, controls the *Line* by the mere presence of the weapon against the opponent's sword.

Foible

> See *Debole*.

Footwork Void

> Footwork action used to move the fencer out of the path of an attack of the opponent.

Forte

> Lower half of the blade from the hilt to the mid-point; slower but stronger part of the blade; primarily used for defence.

Fourth (hand) Position

> With the knuckles inward and the palm upward

Front Edge

> See True Edge.

G

Gather

> A gather moves the rear foot forward up to the position of the front foot; this moves the body slightly forward this is often used as a preparation step.

Gauntlet

> A leather glove with a mail covering to protect the hand from cuts, examples also show a second layer of leather over the mail, also plate examples with mail palms.

Good Guard

> A good guard will: close a Line, have easy offensive potential, allow the fencer to be balanced, and the fencer to be comfortable.

Guard

> Strictly a position in which the fencer closes a Line, however it is often used as an alternate to the word Ward.

Guard of First

> A position in which the arm is held above the shoulder with the weapon pointed at the opponent, with the False Edge downward. This position is the first place where the weapon is pointed at the opponent after drawing the weapon from a scabbard; also known as *Prima*, or High Ward as described by Giacomo di Grassi.

Guard of Fourth

> Fourth is a position with the hand across the body toward the inside, the point toward the opponent, with the palm upward; also known as *Quarta*.

Guard of Second

> The position in which the arm is held outstretched from the shoulder, either toward the front or to the side. In any case the weapon remains pointed at the opponent and remains at shoulder-height; also known as *Seconda*; the ward with the arm out to the side is also known as Broad Ward and is described by Giacomo di Grassi.

Guard of Third

> The position in which the arm is down by the fencer's side, the weapon pointed toward the opponent; also known as *Terza*, or Low Ward as described by Giacomo di Grassi.

H

Half-

> In footwork, used to describe the movement of a single foot; both Paces and Passes require the movement of both feet, as such there can be Half-Steps, Half-Paces and Half-Passes.

Half-Disengage

> A Disengage which changes the engagement from a High Line engagement to a Low Line engagement or vice versa.

Half-Inquartata

> Also known as a *Demi-Volte*; a footwork and body movement in which the rear foot is moved behind the front foot, which is designed to displace the body from an attack against the fencer, primarily used for defending the High Inside Line.

Half-Time

> An attack against the opponent's action and is designed to interrupt and arrest the opponent's attack before it is completed; an action which is half In Time and half Out of Time; actions include Stop Hit, Stop Cut, Stop Thrust.

Hard Engagement

> When the blades of the weapons are in physical contact.

High Line

> Those parts of the fencer which are above a horizontal line drawn through the position of the hilt; includes the High Inside Line and the High Outside Line.

I

Imbroccata

> A Thrust delivered from above meaning that the hand of the fencer has to drop to deliver the attack.

Impact Cut

> Delivered in a similar manner to a cleaving or chopping Cut, but also different as the impact is not the final result; impacting portion of this Cut is merely to allow the blade to bite into the target in order to allow the slicing action to cause more damage; the impact and slicing action are not separate; they need to be performed as one smooth action.

In Distance

> Means that the fencer is within striking distance of the opponent or vice versa, this may not be an immediate attack, but it is in range to be threatening.

Inquartata

> Also known as a *Volte*; a footwork and body movement with a larger movement than the *Half-Inquartata* as the back foot moves further across in order to increase the angle in which the back foot can go far enough that it is almost parallel with the front foot, that is designed to displace the body from an attack against the fencer, primarily used for defending the High Inside Line, in this particular case it can go some way to also protecting the Low Inside Line as well.

Inside Line

> The side of the vertical line drawn through the hilt which is closest to the body, for the right-handed fencer the Inside Line is on the left; includes the High Inside Line and the Low Inside Line.

In Tempo

> See *In Time*.

In Time

> An action performed with the correct Timing resulting in the opponent being struck and the fencer not being such, it is also a situation manipulated to result in such; one which is performed at the most suitable instance for that action; related to the concept of Priority, and affected by Distance; also known as an action *In Tempo*.

J

Just Distance

> Does not actually have a measurement in Time or Distance as it is dependent on the situation in which the combatant finds himself, it is the distance at which the fencer is able to strike the opponent while not being struck.

K

Key Steps

> Form the foundation of all footwork; consist of the Advance and the Pass Forward.

L

"Layers of Defence"

> The concept of using more than one defensive action; principle is based on the idea of redundancy and the fact that any one action is improved by the use of second or further actions.

Lines

> The theory concerned with the division of the combatant and then how these divisions are then defended; there are four quadrants or lines which the fencer is divided into: High Inside, High Outside, Low Inside and Low Outside, the size of these all relate to the position of the hilt of the fencer's weapon.

Low Line

> Those parts of the fencer which are below a horizontal line drawn through the position of the hilt; includes the Low Inside Line and the Low Outside Line.

Low Ward
> See Guard of Third.

Lunge
> (footwork part) a large Half-Pace moving the front foot forward a distance usually to extend the distance of an attack; execution of this Step is important, the power and speed of the lunging step is derived from the explosive use of the rear leg pushing the body forward; the front foot is merely lifted slightly to release the pressure which has built up and to stop the Lunge at its other end; (the attack) simply a Thrust with footwork, it is designed to extend the range of the Thrust by adding a Half-Pace to it.

M

Mandritta
> A term which applies to Cut and Thrust equally refers to an attack which originates from the right side of a right-handed fencer, so, the sword-side.

Manipulation of Distance
> Achieved primarily through the use of footwork actions, though body and arm actions can have an effect, the fencer should be aware of these in the opponent.

Manipulating Time
> See also Breaking Time; use of techniques to lengthen or shorten Cadence or *Tempo* to suit the fencer.

Measure
> See Distance.

Mezzo
> Italian word for "middle" or "half"; middle part of the blade which is half *Forte* and half *Debole*, has some of the characteristics of both; see also *Tondo* if referring to a horizontal Cut.

Mezzo-Cavatione
> See Half-Disengage.

Misura
> Italian word for *Measure*.

Montante
> A vertical Cut delivered upward.

Movement Creates Advantage
> Relates to the "Advantage of the Circle Over the Line"; movement Off-Line creates advantage due to the change in Distance and also Time, this advantage can be used in both in defence and offence.

N

Narrow Distance

> Combatants are a single *Tempo* away from one another; a simple thrust or Time of the Hand can reach the other combatant.

O

Off-Hand Parry

> A Parry made with the off-hand not carrying a defensive device; has the same options of Beat and With Opposition as a sword does; can cover the four quadrants made by the two Lines as the sword does; has the option of grasping the blade should the fencer choose to; best made with the palm of the hand.

Off-Line

> According to "Advantage of the Circle Over the Line", when a combatant makes a movement off the direct facing of the opponent, and thus, the line between the two combatants when facing one another.

On-Line

> According to "Advantage of the Circle Over the Line", when in direct facing of the opponent the line that exists between to combatants facing one another.

Open Line

> A Line which is vulnerable to an attack by the opponent.

Opposing Guard

> See Counter-Position.

Out of Distance

> Means that neither of the combatants is within range to make any sort of meaningful threat.

Out of Time

> Where an action is performed where there is not suitable *Tempo* to perform the action, usually resulting in the fencer being struck; where an action is performed which is not suitable to the situation; there are actions which will be performed deliberately performed Out of Time to gain an advantage, such as *Counter-Time*; related to the concept of Priority and affected by Distance.

Outside Line

> The side of the vertical line drawn through the hilt which is furthest from the body, for the right-handed fencer the Outside Line is on the right; includes the High Outside Line and the Low Outside Line.

P

Pace
> Footwork where the fencer's feet do not cross over one another.

Pace Backward
> See Retreat.

Pace Forward
> See Advance.

Pace Left
> See Traverse Left.

Pace Right
> See Traverse Right.

"Panic Space"
> The closest a fencer will allow an opponent's attack to come before reacting to the attack.

Parry
> A primarily defensive action in which the fencer places an object in between themselves and that of the opponent to defend against an attack; this may be made with weapon or off-hand; and may be made as a Beat or With Opposition.

Parry of First
> Made with the True Edge; covers the Low Inside Line.

Parry of Second
> Made with the True Edge; covers the Low Outside Line.

Parry of Third
> Made with the True Edge; covers the High Outside Line.

Parry of Fourth
> Made with the True Edge; covers the High Inside Line.

Parry with Opposition
> Guides the opponent's weapon away after gaining contact and maintains it.

Pass
> Footwork where the fencer's feet do cross over one another, like motion of walking normally.

Pass Backward
> The front foot is drawn back past the rear foot until the toe lines up with the heel or a little past it, the rear foot then simply regains its position in the guard.

Pass Forward
: The rear foot moves forward passing the front foot to land equal with the big toe of the front foot or a small distance ahead of it, the front foot then passes the rear foot in order to regain its original position ahead of the rear foot.

Percussion Points
: Two spots on the blade where the blade will do the most damage in a Cut if it is started there one on the *Debole* and one on the *Forte*; on the *Debole*, located approximately a hand-span from the point; on the *Forte*, located approximately a hand-span from the hilt.

Press
: Uses an increase in pressure against the opponent's blade to open a *Line* through which the fencer can attack; see also Pressure Glide.

Pressure Glide
: Takes the concept of the Press a little further as it uses the increase in pressure not only to displace the opponent's weapon, but also to place the fencer's weapon into *Line* and even start the delivery of the attack; the point of the weapon will move closer to the opponent as the pressure against the weapon increases, so that all the fencer has to do is to continue extending his arm to deliver the attack.

Prima
: See Guard of First.

Priority
: A concept related to Time and actions which follow this concept are typically performed In Time; related to Cadence and determines what a fencer should be doing at a particular time; designed to have the fencer think about what he needs to do at that particular time and how he can go about gaining the advantage in the current situation; if a fencer is not in possession of Priority he should be defending and is in the defensive role, if he is, he should be attacking or making some action in that direction, thus in the offensive role; also relates to Breaking Priority.

Punta
: See Thrust.

Q

Quarta
: See Guard of Fourth.

R

Reactive

> Related to the concept of Priority; the fencer who is responding to an action, the defensive role.

Recovery

> To return to a Ward after an attack is made, often the most vital part of the process.

Retreat

> Also known as the Pace Backward; the exact reverse of the Advance and allows the fencer to move directly backward; the back foot is moved backward the length of the foot, and the front foot follows.

Ricavatione

> See Double Disengage.

Riposte

> A counter-attack made from a Parry.

Riversa

> A term which applies to Cut and Thrust equally refers to an attack which originates from the left side of a right-handed fencer, the offhand-side, sometimes called a Cross-Blow.

S

Second (hand) Position

> Palm downward and the knuckles to the outside.

Seconda

> See Guard of Second.

Senso di Ferro

> Also known as Feeling Through the Blade; Italian, meaning "sense through steel"; also known as *Sentiment du Fer* in French; being able to feel through the weapon as to what the opponent will do.

Sentiment du Fer

> See *Senso di Ferro*.

Single Time

> An action where the defence and counter-attack are blended into a single action, but the defensive action is clearly made as a Parry, or at least the beginning action of one.

Slicing Cut

> The weapon is placed against the target, pressure is applied and the weapon is pushed or drawn along the target; it is important that the pressure of the blade against the target is maintained while the action is performed; also a good practice technique for the Impact Cut.

Slip

> Moves the front foot backward to the rear foot; this moves the body slightly backward and is often used as a simple limited defence or a preparation.

Slopes

> Also known as Diagonal Steps; change the way that the fencer is facing the opponent, also advance upon the opponent but to the side of the opponent; two work the same way as Paces and two work the same way as Passes, depending on the facing of the fencer.

Soft Engagement

> Where the weapon is placed in a position to gain advantage without actually touching the opponent's weapon.

Squalembrato

> A diagonal Cut delivered downward.

Step

> Any single motion of using the feet in footwork this includes all Paces and Passes; requires the movement of both feet.

Stoccata

> A Thrust in which comes from below meaning that the fencer has to raise his hand to deliver the attack.

Stop Cut

> A Cut made in Half-Time, usually made against the opponent's attacking arm, but may also be made against the body or head to arrest the attack.

Stop Hit

> See Stop Thrust

Stop Thrust

> Also known as a Stop Hit; a thrust made in Half-Time, usually made against the opponent's attacking arm, but may also be made against the opponent's head or body to arrest the attack.

Stramazone

> Also known as a Tip Cut; uses the very tip of the weapon to Cut; it is still using the edge of the weapon in order to do damage against the opponent, it is merely that it is the very tip of the weapon that is being used in this instance; the Cut usually results in a small Cut, so is usually aimed at vital targets.

Stringere

> The application of a small amount of force against the opponent's weapon to force it out of Line while the fencer's weapon is moved in Line, this is the Hard Engagement option; also applied where the blade is merely placed into a position where it dominates a position where it can attack, and does not necessarily have to move the opponent's blade; to achieve this, the fencer needs to angle their blade properly in the correct angle, possibly along with their body position to achieve the same result, this is the Soft Engagement option.

String of Engagements

> From the performance of *Stringere* to the performance of the Double Disengage is what could be called a string of Engagements; each action which follows is designed to counter the previous action.

Strong

> Pressure exerted upon the opponent's fashion in a strong manner.

T

Taking the Blade

> Describes a group of actions which are designed to gain or regain control of the Engagement, usually through a change of Engagement and Line.

Tempo

> Used to describe an action or inaction; not a concrete measure but fluid and dependent on the movement of the fencer performing the action or inaction, and may be manipulated to be shortened or lengthened.

Terza

> See Guard of Third.

Third (hand) Position

> The knuckles toward the ground and palm inward.

Thrust

> Delivered with the point of the weapon against an opponent with the intent on causing damage through the penetration of the point; the primary action in this form of fencing, due to the nature of the weapon being used; also referred to as a *punta* or *botta* in naming an attack.

Time

> One of the founding principles upon which all fencing is based, governs how much time it takes to perform an action and is interrelated with the concept of Distance. Usually divided up into portions of Time, or actions, or *Tempo*. Time is related to the action and inaction of the fencer; often called *Tempo*.

Time Disengage

> A Disengage is performed around the position where the opponent's blade will be rather than where it is; this action is most used against an action in motion; action utilises much of the theory of Absence of Blade in that the weapon does not come in contact with the opponent's weapon before the action is performed, but only may once it is completed; action itself is the same as a normal Disengage, the point is moved under the opponent's weapon to change the engagement; the difference is that the weapon is always in motion and does not come into contact with the opponent's weapon before or during the action.

Time of the Hand and Foot

> A principle which explains how the fencer should move; The body is divided into Hand and Foot, the hand moves before the foot in most instances. This means the weapon before the person.

Timing

> The practical application of the knowledge of Time.

Tip Cut

> See *Stramazone*.

Tondo

> A horizontal Cut delivered parallel to the ground; may be divided further into upper, middle and lower targets, thus *Alta*, *Mezzo*, and *Basso* respectively.

Training Distance

> The Distance at which drills are conducted so that the skills performed are effective so that the student can learn, often much closer than Combat Distance.

Traverse

> A pace which allows the fencer to move directly right or left of his current position; regardless of the Ward taken or the foot position, it is always the foot in the direction which is required that is moved first.

Traverse Left

> Also known as a Pace Left; the left foot is moved sideways about the length of the foot, the right foot is then also moved left the length of the foot.

Traverse Right

> Also known as a Pace Right; the right foot is moved sideways about the length of the foot, the left foot is then also moved right the length of the foot.

True Art

> Considered to be contained in those actions which are a direct attack upon the opponent with no deviation in their delivery. An offensive action which has the intention of striking the opponent directly.

True Edge
> Sometimes called the Front Edge as it faces toward the opponent.

True Edge Parry
> Where the True Edge of the sword is used to Parry; all of the parries presented in this treatise are True Edge Parries.

U, V

Very Narrow Distance
> Closer than Narrow Distance; at this Distance when the bodies of the combatants are close it is usually awkward to move the tip of a sword into strike as such it is most useful to use the edge. However this Distance can also be measured where only part of the combatants has come within this distance, usually the hand, arm or weapon; this is usually measured when a strike is made against an attacking the hand or arm in Half-Time.

Void
> A defence by displacement; based on the simple principle of moving the target of the opponent's attack away from the attack, or in other terms, not being where the opponent's attack is; three types: feet, body, and feet and body together.

Volte
> See *Inquartata*.

W, X, Y, Z

Ward
> Position from which to launch an attack or defence from, for the most part Wards are not defensive positions, sometimes called a Guard, but not the same thing.

Wasting Time
> Occurs when an action is performed lazily or sloppily. So, the action is performed without Timing.

Weak
> Pressure felt through the blade which has a yielding pressure.

Wide Distance
> The combatants will be more than a single *Tempo* away from one another, and in some instances may be two *Tempi* away from one another; the combatants are a Lunge or slightly more away from one another; to cross this Distance will require at least a Time of the Hand and a Time of the Foot, though these may be combined in a Lunge.

Window Parry

Called such because the make a "window" to look through with your arm or sword if they are performed properly, primarily designed to protect the High Line.

HENRY FOX

his Practise.

In Two Bookes

The first intreating of the Arte and Science of the vse of the Single Rapier, with such sundrie notes as applie to that Arte.

The second, of Honor and Honorable Quarrelles

St Florian de la Riuiere
Sword and Book Enterprises

A.S. LVII

TO HIS GRACE

the ſingular good Lord, *Gabriel* de Beaumont, *Duke* of Lochac, Firſt *Baron* St Florian de la Riuiere, *Knight* of the Moſt Honorable Order of the Chiualrye, *Maſter* of the Moſt Honorable Order of the Pelican, Companion of the Moſt Honorable Orders of Leaf of Merit, Lochac Order of Grace, Miles Regni, Lily, Rowan, and Siluer Tear, &c

IN as much as I haue endeuoured to produce this treatiſe of a moſt honorable ſubiect, it is proper to dedicate ſuch a worke to a moſte honorable Lord who has demonſtrated ſuch skill at armes to the which could be compared to the great Pericles in meaſure of honor, valoure and atchieuement, and in the execution of ſuche atchieuementes and manie others has demonſtrated ſuche a noble minde which commaunds ſuch skil and reſpecte iuſt as the noble Cicero of the aunciente Romanes: It

is my

The Epistle Dedicatorie

is my greate honor to presente the worke before you for your perusall and edyfication on subiects beinge the of the vse of the Rapier alone and a second part on honor and honorable quarels and to dedicate suche to you: In so sayinge that suche a subiecte would be most appropriat for your reading and vse in that you haue chosen to grace the field wyth such an honourable weapon and that such other noble lords may also be informed as to the appropriat forme and methods of the vse of such a weapon but also the appropriat caryage and presentation in honourable companie: While this worke is fourmed from the efforte whych has been placed within it and is formed of my owne works and knowledg, it is hoped that you will accepte suche an vnworthie gift of wordes bearing your name and by vertue of it bearinge suche a noble name ennoble the work itselfe by its presence and thus hopefullye fill the debte of the presence of your name bye that which is founde in the pages of the text found herein.

In the production of works created and formd for the instruction and education of Gentlemen, yt is thoughte that no knowledge is better than that of Armes and those subiectes to which they are associated beeing that of skil at Armes is the true profession of the Courtier: Howeuer, suche is noted that it is better to seek honoure through peacefull means, this work is presented in order to preserue lyfe where it is threatened by assaulte and placed at risk due to those quarrelles which do arise between Gentlemen: Such the purpose of this treatise is not to encourage menne into foule or cruel murthers but vse suche skils and knowledge herein expressed to defend their liues and honor and seek renowne for the execution of the skills shoulde they find themselues in a situation where the resort to Arms is the only choice for a resolution to the situation.

I do

The Epiftle Dedicatorie

I do humblie afk you to accept this work as a gift to you in reflection of your skill and honourable nature and in feruice to the protection of your life and honoure and hope that fuche a gift will bringe ioy to reade and that the fubftance within is of vfe to the protection and long life: Such it is prefented in honorable feruice with fuch humble and honorable affection toward yourfelfe and to your moft illuftrious Lady in the hope that all your wifhes in this life are gayned and that the intent of the fkills and knowledge found within the pages herein do ferue you as well as the knowledge and skills upon which they are bafed upon haue ferued me.

Yours in moft Dutifull Seruice to Your Honour,

Henry Fox.

The Authors Epiſtle vnto diuers Noble-men and Gentle-men.

Anye treatiſes haue been penned extollinge the vertues of various different theories and the combatiue arts aſſociated with them: For the moſt part theſe reſulte in treatiſes with diſparate theories and ideas about how the ſworde ſhould be vſed and often reſulte in confuſion as to howe the weapon ſhoulde be vſed in different ſcenarios due to the different approaches taken by the different proponents of theſe theories. This worke is beeing written in order to collect and organize the collected knowledge of one ſwords-man in a ſingle place: The method and theories preſented are one which is of my own; which means it is newe, but is bayſed vppon the collected knowledge of thoſe theories aſſimilated frome othere theorists and learnt while vſing the weapon againſt various opponents ouere my extended period of time combatting againſt ſuch opponentes: This manuall is not merelye repeatinge the theories and principalles of other maiſters theories as ſome will wante to do but is a collection of various elements frome various maſters collected in a ſingle method. Thus while the methode is new, it will alſo be familiar to thoſe proponents of the Arts of Defence and their various ſtudentes.

From the various workes written by various maiſters and theorists it wyll be noted that ſome will write their practiſes purelye from theorie, hauinge no experience in the practice of the Arte. Some, on the other hand, write purely from the point of view of, and indeed learn, their Art only from the vſe of the ſwoord, denying the vſe of anie perticuler theory and thus gaining theyr knowledge through experience with the weapone onelye: Both of theſe practiſes are flawed and need to be addreſſed; thoſe which learne onlie from theorye haue no practical experience and thus no knowledge of how the weapon actually mooues in an encounter with another baſing their practiſe on mathematicall and phyſical theory but wyth no vnderſtanding of the preſſures of battaile and how they relate to its practiſe; those who learn only from practiſe alſo haue their method flawed as they do not vnderſttande why their method workes or does not from the pointe of view of theorye and thus can not explain why or how the methode worketh adequatelie for another to learne it ſaue by practicall demonſtration: That whych is miſſed in the pure theorye is found in the practicall and that which the practicall is miſſing is found in the theorie, thus bothe approaches neede to be combined in ordere to gain a compleat vnderſtanding of a practiſe of defence. It is due to the flaws in bothe of theſe methods that this worke will be preſented and wyll demonſtrate to haue thoſe practical elementes of the ſwoorde baſed vppon a theoreticall baſis but applied to the actuall practical vſe of the weapon: Thus the method preſented will prouide both a theoreticall and practical baſis for the practiſe which is preſented in this manual.

For the preſentation of the method deſcribed in this manuall and ſuche is the nature of the ſkiles preſented that theye are diſplayed in ſuche a faſhion that the foundations of the Arte

are

The Authors Epistle

are first presented in the theoretical elements which are then supported by the practical elements, with sundrie notes to follow which applye to their application in a practical fence. It is important that the foundations are first layd and the theorye presented in order that the mind is in suitable condition to be able to accept the practicall elements thus resulting in a vnification of minde and bodye to the purpose of the arte presented here. The theoreticall elements presented describe those elements which can onlye be seene in a practical sense with the knowledge of them in a theoretical sense due to speede of the techniques and the nature of the skilles presented. VVythoute the suitable explanaytion prouided by the theoreticall elementes the practicall can not be vnderstoode properly and thus vtilised in suitable fashion in a practical forme. The practical and theoreticall elementes neede to be presented and linked as suche in order for the reader to gayne the greatest benefyte frome bothe and thus be hable to appreciate and atchyeue the moste frome the practise presented.

One of the Vertues of the swoorde is that it reflectes the Nature of the indiuiduall who wields it and as suche thys manuall is designed to promote onlye those moste noble qualities and encourage the reader to engage onelye in those practices which wyll promote his Honor and Renowne through the vse of the sword. The inner nature of the indiuidual is reflected in his physical actions and those things which are quantifiable by presented actions. The nature of the sword is that in its speede it does not allow sufficient time for an indiuidual to carefully couer those negatiue aspects of his nature sufficiently to be hidden. Thus a methode which is based on base-borne attributes of pure aggression and brute force wyll be exposed as suche againste a practise which promotes the more nobler qualities of the spirite and the intellectuall facilities of the indiuidual.

VVhile this manual doth teach an Arte with a weapon which in itselfe is violence, it is not designed so that it wyll promote suche arrogance and confidence in men that they, expanded by their confidence, will goe out and seeke quarrelles with others in ordere to presente theyr skills vppon the fielde, but doth promote the defence of Honoure and lyfe wythin the pages and skills presented, should a Gentleman find himselfe in such a situation where such skills are required: It is true that some will teach others that due to their skills they haue the right to be so confident that they shoulde not suffer anye insulte whatsoeuer and shuld goe and seeke those situations where they can present theyr skiles: This manuall insteede woulde promote that the Gentle-man should not go out an seeke quarels in order to demonstrate his skill and Honoure, but kepe them so that theye maye be vsed where such a situation is founde that he has no other option but to seeke resolution by bloud. The nature of lyfe is that Gentle-men togither or passing one another may fall into a quarrell and it is vp to the participants to ensure that such a quarell is handled in such a manner as to promote and increase Honoure amongste theme rather than degrade it: Should such be the case; the instruction found herein is designed to promote such Honoure amongste those inuolued as woulde be expected by theyr rank and station as Gentlemen and ensure that the quarrell remains Honorable and also the result of such a quarel.

No

The Authors Epistle

No man shoulde deliberately go out and seeke others to doe violence vppon for their owne benefite: The skills presented in this manual and thus the violence which results from their vse shoulde be reserued for those cases where it is required and Honor is so touched that yt can not be redeemed except by violence and the shedding of bloud: There are those belieuing that the onlye waye to Honoure and Renowne is through violence will make a quarrell out of the simplest insult and require bloud as restitution from such an insulte with no regarde for any compromise in the situation: Such men are heade-strong and will only bring themselues to griefe and earne themselues Notoriety and the Reputation of a duelist or street-brauler: The Gentleman shoulde aspire to heights which are well aboue thys and be onlye seene to be resortinge to violence where Honour would require it and be amenable to such other resolution should it be suitable in the situation: Only in those times where their Honor is so touched that only bloud can expiate the iniurie done and where the result of such an encounter will result in Honoure and Renown shuld the gentleman seeke violence vppon his opponent in the quarrell.

The skills and knowledge presented herein are designed for the preseruation of Lyfe and Honoure and to increase the Renown of the Gentleman, not so that he maye go out and earne himselfe the Reputation of a duellist or streete-brawler: Violence which is done without Honour earns the gentleman nothinge but a base reputation frome which it is difficulte to recouere: The knowledge of how to vse weapons shoulde onlye be vsed in those times where a Gentleman will earne himselfe a reputation for Honoure and gayn Renowne for his exploytes with the sworde: Suche achieuements liue on past the time of the actual encounter and enrich a mans Reputation and standing and this is to his benefyte. To learne the Art of the Sword merely to be able to go and do violence vppon others is base and shoulde be below any person who is of noble nature: It is true that the Art is the Art of Defence and thus should alwayes be considered as suche and thus vsed for defensiue purposes and not for the ability to merely go out and do violence vppon others.

Your most humble Seruante,

Henry Fox.

Authors Epistle to the Gentle Reader

For men to attaine true greatneſſe there is but one path and that is through the Artes and Sciences, and in this there are two primarye pathes whych a man can follow, Armes and Letters: In this it can be ſeene that theyr greatneſſe is ſpread either by the worke of their muſcles in Armes or the ſweat of their mindes in Letters: It ſhulde be noted that Armes has been put before Letters ſimply by the fact that a noble Lord gaineth and maintaineth his ſtate through the vſe of force and thus through the vſe of Armes: Howeuer, ſuche nobles will alſo be noted to be ſtudied in Letters in ordere that they can maintayne theyr poſition in ſuche an intelligent waye in order that no flaw can be noted in their defences and thus allow challenge frome another through the force of Armes: Thus it ſhoulde be noted that while the force of Armes may be preferred and be ſeen to be the primary by ſome the vſe of knowledge and thus Letters ſhold not be ſecondary to the pointe of neglecte: Suche ſhoulde alſo be noted that there are thoſe Arts and Sciences which do not fall directlye vnder eyther Armes or Letters and theſe ſhoulde not, due to this fact, go neglected: Indeed for a Gentleman to be complete, and a true Gentleman of note, ſuch an indiuidual ſhould cultiuate his knowledge in all of the Arts and Sciences in order to increaſe his knowledge and ſtandinge, thus it ſhould be noted that all of the Arts and Sciences carrye ſuch nobilitie that they ſhould all be of note to all.

The ſearch for knowledge ſtartes euen at an earlye age which continues in the ſearche for knowledge euen in old age, ſeeking all that which can be known by a man: This ſearch for knowledge is what driueth a man, be it for his owne perſonall benefyte or for the benefyt of the wider communitie, ſuche a ſearch is noble regardleſſe of the knowledge which is ſought: So it is that all greate men do ſeek the truth in all thinges that can be founde in the Arts and Sciences and true alſo in the artes of weapons alſo. Some ſeek ſuch knowledge of wepons through the writings of others and theories preſented baſed vpon the phiſical Sciences while others do ſeeke ſuche knowledge onlye through the vſe of Armes in a phiſical approche in order to gaine knowledge: True it is that both will finde truths in their methods and gayne ſome vnderſtanding of the operation of weapons againſt another but the greater method which gains the moſt benefyt is a combination of both, thus ſeeking the truth of the artes of weapons through both Armes and Letters: This ſearch is deſigned to bringe the ſelfe out of the darkneſſe of ignoraunce to knowledge through the purſuite of the ſkills and knowledge of the Arts and Sciences found in ſuch vſe of wepons and ſuch knowledg of the vniuerſe therefore which is aſſociated with ſuch purſuits in order to enrich the lyfe of the man who ſeeks ſuch: Thus the ſearch itſelf for the truths of weapons is in itſelf noble and to be praiſed in any who would vndertake it.

There are manie different pathes to take to finde the truth, but in the ende a man will finde that all paths will lead to the ſame truth in weapons in that the Arte is one which encompaſſeth manie different thinges: Thus the ſearch which has reſulted in the production of this treatyſe has reſulted in one methode whych has beene deueloped from ſeueral different paths and viewes of the Artes of the Swoorde. finding in the ende that whyle ſome theoryes and aſpects of the Arte are different in the ende that the ſumme of theyr commonalities is far greater than their differences and that ſuch an approche can be applyed to other Arts and Sciences for a ſimilar reſult and thus knowledge of a greater expanſe of knowledge than was firſt realiſed. The practiſe preſented in theſe pages was baſed on a foundation which can be diſcouered in many other practiſes of the ſword and then taking ſuch a foundation and bringing ſuch to greatneſſe and perfection of the Arte through practiſe and dilligence in the practiſe of the ſkiles of the Arte: The ſkills expreſſed and deſcribed in this worke are founded vppon that which has beene diſcouered ouer an extended periode of time of practiſing with the weapon primarie to the practiſe and engaging with ſuch opponents who would and in the reſearch of various methods and theories of the vſe of the ſword, reſulting in the diſcouerie of the method preſented through thoſe pathes which lead to the truth of the ſword deſcribed herein and diſcarding only that which is not

founded

To the Reader

founded in true defence.

The Arte and Science which is expressed in these pages is designed for the defence of Lyfe and the Realm, and thus is based vpon the moste Noble ideals of Honor and Dutye: Suche are the skills that while there is violence expressed in theyr method they shoulde only be vsed for the most noblest purposes of the defense of Honoure, the selfe and the Realme and not for the simple abuse of others. The reader shoulde keep in mind that it is the actions of the indiuidual which expresse the nature of the indiuidual and not the methode in which they are vsed, thus a noble methode suche as that which is expressed herein maye be vsed either in noble fashion or not so and that it is vp to the indiuidual to ensure that such skills are only to be vsed in a time of strife and discord where no peaceful remedie is possible: The knowledge presented here is not for the creation of suche ouerconfident indiuidualls that they woulde vse the skiles in braulls and affrayes for the creation of theme as braggarts and brawlers and thus earne themselues the Reputation of street-braulers and duellists: These skils are design so that a Gentleman maye haue the knowledge to be able to maintain his Honor and gaine Renowne in an encounter with another should the situation require it, and thus is the nature of all the true Artes of Defence: This Arte is the Arte of Defence and should be approached as such: It is not designed to giue the knowledge to suche that woulde vse the skiles presented in ordere to committ cruell murthers agaynst their neighbours: The skills presented herein should be vsed in defence of the selfe or ones companions should the occasion require.

The practise of Armes has prouen in manye cases to be of greate benefyte to the person who woulde engage in it: Being that it is a true exercise of bothe the minde and the bodie it giues the benefite to bothe in which other exercises maye focus on either the Art of the Swoorde giues benefit and exercise to bothe: From the more phisical side the practise of Armes in a diligent fashion not onlye prouideth the Gentleman with the skills and means to defend himselfe but also vses his muscles enhancing him phisically in his pursuit: From the mentall syde of the persone, the vse of the knowledge of the Arte increaseth the thinkynge abilitye of the practitioner in that he gaines the abilitie to problem-solue situations: The pure exercise of the mind to diuine the best defence againste the assaulte of an opponente increaseth the mentall faculties of the practitioner thus benefyting him in other situations. The Art of the Sword is the definition of Art and Science in combination into a single pursuit being that it is of both minde and bodie: The minde interpretes and gaynes knowledge of the Science while the bodie practises the Arte as defined by the Science in a practical fashion: In this it shuld be noted that the lack of eyther the minde or the bodie in this will result in the lack of either Art or Science in the practise and thus it must be a combination of both bodie and minde to ensure that the skiles are vsed in their correct fashion.

Without doubt the practise of the Art of the Sworde prouydeth greate benefyte to the bodye of the practitioner and indeede it increases the longeuitie of the indiuidual who woulde choose to practise it: This is not onlye due to the obuious benefite of the indiuiduall being able to defend himself in an armed encounter but the phisical exercise of the Arte alonge wiyh diligente practise in it prouidinge suche mouement of the bodye and exercise of the limmes that can onlye assiste the practitioner phisically. Some of the benefyts of the mind haue already been expressed in that it increases the mentall faculties of the practitioner and increases his abilitie to solue problems, but the practise of the Art and Science of the sword is also goode for the temperament of the indiuiduall in that the practise and learninge as well as the exercise of Armes teaches patience and controll ouer the emotions in order to haue a greater aduantage ouer the opponente: This abilitie to control that which is internall can then result, with the correct application, the abilitie to gaine aduantage ouer the opponent and such abilities can be vsed in other situations for the same aduantage.

While the work presented is primarily addressed to the Gentleman it has been prouen that such phisical skills are also vseful to Ladies in that they prouide similar benefytes, euen shoulde they not be required on the same leuel and for the same reasons: A true Lady will no doubt haue the benefyte of a true Gentleman to defend her Honour shulde it be required and thus the purelye phisical skills founde in the Art of the sword may not be of immediate benefite to her: Howeuer, in such situations where a Lady is found without a Gentle-man to defende her, suche skills canne be of great benefyt to her: Euen should such a situation not

euentuate

To the Reader

euentuate the Lady can gaine all of the phifical and mentall benefites which haue been defcribed herein and thus the purfuit and practife of armes is fuitable to thofe ladies who would choofe to engage in it as much as it is fuitable to men who would want to do the fame.

      Of all the things that can be faid about the arts of defence it fhould be noted that it is the indiuiduals application of the skiles which gaineth or reduceth the benefyte of the fkills vfed: It is alfo the indiuiduals application which refulteth in whether or not thofe skills are practifed for noble or ignoble reafones and refults: Shoulde the indiuidual choofe the fkills can be vfed for the greateft Renowne and Honoure or the greateft Notoriety and Difhonor found: The skills found in this work are defigned to be vfed in the moft nobleft of fituations and for the moft nobleft of reafons found, in the defence of Lyfe and Honor the two moft prized poffeffions.

Fare-well.

The First Booke

An Aduertisement of the Principels of the Arte Expressed Herein

He principels vpon which something is based are the foundations vppon which they are layd, and the other parts of the methode are those which are laide vppon those principalles: It is therefore important that such principels are presented first in order that the reader may vnderstand vpon what foundations the rest of the Arte being discussed is founded: An explanation of such principels is also essential in order for the reader to vnderstand what is meant by the principels as presented by the author.

The principalles are those elements which will vnderlie all of the following theoreticall and practicall elements of this treatise: It is vpon these principels vppon which the practicall and theoreticall elements presented herein are based and the knowledge of such principles is most essential in order to vnderstand the perspectiue from which the presented information which is present. There are fiue principles which are the most important to the vnderstanding of the materiall and instructions founde in this manual and they are founde below.

1. Being the Arte of Defence, defence will alwaies haue prioritie ouer offense.
2. The straight line is the shortest distance between two pointes.
3. Euery mouement is accomplished in tyme, and euery in mouement is tyme vsed.
4. Practise is required in order for the fencer to improue.
5. Fencer who dominates mouement and action dominates the combate.

These principalles are the fundamental rules vpon which my practise of fensing is based: An explanation of the principels is important in order for them to be completely vnderstood. Ech needeth to be discussed in a litle detail in order that they can be vnderstood properlie and thus demonstrated to be important to the following theoreticall and practicall elements and expressed in such: Thus the explanation of the principels that followeth.

The First Principel describes what the intire art is based vpon and thus is one of the most important: It is the Arte of Defence and as such the prioritie is that the combatant is able to defend himselfe and kepe himselfe safe as the prioritie: Thoughts of offending the opponent should onely be considered once the combatant has successfully defended himselfe from the opponent. This being said, howeuer, the successful defence should alwaies be followed by an action of an offensiue nature.

The Second Principalle is a simple statement of fact, but alludes to other elements whyche are important for the knowledge of the swordes-man: The streight line being the shortest distance between two points meanes that any offensiue action which follows a straighte line to the oppo-

opponent

The firſt Booke

nent is more effectiue than one that does not. Following this principel, the poynt has the aduantage ouer the edge due to the ſtraight line that is vſed by the pointe, though the edge ſhould not be diſcarded as it has tymes of vſefulneſſe.

Diſtance affects Tyme and Tyme affects Diſtance and theſe two elements are preſent in this perticuler principel in that it deſcribes an element which inuolues both Time and Diſtance: The ſtraight line being ſhorter in diſtance is alſo ſhorter in tyme taken: As ſuch the combination of Time and Diſtance is eſſential knowledge. The Third Principalle deſcribes the importãce of Time.

As euery mouement is accompliſhed in tyme and euery mouement reſults in time vſed preſents the ſimple fact that the ſmaller amount of time vſed in an action, the more effectiue it is: Extraneous mouements in the performance of an action vſe and waſte time and thus make it leſſe effectiue than it could be. This is diſcuſſed in the Fourth Principel.

Practiſe is required for the ſwordſman to improue. This improuement is the reſult of the refinement of the skiles which he poſſeſſes and the introduction of new ſkills: The refinement of the skills reduceth and remoueth extraneous mouements in the perfourmance of actions and thus makes the combatant more effectiue: Practiſe is of great importance to the combatant if he wiſhes to improue and maintain his ſkills.

Once a ſwordeſman has attained a leuel of skill he is able to vſe this ſkill in order to manipulate encounters betwene himſelfe and his opponents: Thus through vſe of theſe skills, the combatant is able to applie the Firſt Principalle and is able to dominate mouement and action dominates the interaction between him and his opponent. This is where the knowledge of Time and Diſtãce becomes eſſential in order to know how it can be manipulated: Through this the opponent will be able to manipulate the encounter to his aduantage.

The principelles which haue beene preſented are thoſe vppon which this diſcourſe is baſed. Theſe principalles ſhoulde be kept in minde bothe as the manual is reade and alſo as the combatant perfourmes the actions of fencing: Theſe principels will apply both in a theoreticall and alſo a practicall ſenſe. The following elements of theorie will reinforce the ideas preſented here and go into a more in-depth explanation of manie of the principalles preſented here.

Of Tyme

The first Booke
Of Tyme

Yme is one of the keystones of the Arte of Defence and it is verie much related to Distance: Tyme and Distance are the two primary principles vppon which all sword-play and indeed all martiall combate is based: There are euen places where it is almost impossible to separate Tyme from Distance and vice versa: Tyme is one of the roote concepts vpon which fensing is based: If the Arte of Defence is to be vnderstood, then Time must first be vnderstood.

The Thirde Principle, euery mouement is accomplished in Time, and in euerie mouement is Time vsed was described preuiously and describes some of the importãce of Tyme: The important parte of this is that in order to vnderstand Tyme it is related to all mouement: Thus it can be seen that Tyme is a part of euerie motion in fensing. The idea of the relationship betwene mouement and Time is the key to vnderstanding Time in swordplay and those concepts which surround it.

Tyme is often called Tempo, and this is related to actions: Tempo is vsed to describe actions rather than portions of Tyme, though sometimes they are the same: These portions are alwaies associated with actions or inaction on the parte of the combatant both being necessarie to one another. Tempo is not vsed to describe cadence or the flow of a combate: This is a different concept and will be described further on. It is important that Tempo is not concrete but is fluid and may be extended or shortened through manipulation.

Tyme and Timing are two different thinges and it is possible to haue one and not the other: In some waies it is the difference betwene what is found in treatises and what is seen in actuall mouement. It is possible to vnderstand Time but not haue Timing: Timing is the practical application of the knowledge of Tyme and comes about through the practicall vse of weapons and takes time to deuelop. Knowing Time is knowing how long the blow will take, Timing is actually deliuering the blow at the correct Time in a combatiue situation. This is the difference between theoreticall knowledg and practicall knowledge of the same actions.

Included within this concept of Time is also the proper performance of an action in order that it taketh the appropriate amount of tyme in deliuery, and thus arriues with the appropriate Timing, this includes vsing and wasting Time: Time is vsed when an action is performed properly, the Tempi are vsed properly and the blow is deliuered with timing: Wasting Time happens when an action is performed lazilie or sloppilie and thus the action is perfourmed without Timing. In order to perfourme an action efficientlie and thus with Timing it is important to practise this reduceth the amount of time taken in the perfourmaunce of the action as the more practised actions are more efficient in their mouements: This applies to all the actions of the Arte of Defence from the simplest to the most complexest: The idea of a technique being performed with Timing is seene in the concept of an action performed In Time, which will be discussed later: This is most vsually applyed to an offensiue action.

Cadence is the vsual consideration of Tempo as the tearme is thought of: This considereth the flowe of combate between two combatants and how this relates between the combatants: This is different to other concepts of Tyme found in swordplaie as it is not segmented but considereth how fast actions are perfourmed and the reactions from the combatants: Cadence is determined by the actuall perfourmance of the actions and the gaps between them: It is important that Time in fencing is fluide and flows between the combatants and is not rigid or like

turns

The firſt Booke

turns: Actions occur actiuely, as a reſult of another action, ſimultaneouſly or euen independent of the action of the opponent: Cadence decides how faſt the actions between the two combatants are performd. This is alſo determined by reaction time and ſkill.

Related to the concept of cadence is the idea of Prioritie: This perticuler aſpect of fenſing is moſt important when in doſe but is alſo important outſide of ſuch: If a combatter is not performing an offenſiue action they do not haue Prioritie and as ſuch ſhould be looking to their defence: The combatant with Prioritie is the one who is actiuely attacking: There are ſome ideas which will be diſcuſſed later on which will relate back to this concept: The moſt important part of Prioritie is that the fencer who doeth not haue Prioritie ſhoulde enſure that they are ſafe before any other action is perfourmed. Breaking Prioritie is how to gain it, what needeth to happen is that the defenſiue player needeth to become the offenſiue player and in ſuch gain Prioritie: This is alſo related to the idea of Breaking Time, which will be diſcuſſed vnder Manipulating Time.

In general, either the hand mooues or the foot moues and the bodie will followe: This brings about conſideration of what is called the Time of the Hande and the Tyme of the Foote: Theſe two concepts diſcuſſe which ſhould be moued firſt the hand or the foot and the ſpeede of ſuch: It alſo conſiders how the body ſhould follow. The Time of the Hand diſcuſſeth the mouement of the hand and thus the weapon attached to it: It alſo conſiders the mouement of the arme as well, regardleſſe of whether it holds a weapon or not: The Time of the Foot conſiders the mouement of the foote and the legge, in other words footwork: There is a thyrde Time and that is the Time of the Bodie: This is where the bodie and head are mooued.

The Time of the Hand is the faſteſt and for the moſt part will be moued firſt: The Time of the Foote is ſlower than the Time of the Hande and for the moſt part will be moued ſecond: The Time of the Bodie is the ſloweſt and will always be moued laſt: Theſe are the True Times of the hand, foot and body: There will be few exceptions to this rule.

A Falſe Time is one that will lead the player into a daungerous ſituation: Anie mouement of the bodie, regardleſſ of torſo or head, which happeneth before a Tyme of the Hande or the Foote is a Falſe Time. In attack, the hand will be moued before the foot: This is a True Time: In attack, if the foote mooues before the hand, this is a Falſe Time: In attack if the body moues before the hand, this is a Falſe Time. In moſt caſes in defence, it is the Time of the Hand that will be moued before the Time of the Foot: This is a True Time. In mouement acroſſe the ground, the foote will be moued before the body: This is a True Time: In mouement acroſſe the ground, if the body moues before the foot, this is a Falſe Time.

A practicall example of the times is as follows, if a combatter mooueth his bodie into diſtance of his opponent before his weapon, there is a high chaunce that he will be ſtruck: If the ſame fencer moues his weapon into diſtance before his bodie, the opponent will haue to react to the wepon before attacking the combatant. This demonſtrateth the importance of the vſe of the Tyme of the Hand before the Time of the Foot: This demonſtrateth the danger of the Falſe Times and the aduantage of the True.

While Time has been diſcuſſed in ſome quite general termes, there are ſome more ſpecific aſpects of Time, and tearms which accompanie it, which are vitall in order to vnderſtand Tyme and thus fencing: Theſe terms relate to ſpecific inſtances in the flow of combat: Theſe inſtances are vſuallie vſed in reſponſe to the action of an opponent againſt the combatter: This would implie that they are moſtlie reactiue, but this is not neceſſarilie the caſe.

For the beginner combatant, things are broken down into ſingle ſimple actions in order that the fenſer can learne how to perform theſe actions preciſely, as ſuch in the defence and counter againſt an opponent, the defence and counter are ſeparated into two actions: This fourme of action where the defence and attack are made as two actions is called Double Time: There is a ſingle action for defence, oftene a parrie, and a ſingle action for the counter-attack, often a thruſt: This

The firſt Booke

This enableth the fencer to be ſure of their defence as they can focus on it, and then lead on to the attack in a following action. As a combatter improues and the actions become more preciſe, this can be blended into a ſingle action: It is more important that the combatant is ſure of his defence and thus would be better for the fenſer to ſtaie wyth Double Time vntil his actions become preciſe in their mouements: Euen the more aduanced combatants will ſtill vſe Double Time at leaſt ſome of the time in order to enſure their defence. This follows the Firſt Principle that defence has priority ouer offenſe.

The Single Time reſponſe to an opponents action is a more aduanced technique than the Double Time reſponſe, and it takes a great deal of preciſion in order to perform it properly: The Single Time action blends the defence and counter-attack into a ſingle fluid action: Eſſentially the counter-attack is placed where it will bothe defende the fencer and offend the opponent in a ſingle mouement of the ſword: This requireth the techniques to be perfourmed with preciſion and this takes practiſe, it alſo requires knowledge of many of the aſpects of fencing theory, eſpeciallie Lines: If performed ſloppilie or inaccuratelie the combatant may end vp harmed in the proceſſe: It is important that the fenſer enſures that his defence is in place in order that he is not harmed in the proceſſe of his action, as ſtated in the Firſt Principle. The Single and Double Time reſponſes are vſuallie made in reſponſe to an opponents action and defende as part of their proceſſe: There are other times which attack directly into the opponents attack or interrupt it.

Counter Time is literallie againſt the Time: It is againſt the flow of combat alſo and thus againſt Prioritie: What this means is that the action is performed as a reſponſe to the opponents attacke, but rather than defending, the fencer attackes into the opponents attack: This is an action which requires a greate deal of timing and practiſe: As the combatant is attacking directly into the opponents attack, another form of defence is required in order to enſure that the combatter remains ſafe in his action: Diſregarding the defence can reſult in the fencer being harmed in the proceſſe of his action: This is one way for the fencer to break Prioritie.

Half Time is actually not a meaſurement of Time at all, it more deſcribes the Timing of the action in compariſon to where an action would normally be performed: For the combatter, the Half Time attacke is a direct attack againſte the opponents action and is deſigned to interrupt, and arreſt, the opponents attack before it is completed: It is called Half Time becauſe it happens in the middeſt of the opponents tempo: An example of this is an attacke to the hande made againſt the opponent as he makes a cutte or thruſt againſt the fenſer: The action of the combatant interrupteth the action of the opponent ſo that he can not complete it: As ſuch, there is no need for a defenſiue action required as the attack is defeated before it is completed: Howeuer, it is better for the fenſer to make ſome ſort of defenſiue action in order to enſure his ſafety. This is an aduanced technique requiring a great deal of preciſion and timing on the part of the combatant: If the technique is not performed properly or accurately with the correct timing, the fenſer can be left in a great deal of trouble.

An action performed In Time is an action performed at the correct time reſulting in the opponent being ſtruck and the ſwordſman not being ſuch, it is alſo a ſituation manipulated to reſult in ſuch: The combatant muſt haue timing to act In Time: In moſt inſtances to act In Time the fenſer merely needs to deliuer an attack when the opponent is moſt vulnerable and in ſuch a way that he remains defended: This is entirely dependent on the technique being vſed and is vſed in regard to both ſimple and aduanced techniques: It is the reſult of the opponent being ſtruck and the fenſer not which is the key.

The relationſhips between the various Times are important as it aſſiſts in the vnderſtanding of each one as they are all related: The longeſt Time is obuiouſlie the Double Time as it takes two actions and thus two Tempi of action to vſe: This being the caſe that would mean that the Half Time is the ſhorteſt being the ſhorteſt amount of tyme, but this is not neceſſarilye the caſe: It

is the

The firſt Booke

is the length of the action which determines the length of the Tempo: What this means is that Single, Counter and Half Time actually are all the ſame length due to the fact that they all vſe a ſingle action with the weapon: Other actions performed in the ſame Tempo do not lengthen the Tempo. There is a ſimple relationſhip between Single and Double Time, and indeed between Single and all the other Times: Simply ſtated the Double Time action is the one vſed by beginners as it enſures that the defenſiue action can be the focus and then focus is ſhifted to the offenſiue: The other times, Single, Counter and half all are Times which blend a defenſiue action with an offenſiue action and this muſt be done ſmoothly and preciſely in order to ſucceed: This is the reaſon that Double Time is taught firſt and the others afterward. Single Time, Counter Time and Half Time are often confuſed with one another: Often this is becauſe the theory is not clearly ſtated or the demonſtrations of them do not adequatelie demonſtrate the differences: All three are ſimilar in that they vſe a ſingle Tempo in order to achieue their goal: Howeuer, there are differences. Single Time vſes the weapon in a defenſiue motion in order to defend while at the ſame time attacking: In Counter Time the weapon is often not vſed defenſiuely and the fencer muſt vſe ſome other defence: This is the ſame with Half Time: Thus this is a difference and clearly proues that Single Time is different. Counter Time and Half Time are alſo confuſed, juſt as they are with Single Time. Both, as ſtated aboue vſe a ſingle Tempo in order to atchieue their goals: Both vſe another form of defence beſide the weapon in defence: Howeuer, in Counter Time the counter is made directly into the opponents attack: Half Time, on the other hand, counters the opponents attack before it is completed, interrupting it before it can become effectiue: Thus in Counter Time the attack of the opponent is made and completed, whereas in Half Time the attack is ſtopped part way through the action.

The Manipulation of Time is ſomething that the accompliſhed fenſer will purpoſefully do and ſometimes the more nouice fencer will atchieue by accident: To deliberatly manipulate Time it is important to vnderſtand all of the theory which is aſſociated: Thus, to atchieue it by deſign, it muſt be combined with preciſe mouements of the weapon and body, and haue good Timing: The combatant muſt know when and how Tyme can be manipulated in his actions againſt an opponent: The final element of Manipulating Time is impoſing the change on the opponent and this is the hardeſt part. Both Tempo and Cadence can be increaſed and decreaſed: A ſwordes-man can ſimply take longer to perform an action or can ſpeede vp an action to manipulate the Tempo: The ſame can be ſaid for Cadence: If a fencer wants to increaſe the Cadence then he ſhould mooue faſter and perform more actions: If a combatant wants to decreaſe the Cadence, he ſimply mooues ſlower and perfourmes fewer actions. Increaſing the Cadence is more difficult than manipulating the Tempo as this requires the opponent to reſpond in kind: It is ſimpler to increaſe the Cadence than decreaſe it, but the decreaſe can be made by breaking from the encounter frequently in order to ſlowe it downe: This requireth the effectiue vſe of footwork and Timing. The Times themſelues can be vſed ſo to manipulate the ſituation: Eſpecially, they can be vſed to manipulate the Prioritie. A combatter can really onelye ſucceſsfully manipulate the Time, if he has Prioritie, and thus if he is dominating the incounter: If the fenſer is not dominating it is much more difficult to manipulate the Time. Changing from Single or Counter Time reſponſes to Double Time reſponſes will ſlow the Cadence of the encounter becauſe more Tempi are being vſed: Doing the reuerſe will increaſe the Cadence as the opponent will haue to reſpond faſter to the actions. Breaking the Prioritie and therefore dominance of the opponent is beſt atchieued through the vſe of Half and Counter Time actions: This reuerſes the actiue and paſſiue roles and forces the opponent to react to the combatant. The time muſt be choſen properly in order that this can be atchieued effectiuely: The ſame can be atchieued any time the opponent breaks from the encounter or ſtops an action: This inuolueth being able to read the opponent correctlie and haue goode Timing.

Breaking

The first Booke

Breaking Time is an effectiue method of manipulating Time and manipulating the opponent into a worse situation. Breaking Time is simply atchieued by lengthening the Tempo: This is easiest atchieued by pausing during an action and thus pausing the Tempo. Breaking Time is something which must be done vnexpectedly in order to catch the opponent: The technique is designed to force the opponent to moue out of position and thus open a hole for the fencer to attack: An example of Breaking Time is to make a thrust but pause in the middest of it, and then complete the thrust: If the opponent reacts early to the thrust he will be mooued out of position and past where the blade will be by the time the action is completed: This particular technique taketh a great deal of skill and Timing in order to be able to atchieue its result.

Tyme is one of the keystones of fencing and any fenser who wants to atchieue any real leuel of skill in the Arte of Defence needeth to vnderstande it and be able to applie it practically: It is important that the conceptes which haue beene presented are vnderstoode in order to vnderstand what will follow in the practical elements of this presentation: Any fencer who disregards the principles and theories presented here will haue a difficult time in progressing to their full potential.

Of Distance

Istance, also knowne as Measure is one of the primarie principales of the Arte of Defence and is closelye related to the concepte of Tyme which is another one of the primarie principles and was discussed preuiously. The principle of Distance in sworde-play is not as some would think discussing precise measurements: Instead it is verie fluid in nature rather than being concrete, much like Time: It is not concrete because it is based on elementes which can chaunge and some of them rapidly: Distance is most often increasing or decreasing and is verie rarely static, because the combatants do not often stand still, and there are other variables.

Primarily in fencing it is the distance betwene the combatters pointe and the opponent and also the opponents pointe and the fenser whych is the moste important. These are not set distances due to the facte that this is all dependent on the combatants fighting one another: This is because Distance is not only based on the distance between the combatants, but also the length of the weapons being vsed, the length of the arme of eche combatant, theyr bodies, and euen their steps and the type of step vsed by the combatants: These distances will chaunge dependent on various factors includinge the weapons and the combatants themselues: All of these muste be taken into account when iudging Distance. With regard to this it is footwork which changes Distance most drastically and most often.

There are seueral Measures or types of Measure that need to be taken into account in plaie with the sworde: These Distances extende all the waie from the combatants being too close, to the combatants being farre awaie from one another: There is also an additional Distance which is a concept which is not defined by a perticuler distance, but is a concept which is neuerthelesse important. To begin with there are two types of Distance which are the most general and need to be vnderstood before anie of the others can be discussed: One of these is being In Distance, and the other is being Out of Distance: The first will be diuided into further pieces: The other is much lesse complex. Being In Distance meanes that the fencer is within striking distance of the opponent or vice versa, now this may not be an immediate attack, but it is in range to be threatening: Being Out of Distance simply meanes that neyther of the combatants is within range to make any sorte of meaningful threat: Being In or Out of Distance can change verye quickly as distance is most often incre-

increasing

The first Booke

afing or decreafing.

It has already beene ftated that Diftance and Tyme haue a verie clofe relationfhip: This will be clearly demonftrated as the different elements of Diftance are difcuffed: Thefe Meafures canne actually be counted in meafures of Tyme, or Tempi: This is important as it giues a leuel of meafurement whiche is mofte vfeful in this difcuffion for comparifon. Out of Diftance is a Diftance at which the combatants are not able to reache eche other within a fhorte period of tyme: This is the onlye diftance at which a combatant is fafe, fo long as the fencers do not clofe on one another: At all of the other Diftances the opponent may ftrike in fome form or another; This Diftance is vfuallie two Tempi or more in meafurement of Tyme: What this means is that eyther of the combatants will haue to vfe fome form of Time of the Foot, or maybe two, as well as Time of the Hande to reach the other. Next is to proceed to the meafures which are found In Diftance. The two moft commoneft types of meafure and the ones that will be vfed the moft in fencing, both training and combat, are Narrow and Wide Diftance: Neither combatant is fafe at thefe Diftances, it is also at thefe Diftances that moft of the combate will occur. They may alfo be called Clofe and Wide Diftance. Wide Diftance: At this Diftance the combatants will be more than a fingle Tempo away from one another, and in fome inftances will be two Tempi away from one another: This is effentially a Diftance at which the combatants are a lunge or flightly more away from one another. To croffe this Diftăce will require at leaft a Time of the Hand and a Time of the Foot, though thefe maye be combined in a lunge: What this meanes is that the combatants are relatiuely fafe from one another, though fhould neuer be too relaxed. Narrow Diftance is a Diftance at which the combatants are a fingle Tempo awaye from one another: This meanes that a fimple thrufte or Tyme of the Hande can reach the other combatant: It is the optimum diftance for a thruft, but inuolues dangeroufly little time for the combatants: The combatants need to be extreamely aware at this Diftance and not linger here: This is the Diftance where combate will be actiuely occurring between the two combatants. There is a clofer diftance than Narrow Diftance: This is a Diftance at which combatants will find themfelues, vfually by accident, but fometimes by defign: The Diftance is known as Very Narrow Diftance. At this Diftance when the bodies of the combatants are clofe it is vfually awkward to moue the tip of a fword into ftrike as fuch it is moft vfeful to vfe the edge: Howeuer this Diftance can alfo be meafured where only part of the combatants has come within this Diftance, vfually the hand, arme or weapon: Being meafured againft the ftrike againft the extended arme: The important relationfhip here is the clofeneffe of the clofeft part of one combatant to the other: At this Diftance there is only about half a Tempo and therefore there is reallye no time. This makes this Diftance the mofte daungerous. A combatant who is in Very Clofe Diftance fhoulde be eyther acting againfte the opponent or doing his befte to defende and clear himfelfe from the engagement: It is at this diftance where the idea of prioritie becomes moft important.

There is one more type of Meafure which does not actually haue a meafurement in Diftance as it is dependent on the fituation in which the combatant finds himfelf: The meafure is known as Iuft Diftance and is the Diftance at which it is optimum for ftriking the opponent, for the moft part without the opponent being able to do fo againft the combatant: This is actuallie a principle and not a Meafure, belieued to be at leaft two diftances as for fome it is at Clofe Diftance and for others it is at Wide Diftance: What this meanes is that it is actually verie fluid and not concrete: The moft important thing about Iuft Diftance is that the fwordes-man is able to ftrike the opponent while not being ftruck himfelf and this is highlie dependent on the fituation.

Each one of the Diftances is related to both the clofer and further one: As fuch, the Wide Diftance can become Narrowe and vice verfa, but can alfo become Verie Narrowe quite eafilie: This is the cafe becaufe either combatter may increafe or decreafe the Diftance: Increafing Diftance is knowne as Breaking Diftãce and decreafing is known as Clofing Diftance: It is vpp to the fenfer

The firſt Booke

the fenſer to be able to meaſure Diſtance and figure out whether it is increaſing or decreaſing: This is an important part to be able to vſe Diſtance and alſo manipulate it. In the option between Breaking or Cloſing Diſtance, breaking is vſually ſafer, but it is entirely vpp to the ſituation the fenſer finds himſelfe in: It is importante for the ſwordſman to vnderſtande this perticuler relationſhip, and indeede all of the relationſhips between the different Diſtances. Knowing this will enable the fenſer to arriue at Iuſt Diſtance at the correct tyme when they want to: This inuolues the manipulation of Diſtance and requires the combatant to haue an inſtinctiue knowledge of Diſtance.

The firſt ſtep in the manipulation of diſtance is to know the Diſtances: This means to vnderſtand what it meanes to be at Wide Diſtance or Narrow Diſtance and ſo on: It is alſo important that this is knowen from practicall perſpectiue as well as an intellectuall one: This will require time on the part of the fenſer in order to deuelop an inſtinctiue knowledge of Diſtance and to be able to meaſure the Diſtance without thinking about it: All of the elements which make vpp Diſtance muſt be taken into account in this: Only once the combatant is able to meaſure Diſtance inſtinctiuely, then will it be poſſible for him to manipulate it. Diſtance is manipulated through the vſe of the feet, bodie and armes, though it is mainly controled through vſing footwork: Small mouements of the bodie and armes can make a difference affect it by mouing the ſword, but primarily it is through the vſe of footwork that Diſtance is manipulated: What this means is that the ſwordeſman muſt be able to control their own mouements and be able to vſe the appropriate footwork where it is required and this requires a lot of practiſe.

The meaſurement of Diſtance muſt be done in Tempo and action, meaning the vſe of ſtep, thruſt and other actions needs to be done without thinking, it muſt be a trained inſtinct: It requires much time for the combatant paying attention to their mouements to inſtinctiuely know their Diſtance: Fencing with different opponents will alſo enable the combatant to be aware of different mouements on the parte of other combatters that will affect Diſtance. Once the fenſer is able to inſtinctiuely be aware of their own and their opponents Diſtance and how they both vſe them, then he will be able to manipulate Diſtance: This is vſually achieued by the different combinations of footwork in order to change the length of ſteppe. Circuler actions are the moſt vſeful in this perticuler reſpect, but linear mouements can alſo be vſed: Each fenſer will diſcouer their own particular methods of chaunging and manipulating Diſtance, but it is important that theſe mouements are baſed in and found in the theory of ſwordplay.

The laſt thing that needs to be diſcuſſed is the important difference between the Diſtance which is vſed in training and that which is vſed in an actual encounter between different combatants. Much of the training that is perfourmed with the ſtudente will be at Narrow Diſtance: This is to enable the ſtudent to vſe the correct techniques in the prepared ſituation of training: Howeuer, the Diſtance for combate will moſt commonlye ſtart at Wide Diſtance, or further afield, to enable the combatant to haue tyme to react to the actions of the opponent. Contact betwene the two combatants which occurres at Narrow Diſtance will be very brief, and ſubſtantially ſhorter than in training. The reaſon for this is to enable the ſtudente to vnderſtande what the correcte Diſtance is: If parries, for example, are practiced at Wide Diſtance then the opponent will not be able to reach the ſtudente and this will train them to parrie much too earlie if only the armes are being vſed: Euen where footwork is being vſed on both partes, the Diſtance wyll ſtill be Narrowe in order that the diſtance is kepte the ſame: Onlye when a ſingle ſtudente is vſing footwork for parrying drills will the combatants ſtart at Wide Diſtance: Obuiouſly were a combate to ſtart at Narrow Diſtance it coulde be ouer verye quicklye: Hence, there muſte be a difference between the two: The fencer muſt be aware of the difference between the Diſtance used in practiſes and that used in combats, and learn to vſe the one which is ſuited to the ſituation.

Diſtance

The first Booke

Diftance is an important part of fencing theory and the fwordefman who does not haue at leaft a bafic grafp of it will moft likelie be doomed to failure: It is important for the combatant to vnderftand the different types of Diftance and how they can change and quite quickly: The relationfhip between Tyme and Diftance is alfo vital as the two principles intertwine in many parts of the theory of the vfe of the fwoorde: With this knowledge howeuer the combatant is more likely to fucceed.

Of Lines

Ines in the Arte of Defence include fuch thinges as diuifion of the combatant and alfo the Guard or Ward: This perticuler portion of the theorie is about how the combatant is diuided and the affociated theorie with regarde to howe the fwordfman then defendeth thefe various partes: It is important to realife that while moft of the theory with regard to Lynes feems to be of a more defenfiue nature it is alfo by connection offenfiue as the diuifiõs alfo determine where attacks on the opponent wyll be made: The difcuffion of Lines alfo hath fome ftronge connections to the contacte of blades as founde in engagement and this can not be ignored.

The firft part that will be examined in order to correctly introduce the fubiect of Lines is to defcribe the diuifion of the combatant: There are many different ways to diuide the fenfer into fections in order to delineate thefe areas: The eafieft way to diuide the combatant, and moft common is to vfe a fimple methode which diuides the combatant into foure. The combatant is diuided once horizontallie and once verticallie, through the hilt, and through the vfe of thefe two diuifions four Lynes can be named: To ftart with the areas diuided by each Lyne will be defcribed: The partition which diuides the fenfer horizontally refults in a High Line, aboue the diuifion, and a Low Line below the diuifion: This diuifion madeth at the height of the combatters weapon, through the hylt of the weapon: The verticall line diuides the fwordefman through the hilt of the cõbatants weapon in order to create a left and right fide, or Infide Line and Outfide Line: This is dependent on which hand the fenfer holds their weapon: For the right-handed combatant the Infide Line is on the left and for the left-handed combatant the Infide Line is on the right: The Infide Line is that which is clofeft to the body, and the Outfide Line is that which is furtheft. The combination of thefe diuifions refults in four Lynes, a High Infide, High Outfide, Low Infide and Low Outfide: The foure Lines are clofely related to the parries and attacks vfed by the combatter: Parries clofe a Line in order that it is defended, and it is important that the parry does this in order to be effectiue: This will be difcuffed further in a later fection.

Once the Lines are eftablifhed it is poffible to difcuffe how this theory relates to the defenfiue and offenfiue application of the weapon: In fimple terms an Open Line is vulnerable to attacke and a Clofed Line is not: The parries and other options are vfed to clofe the Lynes: Some of thefe options will be difcuffed here and fome will be difcuffed later on: It is difficult, but not impoffible to clofe multiple Lines at the fame time: It fhould be noted that the clofing of the Lyne does not haue to be actiue, a fimple pofitioning of the weapon and bodye maye be fufficient. The idea of Lynes is to open the opponents Line to allow for an attack and at the fame time clofe the combatants own in order to be defended: The opponents Lyne may be forced open vfing fome fort of blade engagement or other phifical method or the fenfer may be able to conuince the opponent to open the Line, through fome other methode: The combatter may alfo open their own Line in or-
order

The firſt Booke

der to inuite an attack: This is performed through the vſe of feints and inuitations, both of which will be diſcuſſed later on.

There are two termes aſſoſiated with the poſition from which a ſwordeſman ſtarts, one is Guard and the other is Ward: Often theſe two are vſed as ſynonyms of one another: This is not actually the caſe: A Guard is a poſition which cloſes a Line, a ward is meerely a poſition from which an attack or defence is launched: For the moſt parte Wardes are not defenſiue poſitions, though ſome do actually cloſe Lines and can ſerue as ſuch: When either term is vſed in this treatiſe be it known that it is actually a Ward in the ſence deſcribed aboue which is being diſcuſſed. There are manie different guardes which maie be adopted: They are meerely dependent on howe the bodye and the wepon may be placed: Some of them are more vſeful than others as they place a weapon in a poſition of immediate readines: There are foure more common Wardes which can be adopted, the moſt vſeful one being the Third Guard: There are three others which neede due conſideration, and they are quite important in the queſtion of Lines as the Guard names alſo relate to hande poſitions: The hande poſition is important as it will be demonſtrated later on that this is important to engagement: The three others are, with little ſurpriſe, Firſt, Second, and Fourth: In diſcuſſing theſe perticuler Guards it is important that the Guards are deſcribed by hande and ſome bodie in their deſcription: Thus, while the Firſt Guard is vſuallye made with the weapon quite high, the ſame Guard can be called with the arm much lower, but the hand in the ſame poſition. There will be a more practicall and cloſer diſcuſſion of this later in a more practical ſence.

In the diſcuſſion of Lines it is alſo important to examine another theoreticall element which is cloſely related to Engagement, and combines conſideratiōs of Guard, Lynes and Engagement together, and that is Counter-Poſition: Counter-Poſition is aboute poſitioning in a waye that the combatant cloſeth Lynes of attacke while opening theme on the opponent: It is important that the fenſer is poſitioned properly in order for this to work: This perticuler technique, as the name implieth, is deſigned to countere the opponents Guarde, or oppoſe it, as ſuch it is alſo called Oppoſing Guard: The technique is alſo deſigned ſo that there is an open, ſafe ſingle attack from the current poſition againſt the opponent: It is of vital importance that the combatant vnderſtands Lynes and engagement properly in order to be able to vſe this technique: The key to this particular technique is for the fenſer to poſition himſelfe in ſuche a way that the opponent is ſucceſsfully oppoſed, his weapon kept againſt a Cloſed Lyne, while the combatters weapon is in an Open Lyne. More of this will be diſcuſſed in a more practical ſence when Guardes are diſcuſſed, as will Lines.

Of Engagement

Ngagement, or Blade Engagement, is an important concept with regarde to the Arte of the Sworde and muſt be vnderſtood in order to be able to fence properly: It is vital that while this perticuler explanation of Engagement will be from a theoreticall baſis, there are eſſential practical elementes which are baſed vpon this theory: Due to this there will be elementes of theorie which will reappear in the practical ſections about Engagement: This is becauſe the plaie betweene the weapons is part of ſwordplaie which the combatant muſt vnderſtand in order to be ſucceſsful.

In order to properlie vnderſtand Blade Engagement it muſt firſt be defined ſo that the concept is vnderſtood: What ſhould be noted is that there are actuallie two definitions, one which is commonlye

commonlye vſed, and one which will be vſed in this treatiſe: The commonly referred to definitiõ of Blade Engagement ſtates that Engagement takes place in combate where the two weapons come into contact wyth one another: This is actually quite a narrowe definition and taketh awaie from ſome of the important partes of Blade Engagement which are eſſential for a compleat vnderſtanding: For the purpoſes of this diſcourſe Blade Engagement takes place where the blade of the opponent is placed in a poſition near that of the combatters, where there is a tactical reaſon for doing ſo: This doth not require contacte betwene the weapons as it is the poſition of the weapone whych is more important than actualle contact betwene them: Wyth this definition it will be noted that it taketh into account more than is founde in the common definition: This is important as thoſe elements where the weapons are not in contact are as important as thoſe where the blades are in contact.

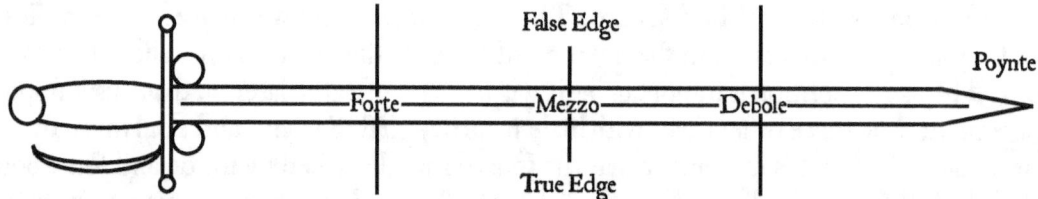

The firſt part to vnderſtanding Blade Engagement is to examine the weapon more ſpecifically it is looking at the blade of the weapon: For the moſt part, the handle and aſſociated hylt does not come into this: The blade is vſually diuided into two halues: The firſt half ſtarts at the hylt and goes to half way toward the pointe: The ſecond part ſtarts at half way and goes to the pointe: The firſt half is commonly called the *forte* and the ſecond half is called the *debole*: There are various other terms which are vſed to deſcribe theſe two parts of the weapon, vſed in other treatiſes: The *forte* is the ſtrong part of the blade and this is becauſe it is located cloſe to the hylt, it is alſo the ſlower parte of the weapon: The *debole* is the weaker part of the weapon becauſe it is located far from the hilt, but it is alſo the faſter parte of the weapon: This being the caſe, the *forte* is more likely to be vſed in defence, and the *debole* is more likely to be vſed for offence, eſpecially for the fact it alſo has the point. There is a thirde parte of the weapon which is the middeſt thyrde of the blade: This parte of the blade is halfe *forte* and halfe *debole*, as ſuch it has ſome of the characteriſtics of both: Of courſe this meanes that it is not exceptionallie ſtrong at eyther: This parte of the blade is called the *mezzo*, the worde meaning the Italyan for halfe: Much of the complex engagement of the bladeſ will moſt often occur about this parte of the blade. The next partes of the blade that needes to be examined are the edges of which there are two: The edge which is moſt commonlie pointed toward the opponent is the True Edge: The other edge whych is cloſer to the combatant is knowne as the Falſe Edge: Both edges of the wepon are important and neede to be conſidered with regarde to Blade Engagement and all other actions: There are ſome claims that the True Edge is ſtronger than the Falſe, and it is for this reaſon that the Falſe Edge is ſo infrequentlie vſed, this is actually not neceſſarily the caſe in all inſtances: There are inſtances where the Falſe Edge will be ſtronger than the True.

The moſt common concepcion of Blade Engagement is with regard to contact betwene the weapons as ſuch this parte will be diſcuſſed firſt: Contact between the wepons for Blade Engagement may be referred to as Hard Engagement, while the meere poſitioning of the weapons may be called Softe Engagement: This helpes delineate betweene the two types of Engagement. With regard to contact between the weapons, this may be an inſtant, ſhort or prolonged contact between them: All of theſe qualifie as Harde Engagement: During this contacte, the combatant is able, with enough practiſe to be hable to feel through the blade: The Italyans call this *Senſo di Ferro*: This giues the combatant a ſixthe ſence of what the opponent will do as parte of his nexte, or euene future

The first Booke

future, moues: This is in no waye myſtical it iuſt requires the fencer to be able to feel through the blade: This can only be atchieued when the ſwordſman ſees the weapon as an extenſion of himſelf, rather than an obiect being vſed: More of this wyll be diſcuſſed in a practical fence later on. There are certaine feelings that will be euident to all: An opponent maye force theyr weapon againſte the combatants, or the combatant may force againſt the opponents weapon: This is called vſing the ſtrong of the weapon againſt the others weak: Yielding againſte the opponents weapon is called vſing the weake againſt the opponent: Both of theſe are vſeful and can be vſed to greate aduantage by the ſwordſman who can feele properlie and take aduantage of the ſituation in which he finds himſelf. The ſecond part of Blade Engagement is Soft Engagement, meerely placing the weapon in the poſition in order to gaine an aduantage: This poſition may lead to Hard Engagement or it might not: A fencer can actuallye influence the actions of the opponent meerely by the poſitioning of his weapon in compariſon to the opponents. There is alſo a methode which vſeth all Soft Engagement, indeed which auoids Hard Engagement totally: This is called Abſence of Blade: In this the ſwordeſman auoids the opponents weapon as much as poſſible, thus denying anye information through Hard Engagement. Both Hard and Soft Engagements can be vſed againſt the opponent with greate ſucceſſe and this will be preſented in a more practical ſenſe further along.

There are ſeuerall techniques which are aſſociated with Blade Engagement including Taking the Blade, Attacks on the Blade and other forms of Engagement: Each one of theſe has a time and place in which it is moſt vſeful, and theſe will be diſcuſſed along with theyr practicall application along with a practical diſcuſſion of Blade Engagement later in the manual. Counter-Poſition relies on knowledge of Lynes and Engagement, this is alſo an example of the vſe of Blade Engagement to atchieue a goal; for the moſt parte this will be Soft Engagement, but Engagement nonetheleſſe.

The principles of Blade Engagement couer a great deal and it is important that eche element is vnderſtood in order to be able to perfourme the Blade Engagements in an incounter with an opponent: In order to be able to do this, the theory of Blade Engagement muſt be vnderſtood firſt. Vnderſtanding is the key to the application of the techniques which will be diſcuſſed in the practical ſection of this treatiſe: Engagement is vital to vnderſtanding and performing the Arte of Defence in a ſucceſsful faſhion and in order to vnderſtand this, the other elements contained within and without muſt alſo be vnderſtood.

Of Practiſe

Ractiſe is ſomething which is eſſential for anie ſkill if the perſon wants to improue their ſkil or euen maintaine it. Practiſe, needleſſe to ſay is eſſential for the Arte of Defence: There are many phiſical ſkiles which neede to be practiſed in order that the combatant is able to perfourme, and it is neceſſarie that the combatant does this: Of courſe practiſe needes to be coupled wyth learning in order to truely improue.

There are alwaies new skiles to be learnt, or different applications for the skiles which haue alreadie been learnt, ſtill, the learning neuer endes: This being ſaide in manie ſcholes there is much focus on the learning of the new rather than the maintaining of the current and olde: Maintenance of the old meanes that the newe has ſomething to be built vppon, without this foundation, the new ſkills maye not be able to be learned or eſtabliſhed as parte of the techniques that the combatant will vſeth: Learning and practiſe go together, one attaineth and the

other

The firſt Booke

other maintaineth: Practiſe ſolidifieth the learnt ſkills: The practiſe alſo encourages the new ſkills to be blended with the olde in order that they can all be perfourmed ſmoothlie. Practiſe is eſſential in order to improue and maintaine ſkill: A ſtudent maie learne ſomething from his maiſter: This ſkill may be learnt and atchieued ſo that the ſkill is knowne: Without practiſe this ſkill will not become a naturall parte of the ſkills which the combatter has, and he will neuer vſe it in an encounter becauſe it is not naturall: This requireth practiſe of the ſkills which haue beene learnt: Further, only through the vſe of the skills of the Arte will the fenſer improue: Drilling is vſeful and allowes the combatant to deuelope patterns to reſpond to, but onelye in an encounter will the combatant be able to practiſe to pick vpp the correct cues from an opponent in order to vſe the ſkil when it is moſt vſeful: Bouting is vſeful for this, eſpecially where the bouting is controlled and both inuolued in the bouting know the aim of it: Both of the indiuiduals inuolued in the bouting muſt vſe their ſkills as they would in a combatiue ſcenario for either to learne and practiſe compleatelie: This is a requirement of the ſtudente and the partner.

Bouting and practiſe ſhoulde be wyth anie partner who will accompanie the combatant in this: Diuerſe opponents will aſſiſt the ſtudent to be prepared for different ſituations as not euerie ſwordeſman will perfourme actions the ſame way, nor wyll they neceſſarilie haue the ſame anſweres to the ſame ſituations: This improues the experience of the combatant and maketh them more complete in their approche. Fenſing with different opponentes will allowe the fenſer to be prepared for vnexpected ſituations due to the differences in approch that the ſtudente maie diſcouer with different opponentes: The more peple the combatant plaies with the more ſcenarios that he will runne into and the more he can be prepared for. It is vital that both the ſtudent and theyr partner are committed to the practiſe and the proceſſes inuolued: This meanes that they ſhoulde bothe be putting their all into the ſituation. It is onely through the full expenditure of ſkill that the ſwordeſman will be able to improue and be able to eualuate their own ſkill againſte another: Shoulde one of the combatters not perfourme with theyr compleate abilitie, then one will be deceiued as to howe ſkilled they are and howe well they knowe theyr ſkills: The only time when there ſhould be an exception to this rule wyll be when one is teachinge the other, or where a perticuler technique is the focus of the bouting, for both ſhould learne and neyther ſhould feele as beinge a meere target: The reſult of ſuch is that the more experienced combatant, ſkilled as they may be, may not vſe all theyr ſkill againſt a newer to teſt what they know: Still in this ſcenario it is neceſſarie to haue the focus on the ſkill-ſet beeing practiſed.

Practiſe needs to be regular: If the ſtudent doeth not practiſe then his ſkills will degrade: This degradation is ſeen acroſſe all elements in the Arte of the ſwoorde. Skiles neede to be practiſed to a degree that the fenſer doth not haue to think about what he is doing: This allowes the combatant to act vſing trained inſtinct: What this meanes is that the ſkill is a parte of the normal proceſſes of fenſing for the ſwordſman: Theſe ſkills will laſt a longer period of tyme without practiſe, but they ſtill need to be practiſed in order to be able to maintaine a high leuel of ſkill: The hours the combatant practiſes ouer the period of the week, on a regular ſituation, are more important, rather than thoſe by which one commits ouer the courſe of a complete ſeaſon, or year, to create the ſkills by which they become a normal proceſs by which the fencer faces the opponent on the field. All aſpects of Arte of Defence muſte be practiſed: This includes the more theoreticall elementes of fenſing ſuch as Tyme and Diſtance: The combatant needs to practiſe theſe and be aware of them in actiõ: This wyll enable the fenſer to take theme into accompt when croſſing ſwordes without hauing to actiuely thinke about them: Tyming is only able to be practiſed by actiuely fencing: It is only through vſe of the ſkilles that the ſtudente wyll be hable to ſee the ſkills in action and thus be aware of their Timing: Thus Timing is improued and maintained through practiſe in both drilles and bouting.

Fatigue

The first Booke

Fatigue will increase ouer time if the skills are not vsed: The practise vsing drills and bouting also allows the combatant to maintaine a leuel of fitnesse due to the actiue nature of the practise: This is not a purely physical concern for the combatant: The fitter he is the longer he will last when fensing, but also the lesse fatigue a swordes-man has the more energy he wyll haue to be able to thinke about what technique is appropriate to the situation and be able to performe it with the correct timing: Practise also maintaines the muscles associated with the actions of fensing, ouer time without practise they will degrade and the combatant will be lesse able. Finally the combatter must practise in the armour and vsing the wepons that he will in an encounter: This is about being fighting fit: Armour is something that needes to be taken into account when practising: Sure a student can practise longer with lighter armour, but then this will be reduced in an actuall encounter: The lighter armour will also not take into accounte the heate of the armoure actuallie vsed and heate has a greate effect on fatigue.

Practise is essential: No swordsman who is serious about what he is doing wyll neglecte practise: Practise is something which should be done regularly in order to maintaine skills. He should focus on what he is doing in the practise and vse his skills compleatlie without any reseruatiõs: This is the only way that he will improue or euen maintaine his skills. The studente shuld seek out different partners to practise with as the experience of doing so will assist him greatly in the future: More to it, the combatant should seek partners with the same goals as him, and thus with the same thirst for real improuement.

Of Wards

Ards and Guardes were discussed a little in the section on Lines in the theorie section. This will discusse similar subiects, but from a more practicall point of view: Of course in order to do this, some of the preuious will be demonstrated in a more practical sence: This is necessarie as the theorie which has been preuiouslie presented is the foundation for the practical elementes which are demonstrated in this and following partes of this treatise.

The Wardes are numbered one to foure: Each one of these represents a hande position and also an arm position: These positions were originallie representing the position of the sword-sman as he draweth the weapon from the scabbard and then prepareth. The Firste is a position in which the arme is held aboue the shoulder with the wepon poynted at the opponent, with the false edge downeward: This position is the first place where the wepon is pointed at the opponent after drawing the weapon from a scabbard: The first position of the hande is also found here in the hand wyth the knuckles vpward is the first position: The following guards represent the following positions as the sword is lowered into position. The Second is a position in which the arme is held out-stretched from the shoulder, eyther towarde the front or to the side: In anie case the weapon remaines pointed at the opponent and remaines at shoulder-hight: The second position of the hande is found in this guarde with the palme downeward and the knuckles to the Outside. The Thyrde is a position in which the arme is downe by the combatants side, the weapon pointed towarde the opponent: The third hand position is with the knuckles towarde the grounde as in the Third Ward. The Fourth is a position with the hande acrosse the bodie toward the Inside, the point toward the opponent, with the palm vpward: The fourth position of the hand is also the same, knuckles to the inside. For some, these Guards will protect Lines, though in truth onely the Third and the Fourth maye do, depending on the positiõ
of the

The first Booke

of the Guarde: Neither Firſt nor Second in theyr claſſic formes are in a poſition to protect any Line, though offenſe is much eaſier from theſe: Theſe foure are Wardes in the trueſt ſence of the word: It is important to delineate betwene hand and Warde poſition in order to reduce confuſion.

The diuiſion of the combatant into Lynes is the ſame as has been deſcribed preuiouſly, a horizontall and a verticall line both which paſſe through the hylt, thus as before the areas aboue are High and thoſe below Lowe; thoſe areas toward the bodie are Inſide and thoſe awaie are Outſide. For the right handed combatter, this would mean that the Inſide line is on the lefte and the Outſide line is on the right. For the left-handed fenſer the Lynes are ſimply reuerſed. Depending on which Guard the combatant is in will depend on which Lyne may be open or cloſed: For example, a ſwordes-man in a Thyrde Guarde has a minimall Outſide Lyne and a muche larger Inſide Lyne; conuerſely the reuerſe is the ſame for a fenſer in Fourth, with a large Outſide and ſmall Inſide Line. Should a fencer wiſh to cloſe a Line, he muſt poſition himſelf in a warde carefullie and cloſe the Line properlie.

The diſcuſſion of what is a Warde and what is a Guarde was made in the Theory ſection, needleſſe to ſay as a tactical conſideration, it is a ſerious one for the combatant: While the terms may be vſed one for the other and vice verſa, the ſtudent of the Arte muſt be ſure of what he vſeth in order to be ſafe: In order to not confuſe the reader it will be vnderſtood that a Ward may be named a Guard in thys manual, but they are all Wards nonetheles: Only if and when yt is ſpecifically ſtated will it actually be a Guard as defined preuiouſly: The diſcuſſion of the difference between a Warde and a Guard leads on to what can be conſidered to be a good Guarde, and thus one aduantageous to the combatant.

A good Guard is one which conforms to ſome ſimple principles, and theſe are all baſed in the theory of the Arte of Defence: In order to vnderſtand what a goode Guard is it is vital to vnderſtand the principles on which it is baſed: What the reader will finde is that this liſt of principalles will actuallie conform to more than one Ward and this is aduantageous. The firſt thinge that a good Guard will do is to cloſe at leaſt one Lyne and do this properlie: This being ſaid, there is no waie for the combatant to cloſe all of the Lynes: This Line, or Lines, ſhould be cloſed enough that a direct attack from the Guard poſition of an opponent will not leaue the ſwordſman indefenſible. Being aware of the open Lines the fenſer will be able to be prepared to defende them, or deliberately leaue them open in order to inuite the opponent to attack there: This forme of inuitation could be ſeen as a feinte as there is a deliberate opening left: More of feints will be diſcuſſed much later on. Following the Lynes and their poſition, the combatter ſhould conſider how eaſie it is to launch an attack or defence from the poſition he is in: This is a conſideration for a goode Guard or Ward regardleſſe of its poſition: There is little poynte for the combatant to be able to be ſafe but vnable to launch an attack: This requires the weapon to bothe be in a threatening poſition and yet to be in a poſition to be able to defende aswell: It is the eaſe of perfourmance of theſe actions whych is the key. In order to be able to launch an attacke or defence, the fenſer muſt be balanced: As ſuch, the combatant ſhould haue his bodie ſtraight and ſupported. The feet ſhould be about ſhoulder width apart for the maximum ballance and potentiall mouement: In combination with this, the knees ſhoulde not be locked, but bente ſomewhat in order to aſſiſt ballance and potential for mouement: Balance allows for a good poſition and the abilitie to moue: What will alſo be noticed is that a ballanced poſition, as deſcribed will alſo be comfortable for the combatant: It is important that comforte is taken into accompt in order that the ſwordes-man is able to maintaine the poſition while preparing to acte: If it is vncomfortable the fenſer will not be able to maintaine it, and thus maye moue out of poſition and leaue himſelfe open at the wrong tyme: In order to be comfortable the Ward ſhould be as naturall to the bodie as poſſible, this, howeuer may take ſome practiſe in order for the Warde to become comfortable for the fenſer: This will alſo aſſiſte to ſtrengthen the muſcl-

muſcles

The firſt Booke

es and prepare them for mouement.

The Third Ward is the one that will be vſed as the Locke Warde throughout this treatiſe as ſuch it will be deſcribed firſt. It has alreadie been noted that ſome of the hande poſition needeth to be taken into account when deſcribing this Ward and it wyll: This Ward is the primarie one as it fulfileth all of the requirements of a goode Guard as deſcribed aboue: The typical Guard will be deſcribed along with ſome examples of different verſions of the ſame Guard: Vnleſſ otherwiſe it is noted it will be the typical Guard of Thyrde and the ſtandard Guarde that is being diſcuſſed anie other will be a variation. To eſtabliſh the typical Ward of Thyrde it is neceſſarie to ſtart from the grounde and then worke vp as it is important to ſtart with the foundation of the Warde: For the right-handed combatant, the right foote ſhould be placed forwarde, the bigge toe poynted at the opponent and wyth the left foote to the rear: The feet ſhould be ſhoulder width apart: The reare foote can be betweene ninetie and fortie-fiue degrees to the forwarde foote: The heeles ſhuld not line vp, but the left ſhould be placed about the width of the foote, or wider depending on preference from the lyne of the front foote. The knees ſhould be bent, ſo that the fencer is ſlightly ſitting in the ſtance: The knees ſhould line vpp with the feet, and hips. The waight of the bodie ſhould be placed between the legges rather than biaſed to one or the other and the fencer ſhould haue a ſtraight back keeping the body vpright. The heade ſhould be held erect: The ſhoulders ſhould be leuel with neyther higher nor lower than the other: The right arm ſhould be placed down by the fencers ſide, not ſtraighte, but the arme ſhould not be fullie bent either: The bend in the arme ſhould place the hande about a palm-width in fronte of the right thighe: The hand ſhould be in Third poſhould ition with the knuckles facing toward the ground: The weapon ſhould be poynted at the opponent and haue the pointe raiſed enough that it lines vp with the top of the ſhoulder: Wyth the hand in thyrde poſition, the falſe edge will be toward the fencer while the true will be toward the opponent: The left hande ſhould be placed in fronte of the right breaſt with the elbowe tucked into the bodie: The palme of this hand ſhould not face the opponent, but be at a ſlight angle. Looking directlie forwarde the fencer ſhoulde ſee the poynte of their wepon directed at the opponent and the tips of the fingers of theyr lefte hande.

There are ſeueral variations which maie be made to the Thyrde Guarde for various reaſons: All variations will be noted in the text where required. The hande poſitions maie be changed: Eyther hande maie be puſhed forward: Vſually one is placed more forwarde than the other, but in ſome inſtances both may be puſhed forwarde: It ſhould alſo bee noted that the hande maie haue a changed poſition, rather than being in Thirde, it may be changed to another poſition. Iuſt as the hand poſition maie be changed, ſo too maie the foote poſition alſo be changed: The feete maie be ſwapped ouer, being the moſt obuious variation, or they maie be placed further apart or cloſer togither. The bodye may alſo be leaned eyther forwarde or backwarde, depending on the ſituation: This alſo alters the Guard. Eche one of the variations in the Guarde will be noted in the text in order to reduce confuſion: Where no alteration is mentioned, it is to be aſſumed to be the Guarde deſcribed in detail aboue: The ſame variations may be applied to all of the following Guards as well.

To eſtabliſh the typicall Guard of Fourth, the feete and bodie ſhould be placed in the ſame poſition as found in the Guarde of Thyrde as deſcribed aboue: This remaineth the ſame in order to maintaine the vpright poſition of the bodie and the ballanced nature of the Guarde eſtabliſhed by the poſition of the feete. Where the Guarde of Fourth differeth is in the poſition of the hands: It muſt, otherwiſe it will remaine as in the Guard of Third: The offhand comes ouer to the right and is placed in the mideſt of the cheſt, once again with the palme of the hande readie to deflect an incoming blade: The ſword-hande is then turned ſo that the hande is in the Fourth poſition, with the palm vpp: The arme is then brought acroſſe the bodie at the height of the elbow in its vſual poſition down beſide the bodie: The pointe of the wepon ſhuld be towarde the opponente at ſhulder height

The firſt Booke

height.

  The Guard of First is one which is not often vſed, but it is ſtill neceſſarie for the ſwordeſ-man to vnderſtand its poſition, and in this waie be prepared for the opponent to take it, or take it himſelf, ſhould the ſituation demand it. To eſtabliſh the typical Guard of Firſt, the feete and bodie ſhoulde be placed in the ſame poſition as found in the Wards of Third and Fourth as deſcribed aboue: This remaineth the ſame in ordere to maintaine the vpright poſition of the bodye and the balanced nature of the Guard eſtabliſhed by the poſition of the feete. Where the Ward of Firſte differs is in the poſition of the handes and armes: It muſt, otherwiſe it will remaine as in the Guard of Thyrde: It is the ſword-arm and hande which is the primarie difference: The off-hand remains in the ſame poſition as in Thyrd: The ſword-arm is extended directly vpward from the ſhoulder: The hande is placed in Firſt poſition with the knuckles vpward, thus the falſe edge will be downewarde: The poynte of the weapon ſhoulde be thretning the opponent: The weapon ſhould be almoſt horizontall in its poſition, though poynting downewarde a litle threatning the opponent.

  The Guarde of Seconde is ſimilar to that of Firſt in that it is not vſed all that often: There are actuallye two different formes of Seconde and bothe wyll be deſcribed. As with Fourthe and Firſt, the feete and bodie remaineth in the ſame poſition in ordere to maintaine balance and mouement: As in the Guard of Firſt, the off-hand remains in the ſame poſition as well. In the firſt verſion of Second the ſword-arm is placed directlie forwarde of the ſhoulder with the poynte of the weapon thretning the opponent: The hande is in Second poſition with the knuckles outwarde and palme downewarde. In the other variation, ſometimes known as Broade Warde, the hande remaines in Seconde poſition, but the arme is directlye outwarde to the ſide from the ſhoulder: The weapon is pointed towarde the opponent as founde in all of the other guardes.

  While Thyrde is the primarie Garde that the combatant will adopte when facing the opponent, knowing the others alloweth the ſcholler to be prepared to face them, or euen vſe them himſelfe: For the moſt parte the other Guardes and variations of Guardes will be vſed as examples for different reaſons in what followes: For the moſt parte theſe wyll be a chaunge in hande poſition rather than the adopting of the compleate Guarde as they haue beene deſcribed. Howeuer, the primarie Guarde that wyll be vſed in this manual is Thirde as it preſents more aduantages for the fenſer, both tacticall and practical, than the other Guardes.

  Once the principles haue bine eſtabliſhed and the typical Wardes ſet, it is then poſſible to examine the Wardes from a tacticall pointe of view: This diſcuſſion is focuſſed on howe the Guards will operate in combate: The approache that will be taken wyll be a much more practicall approche then what has been ſo far: This will take into account thoſe principles founde in the Theorie ſection along with thoſe founde aboue in order to demonſtrate how a Garde is or is not effectiue from the pointe of view of beeing one from which to defende the combatant and alſo ſtrike againſt the opponent. The firſt parte of this is to refreſh about the principles of the oppoſing Guarde whych hath beene diſcuſſed in the Theorie ſection: The tactical principel behind this perticuler approache is to cloſe the combatters Lyne and open a Lyne in the opponent: This is deſigned to giue the fenſer a directe ſafe attack againſt the opponent vſing onelye a ſingle Tempo in order to atchieue it: Thus, wyth this in minde, it is poſſible to looke at the aduantages of various Guardes and theyr tacticall poſſibilities: This, howeuer, muſt take into account the principelles of the Goode Guarde.

  From a purelie tactical poynte of viewe, according to the principalles preſented, Firſte is a horrible Guarde, it is actuallie the worſt: The firſt thing about this Guarde is that it is vncomfortable, the ſworde arm is high in the aire and a greate deale of ſtrength is vſed in order to remaine in this poſition: This is bad for the fenſer as if he relaxes he comes out of Gard: The Guard is alſo not cloſed: It leaues all of the Lynes open, with ſome very limited cloſure of the High Outſide Ly-

Lyne

The firſt Booke

ne: This reſults in a verie flow defence: There is onelye a ſingle directe attack from the poſition all other attacks require additionall mouement: All of theſe factors determine that this is not a goode Guarde from a tactical pointe of viewe. Secondeis not much of an improuement, from the examination of Broade Warde: It is alſo vncomfortable due to its poſition and not perticulerly cloſed from a Lines pointe of view: There are few limited attacks as with Firſt that do not requier ſundrie mouements: The other verſion is better: The poſition can be comfortable if the fenſer is trained in the poſition, it is a cloſed poſition due to the pointe beeing directed at the opponent: Howeuer, it is limited in attack due to the poſition of the arme: A thruſt requires foote mouement the onlie other motion is a cutte. Fourthe is an improuement in that it is more cloſed than the preuious Guards, but it is alſo bound vpp due to the poſition of the armes: This binding along with the poſition of the arme reſults in a limiting of the offenſiue options for the fencer: Howeuer, in compariſon to Firſt or Second, Fourth is a much more comfortable and defenſible poſition. Thirde is the primarie Ward of this diſcourſe for manie reaſons the tactical reaſons are iuſt another reaſon why it is as ſuch: It is the moſt comfortableſt Warde of the four ſtandard Wardes which haue beene diſcuſſed due to its natural poſition: Due to its poſition it has wide options for attack and defence and it is definitiuelie cloſed on a ſingle Lyne if fourmed properlie, which can be defended with minimal mouement. All of theſe factors reſult in Thyrde being the moſt tactically aduantageous Warde.

There haue beene variations for each Guarde which haue bene noted preuiouſlie: From a tactical pointe of view, the changes in the poſition of the Wardes due to the changes found in theſe variations will chaunge the tactical poſſibilities of each of the Guardes: The fencer ſhould be aware of the different variations of the Guardes and howe they affect them: An example of a chaunge in Guard reſulting in a tacticall chaunge is extending the offhand forwarde in the Thyrd Guard: This can nominallie cloſe another Line for the fencer, but can alſo drawe them to attack ſtreight downe the centre Line betweene the hande and the ſworde. The fencer ſhoulde be aware and experimente with different variations in order to be prepared for the changes that reſulte: What ſhould be noted about the Wardes preſented is that for the moſt part they cloſe, or partiallie cloſe the High Outſide Line. Fourth is the exception in this caſe as it cloſes the High Inſide Line.

Once all the tactical queſtions of the Guard haue been examined, it is neceſſarie to examine howe to counter the opponents Guard, therefore denying him the aduantage of the poſition he has taken: With regarde to this the ideall is to deny the opponent an opening whyle creating an opening for the fenſer to attack in compleat ſafetie: Shoulde this not be poſſible then the fenſer ſhoulde be focuſſed on denying the opponenet his attack: This will be preſented with the Counter-Guardes belowe. The Wards canen be countered by other Guardes as preſented, or with litle modification: Theſe counters are baſed vpon the tactical principelles preſented and alſo the principles of the goode Garde. It is of ſignificance that the ſcholler muſte be aware of the poſition of the opponent in all aſpects in his Ward: The various poſitions of the bodie, hands and ſword can change things markedlie as will be ſeene.

The Guarde of Firſte is countered by the Guard of Thyrde due to the oppoſing poſitions: The high poſition of Firſt is countered by the lowe poſition of Third: In this perticuler ſituation it will requier mouement on the parte of the defenſiue fencer as this is not a directe counter without mouement. The Guard of Firſt is alſo countered by a Guarde of Fourth where the hande and arm are raiſed in order to cloſe the Inſide Lyne compleatlie. The Guard of Firſt may alſo be countered by a Guarde of Seconde in the firſt variation due to the increaſed diſtance of the Seconde and the threat preſented by the thruſt which is cloſer to the opponent than his is againſt the combatant. Some will claim that a Guarde of Firſt will counter a Guarde of Firſt, howeuer, no Lines are cloſed and mere threats are made: This is ſimply copying the Garde in order to gain the ſame aduantage:

It is

The first Booke

It is not an approche to countering an opponents Gard that should be made vnlesse the fencer knowes the Guarde perticulerlie well and has additional mouements in minde.

The Guarde of Seconde may be countered by another Guarde of Second: This actuallie different to the example aboue, especially if the first variation Garde is taken: In this perticuler case the fencers wyll be in a neutral position due to the fact that both are thretned and both are closed at the same time: This positiõ requiers one of the combatters to moue in order to gain an aduantage. The Broade Warde maie also be taken against another Broade Warde in ordere to threaten against the same Lyne which is taken: Once again, the fenser must be carefull in vsing this counter as there are reallie no Lynes closed vnlesse the off-hand is able to close a Line: The most effectiue counter to a Guarde of Seconde, in Broade Warde, is a Guard of Fourthe: The position of the Guarde of Fourthe wyll close the Inside Lyne to the opponent, especially effectiuelie where the combatant is able to close and phisically close the Line: Euen where contact is not possible the Ward of Fourth will effectiuely counter that of Seconde. For the first version, a similar Guarde can be vsed, as described aboue, or a first version Guard of Second with the hande in Fourth can be vsed against the opponents Inside Line to close the fensers Inside Line: This is more effectiue than iuste copying the Guarde: This Guarde can also be countered wythe effectiue footwork due to the Guarde relyng on footwork or cutte for effect as such a Guard of Thyrde can be taken also.

The Guarde of Thyrde can countered by a Guarde of Fourth wyth the combatants blade to the opponents Inside, closing the Inside Lyne compleatly: This can be done wyth or wythout Blade Engagement: Interestinglye, the Garde of Thirde maye alsoe be countered by a Guarde of Thyrde to the Outside, the hande is turned to Seconde in order to close the Outside Line, or with a Garde of Thirde to the Inside with the hande in Fourth: This is dependent on where the fenser seeketh to strike the opponent, and also the position of the Guarde relatiue to the opponent: In this particular case it is the hande which assisteth in closing the Lyne and mouing the opponent out of Lyne.

The Guarde of Fourthe maie be countered with a Gard of Thirde to the Inside: This is designed to close the Outside Line: The hande is turned in Seconde in order to reinforce the position. A Guarde of Seconde, in the Broade Warde could also be vsed so long as the wepons are placed together and the Seconde is to the Inside of the Fourth: This requiers positioning on the parte of the fencer in Seconde. It is ironic that the Guarde of Fourthe has so fewe counters but can counter seuerall other Guardes: This should be taken into account bothe when vsing and againste a Ward of Fourthe.

The best waie to vnderstand and vse the Guardes and their counters is to vse them: A student of the blade shuld practise these with another student in order to become proficient in them: They should also vse some of the variations in order to be aware and more comfortable with them as well. The instructions for the four primarie Guards should be read carefullie and the position of the combatant considered carefullie, especiallie in refrence to the opponents: Further thought shulde be giuen as to howe the variation maie chaunge the Guarde and the effect this chaunge will haue on the swordes-mans position. It is the Guarde of Third that shoulde haue most attention paide to it as it is the primarie Warde that will be vsed throughout this discourse.

Of the Feet

The firſt Booke
Of the Feet

Ootwork is an eſſential elemente in the Arte of Defence: It is footwork moore than aniething elſe in ſwordplaye that determines Diſtance. The abilitie to vſe footwork properlie is the abilitie to moue acroſſe the feelde in a comfortable and efficient maner and wyth this in minde it is important that the ſtudent vnderſtand footworke and its terminologie: The combatant ſtudente, after training in footwork, be able to vſe the footwork found in the Arte of the Sworde as normallie as he would walking: Key elements of footwork will be found in this diſcuſſion and they ſhould neuer be paſſed ouer in training, alonge wyth practical training in footeworke.

Before anie practicall matters can be addreſſed with regarde to footework, it is important that ſome theoreticall elementes are diſcuſſed: Theſe theoretical elementes are addreſſing the tearms that will be vſed in the diſcuſſion of footwork: Theſe tearmes muſt bee vnderſtood in order that the ſtudent can vſe the tearmes and the appropriate footwork aſſociated with theſe termes: Vſing theſe terms wyll make it ſimple to diſcribe any footework mocion that a ſwordes-man maie wiſh to perfourme. There are foure termes which the combatant needes to vnderſtand; Step, Pace, Paſſ and Half: Theſe four termes can be vſed to deſcribe any footework action which the combatant may wiſh to performe: A Step is any motion of vſing the feet in footwork this includes all Paces and Paſſes: This requieres the mouement of both feete: A Pace is footeworke where the fencers feete do not croſſe ouer one another: A Paſſ is footeworke where the fencers feete doe croſſe ouer one another, like mocion of walking normallie: Halfe is vſed to deſcribe the mouement of a ſingle foote as both Paces and Paſſes require the mouement of both feete, as ſuch there can be Halfe-Steps, Halfe-Paces and Halfe-Paſſes: Theſe terms will be the ſtandard ones vſed in reference to footwork throughout this treatiſe.

One of the moſt important thinges about footeworke is that it needes to be perfourmed without thinking about it: This meanes that it needes to be comfortable, eſſentiallie like walking: What footwork requires ſo that the combatant doeth not haue to thinke about it is practiſe: If the combatant is concerned about hys footwork he will be occupyed with this thought and will not be able thinke about the other neceſſarie aſpects of the vſe of the ſworde: Hence, the footwork muſt be naturall to the combatter: In order to atchieue this ſtate of normalitie in mocion, the combatant needs to do a lot of practiſe ſo that the inſtant reſponſe to a ſtimulus is the correct mocion with footework: The ſcholler ſhould take any opportunitie that he can to practiſe his footeworke and thus enable it to become as naturall in mocion as poſſible.

There are certaine rules, which if the ſtudent followeth them, he ſhoulde not haue anie problems with his footworke: Theſe rules deſcribe the eſſential partes of footwork and its efficient mocion when it is in vſe: For the moſt parte the rules wyll remaine in place as rules, but it ſhould be noted that there are exceptions to theſe rules and the fenſer ſhoulde be aware of theme: Some of the exceptions will be deſcribed in this diſcourſe, but it wyll be noted which rules are moſt likely to haue exceptions to theme.

1   The firſt rule of footeworke is to always remaine balanced: The combatant in his mocion ſhoulde doe his beſt to remaine ballanced and vpright: This is atchieued by maintaining an euen amount of waight betweene the feete and not leaning in anie direction: Ballance is eſſential to be hable to perform anie action in ſwordplaie efficientlie and effectiuelie: Maintaining ballance will alſo preuent the ſcholer from falling ouer: An action which vndermines ballance ſhould be ſtrongly

confidered

The firſt Booke

conſidered before it is vſed, and if it is, the combater ſhould alwaies regaine his ballance immediatelie after the action is perfourmed. The next rules are about mouement and the methode of mouement by the ſtudente.

    2   Secondly, euerie compleate Step in fencing requiers the mouement of both feete in order to compleat it: This being ſaid, each foote ſhoulde be moued once onelye, anie extraneous ſhuffling of the feete afterwarde for correction or otherwiſe waiſtes tyme and energie: There are verie rare tymes where a Halfe-Step wyll be taken and the fencer will remaine at the Halfe-Step: The Step ſhould alwaies be compleated in ſome faſhion euen if it is to returne to the originall poſition.

    3   Thirdly, the knees ſhould alwaies be bent when in Guard: Bending the knees is the firſt parte to making a ſtep, wyth this compleated the ſtepping is more efficient: Bending the knees alſo aſſiſteth with the maintenaunce of ballance and the efficient mouement of the combatant acroſſe the grounde.

    4   Fourthly, the methode of mouement is important: It ſhoulde be cleane and efficient: The ſcholler ſhould not ſhuffle his feete in the ſteppe: The ſcholler ſhould not dragge his feete in the ſteppe: The ſcholare ſhoulde not ſkip or leape or bounce when making a ſteppe: Each one of theſe is deleterious to the efficiencie and effectiue mouement of the feete and therefore footeworke: Eche foot ſhould be picked vpp and placed: Eache foote ſhould glide iuſt aboue the grounde.

    5   Fifthly, the combatant ſhould neuer ſtretch nor ſhrink his ſteppe in order to maintaine it wyth his opponent: This wyll deceaue the fenſer as to the correct Diſtance: The length of the ſtep ſhould alwaies be maintained at the naturall leuel that the combatant is alwaies at.

    6   Sixth, the combatant ſhoulde remaine facing the opponent: There are verie rare occaſions where this manual wyll inſtruct the combatant to haue his backe to the opponent: There are a fewe exceptions to this rule, but this wyll be perfourmed with purpoſe, and the purpoſe deſcribed: In general, howeuer, the fenſer ſhould remaine facing the opponent: This giues the fencer acceſſe to all meanes of offenſe and defence.

    7   Seuenth, wyth regarde to the general rules of fenſing, the combatter ſhould not croſſe his feete in the mouement in fenſing: Obuiouſly there is an exception to this rule when performing a Paſſe: There are alſo other exceptions to this rule, but in generall the combatant ſhould not croſſe his feete as this wyll affecte his ballance and his efficient mocion.

    Footeworke is baſed around two, what wyll be called, Key Steps: The action of theſe two Steppes deſcribes the actions of all of the other baſic footework mocions that wyll be founde in this treatiſe: Of courſe, there are exceptions, but the mocions deſcribed in theſe two Steps will be founde in all butte a verie fewe of the Steps: One Step is the Forwarde Pace, or Aduance as it wyll be referred to in this treatiſe: The other is the Paſſe Forward: Both of theſe Steps preſent the action that will be founde in the followinge Steps. For the Aduance, taken from a Guard of Thyrde, the toe of the fronte foote is lifted the heele is then puſhed forwarde iuſt ſkimming the grounde as ſuch the front foote is moued forwarde about the length of the foote: The reare foote is then moued forwarde the length of the foote: This completes the Step. The paſſe forwarde is much like taking a normal walking ſtep: Taken from the Guarde of Thyrde, the rear foote moues forwarde paſſing the front foote to land equall wyth the bigge toe of the fronte foote or a ſmall diſtance ahead of it, the front foote then paſſes the rear foote in order to regaine its originall poſition ahead of the rear foote. The actions found as deſcribed in theſe two Steppes will be found in the other Steppes which wyll be preſented.

    To ſtart with two ſimple Paces, one which has beene deſcribed alreadie, and the other which is the reuerſe of the alreadie deſcribed one wyll be the beginning: Theſe two Paces are the Aduance and the Retreat: This enableth the combatter to moue forwardes and backwardes: The

                                                                               Aduance

The firſt Booke

Aduance is the forwarde Steppe and has beene deſcribed as one of the Key Steppes aboue: The Retreat is the exact reuerſe of the Aduance and allowes the combatant to moue backewarde. For the Retreat, the backe foote is moued backeward the length of the foote, and the front foote followes: The feete ſhould iuſt ſkim the grounde: What can be ſeen here is that the Retreat is the exact reuerſe of the action deſcribed for the Aduance, and that it is a controlled mouing backewarde. In theſe ſteps the fenſer ſhould end vp back in his guarde as he ſtarted: The feete ſhould be in the ſame poſition as they were before the Step was taken: The ſame can be ſaid for moſt of the Steppes which are deſcribed.

  The Trauerſe is a pace which allowes the combatant to moue directlie righte or lefte of his current poſition: Regardleſſe of the Warde taken or the foote poſition, it is alwaies the foote in the direction which is requiered that is moued firſt: Indeed the ſame thinge can be ſaid for moſt of the Paces: There are ſome exceptions which wyll be noted further alonge. In order to performe a Trauerſe Righte, the righte foote is moued ſidewaies about the length of the foote, the lefte foote is then alſo moued righte the length of the foote. The Trauerſe Left is the ſame proceſſe except the lefte foote moues firſt followed by the righte. If the oppoſite foote is moued firſt the ſwordes-man maie chaunge his facing and the feete will croſſe: This will aduerſely affect the combatants ballance: In no parte during the performance of a Pace ſhoulde the combatants feete croſſe. What wyll be noted is that the Trauerſes are vſing the Aduance as a Key Step in ſimply making the mouement to the ſides rather than forwardes.

  Steps maie be taken in a diagonall direction in order to chaunge the waie that the ſtudente is facing the opponent: Theſe muſt be executed with ſome care: There are two directions which are ſimple and followe the ſtandard rules, and there are two directions whyche are a litle different. For the right-handed ſcholer in Third, it is the forwarde and righte, and the backeward and lefte which are the ſimple ones: The forwarde and lefte, and backeward and righte are the more confuſing ones: The ſimple rule in this particular ſcenario is facing. For the right-handed fenſer in Thirde, to moue forwarde and righte the combatter moues his righte foote firſt diagonallie forwarde on foot-length and followes it with the lefte foot: This is ſimply an Aduance in a diagonall direction to the righte: To moue backeward and lefte, the lefte foote is moued firſt a foot-length followed by the righte foote: This is a Retreat in a diagonall direction to the lefte. The other two directions, forwarde and lefte, and backewarde and righte are a little more complex, but not too much: To moue forwarde and lefte, vſing the ſame combatant in the ſame guard, the lefte foote is moued firſt followed by the righte foote: Now this will briefly croſſe the feete, but it wyll maintaine the facing of the ſcholler, thus he wyll remaine defenſible: To moue backewarde and righte, it will be the righte foote that moues firſt followed by the lefte. What ſhoulde be noted for memorie is that it is the direction, lefte or righte, which determines the foote that wyll be moued firſt: In all diagonall mouements, as in all of the preuious ones the foote ſhoulde onlye be moued the length of a foote or thereabouts, further then this wyll ouer-extend and vnbalance the combatant: As before the combatant will ende vpp in the ſame guard with the ſame foot placement as before: Diagonal Steppes are alſo known as Slopes.

The Paſſe

The firſt Booke

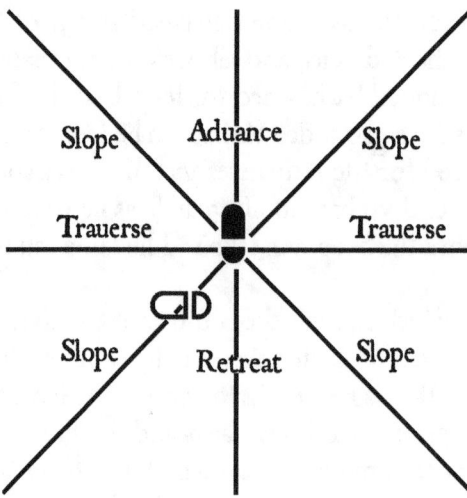

  The Paſſe is different from the Pace in that the feete intentionallie croſſe ouer, this makes it a ſlower ſtep in execution, but it makes vpp for this with the diſtance couered by eche Step which is larger than found in the Pace: Due to the nature of the Paſſe, the fenſer ſhoulde be warie of the tyme it is vſed due to the middeſt parte of the Step where the ſtudente is a little vulnerable due to the feete being croſſed. The Key Paſſe which has been deſcribed before is the Paſſe Forward: The Paſſe in retreate is the exact reuerſe of the Paſſe Forwarde in much the ſame way that in Paces the Retreat is the exact reuerſe of the Aduance: The Paſſe Backewarde is executed as ſuch, the front foote is drawne backe paſt the rear foote vntil the toe lines vp with the heele or a little paſt it, the rear foote then ſimply regains its poſition in the guard. Trauerſes may alſo be performed vſing the Paſſe rather than the Pace as deſcribed aboue: In this particular caſe, in order to moue right, the left foote moues firſt vntill it is paſt the righte foote, and then the righte foote regaines its poſition in Garde: In order to moue lefte, the right foote moues firſt vntil it is paſt the lefte foote and then the lefte foote regaines its poſition in Guard. As ſtated, the Paſſes reſult in an increaſe in diſtance made by the fenſer, but care ſhoulde be taken in their vſe due to theyr vulnerabilitie. The Paſſe in a diagonal direction maie be perfourmed, but will not be deſcribed here as the ſtep is difficult and leaues the fenſer exceptionallie vulnerable: The ſcholer ſhoulde feele free to experimente wyth this Steppe, but greate care wyll be required for its vſe.

  What haue beene deſcribed ſo far are compleat Steppes where both feete are moued and the fenſer ends vp back in his Guarde: There are Halfe-Steppes where onelie one foote will moue, and theſe Steppes can be vſeful to the combatant: What the ſtudent ſhould note, howeuer is that eyther the foote will then haue to returne to its original poſition or the other foote will alſo haue to moue for the ſtudente to regaine his Guard. The firſt Halfe-Steps that will be deſcribed are the Gather and the Slippe: Theſe two Steppes are deſigned to cloſe the feete of the guarde: This is often made as a prelude to a followinge action, or to withdraw the fenſer ſlightlie. The Gather moueth the rear foote forwarde vp to the poſition of the fronte foote: This moues the bodie ſlightlie forwarde this is often vſed as a preparation ſtep. The Slip moues the fronte foote backeward to the rear foote: This moues the bodie ſlightlie backewarde and is often vſed as a ſimple limited defence or a preparation as with the Gather: It will be noted that bothe of theſe mouements are Halfe-Paces. The obuious Halfe-Pace that is made as part of an action is the Step vſed in the Lunge: This is a large Halfe-Step mouing the front foote foreward a diſtance vſuallie in order to extend the diſtance of an attack: The execution of this Steppe is important, the power and ſpeede of the lunginge ſtep is deriued from the exploſiue vſe of the rear legge puſhing the bodie forwarde: The fronte foote is meerely lifted ſlightlye in order to releaſe the preſſure whych

hath

hath built vp and in order to ſtop the Lunge at its other end: Manie will attempt to throw themſelues forward vſing the bodie or ſimply falling ouer and vſing Grauitie: This is an inefficient methode in order to atchieue the gain: More of this Steppe wyll be ſaid in accompanyment to the thruſting action to which it is often aſſociated.

There are other Halfe-Paces and indeed Halfe-Paſſes: The ſchollar ſhoulde be aware that anie mouement of a ſingle foote is a halfe mouement: The ſchollar ſhould feel free to experimente with theſe: The greateſt vſe of the Halfe-Steppe is in order to chaunge the Step parte waie through it: Through this, the fenſer is able to chaunge direction and indeede euen chaunge the Steppe beeing made. There are manie different footeworke actions which maie be made: Some of theſe wyll be deſcribed later on due to theyr aſſociation with other actions. Footeworke is ſomething which the combatant muſt experiment and practiſe in order to be able to perfourme the actions without thinking: The ſwordes-man ſhould be able to reacte with his feete againſt the action of an opponent without hauing to think about it: More footeworke actions wyll be founde throughout this treatiſe, howeuer what has been preſented are the eſſential Steppes which are the keys to mouement.

Of Voids

Here are two defenſiue actions which will be deſcribed to defend the ſtudent againſt the attack of the opponent, the Void and the Parry: Theſe perticuler ſkills are vitall and muſt be learned properlye for the ſtudente to be able to defeat an opponent without beeing ſtricken: It is theſe elementes which muſt be diſcuſſed and learned firſt as they compriſe the foundation for the Firſt Principale being that defence is more important than offence. The firſt defenſiue action that wyll be diſcuſſed is the Void: It is a verie ſimple action, for the moſt parte, and baſed on a verie ſimple principale: Howeuer, there are ſome complex elementes that ſhoulde be noted and taken accompt of: This is the eaſieſt followe on from footework as it vſes the feete in moſt partes of it, and is another mouement of the bodie.

The Void is baſed on the ſimple principalle of mouing the target of the opponents attack awaie from the attack, or in other tearmes, not being where the opponents attack is: There are ſome different waies to do this, but all are baſed on remouing the target of the attack awaie from the attack. The Voids can be broken vp into three types, one that vſes the feete, one that vſes the bodie, and one that vſes both the feete and the bodie: The Voids will be broken into theſe three types. The moſt important thinge is that a Void is moſt effectiue where it moues the ſcholler awaie from the attack in the moſt efficient methode.

For the moſt parte, the Voids vſing the feete haue alreadie beene preſented: Theſe are all footwork actions which haue been diſcuſſed preuiouſlie: This perticuler ſection diſcuſſes vſing them in a more directlie defenſiue purpoſe. The ſimpleſt action in this perticuler caſe is the Retreat: It is a baſic Step which increaſeth the diſtance betweene the opponent and the ſcoler, aiming at hauing the opponents attack fall ſhort: Moſt of the actions deſcribed vſing footeworke aim at doing ſimilar thinges. The Diagonal Steps backward to the lefte and righte can be vſed in the ſame waie as the Retreat to auoide an attack: Theſe are verye ſimple actions but canne be very effectiue. The Trauerſe can alſo be vſed, but ſome care needes to be taken in its vſe defenſiuelie as this requieres ſome Timing in order that the combatant moueth at the correct tyme and in the correct direction: This is becauſe the direction awaie from the attack is not directlie awaie, but to the ſide: The incr-
increaſe

The firſt Booke

eaſe in diſtance from the opponentes attacke is leſſe than in withdrawing directlie awaie. The Slip can alſo be vſed in a ſimilar waie to the Retreat as it moues the bodie awaie from the attack, but the combatant muſt be well aware of their Diſtance as it doth not moue as far as the Retreat ſtep: Ironically, this is alſo its greateſt aduantage as it keepes the combatant cloſe to the opponent, allowing for a quicke counter if the combatter chooſeth.

The bodie maie alſo be moued without the mouement of the feete in order to auoid an opponents attack: Theſe are for the moſt parte ſimple actions: In moſt caſes the bodie is ſimply leant one direction or another in order to auoid the attack: The important thinge in this perticuler ſituation is that the ſcholar maintaines his ballance while performing theſe actions and does not ouerbalance: It is alſo importante that the ſtudente mooues their bodie awaie from the opponents attack the ſhorteſt direction poſſible. The leaning action ſhoulde be centred round a combination of bending and twiſting at the hips and ſhoulders, meanwhile remaining as vpright as poſſible: The body may be bent in any direction he chooſes ſo long as it followeth the principles preſented aboue. Further to this, a ſingle piece of the bodye maie be remooued from the attack alſo: This is moſt vſeful and effectiue when an attack is made againſt a limme it is quite ſimple to moue the bodie parte out of the waie in order to keepe it ſafe.

Of the three types of Void, the mouement of the bodie with the feete is the moſt effectiue as it combines the aduantages of the other two techniques: This maie ſimply be a ſtep added to the mouement of the bodie, or it maie be a purpoſeful technique ſuch as what is knowen as the *incartata* and *half-incartata*: Theſe are two purpoſeful techniques which neede care in their perfourmance, to miſtime them could reſult in the combatant being ſtrooken, as ſuch it is vitall that they are perfourmed with preciſion. It wyll be noted that the techniques are related and that the one is halfe the motion of the other: The *half-incartata* is halfe the *incartata* as the name woulde ſuggeſte, and indeede it is alſo halfe the mouement: In order to perfourme the *half-incartata*, the reare foote is moued behind the front foote, ſo that the bigge toe lines vpp wyth the heele of the fronte foote: From a poſition of the Guard of Thirde, this is effectiue in defending the High Inſide Lyne. The *incartata* is a larger mouement as the backe foote moues further acroſſe in order to increaſe the angle: In this perticuler motion the backe foote can go farre enough that it is almoſte parallel with the fronte foote: For comforts ſake it is enough that the foote is placed one footelength acroſſe from the fronte foote: As with the *half-incartata* this action protecteth the High Inſide Lyne, in this perticuler caſe it can go ſome way to alſo protecting the Low Inſide Lyne aswell. Both of theſe actions can alſo be perfourmed vſing the fronte foote to come behinde the reare in order to defende the other ſide: Care ſhoulde be taken in the vſe of theſe techniques and practiſe ſhoulde alſo be had before perfourming them in an encounter.

Voids are an effectiue forme of defence and can be ſpectacularly ſo when perfourmd effectiuelie: The poſition of the technique can alſo allowe the ſwordſman to ſet themſelues vp for a counter-attack againſt the opponent. While Voids are effectiue againſt thruſts, it ſhould not be forgotten that they are verie effectiue againſt a cutte: In fact, the Void is actuallie a better defenſiue action againſt the cutte than a Parry of any kinde: The cutte parried is ſtopped and then the combatant acteth from a poſition where the opponent can ſtill be effectiue: A cutte voided paſſes by the combatant and muſt compleate due to the nature of the cutte, this vnbalanceth the opponente and leaues a larger opening for the combatant againſt him.

Voids need to be practiſed in order to be effectiue, and they muſt be practiced againſt valid attacks in a ſafe enuironment: The ſcholar who can effectiuely learn howe to Void can actuallie defend himſelf vſing ſimply this technique: Howeuer, it is aduiſed that further defenſiue techniques are taken into account and learnt in order that the ſchollar will be trulie effectiue.

Of the Parry

The first Booke
Of the Parry

He Parry is another defenſiue option, beſt combined with the Void: This increaſeth the effectiuenes of bothe the Parry and the Void, thus making a moore effectiue defence againſt an attacke from the opponent. There are two Parries that can be vtiliſed when vſing the ſingle ſwoorde, one with the ſworde and the other wyth the offhand: The firſt is the more obuious of the two due to it being with the weapon: The ſecond one is one whych is not often vſed and needes to be conſidered as it can be verie effectiue, eſpeciallye when combined with other formes of defence or offenſe: Due to this, it will be the Hand Parry which is addreſſed before the Sword Parry, but before eyther is diſcuſſed, it is important to examine the principalles vpon which they are baſed.

The Firſt Principale of the Parry actuallie applieth to all formes of defenſiue action and it is through this principalle that a combatants defenſiue actions eſpeciallie and actions in generall canne become more effectiue: The principale which is being diſcuſſed is to wait for the opponents attack to arriue before perfourming a defenſiue action: What this meanes is that the combatter ſhoulde wait for the opponents attack to be near the combatant before the action is perfourmed: This inuolues patience and confidence in skill. The newer ſtudent wyll Parry much earlier than the moore experienced one becauſe the moore experienced has moore confidence in his skill: This is baſed on what will be referred to as a panic ſpace: The panic ſpace is the cloſeſt a ſwordes-man will allowe an opponents attack to come before reacting to the attack: In more experienſed combatants this wyll be much more cloſer than in leſſe experienced: This requirs practiſe and confidence in the ſkill being vſed. If the combatant chaſeth the opponents weapon, the Parry will be made much cloſer to the *debole* on the combatants weapon than if he waits: If the opponents weapon is chaſed too much, this can reduce the effectiueneſſe of the Parrie markedlie: The more the combatant waits the cloſer to the hylt and thus further down the *forte* the opponents attack will be receiued: This maketh for a more effectiue Parry: Of courſe if the combatant waits too long he wyll be ſtricken. This means that this perticuler action requiers Timing, iuſt as with all defenſiue actions: The Voids deſcribed preuiouſly will alſo be ſubſtantiallie more effectiue if the ſwordſman waiteth for the opponents attack.

There are two types of Parry, the Beat Parry and the Parry with Oppoſition: It is important that the ſcholer vnderſtands the difference betweene the two parries and the effecte of each and thus how effectiue they can be: The moſt important thing about this diſcuſſion is that both apply to both ſworde and hande. It is eaſier to performe both with the ſword, as the Beat Parry perfourmd incorrectlie can be painfull on the hande, but bothe can bee effectiuelie vſed by the hande: The Beat Parry vſeth the impact of the weapon or hande in order to force the opponents weapon awaye and therefore out of daunger. The Parry with Oppoſition guides the opponentes weapone awaie after gaining contact and maintaineth it. The Beat Parry is much ſimpler to vſe as it ſimplye inuolues ſtriking the weapon away from the ſchollar: The ſame technique vſed can be modified for offenſiue purpoſes in the Beat Attack, diſcuſſed further along in this diſcourſe: The experienced combatant may euen vſe the Beat Parry againſt the opponents debole before the attack arriueth, but this inuolues Timing on the part of the ſwordes-man: Of courſe the diſaduantage of the Beat Parry is that it loſeth Engagement once the opponentes blade has beene ſtrooken and therefore the opponents weapon can not be felt through contact. The Parry with Oppoſition is moſt effectiue when it is executed properlye: It is a ſlower Parrye than the Beat Parry, but it maintaineth contact with

The firſt Booke

with the opponents wepon and therefore is able to feel where the opponents weapon is: There are alſo more options open to the combatant who vſeth the Parry with Oppoſition due to the maintenaunce of contact. Through this cōtact a fenſer can gain an extended period of Hard Engagement where ſeueral Blade Engagement options are posſible. Due to its aduantages, it wyll be the Parry with Oppoſition that will be the primary parrye vſed in this treatiſe: The Beat Parry ſhoulde, howeuer be kepte as an option for the combatant for thoſe tymes where it is aduantageous. Both types of Parry haue their place in the vſe of the ſword, and not iuſt the rapier.

    The offhand as a parrying option, and indeede a defenſiue option, is often forgotten in fauor of the ſword: The combatant who does this reduces his defenſiue options quite markedly. Of courſe, the argument againſt the vſe of the hande as a defenſiue option is that the hand may be ſtrook or hurte in the proceſſe of beeing vſed to parry: The combatant ſhoulde conſider at this pointe in time whether it would be better to poſſibly hazard a little hurte on the hande or poſſiblie a greater hurte againſt ſomething more vital: There are actuallie gauntlets deſigned for the purpoſe of vſing the hande in defence, but ſtill the offhand ſhould be conſidered a viable option euen without this option. It is the palme of the hande that ſhoulde be vſed to parry the opponents weapon: This is more padded than the fingars and as ſuch will be leſſe painfull than vſing the fingers, likewiſe vſing the palme rather than the backe of the hande: To this pointe if a parrie is made and it is miſſed with the hande, the forearme is viable in defence ſo long as the arme is kept ſtraight when the parry is made, alſo when the palm is vſed, ther is more control posſible ouer the opponents weapon. The action of the Hand Parry ſhould be ſmooth: This wyll reſult in a much more effectiue parrie than if it is ierkie, alſo the ſcoler will be able to maintaine greater control of the opponents weapon if the parry is ſmooth. In this action, the opponents weapon ſhould be moued awaie from the bodie and neuer acroſſe it: The ſhorteſt diſtance awaie from the bodie ſhould be choſen, euen if this meanes croſſing the hand acroſſe the bodie. In vſing the hande, the ſtudente ſhoulde neuer attempt to parry too lowe: In meaſuringe this, the ſcholar ſhould put his arme by his ſide and neuer parrie aniething lower than the poſition of his wriſt: If the ſcoler parries anie lower he will haue to leane and this will make him cloſer to the opponents weapon and this is dangerous: As deſcribed before, the combatant ſhould not reach for the opponents weapon but allow it to come and then Parry. The Hand Parry may be effectiuelie vſed againſt attacks on all Lynes: The ſimple thing in order for the combatant not to get tangled is to moue the ſworde out of the waie of the hande: Hence, from the Guard of Third, a Hand Parry to couer the High Inſide Line is ſimple: The Parry for the High Outſide Lyne inuolueth the moouing of the ſworde pointe downewarde in order that the combatters weapon is not impeded: Similarlie, for the Low Outſide Line, the ſworde ſhould be lifted awaie from the Hand Parry: The other two lines ſimply follow the rules as they haue been deſcribed. The action deſcribed is the Parry with Oppoſition vſing the hande: The Beat Parry with the hande is moore than meerely ſlapping the ſword awaie. The ſame rules apply, the action ſhould be ſmooth, the ſhorteſt diſtance awaie from the bodie, do not Parry too lowe, do not reach, and moue the weapone away from the parrie in order not to become tangled: It is the impacte which maketh the Beat effectiue, ſo the impact muſt be ſharpe but controlled, and muſte vſe the palme. In both caſes the combatant ſhould attempt to come in contacte wyth the flatte of the opponents weapon rather than the edge: This makes the Parry more effectiue and is leſſe chaunce for potential damage to the hande. With regard to this, the Hand Parry ſhould not be vſed againſt a cutting attack due to the increaſed potential damage to the hand: There are techniques where the offhand can be vſed defenſiuely againſt the cutte, but theſe are an aduanced technique which wyll not be deſcribed in this treatiſe.

    The Sword Parry is a more natural defenſiue action than that of the Hand Parry, but it is moore complex and muſte be executed properlie in ordere to retaine its maximum effectiueneſſe:

The

The first Booke

The same rules which haue been described for the Hand Parry actually apply to the sword parry, alonge with those described initiallye in the discussion of the Parry. The purpose of the Swoorde Parry is to defende the combatant vsing the sworde againſt an attacke from the opponent: Essentiallye, the swordes-man creates walls againſt the attacks of the opponent: When all of the parries are put together, this creates a Defensiue Boxe with the sworde and parries as the sides of the boxe. With this in mind, it is possible to vse a single Parry to close any one Lyne: This is the primarie purpose of the Parry. Some of the *forte* and *debole* has been discussed preuiously with regard to waiting for the opponents attack to arriue, further to this it is important for the student that he catcheth the opponents *debole* on his *forte* in order that the Parry is effectiue, essentially vsing the strength of his sword againſt the weak of the opponents: Vsing the same principle, the edge of the sword should be put againſt the opponents weapon beinge that the edge is stronger than the flatte: To this the scholar should not vse the flatte of his weapon againſte that of the opponents due to the same reasoning, the opponents pointe may also roll around the studentes blade if the flatte of the blade is vsed to Parry: The Lateral Parry, simply mouing the weapon from one side to the other is simplie lesse effectiue then turning the edge to the opponents weapon. The point position of the weapon in the guard which the combatant taketh can also affect the effectiuenesse of the Parry and the ease of its perfourmance: In the Guards of Thyrde and Fourth, the pointe of the weapon should be as high as the combatants shoulder: The angle of the sworde which is created by the position of the weapon couers more than if it is lower: It is simple that the higher position of the pointe increaseth the defence, but a lower point is faster for the attack: Being that defence is primary, it is important that the point is kept vp. With this position and principles intact, it is now possible to present the parries themselues.

There are two edges on a sword, regardlesse of whether both are sharp or not, and as such two Parries for each Line, one with the True Edge and one with the False Edge: It is the True Edge Parries which will be dealt with here: Some of the False Edge Parries will be mentioned, but not as the primarie parries. The foure Parries whych are demonſtrated here are those designed to couer the foure Lynes: There are other parries, some of which will be mentioned later on. What should be noted is that while the Parry with Opposition is the primary, and that the Beat is secondarie, the easieſt way to consider the parries is to perfourme them as cuts: This will assist with the deliuerie of the parry. The Parry of Firſte is the parry which couereth the Low Inside Line: From the Guard of Thirde it is made as a sweeping action diagonallye acrosse the bodie and down lowe: The Parry should be deliuered as though the fenser has the intention of deliuering a cut to the opponents sword: The point of the weapon should not dragge on the grounde, and as such should be angled slightly forward in order to auoid this. The Parry of Second is the parrye which couereth the Low Outside Line: From the Guard of Thirde, the pointe is dropped and the hande turned outwarde so the edge commeth in contact with the opponents weapon: Once again, this should be deliuered in the maner of a cut againſt the opponents weapon sweeping downward and outwarde: Again the pointe should be lifted slightlie in order to auoid coming in contact with the grounde: The Parry of Thirde couers the High Outside Line: From the Guarde of Thyrd it can be as simple as meerely turning the hande to Seconde position so that the edge of the weapon meets the opponents weapon: This can also be deliuered in the maner of a cutte should the fenser inscribe a "C" in the aire when perfourming the Parry. The Parry of Fourth is couers the High Inside Lyne: From a Guard of Thyrde, the hande is turned to the Fourthe position the weapon is then pushed directly acrosse the bodie leading with the knuckles in order that the edge comes in contact with the opponents weapon: Once again, this parry can, and should be deliuered in the manner of a cutte. These are the foure True Edge Parries designed to couer the foure Lynes: These Parries will be effectiue if perfourmed as described againſt both thruſting and cutte attacks, howeuer as has been mentioned preuiously, auoiding a cutte can be more effectiue than parrying it.

There

The firſt Booke

There are other Parries, as mentioned before which can be utiliſed by the ſwordeſman. For example Falſe Edge Parries can be vſed for Thirde and Seconde: In this particular caſe for Thirde, the hande is turned to Fourth poſition and puſhed outward ſo that the Falſe Edge comes into contact with the opponents weapon rather than the True Edge: The ſame proceſſe is vſed in order to vſe the Falſe Edge rather than the true for the Parry of Second: The hande is turned to Fourthe poſition and the pointe is dropped ſo the Falſe Edge comes into contact with the opponents weapon: Theſe are optional Parries and will require practiſe in order to be effectiue. The parries of Firſt and Seconde can alſo be lifted in order to protect the High Line, but theſe are not ſtandard Parries and as with the Falſe Edge Parries, will require a great deal of practiſe. There are alſo Parries called Window Parries: In theſe, from a Guard of Thyrd, the pointe is dropped doweward: The hande is then lifted with the palme toward the opponent with the knuckles toward the Inſide Line parrying wyth the True Edge: This Parrye is deſigned to couer the Highe Inſide Line: The poſition which reſults is an effectiue poſition from which to deliuer a vertical cut known as a *fendente*. Another intereſting, and finall note is that the Parries of Thyrde and Fourthe canne actually be vſed to chaunge the Guarde from Thyrde to Fourthe and vice verſa. There is alſo the Ceding Parry which is made in reſponſe to the Ripoſte of an opponent, once the opponente has made his Parry and beginneth his ripoſte, the ſworde is drawen backe towarde the combatant while remaining engaged with the opponents weapon into the moſt appropriate Parry: This is the moſt vſeful reſponſe to a Ripoſte as it is effectiue and ſimple and may be vſed in conjunction with other defenſiue techniques. Parries can be extremely effectiue when vſed properly and following the directions here deſcribed.

Defenſiue Combination

He effectiuenes of defence is improued by vſinge moore than one action in the defence againſte an attacke by an opponente: While it is true that an effectiue defence maye be mounted by the vſe of onlye one action in the righte Timing, the vſe of more is moore effectiue and enſures that the combatant is defended from the attack: This is ſomething that the combatant ſhoulde conſidere when performinge a defence againſte an opponents attacke: Eſpeciallie for the newer ſtudente it is better that the ſtudent vſeth moore than one defence in order to be ſure of his defence. The principale vpon which this is baſed is founded on redundancie and the aduantage of many ouer one.

The concept of vſing more than one defenſiue action againſt an attack is what for the purpoſe of this treatiſe is called Layers of Defence: This principle is baſed on the idea of redundancie in defence and the fact that any one action in defence is improued by the vſe of ſeconde or further actions: An attack may be warded off by the ſwordsman vſing a ſingle action when it is performed properlie and with the correct Timing: More effectiue is when multiple actions are perfourmd. A ſingle Parrie of hande or ſword may be vſed to defend againſt a thruſt, but the ſame Parry will be increaſed in effectiueneſſe through the vſe of another defenſiue action: If the Parry faileth to ſtop the attack and it is the combatants only defence, the combatant will more than likely be ſtroken: If there is an additional defenſiue option placed in the waye of the attacke, then the attack has to paſſe through two defences in order to ſtrike the combatter rather than only a ſingle one: Further to this if a thirde defenſiue option is vſed then the defence increaſe further: It is beſte, eſpeciallye for the newer ſcholar, that multiple defenſiue actions are vſed againſt the attacks of an opponent in ordere to be

The firſt Booke

to be ſurer in his defence.

A thruſt made againſt the High Inſide Line againſt a combatant in a Guard of Thyrd may be parried by a Parry of Fourthe: Executed with the correct Tyming and perfourmd accuratelie, this will be an effectiue defence againſt the thruſt: If the combatant miſtimeth the Parry he will be ſtrake by the thruſt: If, howeuer, the combatter combined the Parrie of Fourthe with a Voide of his bodie, then he has increaſed his chaunces of remaining ſafe from the attack: This is becauſe the thruſt now has to defeat two defences in order to ſucceed: The ſcenario preſented demonſtrates how the vſe of a ſecond action can improue defence for the combatant. Againſt a thruſt againſt the High Outſide Lyne a combatant may make a Parry of Thyrde, or he may make a Parry of Thyrd and vſe a Voide, he may alſo vſe his offhand to ſupport the Sworde Parry: Added to this he maie alſo vſe footeworke to drawe himſelfe away from the opponents attack. Eache one of the ſundrie actions mentioned for defence wyll increaſe the defenſiue potential of the whole. The ſcoler ſhould practiſe the vſe of defenſiue combinations as a parte of hys ſtandard training this wyll allow the ſcoller to deuelop defences againſt the opponents attacks: Further, the vſe of multiple defences will alſo aſſiſt in the deuelopment of the ſkills required to performe multiple actions againſt an opponent regardleſſe of whether theſe actions are defenſiue or offenſiue.

The principalle of Layers of Defence is primarilye deſigned to increaſe the defenſiue potentiall of the combatant againſte an attack of the opponent: Howeuer, the vſe of this perticuler principalle in the vſe of multiple actions againſt a ſingle attacke at a ſingle time increaſeth the mobilitie of the ſwordſman and increaſeth the familiaritie of the combatant with the mouements of his own bodie: The abilitie to vſe multiple actions againſt an opponent can onelye be ſeene as an aſſet to the combatter as this abilitie will allowe the combatant to perfourme more and more complex actions: Such training is not only building phiſical bodye motion, but is alſo mentall as it beginneth to allow the ſtudente to deuelope the mental abilitie to perfourme multiple actions at the ſame time: Being able to performe multiple actions at the ſame time will reſult in a great aſſet as the ſcholar progreſſeth. What ſhould be noted is that the defenſiue combinations which haue been preſented here are onely a ſmall portion of thoſe poſſible againſt an attack: What the combatant ſhould be conſidering is how another action canne be vſed againſt the attack made by the opponent: Some practiſe ſhould be taken conſidering various attacks and then multiple defences againſte it vſing multiple actions in order to find the moſt effectiue combination for each type of attack: In this way the ſcholler will alſo haue opened his mind to different options that are auailable againſt different attacks.

Of the Thruſt

The first Booke
Of the Thruſt

He Thruſt is an attack deliuered with the poynt of a weapon againſt an opponent with the entent on cauſing damage through the penetration of the point: The pointe is proiected primarilie through the vſe of the muſcles of the ſhoulder and arme to a poynt in ſpace: When vſed offenſiuelie againſt an opponent, this ſpace will be occupyed, but the deliuerie is the ſame as it woulde be deliuered againſte any target regardleſſe of the ſituation: This is a technique-focuſſed action.

The Thruſt is the primarye offenſiue action in this forme of the Arte of the Swoorde: For moſt, the Thruſt would ſeeme like a verye ſimple action which would neede verie little inſtruction and would maruell at the amount which has bene written about it: Howeuer, there are certaine details which neede to be emphaſiſed in order that the Thruſt can be deliuered properlie by the fencer and thus maximiſe the offenſiue potentiall of this perticuler action, meerelye haphazardlie throwinge the poynte at the opponente is not ſufficient in order to be effectiue.

The Thruſt is the primarie offenſiue action in the Arte of Defence due to ſeuerall reaſons, which will be explained: The Thruſt is the moſt efficient methode of deliuering an attack: It is quicker than a cutte due to the principalle of the ſtreight lyne and alſo vſeth leſſe muſcle power to cauſe damage: The weapon itſelfe actuallie biaſes fenſing towarde the Thruſt: The weapon hath a ſmall croſſe-ſection, and is longe and poynted: The ſmall croſſe-ſection reduces its effectiueneſſe in cutting, but the cutte ſhoulde in no waie be neglected as it is alſo a vſefull offenſiue toole: The lengthe of the weapon increaſeth the aduantage towarde the Thruſt due to the reache of the weapon. This is a weapon deſigned for gentlemanlie conteſts, and not for the battelfield; it is deſigned to ſettle matters of Honor betweene Gentlemen.

Much has been ſaid about the importance of ſpede, but it is accuracie which is more important than ſpeed: There is little vſe hauing a Thruſt which is faſter than anothers, if that Thruſt can not arriueth at its intended target: It would be better for the ſame ſwords-man to posſeſs a ſlower Thruſt that can be deliuered to the target of his choiſe rather than hauing a faſt thruſt which he has little or no control ouer. This is a technique-focuſſed action rather than one which meerelye vſeth muſcle power in ordere to deliuereth it: If the powere vſed is not focuſſed in the correct direction it will be of little vſe to the combatant. The concepte of the ſpeede of a Thruſt is actually a fallacye: There are thoſe who wyll claim that ſome experienced Gentleman has a faſt Thruſt and this is due to the ſpeede and powere at which he deliuereth his Thruſt: This is inaccurate, the ſpeede of the Thruſt is not due to ſimple muſcle powere but actuallye due to the efficiencie of motion which the ſworde-ſman vſeth in order to deliuer the Thruſt: There is ſome muſcle powere vſed in order to mooue the weapon, but the primarie reaſon that an accurate Thruſt is faſt is due to the preciſion in the methode of deliuerie: This ſimple fact can be related to all the actions of ſwordeplaie.

The actions of the experienced ſwordes-man are faſter due to efficiencie: The combatant will attempte to vſe as little energy as poſsible in the vſe of an action and as ſuch it needs to be executed in the moſt efficient manner poſſible: The leſſe extraneous actions which are vſed in the performance of an action, the more efficient it wyll be and thus will ſeeme to be quicker, euen if this is not the combatters intention: This efficiencie is a reſult of practiſe and alſo experience, the more comfortable a ſcholler with a ſet of actions, the eaſier it will be for the ſcholler to perfourme theſe actions and thus the ſeeminglie faſter they will be: The important thing with regarde to this is that it is technique which is important not the brute power of the combatant.

There

The firſt Booke

There are different fourmes of Thruſt all of which relye primarilye on the ſame technique: What differentiateth theme is the direction in which they are deliuered: It ſhoulde be noted that a Thruſt is named for the methode and direction from which it is deliuered and not in which it lands: This is due to the fact that the ſame Lyne can be targeted by different Thruſts rather than iuſt a ſingle one: It is due to this that the Thruſt are named for the direction in which they are deliuered rather than the Lyne which they target. Similar to the Lynes, there are foure directions which will define the type of Thruſt being deliuered: They are from below, from aboue, from the righte and from the lefte: Of courſe, depending on the ſituation, theſe names can be combined to giue a horizontall and verticall direction: The horizontall is giuen before the verticall for both cuttes and Thruſtes: In the ſame waie, a Thruſt deliuered purely from a ſingle direction will haue onlye one name.

The primarie Thruſt is the Thruſt that comes from belowe meaning that the hande of the ſtudente has to riſe in order to deliuer the Thruſt: This is called a *ſtoccata*: It is a Thruſt which could alſo be referred to as a normal Thruſt as it is the moſt common deliuered. The Thruſt deliuered from aboue meaning that the hande of the ſchollar has to droppe in order to deliuer the Thruſt is called an *imbroccata*: The ſimpleſt and moſt obuious poſition from which this can be deliuered is from the Guard Firſt: Howeuer this is not the only poſition from which it can be deliuered: For example an *imbroccata* can be deliuered from a Guard of Third againſt the foote or legge of the opponent. The two tearmes for thoſe Thruſts which come from the lefte and righte actuallye applie to both cuttes and Thruſtes: A Thruſt or cutte delyuered from the righte ſide of the fenſer againſte the opponent is called a *mandritta*: A Thruſt or cutte deliuered from the lefte ſide of the fencer againſte the opponent is called a *riuerſa*: This is ſometimes called a croſſe-blowe becauſe the arme has to croſſe the bodie: More will be ſayde of the deſcription of the cutte in a ſection further on in this treatiſe. Vſually to delineate between a cutte and a Thruſt, in the left and righte blowes, the word *punta* wil be added to thoſe which are Thruſts: The *ſtoccata* and *imbroccata* only will refer to Thruſts as there are further names for the cuttes: What ſhould be noted is that for the lefte-handed fenſer theſe will be reuerſed due to the chaunged poſition of the ſwoord.

The Thruſt for the moſt parte is a ſimple action, but miſtakes are often mayde in its execution: Care needeth to be taken in order that the Thruſt is executed properlie and thus effectiuelie: There are ſome common miſtakes which are often made in the execution of the Thruſt and they wyll be noted as the examination of this technique takes place. It muſt be noted that power is not required in the execution of the Thruſte: The ſimple deſign of the weapon and the Thruſt itſelf utiliſing the deſign of the weapon meaneth that only a ſmall amount of preſſure is requierd in order to do damage to the opponent: The ſimple execution of the Thruſt along with the wepons own weight is ſufficient.

The firſt thing that ſhould be noted with regarde to the technique of the Thruſt is that it is the ſhoulder which is the prime mouer in this action: The elbowe, wriſte and hande meerlye guide the poynte to its target: This enables a larger muſcle group to perfourme the maior action and thus vſeth leſſe energie: It is the ſhoulder that ſhoulde moue firſt, if one of the other ioints or partes of the arme moues firſt then the poynte could be throwen off target and wyll reduce the effectiueneſſe of the technique as a whole. Though the ſhoulder muſt mooue firſt it is not meerelye that the arme will ſwinge forwarde and backwarde: There needeth to be purpoſe in the action, and each Thruſt needeth to be perfourmed as a ſingle purpoſeful action: While the action has ſome velocitie in its action in no waie is the arm throwen: Each part of the arme actiuateth ſingley and doeth its purpoſe in the action: This is controlled by the ioints and the muſcles. While it is the ſhoulder that actiuates the Thruſt, it ſhould not moue foreward before or after the Thruſt is made vnleſſe another action is made after the Thruſt: If the ſhoulder moueth forwarde before the
Thruſt

The first Booke

Thruſt is mayde, the opponent wyll vſe this as a cue as to when the combatant will Thruſt and be able to auoid or counter it: If the ſhoulder moueth forward after the Thruſt, the combatant may force the poynt off target and wll alter the diſtance to the target: This is eſpecially important in practiſe ſo that the fenſer doth not deceiue himſelf as regard to his own Diſtance.

Iuſt as the front foote and toe is vſed to pointe the bodie toward the opponent, ſo too ſhould the hande and fingars poynte at the target when the Thruſt is made: This ſimple concepte and action will aſſiſt in the accuracie of the Thruſt. The ſhorteſt diſtance between two pointes is a ſtreight line as ſuch the ſhorteſt diſtance between the pointe of the wepon and its target is alſo a ſtraight line: It is this lyne that the poynte of the weapon ſhould follow when the Thruſt is made: The foremoſte foote ſhoulde be poynted at the target as this aligneth the bodie, as this asſiſteth wyth accuracye: The poynte ſhould neither moue vpward nor dippe in its action: The point ſhould moue directlie from its currente poſition to the target: Any deuiation from this will affect the Timing of the Thruſt and the accuracie of it.

The poſition of the hande needs to be conſidered with regard to the Thruſt, this applieth both before, during and after the Thruſt: The hand itſelf, for the moſt parte ſhoulde not chaunge poſition in the proceſſe of deliuering the poynte to its target: Changes in hande poſition will affect the direction of the pointe and maie moue it off target. Some will argue that the hande ſhoulde bee turned to Fourthe poſition in the Thruſte when it is compleated, or euen during the Thruſt: The only reaſon that this ſhould be done is in order to turne the edge towarde the opponents weapon: Some alſo claime that the hande ſhould be turned to Second poſition at the completion of the Thruſt: The ſame reaſon as before applieth: The hande ſhould remaine in the ſame poſition as it was at the beginning of the Thruſte throughout the action in ordere that the poynte remaineth on target. Some will claim that twiſting the hande and the arme during the Thruſt will increaſe velocitye and make for a more effectiue Thruſt: It maie indeed increaſe velocitie, but the deuiation in the hande can reſulte in a deuiation from the intended targete of the combatant. The ſimpleſt action in the Thruſt is the moſt efficient and will turn out to be the moſt effectiue: This is ſimplye becauſe anye extraneous mouement of the hande or arme has the potentiall to deuiate the poynt and alſo will vſe extra energie: Theſe two factors wyll reſulte in the Thruſte being leſſe effectiue. The combatant ſhould keep his Thruſt as ſimple as poſſible.

The Lunge is ſimplie a Thruſt with footeworke: The Thruſt itſelfe has a limited raunge, limited to the length of the ſworde and the length of the arme: The Lunge is deſigned to extende the range of the Thruſt in order to reach further targets by adding a Halfe-Pace to it: The footeworke attached to the Lunge can alſo be vſed in order to change the direction of the attaque againſt the opponent, this relateth to a modification of the normal Lunge. The ſtandard Lunge proiects the ſwordſman ſtraight forwarde, the modified verſions vſe other footework to change the direction of the attack: Theſe will be examined after the details of the ſtandard Lunge haue been inueſtigated: To ſtart with the principales behind the Lunge need to be inueſtigated.

Firſt of all and moſte importantly, the Lunge is one of the places where the importance of moouing the hande before the foote is demonſtrated: In the Lunge a Thruſt is made and then the ſtep followeth, hence hande before foote: This is a verie ſimple view of the Lunge, howeuer if the foot moues firſt, there is moſt likely that the ſcholler will be ſtroken before the attack is completed. Secondlie, the ſpede and power of the Lunge in its mouement commeth from the power generated by the legges: This is important if it is to be perfourmed properlie: Many wyll attempte to throwe themſelues at the grounde vſing their forwarde foote to ſtop them as the action of the Lunge: This is an inefficient methode and it is flawed: The power muſt be generated by the legges in order to proiecte the combatant forwarde in the Lunge: An in depth diſcuſſion of this wyll bee made. When the Lunge is thought of, it is a large ſtepp which is made in order to drammatically increaſe
the range

The firſt Booke

the range of the Lunge, howeuer a ſimple Half-Pace is ſufficient for the action to be called a lunge: Bothe of theſe actions relate to the ſame actions and the ſame principles: The action of the arme is ſimply the Thruſt which has already been diſcuſſed: The ſame action is vſed in this perticuler ſituation: The footwork action has alreadie been diſcuſſed ſomewhat in the ſection on footework, but more detail is required: Theſe two actions need to be combined in order to compleat the Lunge.

Eſſentiallie this is a Halfe-Pace as has beene deſcribed: The ſame principalles followe: The front foote needs to be picked vp and placed, gliding aboue the grounde not dragging: The ſpeed of the Lunge is made through the efficient vſe of the muſcles of the legges and nothing more: The power of the Lunge is generated frome the rear leg, more ſpecifically the muſcles of the vpper leg: The action of the legge is to ſtraighten the legge and thus moue the combatant forward: It is important that the combatter vnderſtandeth that the energie generated by the rear legge needs to be directed forwarde and not vpwarde as ſome wyll doe: This needeth to be executed exploſiuelye: The ſtudents rear foote ſhoulde alſo remaine ankhored and ſhould not dragge in anie waie. In the Lunge the Thruſt is made firſt and the deſcribed footeworke motion followeth: The Thruſt ſhould be made as has alreadie beene deſcribed and ſhould be almoſt compleat before the foote mouement beginneth: Howeuer, the action of the Thruſt ſhould not dragge the ſcholer forwarde in the action of the Lunge; the forward motion muſt be generated by the legges: The Lunge will require much practiſe in order to perfect and become the moſt efficient that it can be.

Something has alreadie bene ſaide of Thruſting actions which can be made againſt the opponent vſing different angles in ordere to atchieue a greater reſult: Eache one of theſe actions can be further enhanced through the vſe of footework: In moſt caſes a ſimple Pace will increaſe the effect of the attacke: The Lunge action deſcribed aboue can be projected in different directiõ, including to the rear: This is a difficult action and the ſtudent ſhould conſider carefully how to atchieue this. Howeuer the lunging actions forwarde and off at an angle will increaſe the effecte of a Thruſting attack. The *punta mandritta* can be enhaunced through the vſe of a lunge in a forwarde and righte direction: This will increaſe the angle of attacke on the opponent and make it more difficult for them to defende. The *punta riuerſa* is a Thruſting action which breaketh one of the rules of footeworke: In this the righte foote croſſeth ouer the lefte, moouing lefte and forward, in order to project the attacke in the correct direction: The attacke is directed around the opponents defence: Executed correctlie, the combatant ſhoulde be in little daunger due the attack being made againſt the opponent and the neceſſitie of defence on his parte. One of the things that maketh the Lunge a ſucceſsful action, which is often forgotten, is the Recouerie.

The Recouerie is an important part as it moueth the combatant out of the poſition founde at the end of a Lunge and back into a more defenſible poſition: In moſt caſes, this meerely inuolues the compleation of the Pace which was ſtarted from the Halfe-Pace made by the Lunge: This Recouerie maie be made forward or backwarde. In the forward Recouerie, the ſtudent merely compleateth the forwarde Pace which was ſtarted: In the backeward Recouerie, returns to his original ſtarting poſition. For the *punta mandritta* and *punta riuerſa* it is better for the ſcholar to complete the ſteppe moouing forwarde than it is to returne to the original poſition. The importante thinge that ſhould be noted with the Recouerie is that it breaks the rules with regard to Timing: In this particular inſtance, the foote will mooue before the hande: The ſcoller ſhoulde returne to a normall Guarde poſition with his feete before returning the weapon to his Gard: Proceeding in this manner means that the ſtudente will remaine with his weapon poynted at the opponent vntil he has returned to a Warde, thus the opponent remains vnder threat. The Recouer Backeward is vſeful to mooue the combatant awaye from the opponent after the attack: The Recouer Forwarde is vſeful to followe the opponente and keepe him on the defenſiue: If another opening is founde during the Recouer Forwarde, once the feete haue beene returned to poſition another Lunge may be made,

The firſt Booke

be made, eſpecially as the arm is already in poſition: It would ſuggeſt due to this that a tactical conſideration ſhould be made that a combatant on the defenſiue, againſt an opponent lunging, ſhould not vſe a ſimple Retreat Step in defence but ſtep off-line in defence this reduceth the chance of the opponent being able to follow his Lunge with another after the recouerie.

The Thruſt is the primarie attack found in the Arte of Defence due to the ſhape and nature of the weapon: It doth not requier the brute force of the cutte, and is much quicker due to the direct lynes that it takes: Howeuer, the Thruſting actions neede to be executed correctlie in order to be their moſt effectiue. The Lunge is a ſimple extenſion of the Thruſt adding a footework motion on to the Thruſting action in order to increaſe its range: The Timing of this action muſte be performed properlie in order to be effectiue, any dereliction in this perticuler action will reſult in the Lunge being leſſe effectiue and the ſtudent potentially being in daunger for his lyfe. The Lunge is only really ſucceſsfully completed with the addition of the Recouerie, which alſo muſt haue attention paid to it manie a fenſer has neglected his Recouerie to his demiſe.

Of the Cutte

He Cutte is an attack delyuered wyth the edge of the weapon: This canne be perfourmed with eyther edge in at leaſte two different methodes, bothe of whych are attempting to cut the target open. While the Cut is a ſecondarie attack to the thruſte, it is ſtill importante for the ſtudente to knowe this attack and vnderſtande howe to perfourme the Cutte properly: Meerely ſmaſhing the edge of the weapon into the opponent wyll not doe ſufficient damage to be effectiue: There is technique inuolued which is important in the deliuerie of the Cutte in order to make it effectiue.

With regarde to the rapyer, the Cutte is a ſecondarie methode of attacking the opponent, but it is ſtill a vſeful one to know: It has the diſaduantage that it is ſlower than the thruſt in its perfourmance, but it has the aduantage of being more vſeful at cloſer ranges where the poynt cannot be turned on to the opponent: This being ſaid, it is poſſible to ſucceſsfullie deliuer a Cutte and be effectiue at ſome diſtance: It is not neceſſarie to be at the Very Narrow Diſance in order for the cut to be effectiue: This is a matter of technique rather than the raunge at whych it is delyuered or the power of the combatant who is deliuering the Cutte. In combat with the rapier there will be opportunities to vſe the Cutte and the ſcholer ſhould alwaies attempte to take aduantage of theſe opportunities: One cleare opportunitie for a Cutte is when a thruſt has miſſed the opponent, with the pointe paſt the opponent with the edge cloſe to the opponent, and is onely one example: There are ſeueral other tymes where the ſimilar opportunities wyll be preſent: In order to take aduantage of theſe opportunities, the ſtudente has to be aware of them and not be too focuſſed on deliuering the thruſt.

The rapier hath two edges and thus has two edges to cut with: The important thinge with regarde to this is that both edges can be vſed to cut wyth: Often the Cutte is focuſſed on the True Edge with the Falſe Edge all but ignored: It is important that the Cutte with the Falſe Edge can be iuſt as effectiue, and indeede more effectiue in ſome inſtances; iuſt as the Cutte with the True Edg can be deliuered from a multitude of different directions, ſo too can the Falſe Edge: In ſome inſtances, the name of the direction will actuallye be chaunged in ordere to ſuite the Falſe Edge rauther than the True Edge: This is ſimplie becauſe the blowe is eaſier to deliuer with the Falſe Edge than it is with the True Edge.

In examining

The first Booke

In examining the directions of the Cutte, it muſt be remembered that eche maie be deliuered wyth both the True Edge and Falſe Edge. Some of theſe directions haue already been diſcuſſed vnder the thruſte, two to be precyſe the *mandritta* and the *riuerſa* each beeing a deſcription for a Cutte which comes from a particular ſide of the ſwordes-man againſt the opponent: The *mandritta* is ſometimes called the right blowe beeing a normal faſhioned blowe, and the *riuerſa* called a croſſe-blow in that it comes acroſſ the fenſer: Theſe are vſed to deſcribe all of the blowes which come from one ſide or the other. The ſimpleſt and moſte commonlie throwen Cutte is the *tondo*: This is a horizontal cutte deliuered parallel to the ground: They may be deliuered to the vpper parte of bodie, middle or lower: Each one of theſe has a name, from the vpper to lower they are, *alto, mezzo*, and *baſſo*: Thus, for a right-handed combatant, a horizontal blowe thrown from the right at the middle of the opponent is called a *mandritta mezzo tondo*. Mouing to the Cutte perpendiculer to the *tondo* the vertical cutte is found: A vertical cutte deliuered downeward againſt an opponent is called a *fendente*: Of courſe, if it is to one ſide or the other the righte or left delineation may be vſed as it is for all cuttes: Anye exceptions to this wyll be noted. A vertical cutte deliuered vpwarde againſt an opponent, followinge the ſame lyne as the *fendente* is the *montante*: This may be delyuered wyth eyther the True or the Falſe Edge, though moſte commonlye it is delyuered with the Falſe. The laſt direction for the cuttes that needes to be diſcuſſed is the diagonal line: A downward cutte on a diagonal is called a *ſqualembrato*. The vpwarde cuttes with the Falſe Edge are called a different name for each: For the *mandritta* ſide the Falſe Edge cutte on the diagonal vpwarde is called a *falſo dritto*, for the *riuerſo* ſide, it is called a *falſo manco*: Vpward cuttes with the True Edge along the diagonal line are alſo poſſible theſe are often not vſed due to the difficultie in order to deliuer the cutte. Experimentation with the cuttes is vſeful to diſcouer which cuttes are eaſier with which edge.

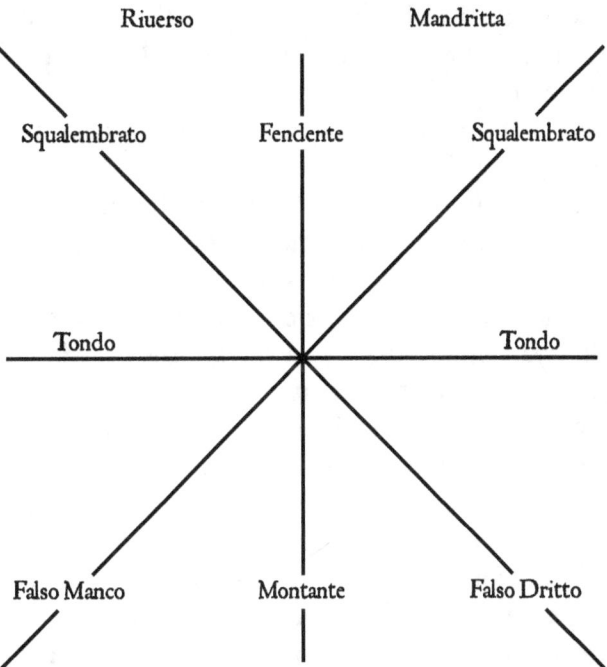

Diſtance is an important factor when conſidering the Cutte. There are two optimum places on the blade for cutting: One is located on the *forte* and the other is located on the *debole*: In both caſes, they are located approximatelie one hande-ſpan from the hylt and poynte reſpectiuelie: In a purelye cutting weapon theſe maye be referred to as the inner and outer percuſſion pointes: It is at theſe points which the ſcholar will gaine the greateſt amount of impacte and the cleaneſt blowe when vſing the weapon to cut: Should a ſcoler wiſh to cutte properlie, it is theſe parts that the ſchollar ſhould focus on and it is theſe partes which will determine the diſtance: Of courſe, the entier edge and

The first Booke

and poynte maie be vſed to cut, but theſe ſpecific ſpots wyll gaine the combatter the moſt leuerage and aduantage. The Cutte with the tip, or *ſtramazone* is a cutte which has not bene addreſſed at this pointe and wyll be addreſſed ſeparatelye as while the technique is muche the ſame as the other cuts, it is a different ſorte of blowe. The outer percuſſion pointe, that which is located on the *debole* can be vſed at ſome range againſte the opponent: This is becauſe it is ſimple inough to extende the arme and vſe the outer parte of the wepon againſt the opponent: This wyll moſt often reſult in the cleaneſt and ſafeſt cutte: Howeuer, the ſame part of the weapon canne be vſed in cloſe, ſhoulde the combatant require. The cutte at cloſe is often facilytated through the vſe of the inner poynte that located on the *forte* this is vſually a rough and tumble affair called Cloſes and Grypes: This is a ſubiect which wyll haue ſome attention paide to it in a later parte of this treatiſe. The vſe of theſe ſpecific ſpots on the weapon in cutting wyll reduce the potential for the weapon to ſimplie bounce off the opponent and for the cutte to be ineffectiue: In the caſe of the rapier, it is the technique of the Cutte which reſulteth in it being effectiue or not anie brute force applyed by the combatant. This is an important pointe and emphaſiſeth the importance of technique.

There are two methodes of cauſing damage with a ſword againſt an opponent, one which is focuſſed on the impact and the other which is focuſſed on ſlicing: While many wyll ſeparate theſe two and ſaye that theye are diſtinctiue, euen when a ſwordſman is vſing an impact cut, with the rapyer it is neceſſarye to inuolue ſome of the technique inuolued in the ſlicing cutte: This is ſimplie due to the profile of the rapiers blade: The ſhape of the weapon wyll determine the moſt ſucceſsful method for cutting: The angle of the edge is an important factor, it a primarilie cutting wepon the edge will be wide and the angle will be low: This is not the ſituation in the caſe of the rapyer; yt has a narrowe edge and ſharpe angle on the blade: This makes the profile of the wepon determine that it is ſimply not ſuited to the ſtile of cleauing blow that is found in weapons ſuch as the longſworde: It is due to this angle of the blayde that the ſlycinge action in the caſe of the raypier becomes vaſtlye more important than any ſorte of impacte or cleauing action: This ſimple fact chaunges the ſtyle in which the cutting attack with a rapyer is deliuered.

To ſtart with it will be the purelie ſlicing cutte that wyll be examined: In this caſe, the weapon is placed againſte the target, preſſure is applyed and the weapon is puſhed or drawen along the target: It is important that the preſſure of the blade againſte the target is maintained whyle the action is perfourmed: This action has much in common wyth howe a knife is vſed to cutte bread: An important note ſhould be made at this poynte in tyme that the weapon maye be puſhed or drawen by the combatant; both of theſe actions are equallie valid in the vſe of the cutt: The puſhing action is one which wyll force the hylt cloſer to the opponent, and the drawing will pull it awaie from the opponent: Each has its particular vſe in its perticuler ſituation, and the ſame actions can be vſed in both the purelie ſlicing cutte and the cutte with impact: The ſlicing cutte is one which will moſt likelie be vſed in the cloſe, but doth not preuent it from being vſed at range. The technique which is preſented is good practiſe for the following impact cut: It ſhould be noted that the ſlicing cut doth haue its limitations, it has a tendencie to be ſlower, and is moſt effectiue on expoſed flesh, it alſo, in ſome caſes, ſeemeth to be lack in ſome cutting abilitie againſte ſome different targets.

The cutte with impact is deliuered in a much more flambouyant faſhion. In fact it is deliuered much as a cleauing cutte would be, but it is not the impacte which is the primarie aime: It is true that if the blowe is deliuered too harde the weapon wyll ſimplye bounce off and the cutte wyll be ineffectiue: This is due to the ſhape of the weapon: The impacting portion of this cutte is meerelie to allow the blade to bite into the target in order to allow the ſlicing action to cauſe more damage: The ſlicing action is the ſame as deſcribed preuiouſlie excepte that the blade has alreadie beene put into poſition for the cutte: What ſhould be noted here is that the impact and ſlicing action are not ſeparate; they neede to be perfourmed as one ſmooth action in order to be effectiue: This meanes that the weapon ſhould flow, lead to the target, byte and cutte all in one ſmooth action:

The first Booke

ion: Any flowing or stopping will destroy the momentum of the cutte and reduce the effectiuenes of it: Slowing in anie forme during anye cutte wyll allowe the opponente tyme in whych to mounte a defence or perfourme some other action in ordere to counter the cutte beeing perfourmed: The cutte wyth impacte will most likelie be vsed at some distance due to the preparation required for it howeuer this doeth not preclude it from being vsed in closer.

The *stramazone* is a different style of cutte to those which haue been described euen though it vseth manie of the same principales which haue been described for the other cuttes: It is different in that this cut onlye vseth the verie tip of the weapon in order to cutte: This is the reason why it is sometimes called a tippe cutte: What should be noted here is that it is still vsing the edg of the weapon in order to do damage against the opponent: It is merely that it is the verie tip of the weapon that is beeing vsed in thys instance: It is a scratching cutte which resulteth in small cuttes, howeuer, these cuttes can be iust as debilitating, if not more so in some instances, as those perfourmed by the other forms of Cutte. The *stramazone* is vsually deliuered against those targets which will cause the moste problems for or damage to the opponent: In this perticuler instance the primarye targets are those exposed viytal areas such as the throat, or against simply debilitating targets such as the forehead in order to blinde the opponent with bloud in his eies: This cut should not be aimed at the chest due to the relatiue protection of the ribbe cage: Thus this cut should be aimed at softer, fleshier targets. It has been claimed that there are two methodes in which the *stramazone* maie be deliuered: One version of this is verye vigorous and the other whych is somewhat lesse so: One method is to deliuer the cutte in much the same waie as found in the impact cutte aboue, and the other is to place the poynte on the target and then draw it acrosse: The seconde methode described here is one that wyll not be vsed in this treatise as if the swordes-man can playce his pointe in this manner a thruste maye much moore easilie be delyuered and will cause moore damage, thus the effectiuenesse of this methode is clearly disputed: It is of vital importance that the combatant has hys Dystance correcte for the deliuerie of the *stramazone*: If he is too farre he will simplie misse the target, if he is too close the tippe of the weapon maie simplie impact on the opponent and bounce off or the cutte will simplie be ineffectiue: The combatant must be at a distance where iust the tip of the weapon wyll reache the target and thus onelye this parte will come in contact with the target: This should be practised in order that the combatter is able to do this before attempting this cutte in an incounter: The deliuerie of the cutte itselfe is much the same as the impacte cutte described aboue, with onely the tip coming in contact with the target: It shoulde be one smooth action which deliuereth the poynte to the target passes it acrosse the target without anie slowing: The tip should literallie scratch the target, a small, short, sharpe cutte. This is a verie vigorous style of cutte: Its true effect relieth on the speede at which the cutte is deliuered rather than any real impact of the weapon on target; there is verie litle if anie power in this cutte, it is the slicing action of the tip which doeth the damage.

Of the Deliuierie

The first Booke

Of the Deliuerie

N attack againſt an opponent is ſomething which vſes the techniques which haue been preuiouſlye deſcribed: This is an introduction to the concept of the attack and ſome of the elementes whych are inuolued in perfourming a ſucceſsful attack againſt an opponent: This will focus mainly on thoſe practical elements, ſome of which haue beene preuiouſly deſcrybed in the techniques of the offenſiue actions aboue, but moore on the deliuerye of theſe techniques againſte an opponent: Eſſentiallye this is an introduction to vſing the offenſiue skills which haue beene deſcribed preuiouſlye, deſcribing the other elements which muſt be taken into account and leading on to other partes of the treatiſe which wyll follow and improue the abilitie of the fenſer to deliuer a ſucceſsful attack againſt an opponent.

There is much ſaid about defenſiue and counter-offenſiue actions in manye different workes on the ſubiect, but actuallie verye little about actual offenſiue worke agaynſte an opponent: Offenſiue actions are deſcribed, but verye little is deſcribed about their ſymple application without ſome ſorte of offenſiue action frome the opponent: This puts the ſwordes-man on a verie reactiue rather than actiue footing in hys combatting, as a reſult he ſtandeth waiting for the opponent to act rather than taking the initiatiue where the opportunitie is preſent: It ſhuld be noted, howeuer that this treatyſe would not and doeth not claim that the attaque is ſomething that ſhould be taken lightlie, or ſeene as a ſimple matter of deliuering the attaque, quite the contrarie: There are manie elementes which muſte be diſcuſſed in order that the ſchollar vnderſtands howe a ſucceſsfull offenſiue action vſing eyther the poynte or edge is deliuered againſt an opponent: This is meerelye an introduction to ſome of thoſe conſiderations which muſt be made by the combatant.

The firſt thinge that muſt be addreſſed is the technicall aſpectes of the attack itſelfe: Theſe are details which are vital for a ſucceſsful attack: The firſt thinge is that the attack muſt be executed properlie: There is little vſe for an attack which is perfourmed without thought or which is ſlack in its execution: Such an attack has a high chaunce of being ineffectiue againſt euen the ſimpleſt target, thus the attacke muſte be perfourmed vſing the correcte technique: Following this, the theoreticall principals which vnderpin the attack need to be taken into account, Tyme and Diſtance being two of the moſt vitall: Without theſe principales the attacque maie faile due to manie reaſons including ſuch ſymple thinges as being Out of Diſtance or lacking the Tempo to compleat the action ſucceſsfullie: All of the principles muſt be taken into account in order that the attack is ſucceſsful.

In ſome inſtances a ſtudente will ſimplie throwe out an attack attempting to vtiliſe as much muſcle power in order to make the attack faſte: This often reſulteth in an attack whch is wylde and inaccurate: Such an attack is in manie inſtances worſe than making no offenſiue action at all: It is the accuracie of an attack which is the moſt vital element of the attack: This accuracie is parte and parcell of the technique and the perfourmance of the action as well as beeing able to ſtryke the intended target: The accuracie of an attacke in its deliuerie againſt an opponent is vital; it is more important to be able to hit anie target that the ſwordſman requireth or chooſeth to than being able to deliuer a blowe with greate velocitie: The technical aſpects of anye attack needes to be conſidered ſeriouſlie in order for the attack to be ſucceſsful.

Once the technical aſpectes are dealt with it is poſſible to examine ſome of the tactical conſiderations: Theſe are conſiderations of when the blowe is delyuered and where the blowe is deliu-
deliuered

The first Booke

ered. The optimum Tyme to deliuer an attaque agaynſt an opponent is when hee is the moſt vulnerable: The optimum Place to delyuer an attaque againſte an opponent is where he is moſt vulnerable: Recogniſing the Time and Place for an attack commeth from being able to read an opponent, this is ſomething which will be diſcuſſed in ſome detail in a latter parte of this treatiſe.

What any ſcoler, euen a new ſcholer, ſhould be able to recogniſe is when a Lyne is open or cloſed: An attacke made againſte a cloſed Lyne for the beginning ſchollare is a waſte of Tyme as the opponent is eaſily able to defend againſt it: The techniques for opening Lines are ſomething which wyll be diſcuſſed later in the diſcourſe: For the ſtudente at this pointe in tyme, it is better that the ſcholar only attaque an open Lyne: This is a place where the opponent is vulnerable to attack: The attack to an open Lyne, euen if the opponent defendeth againſt it, is much more vſeful than an attack againſte an alreadye cloſed Line: This is ſymplye due to the fact that the opponente has to vſe Time and energy in ordere to cloſe the open Line, whereas a cloſed Line is alreadie defended and therefore needes no attention paid to it: With this in place, the combatant needes to conſider his own defence againſt the offenſiue or euen counter-offenſiue actions of the opponent: With regarde to thys the combatant ſhoulde cloſe the Line in whych the opponents weapon is found: This is atchieued through the vſe of footeworke or Blade Engagement, the ſeconde of which wyll be found in a later parte of this treatiſe, the firſte of which is founde vnder the deſcription of defenſiue actions preuiouſlie deſcribed: Shoulde the fenſer chooſe that an attack with the edge is the moſt ſucceſsful waie to approach an opponent, he ſhould conſider how he wyll cloſe with and recouer from the opponent: Theſe ſorts of conſiderations will be diſcuſſed in the portion of the manuall about Cloſes and Gripes, the cloſe-quarter element of rapyer combate. Muche has bene diſcuſſed ſo farre about the optimum Place for an attacke to be deliuered; little has been ſayde about the optimum Time in which the attack ſhoulde be deliuered: Tyme is able to be manipulated in order to ſuite the actions of the combatter: This is a concepte and a ſkill-ſet which wyll require a great deal of practiſe on the parte of the ſtudente: The theoretical concepts haue alreadie bene diſcuſſed preuiouſly wyth other elements of Theorye, but it is the application of theſe conceptes which the fencer needeth and theſe too wyll be deſcribed in a later parte of this treatiſe.

Wyth theſe conſiderations in minde, both technical and tactical, there is a greate deal that needeth to be conſidered in order that the combatant is able to deliuer a ſucceſsful attack againſt an opponent: Eche one of theſe needeth to be conſidered and the releuant ſkills practiſed in order for the combatant to be able to deliuer a ſucceſsful attack againſt an opponent: In anie place where ſome thing is lacking the ſchollar can find himſelf in a great deale of trouble. Simplie deliuering the blow of poynt or edge againſt an opponent is not ynough: There are things which the ſtudente needeth to conſider in order that the attack is ſucceſsful and that the ſcholar is not alſo ſtrooken in the proceſſe of making the attaque againſt the opponent.

Of Blade Engagement

The first Booke
Of Blade Engagement

Lade Engagement is one parte of fwordplaye which the fwordes-man wyll, in fome waye, haue to participate in when engaged wyth an opponent whether he liketh it or not: This is one of the mofte importante interactions betweene the combatant and the opponent and it is all perfourmed through the weapons and their pofition: It is one of thofe tymes when the weapon becometh the focus rather than anye other elemente: Blade Engagement is an importante concept and inuolues a fet of fpecific techniques which the fcholar wyll find vfeful in his engagement wyth opponents: Vfed correctlye thefe can be vfed to defeat an opponents attack by a meere pofitioning or re-pofitioning of the weapon: Vfed incorrectlie it can leaue a fcoller expofed and at the mercye of the opponent: Thefe techniques can alfo allowe a ftudente to dominate an opponent in his engagement with the blade.

The firft thinge that is requiered in order to vnderftand Blade Engagement is a definition of what it actuallie is. Commonlie it is regarded that Blade Engagement only applieth when there is fome contact betwene the weapon of the combatant and that of his opponent: This definition is fomewhat narrowe and needeth to be expanded fomewhat. Blade Engagement is inuolued bothe when the blades are in phifical contact and alfo when there is a lacke of contact betweene the weapons: It is actuallye the pofitioning of the weapons that is importante: Thus there are fourmes and methodes of Blade Engagement which do not actuallie inuolue contact between the weapons, examples of this are the Tyme Difengage and the concept of Abfence of Blade, both of which are difcuffed below: A wepon can be confidered engaged both when the weapons are actuallie in contact, but alfo in a pofition where the blades are not actuallie in contact but are in a pofition where the combatant is denyinge a Line to the opponent, or euen caufing other aduantage or difaduantage due to the meere pofition of the weapon or the combatant.

The weapon needeth to be diuided in order that the partes of the weapon are knowen and the releuant knowledge about ech parte of the weapon is knowen: The firft diuifion that the fenfer requires is with regarde to the edges: On the rapyer there are two edges one which lines vpp wyth the knuckles and the other which lynes vp with the backe of the hand: The one whych lines vp with the knuckles and is faced toward the opponent in the Guard of Thyrd is the True Edge: The other edg which is clofer to the fenfer in the fame gard is known as the Falfe Edge: Thefe edges wuld haue become apparente in various other partes of this treatife preuiouflie: It is commonlie thought that the True Edge is ftronger than the Falfe Edge and as fuch the True Edge fhould be vfed all of the tme: This is not actually the cafe: The Falfe Edge is actuallie as ftronge, and in fome inftances, ftronger than the True Edge and as fuch both fhoulde be able to be vtilifed by the fenfer with equal comfort. The next diuifion that needes to be made is through the middeft of the weapon fo it is diuided into halfe: One halfe comprifeth the poynt and partes awaie from the hylt, the other comprifeth the halfe which is clofer to the hylte: The former is called the *debole* and the latter called the *forte*: Thefe two partes haue been noted in other partes of this treatife: There is, howeuer a thyrde parte of the weapon called the *mezzo* which is the middeft of the blade: This part of the blade comprifeth halfe *forte* and halfe *debole*: It is about this part of the weapon that moft of the Blade Engagement practifes will be made: This parte of the blade has the aduantages and difaduantages of both partes of the weapon and thus thefe aduantages and difaduantages need to be vnderftood in order for it to be vtilifed properlie: The other two partes of the blade which are vfeful for Blade Engagement are the inner and outer percuffion pointes which were difcuffed preuiouflye.

Eache

The firſt Booke

Eache parte of the weapon has its owne purpoſe, aduantages and diſaduantages, and for the ſtudente to be able to perfourme the actions of Blade Engagement ſucceſsfully each parte of the weapon muſt be familiar to him, without this vnderſtanding, the ſcholler will haue a greate deal of trouble perfourming the actions.

The concept of Abſence of Blade is to come into contacte wyth the opponents weapons as little as poſſible, and not at all if poſſible: This means that the combatant vſing this particular tactick will vſe a lot of Voids in defence and verie little Parries of the ſworde: The idea behinde this perticuler approche is to denye the opponent the information that he would haue gained through contact betwene the blades: This can be vſed by the combatant verye effectiuellie but he has to be aware of his owne poſitioning and that of the opponent: The influence of Abſence of Blade ouer the opponent is atchieued meerelye through the poſition of the weapon and the bodye in compariſon to the opponente: This canne be clearlye related to Oppoſing Poſition in that in bothe ſituatiõs an aduantage is gayned through poſitioning the weapon and primarilye without coming into contacte wyth the opponents weapon: This method is ſometimes vſed, in the moſt rudimentary faſhion by nouice fencers, who are vnſure about Blade Engagement and thus ſtay at diſtãce from their opponent. There has to be a reaſon to vſe Abſence of Blade againſt an opponent: One reaſon would be where the opponent is ſtronger than the combatter, or where the opponent clearlie has a moore dominant poſition where the blades are engaged, or where the opponente clearelie knowes moore about Blade Engagement wyth contact than he does without contact: The combatant needes to be ſure of his Diſtance wyth regarde to Abſence of Blade and alſo his own poſitioning as it is theſe two elements which compriſe the primarie elements in his defence: Sure the weapon or hande maie be vſed to Parry, but thys reſults in blade contact and thus loſſe of Abſence of Blade. In ſome inſtances Abſence of Blade will be vſed with engagement of the opponents weapon, but this engagement will onely be at the choiſe of the ſwordſman: This takes the aduantage of bothe fourmes of Blade Engagement: The aduauntage of Abſence of Blade when combined with direct contact in this faſhion is that the opponent has a much ſhorter Tyme in which to reacte to the actions of the combatant due to the ſhortened period of contacte betweene the weapons: The poſition of aduantage is alreadye gayned and the contacte happens as a parte and parcel of the offenſiue action as a reſult of the aduantage gained through the poſition eſtabliſhed by the ſwordes-man.

Blade Engagement inuoluing contact betwen the weapons is muche more complex and inuolues manie different elementes that need to be taken into account: Much of the information founde here is alſo important for the ſtudente vſing Abſence of Blade as ſome of the techniques maye alſo be vſed through this perticuler methode. Blade Engagement with contact is the moſt commonlie thought of methode of Blade Engagement when thoughts of Blade Engagement are preſente: As ſuch in order to ſimplifie things, Blade Engagement vſing Abſence of Blade will be referred to as Abſence of Blade and that vſing more contact betweene the weapons wyll be called Blade Engagement: This being the caſe, the reader muſt realiſe that both are actuallye methods of Blade Engagement and are iuſt as releuante to the vſe of the rapyer as one another. In Blade Engagement the moſte importante thinge is the contact betwene the wepons, this being ſaid it is therefore vitall for the ſcholar to be able to feele through the weapon in order to be able to find out what the opponent is dooing and thinking: This feeling through the blayde is referred to as *ſenſo di ferro* in the Italyan, *ſentiment du fer* in the French, *tacto* in the Spaniſh, and *fülen* by the Alamanes: The fact that it is preſent in the languages and treatiſes of theſe many nations preſents example of its ſignificance: For conuenience, it is the Italyan *ſenſo di ferro* that will be vſed throughout this diſcourſe: This idea relateh to an almoſt ſixth ſenſe where the ſwordeſman is able to feel through the blade of his weapon as if it were an extenſion of him: The abilitie to do this alloweth the ſwor-
ſwordes-man

The firſt Booke

ſwordes-man to feel what the opponent is doing before the opponent actuallie moues and ſupplies a ſort of precognition of what the opponent plans to do, but this is only if the ſcholar is practiſed in this.

Along wyth this feeling through the blades, the ſcholer ſhould alſo be aware of the degree of preſſure exerted by the opponent vpon hys weapon: Thus the ſtudente will be able to feele a ſtrong preſſure or a weak preſſure: This can be related purelie to ſtrength, but alſo to other aſpectes ſuch as the poſition of the blade: What muſt be cleare to the ſcoler is that there is aduantage in both: Clearlye the ſtrong may puſh awaye the weake, and in ſome inſtances the ſtrong maie reſiſt the ſtrong: The former will reſult in aduantage, the latter in a neutral poſition where neyther weapon will moue: What is not realiſed by ſome is that the weak vſed againſt the ſtrong can alſo be vſed as an aduantage: If the combatant yeeldeth to the opponents ſtrength, this can reſult in the opponent being mooued out of poſition and out of Line, thus leauing the combatter a Line through which to attack: The vſe of weak againſt weak will reſult in the ſame ſituation as that founde with the ſtrong againſte the ſtrong: This is ſomething which the combatant ſhoulde be well aware of: The tacticall games that can reſult between the combatters as a reſult of the ſimple vſe of the ſtrong and the weake are moſte intereſting. What ſhould be noted howeuer is that the ſtrong and weake principle is principallie applied when the blades are in contact at the *mezzo* or *debole*: But the ſame aboue can reſult where the weapons are in contact *forte* to *forte*: A weapon is always ſtrong regardleſſe of the ſtrength applied at the *forte* where the opponents *debole* is againſt the ſchollars *forte* at which the ſcholler has the aduantage.

Gaining aduantage when combating with a rapyer is all about being in a dominant poſition, it inuolues the combatant being in a poſition where he has an aduantage ouer the opponent: For the moſte parte this inuolueth the combatant hauing his weapon in an open Line where an attack can be made againſt the opponent: For the combatant vſing Abſence of Blade, this is atchieued by poſitioning the weapon in an open Line: Once achieued the ſcoller ſhould attack immediatlye along that Lyne: For the combatter vſing Blade Engagement this inuolues the vſe of *ſtringere* in ordere to open a Lyne. *Stringere* is the application of a ſmall amounte of force againſte the opponents weapon in order to force it out of Lyne whyle the combatants weapon is mooued in Line: It is importante to note that the ſtudentes weapon doeth not ſmacke into the opponents weapon it is placed there and then preſſure is applied to it: The ſcoler ſhoulde vſe the edge of the weapon in ordere to gette the beſte feeling through the weapon and alſo the beſte preſſure for the action: Depending on the ſide the preſſure is applied wyll determine whether the Inſide or Outſide Lynes are opened: The poſition of the wepon in either the High or Low Line will determine whether it is the High or Lowe Line which is opened: The ſecond aduantage of the vſe of *ſtringere* is that the location of the opponents weapon is knowen when this technique is applied: This wyll alſo ſhut the opponents weapon out of Line and thus wyll not be threatening the combatant: Once the *ſtringere* is applyed, and the aduantage is gayned, the ſwordes-man ſhoulde attacke immediatlye. There are other techniques which can be vſed to open a Line to the opponent, and iuſt as with the *ſtringere* once this is atchieued a ſtraight attack ſhould be made along the Lyne which has bene opened as ſoon as it is opened. *Stringere* is alſo applyed where the blade is merely placed into a poſition where it dominates a position where it can attack i.e. into an open Line: It doth not neceſſarily have to moue the opponents blade: The fenſer, to achieue this, needeth to angle their blade properly in the correct angle, poſſibly alonge with their bodye poſition to achieue the ſame reſulte as hath been expreſſed wyth the Hard Engagement option preuiouſly: Once this Soft Engagement option has been atchieued, as with the Hard Engagement option, an attack ſhould be made into the open Line created by the poſition.

The important thing with regarde to *ſtringere*, Blade Engagement and indeede all techniques of ſwordplaie, there muſt be purpoſe behind the technique: A technique ſhould not be perfourmed

The first Booke

perfourmed for no reason a schollar must haue a cleare reason for perfourming a technique againſt an opponent, and the primarie reasons shoulde be that it eyther defendeth the scholler or gaineth an aduantage ouer the opponent: An action performed without a purpose wasteth time and energy and can also leaue the scholler vulnerable to an attack by the opponent.

Stringere is vsed in order to open a Lyne: This is performd in order to attack, shuld the student not responde to this particular action he will be strok, as has beene described aboue: Regardlesse of the choise of technique vsed the optimum response to hauing a Line opened and the opponents weapon in place to attacke is to close the Lyne again: This maye be atchieued through seuerall different techniques includinge the vse of footeworke: What will be presented belowe is some of the options vsinge Blayde Engagement. The countere to *stringere* when vsinge Blade Engagement is to performe a Disengage. This may be perfourmed vnder or ouer the opponents blade, but its purpose is to close the Line which the action of *stringere* has opened. The Disengage is an action to chaunge the Lyne of engagement and indeed also counter *stringere* by closing the Line as a result: This action is perfourmed by shiftinge the poynte of the wepon vnder and arounde the opponents weapon to moue to the other side of the weapon, or by shifting the poynte ouer the opponents weapon for the same result: It is encouraged that the Disengage vnder is performed more often as the Disengage ouer, or Cut Ouer, can leaue the combatant exposed for a short amount of tyme while the point is not in Line: It is true that the Disengage vnder, called for the purposes of this manual the Disengage, leaueth the combatant exposed also in the middle of its perfourmaunce, but this is a shorter period of tyme as compared to the Cut Ouer. The action of the Disengage, eyther ouer or vnder changeth the Line of engagement and opens the opponent to attack: This aduantage should be taken aduantage of immediatlie, attacking as a result. Of course, there is also a counter to this action: This action is called the Counter-Disengage: It is performd in order to chaunge the engagement backe to where it was when the *stringere* was perfourmed: Essentiallie the action of the Counter-Disengage is to perform a Disengage around the opponents Disengage, or indeede in response to the Disengage of the opponent: As can be expected, there is also a counter to the Counter-Disengage: With little surprise this is a second Disengage performd in order to counter the Counter-Disengage: Vnsurprisinglye, this is called a Double-Disengage: Thys is a seconde Disengage perfourmed in order to counter the Counter-Disengage: The actiõ itselfe is actuallie the same as the Disengage.

From the performance of *stringere* to the perfourmaunce of the Double-Disengage is what could be called a string of engagements: Eache action which follows is designed to counter the preuious action. The importante thinges to note here are that at eache completion of an action there is the opportunitye for an attacke made by the persone who has compleated their action, and it is this which should be the focus rather than a simple battle of changing engagements: Also eache action is perfourmed in response to the preuious action: There is little poynte to perfourming a Counter-Disengage if the opponente has not perfourmed a Disengage and so forth: Once again, this comes downe to purpose and the purpose of each of these actions muste be vnderstood in order that they can be vsed effectiuelie.

There are two further actions which chaunge the engagement and are designed to do this: One is the Half-Disengage, and the other is the Time Disengage: What should be noted here is that each of these are a Disengage and therefore is the start of the responsiue actions: Eache can be countered by a Counter-Disengage perfourmed effectiuelye in response to the action: The firste action is the Halfe-Disengage: This is a disengage which changeth the engagement from a Highe Lyne engagement to a Lowe Line engagement or vyce versa: What shoulde also be noted in this engagement is that it wyll also chaunge the engagement from Inside to Outside or vice versa as the normal Disengage does: The actiõ itself is exactlie as it is described a half a Disengage: Therefore the action of the Disengage is stopped halfe waye through in ordere to chaunge the Line alonge the vertical

The first Booke

vertical engagement: The poynte is therefore placed aboue or belowe the opponentes weapone in order to chaunge the Line along the vertical line of engagement. The Time Difengage is an action while fimple is fometimes difficult to grafp due to the fact that it is different from the other forms which haue been prefented fo far: Each of the actions which haue been defcribed aboue worke around the actual and phifical placement of the opponents weapon, the Time Difengage does not: The Time Difengage workes arounde the pofition of the opponentes blade in Tyme, and thus in motion rather than being ftatic. In the Time Difengage, the Difengage is perfourmed around the pofition where the opponentes blade wyll be rather than where it is: This action is vfed againfte an action in motion: For example a Time Difengage can be vfed in refponfe to the performaunce of *ftringere* before the *ftringere* actuallye comes into contacte wyth the fenfers weapon: This particular action vtilifes much of the theory of Abfence of Blade in that the wepon doth not come in contact with the opponents weapon before the action is perfourmed, but onely may once it is compleated: This is an action which fhoulde be perfourmed in concert with an attacking action, moft fimplie a thruft, in order to be effectiue: The action itfelfe is the fame as a normal Difengage, the poynte is mooued vnder the opponents weapon in order to chaunge the engagement: The difference is that the weapon is alwaies in motion and does not come into contact with the opponentes weapon before or during the action: The other difference is that it can be perfourmed while the combatant is preparing to thruft, and thus chaunge the Line of the attack as it is perfourmed: This is one of the few times when the poynt of the weapon maie deuiate from its target in the performance of the thruft.

    Attacks on the Blade are actions in which the fwordes-man vfeth their weapon to open a Lyne in the opponent in order to attack it: Some of thefe are fimple actions of force where others are much more fubtle: Eche one regardles of the methode it vfeth to difplace the opponents blade has technique behinde it: None of the actions meerely bafh the opponents weapon out of the waie.

    The Beat is one of the fimpleft actions vfed in order to difplace the opponents weapon: It is alfo one where manye people will make miftakes in its deliuerye: The Beate is an Attack of Force and it vfes impact power to mooue the opponents blade out of Line: This action was brieflie mentioned vnder the Parry preuiouflie: This is the action in its offenfiue mode: The vntrained fcoller will often, by inftinct, attempt to fwat their opponents weapon out of the waie in order to delyuer an attack: In fome waies this is the beginnings of the Beat: The Beat, howeuer, vtilifeth this action and addeth certaine pointes in ordere to be more effectiue: The firft point heere is that the fcholler fhould aime to vfe the percuffion poynt againft the opponents percuffion point: Thefe pointes were difcuffed when addreffing the Cutte: Secondlie, the fcholar fhould be vfing the edge of his wepon againft the opponents: The flatte wyll be fubftantiallie leffe effectiue and will often leade to the poynte beeing out of Line: Thirdlie, the fcholler fhoulde be vfing his wrift and fingars to generate the power for the Beat, the arme fhould not withdraw in anie waie to generate power: The fimple action of the wrifte directing the action againfte the opponents weapon combined with a vigorous clofing of the hande is all the power that the ftudente will requiere in order to delyuere this action. Vfing thefe three points, from a Guard of Thirde, the hande is turned to Fourth if the combatant is on the Outfide of the opponents weapon or Seconde if he is on the Infide of the opponents weapon: This fhould be combined with the vigorous actions of the wrifte and fingars in order to compleate the action. The correct perfourmance of this action wyll be fufficient to beate the opponents weapon out of Line and leaue an opportunitie for an attacke: The thruft which followeth fhould be a fimple extenfion of the poynte from the pofition the fcoller finds himfelfe in: If too much power is vfed the poynt of the fcholars weapon will alfo be out of Line: The Beat is about the correct deliuerie and amount of force in the correct place. The Beat is moft vfeful againft opponents who leaue their poynte out longe, efpeciallye if they are holding theyr weapon too loofe or too tight. In the Beat, the place is as importante as the tyme of the deliuerye:

                                                                                                                            The

The firſt Booke

The beſt defence againſt a Beate is to Diſengage as the Beate is delyuered, another defence is to vſe the powere of the Beat in ordere to moue the poynte of the weapon back into Line, or ſimplie not place the weapon in a poſition where it can be beaten.

While the Beate vſes impact force againſt the opponents blade, the Preſſe and related actions vſe an increaſe in preſſure againſt the opponents blade in order to open a Line through which the combatant can attack: While the Beat vſeth impact to diſplace the opponents weapon, the Preſſe and aſſociated actions do not: In fact, impact when vſing theſe techniques reduces the effectiueneſſe of their deliuerie. The key piece of theorie which is required for the vſe of theſe techniques the weak and ſtronge partes of the blade: Eſſentiallie the Preſſe places a ſtrong combatters weapon againſt a weak opponents weapon and forces it out of the way by increaſing preſſure: The Preſſe is the ſimpleſt forme of this kinde of Attack on the Blade: The *mezzo* of the blade is vſed againſte the *debole* of the opponentes and the weapon is forced awaye by preſſure of one on the other: The ſame can be vſed where the ſcoler places the *forte* of his blade againſt the *mezzo* or *debole* of the opponents: The opponents weapon needes onelye to be moued enough ſo it is out of Line of the ſcholer: The ſcholar muſt vſe the edge of the weapon againſt the opponents: The flat is vſeleſſe for this technique: The weapon ſhould not impact on the opponents wepon, but be placed there: The increaſing preſſure ſhould be made as the combatant moueth his weapon into Line at which time an attack ſhould be made: This is the principle of all of the preſſures. The Preſſure Glide takes this concept a little further as it vſeth the increaſe in preſſure not onely to diſplace the opponents weapon, but alſo to place the combatants weapon into Line and euen ſtart the deliuerie of the attack: In this perticuler caſe the poynt of the weapon will moue cloſer to the opponent as the preſſure againſt the weapon increaſeth: So much ſo that all the ſtudent has to do is to continue extending his arm in order to delyuere the attack at the end: In this particulare caſe the blades wyll come into contact with the ſcholars *mezzo* on the opponents *debole*, the ſcholler will mooue his weapon forwarde increaſing the preſſure on the opponents weapon forcing it out of Lyne: The poynte of the ſcholers weapon wyll graduallie be further and further into Line: At the final poynte of extenſion, the ſchollars *forte* will be againſte the opponentes *mezzo*: Wyth the angulation of the blayde the combatants *debole* will not come into contacte with the opponentes weapon due to the reſultant poſition at the completion of the action: In this waie the combatant will alwaies be in the ſtronger Blade Engagement poſition: If the ſtudentes poynte is not forced cloſer and cloſer to the opponent whyle the opponents is forced further and further out of Line, then the action is being performed incorrectlie. The beſt defence againſt this attack is to catch the opponents blade by performing a Parry againſt the increaſing preſſure: This can be enhanced by retreating in order to chaunge the Blade Engagement: Chaunging the Blade Engagement is the keye to defeating the Preſſe and related actions, making the ſchollers weapon ſtrong againſt the opponents.

The Flowing Attack is vnlike the Beat or Preſſure in that it vſes very little contact between the weapons: In ſome inſtances it maye not euen come into contact wyth the opponents weapon at all: This Attack on the Blade is all about the placement of the weapon rather than forcing the opponents weapon out of the waie: It is a verie ſubtle but verie faſt attack reſulting in a ſimple thruſting attack at the ende: In manie wayes it could be miſtaken for a ſimple extenſion of the arme into a thruſte againſte the opponent: This action controls the Lyne by the meere preſence of the weapon againſt the opponents: There ſhuld be no preſſure againſt the opponents weapon during this action and there ſhould be no impact agaynſt the opponents weapon eyther: The Flowing Attack is perfourmed by the placement of the weapon in Line againſt the opponents: The meere poſition of the weapon makes the opponents weapon out of Line. The attack itſelfe is perfourmed verie cloſe to eyther edge of the opponents weapon: The edge of the ſcholars weapon ſhould be turned towarde the opponents weapon in order to cloſe it out of Line: From this poſition, the combatant extends
the weapon

The first Booke

the weapon toward the opponent vſing the poſition of the weapon cloſe to the opponents in order to open the Line and attacke in a ſingle flowing action: The poſition of the weapon preuenteth the opponent from replying downe the ſame line: This is a faſt action and ſhould be performed vigorouſlie. The defence againſt the Flowing Attack is to Parry in the direction of the weapon in order to cloſe the Line: A Retreat Steppe in this inſtance is aduantageous.

  Controlling the opponents weapon is one of the keys to being victorious in a combat wyth an opponente there are Blade Engagement actions whych aſſiſts in this: They are often referred to as a group of actions called Taking the Blade: This eſſentiallie deſcribes the action of taking the controll of the weapon awaie from the opponent and placing it ſomewhere it is of more vſe to the fenſer. Vſing theſe actions a ſwordes-man canne chaunge the Lyne of Engagement or euen regaine controll of the encounter through a chaunge of engagement: Theſe actions are all verye ſimilare in their perfourmance and alſo purpoſe: For thoſe actions where the Line of engagement is changed by the action, the ſcholer ſhould always engage the opponents blade with his *mezzo* or *forte* depending on where the blades ſitte: Should the ſtudente attempt to do this wyth the *debole* he will not be able to gaine a ſufficient mechanical aduantage or control ouer the opponent: In order to mooue the opponents weapon, the ſcholar will need to turn hys hande: The direction is determined by where the ſcoler wiſheth to direct the opponents weapon to: The hande maie be turned eyther clockwiſe or anti-clockwiſe depending on the deſyre of the ſcholler, but ſpecial note and attention ſhould be paid where the pointe of the opponentes weapon croſſes ouer the bodye of the ſcholar: The hande ſhoulde be turned about the wriſte: There ſhould, for the moſt parte, be verie little mouement in the reſt of the arm: The ſchollar ſhoulde vſe a circuler action in the turne in order to turn the opponentes weapon to the location requyered, and not further: Eache direction that the blayde can be mooued, verticallie, horizontallie and diagonallie can haue its owne name, but the principale of the action and its perfourmance is much the ſame: The onely difference really is the direction in which the opponents weapon is moued: Should the principles of the actions preſented aboue be followed, the combatter ſhuld haue little difficultie figuring out howe to moue the opponents weapon in anie direction he maie chooſe, for the purpoſes of referring to theſe actions later, the term Bind will be vſed to deſcribe the action, and a direction indicator wyll be vſed.

  There is an action, as indicated preuiouſlie, that enableth a ſwordeſman to regaine control ouer the weapons during a combat: This is called an Enuelopment. Externallie it looks like a muche the ſame as the action of the Binde whych has beene deſcribed preuiouſlie except that in this action the blade compleateth the circle and looks like it has come back to where it ſtarted, this is not actuallie the caſe as a chaunge of Blade Engagement has alſo occurred duringe the perfourmaunce of this action: The purpoſe of this action is to regaine control ouer the blade and this is atchieued through this chaunge of Blade Engagemente. A combatants weapon has the aduauntage where the *debole* of the opponents weapon is placed on his weapon neaer the *forte* of the wepon: Shoulde the reuerſe be the caſe then the combatant is not in control: The Enuelopment is vſed to gayne this controll: To perform the Enuelopment, the ſcholer ſhould lift their point ſo that their *debole* is about the opponents *mezzo*: This will gaine the ſcholar a meaſure of ſtrength on the weapon and alſo ſome control as well: Should the ſtudents weapon be on the Outſide of the opponents weapon, the weapon ſhoulde be turned to the Inſide: Should the ſchollars weapon be on the Inſide of the opponents weapon it ſhoulde be turned to the Outſide: The important thinge about this turning, and indeede with all actions of Taking the Blade, is that contact muſte be maintayned throughout the entyre proceſſe: Otherwiſe the ſcoler will loſe control of the opponents weapon: The circulare motion of the hande ſhould be a compleate circle, but not more than a compleat circle the weapon ſhould end vp on Line when it is compleated. The circulare action with the hande ſhoulde ſhift the engagement ſo that the opponents *forte* will end vpp on the combatters *debole*: If it does not then more angulati-
                           angulation

The firſt Booke

ion of the blade is required in the turning. It ſhould be noted that this wyll be in the ſame Line as when the action ſtarted: The ſcholer ſhould giue ſome conſideration to couering that Lyne as ſoone as the action is completed.

In the caſe of both the Bind and the Enuelopment, they are actions which can be countered: The countering is atchieued by the application of force at the correct tyme in order to ſtop the turning mocion of the actiõs: In the actions deſcribed, there is a ſpotte in all of them where the engagement is not ſo ſolide betweene the blades: This maie be accompanied by a ſlipping feeling between the blades: Should a combatante wiſh to ſtop the action which is being perfourmed, all he has to do is to turne his weapons edge towarde the opponentes weapon at this poynte and holde firme with his weapon: In moſt inſtances it will reſult in both weapons meeting at the *mezzo* of each, which is a neutral poſition: The important thinge is that the force needeth to be applyed at the correct tyme in the action. Againſte ſome actions allowing the actions mocion to carre the ſworde and then continuing with the velocitye of the weapon can alſo be effectiue, but the ſtudente needs to be aware of the conſequences of following the action and the potential harme inuolued: As in all actiõs which ynuolue Blade Engagement, information is paſſed betweene the two combatants during the contact betwene the weapons, and care needes to be taken in theyr perfourmaunce: Should the applicable theorye be followed and note taken of the engagement, then the ſcholler ſhoulde be able to applie actions of Blade Engagement ſucceſsfully againſt the opponent.

In Tyme

N action in ſwordplay can be deſcribed as being In or Out of Time: This is vſuallye determined by whether the action is mayde at the correct moment and is ſuited to the ſituation: Eſſentiallye, an action whych is perfourmed In Tyme is one which is perfourmed at the moſte ſuitable time for that action: An example of an action perfourmed In Tyme is a thruſte which is directed againſt an Open Lyne on the opponent where the poſition of the thruſt preuenteth an immediat counter-attack from the opponent: The attack is alſo mayde where the opponent is ſtationarye and not attacking hymſelfe: This is becauſe the combatant is makinge hys attack while the opponent is ſtationarie and thus not acting againſt the combatant, and againſte an open target: This concepte hath alreadye beene diſcuſſed in the Theorye: It is the practicall applicaytion which is important here.

Another important elemente of determining whether an action is perfourmed In Time is whether there is the correct amount of Tempi auailable for the action to be perfourmed: Of courſe for a ſimple thruſt onelye a ſingle Tempo is required, but for a moore complex action, more Tempi wyll obuiouſlye be required: Vſinge the preuious example, if the two combatants are at Narrow Dyſtance, a ſimple extenſion and thus a ſingle Tempo wyll onely be required: Shoulde the combatants be at Wide Diſtance, the ſcholer may haue to cloſe on his opponent, and this maie requiere the expenditure of an extra Tempo to moue forwarde, if this is the caſe, the ſcholler may find himſelfe Out of Time for his action, where both combatants mouements haue to be taken into account that thinges get more complex. Shoulde the ſchollar in the example vſe a lunge and thus a ſingle Tempo, the ſame ſituation as deſcribed aboue wyll ſtill reſult and thus he wyll be In Tyme, ſo long as the Diſtance is correct: This alſo giueth a practicall example of the influence of Diſtance on Tyme.

Whether

The first Booke

Whether an action perfourmed is In or Out of Tyme is dependent on the situation more then the action perfourmed: The same thruste mayde by the combatant in the example woulde be Out of Time if the opponent was thrustinge at the same time, and of course the resulte woulde be worse for both: The same thrust would also be Out of Tyme if the combatant was not in position, or if the opponente had the entended Lyne couered, as this would requiere additional Tempi to open or chaunge Lynes: Should the opponent be attacking first a correct action In Time would be a defence of some kinde, and thus a defence againste the in-bound attack of the opponent: Thus the student must be aware of the situation in order to determine the correct response and thus remain In Time. For the most part, where the opponent attacks first, the action In Time will be a defensiue action of some kinde by the scholler: This follows the First Principalle: Obuioussie where the situation is correct and the schollar attacks first, it is the attack which will be In Time.

Of course there are those situations where the swordes-man will deliberatelie moue Out of Time in ordere to atchyeue his goal: Thus it is vseful to determine whych of the other Tymes which are vsed is In or Out of Tyme: This is bothe for demonstration purposes and also for theoreticall application of these Tymes. Double Time is a vse of Tyme in the Arte of Defence which clearlie falls within the idea of In Time: The opponent attacks, the combatant responds with defense firste, reacting to the Time presented, and then followes with his counter-attack, vsing two Tempi: Single Time workes in muche the same fashion as Double Time except the two actions are blended ynto a single action: The defensiue action is combined with the offensiue action in a single Tempo in response to the attack of the opponent, the fact that the combatant respondeth wyth the defence againste the attaque meanes that it followeth the Tyme present and thus also falleth within the idea of In Tme. The remayning two Tymes which are vsed in swordplaye, Counter-Time and Half Time do not reallie followe this format and are as suche not so easye to deale with: The action in Halfe Time is one which is bothe offensiue and defensiue in the same instant, but without the deliberatelie defensiue action of Single or Double Time: The action in Halfe Time attacks the opponents attack before it is compleated, intercepting it before it striketh: Thus this is an offensiue action in a situation where the combatter should be defending himself and thus is Out of Time, yet is also a defensiue action in that it is countering the opponentes attacke, and as such is In Time: This makes half time truly *half*, half In Time and half Out of Time. The action of a Counter-Time response is one which is an offensiue action directed againste the opponent while he is attacking, an attack launched to counter an attack, of course, this resulteth in an attack where a defensiue action shoulde reallye be made, thus makinge the action of Counter-Tyme, Out of Tyme: There coulde be some argumente that this action also counteres the opponents offensiue action and thus would make it In Tyme, but the very name of the action, Counter-Tyme, demonstrates euidence to the contrarie as it is literallie against Time.

The actions which are In or Out of Time are dependente on the situation in whych the combatant findes himselfe: In a normall situation at Narrow Distance the difference betwene an action In or Out of Time can mayke a big difference, at Wide Distance it is lesse importante, but still needeth to be considered: Thus Tyme and Distance are related once again: Of course, should the combatters come within Narrow Distance and engage in Closes and Gripes, the difference betweene beeing In or Out of Time can decide the outcome of the encounter: The concept of Priority in this situation is moste vseful and is related verye muche to beeing In and Out of Tyme: The In Time action at this Distance is determined by Prioritie: If the combatant is acting he acteth offensiuelie, if reacting, defensiuelye: The onelye waye to breake this pattern is to vse an action Out of Time, but this must be done at the correct Time or the scholar will find himself strook: More will follow about actions at this Very Narrow Distance, and the elements which surround it.

Of Prioritie

His Practice in Modern and Elizabethan English

The first Booke
Of Prioritie

He theoretical elementes in regarde to Prioritie haue alreadye beene discussed: This is a more practical discussion of howe it operates in combat: The first thinge to be noted is that Prioritye is primarilie related to close combat, Closes and Gripes, howeuer the same principles can be applyed at Narrow and euen Wide Distance: There will be a further discussion of Closes and Gripes later in which the conceptt of Prioritie wyll be demonstrayted to be significant and thus requires special attention: For the purposes of the current discussion it is the application of Prioritie in general: This is a discussion of the actiue and the reactiue, the attacker and defender.

The swordes-man wants to gaine Prioritie in order to be able to act against the opponent: The opponent also wants to gaine Prioritie in order to act againste the combatant: Priority describes the condition of the requiered action of the combatant or the opponent: If the opponent attacks firste, the Prioritie, and indeede the In Tyme responfe is to mount a defence againste the attacke, thus in this ynstance the opponent has Prioritye and the combatant does not: Actiõs performed following Prioritie also follow Tyme and are performed In Tyme: Another way to describe this is to say that the combatant who attacks first is the actiue and the other is the reactiue: In Prioritie the combatant muste responde to the action of the opponent if they are the reactiue: A simple example follows as suche: two combatters, Arthur and Bartolomeo, meet one another on Garde and Arthur maketh a thrustinge attack againste the other, thus gaining Prioritie: Bartolomeo must respond to the action and as such Parries the thrusting attack: One acts, the other reactes: Once the Parry is made Bartolomeo maye then counter-attacke Arthur, thus gaining Prioritie, to which Arthur muste responde: This simple example describeth how Prioritie is gained and chaunges in a simple fashion, obuiouslye things can be much more complex.

Where one attacks before the other, the other must follow or be able to immediatlie counter the attack: One combatant maie remaine on the actiue and the other maie remaine on the reactiue if the situation playeth out that waye: This is something which can happen at close quarters due to the minimal Dystance and minimall Time: Howeuer, at Distance where the Dystance is longer and so is the Time, the Prioritie can chaunge, though it maie not alwayes work out as such. In general, the longer the Distance and Tyme, the more chaunces the reactiue combatant will haue to chaunge to being the actiue: Obuiouslie, the shorter the Time and Distance the lesse chaunces the combatant will haue to change the Prioritye: This demonstrateth a relationship betwene Time, Distance and Prioritie.

The mayne application of this concepte is in close combat: In thys situation the combatters neede to be aware of what is going on in order to be able to act efficientlie and to their own benefit: Should Arthur and Bartolomeo find themselues at the close the importance of Prioritie increaseth greatlie, should Arthur cutte at Bartolomeo in the close, Bartolomeo will haue little Tyme to react and wyll thus vse a Tempo to defend, at which Time Arthur may spende another to attack again: This situation will leaue Bartolomeo on the defensiue as if he doth not defend he will be striken by Arthur: This is what Prioritie reuolues around, the action a swordsman must take in order to suruiue the incounter wyth the opponent: The onlye way for Bartolomeo to suruiue is to continue to defend while trying to either leaue from the incounter or finde a place in which he can chaunge the Prioritie.

Euery

The first Booke

Euery combatant ſhould do his beſt to get on the actiue or offenſiue, remembering to enſure his defence in the proceſſe, and to ſtaie there: Following Prioritie and remaining In Time, the reactiue can only defend: If he is to change this ſituation he muſte either diſengage from the incounter and ſtart again, or go Out of Time. In order to change the ſituation ſomething needs to change in the ſituation: The combatter needeth to make Tyme to make that change and then force that chaunge on the ſituation and the opponent: Manipulating the Time is one way to atchieue this end, as is chaunging the Diſtance or the Blade Engagement: An example of changing Prioritie woulde be if Arthur makes his cutte *mandritta ſqualembrato* againſt Bartolomeo, and inſtead of ſimplie Parrying to block Arthurs weapon, Bartolomeo vſeth an angled Fourth to deflect the cutte and haue it ſlide toward the hylt ſtopping it, he chaungeth the Blade Engagement and giues himſelfe Tyme to reſponde with a *riuerſa tondo*, thus chaunging the Prioritie: Indeede the action of the Parry and the Cutte can be perfourmed as one ſingle fluid motion, giuing him euen moore Tyme: This is onlye one example of how the chaunge can be made.

One waie of thinking about Prioritie is what canne the ſwordes-man do in a ſingle Tempo or action in reſponſe to the current action? In this waye eache action is meaſured againſte that of an opponent: One attacks, the other defends: One action eache at a time, this taketh into account the action of an opponent as well as the action of the combatant: The ſcoler needeth to be thinking about Prioritie in this manner in order to be able to vſe it properlie: The actions haue nothing to do with the ſpeede of the actions, meerely the actions themſelues: Eache action needs to be taken into account: An attack is made, one action: The weapon is withdrawn after the attack, one action, and ſo forth: Euerye action of combatant and opponent needeth to be taken into account in this perticuler proceſſe: Each inſtance that the actiue combatant is not attacking the defenſiue combatant, there is an action whych can be perfourmed in order to chaunge the Prioritie: In this waie more actions can be founde which can be vſed to chaunge the Prioritie. The difference between Very Narrow, Narrow and Wide Diſtances ſhould be taken into account through this particular proceſſe: At wider Diſtance there wyll be more opportunitie for actions which neede to be taken into account.

Prioritie is deſigned to haue the ſcholer think about what he needeth to do at that perticuler Time and howe he can go about gaining the aduantage in the current ſituation: In ſome inſtances there will be a verie ſimple reſponſe to the current ſituation and in others it may be much more complex: The neceſſarie thing for the ſchollar is to enſure that the action which is perfourmed enſureth that the scholar remaineth guarded againſt the attack of the opponent: The idea of Prioritie delineateth betweene the attacker and defender, actiue and reactiue combatters: The actions and deſcriptions of changing the Prioritie are not neceſſarye as there are manye and varyed methods of atchieuing the reſult which is requiered: Prioritie is a concept which can be applyed to all ſituations in fencinge and one whych the fencer ſhoulde conſider at all tymes.

Of Double Tyme

The first Booke
Of Double Tyme

Ouble Time is the firfte form of Time that the ftudente wyll bee introduced to when they ftart to fence in this methode: This forme of Fenfing Time feparateth the defence and the counter-attack againft the opponent into two actions: It meaneth that the actions can be feparated for practife and that the fcholer can be fure of theyr defence before launching a counter-attack againfte the opponente: This forme of Time has alreadie beene defcribed in the Theorie fection and it is the application of this in a more practical fence that is to be defcribed.

    Shoulde the opponent launch a thruftinge attack againfte the combatant, feuerall refponfes could be made: The obuious refponfe to the attack wuld be to Parry the opponents attack and then launche an attaque backe agaynfte them: This is the definition of the Double Tyme refponfe to an opponents attack: The aduantage of this is that the fcholar canne make fure that the Parry has been effectiue againfte the attack before the counter-attack is launched: This is the definition of the defenfiue playe, being that the defence is primarye and the counter-offenfiue action is fecondarye to enfuring that the defence is effectiue: This forme of refponfe will be flower than other fourms of refponfe which wyll be defcribed later on in this manual, but the aduantage is that the defence can be enfured before the counter-attack is launched: The other aduantage is that this forme of fwordeplaie alfo followeth the Firft Principale: The defenfiue action of the Parry canne be increafed by the vfe of Voids or Footeworke to enfure that the fcoler is fafe from the attack of the opponent.

    The combatters, Arthur and Bartolomeo, ftart in a Guard of Third, Bartolomeo maketh an attack to the High Outfide Line of Arthur: In refponfe, Arthur perfourmes a Parry of Thirde with oppofition to couer the Line, and alfo perfourms a Halfe-Pace in retreat in order to increafe the Diftance: The defenfiue action here defcribed vfeth two actions in a fingle Tempo in order to enfure that Arthur is fafe then he mooues to his counter-attack: Vfing the engagement made through the Parry Arthur thruftes along the Infide Lyne of Bartolomeos fwoord and ftriketh him in the cheft vfing a *ftoccata* and placing him backe in Diftance by the return of the foot vfed in retreat: The counter-offenfiue action againfte the opponent vfeth a feconde Tempo thus compleatinge the action defcribed in two Tempi, being a perfect example of a Double Tyme refponfe to a thruftting attack againft the High Outfide Line: The action defcribed feparates the defenfiue action, in this cafe a Parry of Thyrde, from the offenfiue action, in this cafe a thruft in *ftoccata* vfing the alreadie engaged blades: This is the definition of a Double Time action. The aduantage of perfourming the actions in this manner is that the defence can be enfured before the counter-attack is launched in order to kepe the fcholler fafe from the initial attack: This is a forme of Fenfing Time, and a methode of defence that the fcoler fhoulde familiarife himfelfe with: This forme of attaque and counter-attack conformeth to bothe the concepts of In Time actions and alfo Prioritie: Anie actiõ where the defence and counter-attack are feparated as fuch is a Double Tyme refponfe.

                                                          Of Single Tyme

The first Booke
Of Single Tyme

Ingle Time is the next logical ſtep in diſcuſſion from Double Time: The difference betwene Single and Double Tyme is that while in Double Time the actiõs of defence and attaque are ſeparated, in Single Tyme the defence and counter-attack are blended into a ſingle action, thus vſing a ſingle Tempo: It is often ſeene that in a Single Time action there is a ſimple blur of motion as the ſwordeſman attacks into the opponents attack, but this is not actuallie the caſe: While the reſult of a ſucceſsful Single Time action may appeare as ſuch there is an action of defence preſent in the reſponſe to the opponents attack: The reaſon why it maie appeare as though the ſwordſman has meerelye attacked into the opponentes attack is that the actions of defence and counter haue beene blended into a ſingle action: There is actuallie a defenſiue action performed in the Single Time reſponſe, but it is combined with the counter-attack, making it difficult to notice in the action.

The opponent attacks the ſcholar and the ſcholler launcheth out of his Garde perfourming a reſponſe which both cloſes the Lyne, thus defending him, and attacks the opponent all in a ſyngle action: This is the eſſence of the Single Time reſponſe: It is much faſter than the Double Time reſponſe as it combineth what is done in two Tempi into a ſingle Tempo: It is howeuer important that the ſcoler is accurate in his defence otherwiſe he can finde himſelfe empald vppon the opponents weapon: The Single Tyme reſponſe relieth vppon the combatant being accurate in his defenſe and his attack: He combineth the ſimple actions of Parry and Thruſt into a ſingle action vſing a ſimple action which defendeth and offendeth in a ſingle Tempo.

In the demonſtration of the Double Time reſponſe the combatters ſtarted in Guarde, one attacked the other defended, vſing two actions and then counter-attacked, vſing the ſame demonſtration the Single Tyme reſponſe can alſo be demonſtrated: The combatants, Arthur and Bartolomeo ſtart in a Gard of Third, Bartolomeo maketh an thruſt to the High Outſide Line of Arthur: In reſponſe, Arthur cloſeth the Lyne by turning his hande into the ſeconde poſition to engage Bartolomeos blade wyth the True Edge, and in the ſame motion thruſteth forward with a *ſtoccata*, ſtrikinge the Bartolomeo in the cheſt: Footworke motions may be vſed to enſure the ſafety of the defence and the ſucceſſe of the attack, moſt likelie they wyll be of a forwarde nature: The defenſe and counter are bothe preſent as they were in the Double Tyme reſponſe to the ſame action, howeuer in this inſtance the defence is to merely cloſe the Line by the turning of the hande: What ſhould be noted is that this is the ſtart of the Parry of Thyrde: The turning of the hande cloſeth the Lyne and alſo prepareth for the thruſt with oppoſition which is perfourmed once the hande is put into poſition: The thruſt is then made from this poſition as a compleacion of the action rather than as a ſeparate action as in the Double Time reſponſe. The Single Tyme reſponſe is faſter than that of the Double Tyme reſponſe but the ſcholler muſt be ſure that his defence is ſufficient to defend him againſte the attack of the opponente: Thus the ſtudente muſt be familiar wyth the action: Without the defence, the ſchollar maye ſtrike the opponent, but is likelie to be ſtrooken: The ſcoler ſhoulde be ſure of his actions before attemptinge to perfourme the Single Tyme reſponſe to the attack of an opponent.

The Single Tyme reſponſe to the opponents actiõ can be extremelie effectiue as the action giueth the opponent verie little time to reſpond to the counter-offenſiue action: The ſtudente ſhoulde practiſe the ſymple actions of defence and attacke before attempting this forme of reſponſe: The relationſhip between Single and Double Tyme is cloſe as the actions of one canne prepare the
ſcholare

scholare for the actions of the other: In order to perfourme a Single Tyme responfe properlie, the combatant needeth to be hable to perfourme the actions of defence and counter-attacke in a fyngle Tempo, but clofe the Lyne of the incoming attack of the opponent properlie: Defence is ftill a vital parte of the action in Single Time, without it both the combatant and the opponent are likely to be ftroken. While it would feeme that Single Time refponfes go againft both Prioritie and Time, it is not actually the cafe as a defence is being mounted againft the opponents attack before the counter is made.

Of Counter-Time

He action in Counter-Time is directed againfte the opponent when they attack: This is an action which is performd againft Tyme, where Double Time, defence then attaque, is feene as the normall refponfe to an opponentes attack: This is literallie againft Tyme: When an attack is performed by the opponent the vfuall refponfe is for the combatante to make a defence of fome kinde and then mount an attack: In the cafe of Counter-Time the attack and defence are perfourmed in a fingle motion, but vnlike Single Time no fpecific thought is really made about the defence: Sure the combatant doth thinke about defence, but this is made as a confequenfe of or adjunct to the attacke whych is made againfte the opponent: The defence is vfuallye couered by fome other afpect fuch as the pofition of the weapon in comparifon to the opponents, Footeworke or the Voide: This is not a clear defence as is found in Single or Double Time.

Some examples of Counter-Time neede to be made in order that the fcholer vnderftands exactlye howe this methode operateth: Vfing the common example prefented in bothe Single and Double Time, the differences will be demonftrated as to how Counter-Time differs: Arthur and Bartolomeo ftarte in a Guarde of Thyrde, Bartolomeo maketh an attack to Arthurs High Outfide Lyne: In refponfe, Arthur launcheth a ftoccata againfte the Bartolomeo clofinge the Lyne with his weapon preuenting the Bartolomeos weapon from coming backe in and ftrikinge him: This defenfe can be enhanced by a diagonal ftep to the forward and towarde the Outfide Line: The weapon fhoulde ftrike Bartolomeo in the cheft: This is a Counter-Time refponfe to an attack with a thruft to the High Outfide Line. Arthurs pofition needs to be exact in order for him to remaine vntouched: This is a verie precipitous refponfe to the attack of his opponent: An example needeth to be made of a refponfe to a Cutte: Should the Bartolomeo deliuer a cut riuerfo mezzo tondo againft Arthur, the fame refponfe can be mayde, catching the Cutte wyth the forte of the weapon in the thruft: What fhoulde be noted is that it is the pofition of the weapon alonge wyth the footeworke whych both defendeth Arthur and enhanceth hys attack againfte Bartolomeo: Vfing thefe refponfes, the refponfe maie be made againft eyther a thrufte or a Cutte: Indeede vfinge the correct pofition and the correct refponfe the combatant maie alfo delyuer either a Cutte or a Thrufte in refponfe to the attack of the opponent: The thruft is vfed as the primarie example as this is the moft aduantageous attack in manye inftances.

The Counter-Time refponfe is effectiue due to the fpeed of the refponfe to the opponents attack: This fpeed of the refponfe leaueth verie little time for the opponent to refpond: Indeed it leaueth euen leffe due to the commitment to the attacke mayde by the opponent: The Counter-Time

The first Booke

Time responſe is also effectiue due to the fact that it is againſt Tyme and is the vnexpected reſponſe to an attack: The normal reſponſe is to make a defence firſt and then counter-attack, the Counter-Time action in manie waies putteth the counter-attack firſte and the defence is a conſequenſe of poſition: Wythe regarde to the ſpeede of the mocion, the Counter-Time reſponſe is actuallye quicker than the Single Time reſponſe in that for Single Time to happen the opponents attack has to be compleated, whereas in Counter-Time the opponents attacke is not compleated: Howeuer, euen with all the aduantages of this perticuler reſponſe noted, care needes to be taken in its vſe as it is riſkie vnleſſe the defenſiue options are couered properlie: If the ſcholar is out of poſition by verye little then he can be ſtruck by the attack of the opponent: This is a preciſe reſponſe and not meerelye throwing an attack againſt the opponents: The Counter-Time reſponſe being againſt Time is Out of Time in that it doeth not defende before an attack is made: It is alſo againſte Prioritie in that the fencer ſhoulde be defenſiue and is not, but alſo ſhould be noted that it is one of the wayes to change Prioritye, forcing the opponent to defend againſt the attack of the combatant rather than compleating his owne and thus forcing hime on the defenſiue. The Counter-Time reſponſe is verie effectiue but needeth to be practiſed and vſed properlie in order to be effectiue.

Of Halfe-Tyme

Or ſome ſcholars of the blade, the concept of Half-Time is difficult to fathome as it is thought that it inuolueth diuyding a Tempo, and in ſome wayes it doth: The Tempo which is diuided is that of the opponent rather than that of the cõbatant: The action in Half-Time is deſigned to interrupt the action of the opponent and thus preuent him from completing it, thus cutting the Tempo: Half-Time interrupteth the action of the opponent and preuents it from beeing compleated rauther than allowing the action to be compleated as it is in the other Tymes deſcribed: The reſponſe of the ſwordes-man to the attack of the opponent is to make an action againſt the attack itſelfe.

The action in Halfe-Time ſhoulde ſtoppe the opponentes attack from beeing compleated: Howeuer, other defenſiue actions ſhould be taken in order that the combatant is not ſtriken: This maie be in the form of the poſition of the bodie or weapon, Footework or a Voide. The thing that differentiateth Half-Time frome the other Tymes is that rauther then aiming to deliberatelie attack the opponent it attacketh the opponents offenſiue action: Thus ſtaying it in the middeſt of the Tempo, hence the name Half-Time: This action againſte the opponents attacke is effectiuelye an attack and defence in the ſame action: The counter by the ſcholar attackes the opponent but this is done in order that the attaque of the opponent is defeated and thus the ſcholler is defended from the attack: An example of the action followeth as ſuch; Arthur and Bartolomeo ſtart yn a Guarde of Thyrde, Bartolomeo ſtarts to make an thruſt to the High Outſide Lyne of Arthur: In reſponſe Arthur performs a Slope forward to the Inſide and thruſtes *ſtoccata* to Bartolomeos forearme before the thruſte is compleated: Another reſponſe to the ſame attacke inuolueth the Arthur Trauerſinge to the Inſide and performing a *falſo dritto* to the wriſte or forearm of the attacking arme of the opponent: In all inſtances, the opponents attack is interrupted before it is compleated and the combatant perfourmeth a Footeworke action in order that he is not ſtrook by ſome action of the opponent.

The action in Half-Time is effectiue due to the ſpeed and Tyme of the reſponſe: The opponent has really no tyme to reſponde in that the combatter interrupteth his action before it is all-

allowed

The first Booke

wed to be compleated: Euen from a purelye theoretical pointe of view the opponent has no Tyme as it is caught in the midle of the action and therefore in the middeſt of the Tempo: The other aſpect whych maketh the Half-Time reſponſe effectiue is that the counter is agaynſte the opponents attacke thus the ſchollar doeth not haue to cloſe particularlie farre in order to reache the opponent, vſing the Very Narrow Distance of the opponents weapon, arme and hande. The riſke of the vſe of the Halfe-Tyme is if the attack is not accurate in the attack and the opponentes attack is allowed to be compleated: Thus care needes to be taken in the vſe of this form of Tyme. The action of the Half-Time reſponſe to the opponentes action is both In and Out of Time, iuſt as it is bothe for and againſt Prioritye, and indeede it is for the ſame reaſon: The action is In Time and for Prioritie in that the action defendeth againſt the opponents attack, but it is alſo Out of Tyme and againſte Prioritye in that rauther than ſome purelye defenſiue action vſed againſt the opponent, he is vſing an offenſiue one, thus attacking where the ſtudent ſhuld be defending. The action in Half-Tyme is verye effectiue if vſed and executed properlye, iuſt as wyth the othere Tymes, it doeth ſtand out in that it catcheth the opponent in a half Tempo rather than allowing him to compleat his action and reſponding to this.

Cloſes and Grypes

Loſes and Gripes is the parte of combate where two combatants come into cloſe contact with one another: This form of incounter with an opponent maie or may not occur during an incounter, howeuer it is important to vnderſtand the reaſons for it happening and how to deal with the ſituation regardleſſe: The elements preſented heere are all baſed vpon the theoretical elements which haue been preuiouſlie diſcuſſed: Some of theſe elements are more important than others: Cloſe work is vſuallye the reſult of the combatters entering Verie Cloſe Diſtance: This is the diſtance at which cloſe worke happens and where the principles preſented will applye: Some of them maie applie at wyder Diſtances alſo, but their primarie effect is in the cloſe.

Cloſes and Gripes, cloſe quarter combat, or cloſe work happens for two real reaſons: Either the ſituation was deſigned by one of the combatants, or the combatants haue failed to control Diſtance: The ſecond option vſuallie happens when two ouertlie aggreſſiue combatters come into contact with one another: It can alſo happen with one more aggreſſiue combatant and the other who loſes control of the diſtance between the combatants: A ſwordes-man maye alſo deſign to cloſe with the opponente and this alſo needes to be conſidered as there are thoſe reaſons where a combatant maie chooſe to cloſe with the opponent in order to affect contact in cloſe contact.

A combatant maye chooſe to engage in Cloſes and Grypes where he is the ſtronger of the two combatants: This may enable him to haue more control ouer the ſituation: On the other hand a combatant who can moue quicklye maie alſo chooſe cloſe contact due to his ſpeed: This bringeth into accompt other reaſons for chooſing cloſe contact: Weapon length may dictate that the ſcholer may haue the aduantage in the cloſe: A ſcholler may alſo chooſe to engage in the cloſe where his ſkil leuel is clearlie aboue the opponents and he belieueth that he can gaine an aduantage ouer the opponent in the cloſe: Obuiouſlye a combatant in all of the oppoſite ſituations will decide that action at the cloſe is not aduantageous to him and will moſtly chooſe to auoid it: A ſimplie weaker or ſlower combatant will chooſe not to put himſelfe in a ſituation where thoſe attributes he does not haue are the primarie: Clearlie a combatter with a longer weapon will want to ſtaye moore at range in order to take aduantage of the length of the weapon: Alſo it is vnlikelie that a combatant with leſſe ſkill in the cloſe

The first Booke

the clofe will choofe to put himfelfe in fuch a fituation where he has little or no aduantage.

The action of the Clofes and Gripes can be verie confufing and is verie quick due to the clofeneffe of the combatants: Manye fcenarios could be defcribed and prefented here and ftill elements woulde be miffed in the defcription: The action at the clofe is quite varied and manye different things can affect the outcome of the incounter. Rather than giuing precife defcription of euerie incounter poffible, fome moore generall rules wyll be prefented: This is moftlye due to the fact that much of what happeneth at the clofe happeneth often by inftinct rather than defign: The ftudente needes to act and reacte to the fituation he is placed in rather than attempting to finde the perfect anfwere to the fituation: This is the firft element that muft be vnderftood, the fcholar fhould follow his inftincts rather than fighting them: This primeuall inftinct is vfeful to the fcholler and fhould be harneffed: With the generall defcription prefented, it is then poffible to examine the important elementes prefente in order to maximife the aduantage for the fcholler and to keeping intact.

The concept of Priority as prefented is vitall to the ftudent in order for him to furuiue the clofe: If the fcholar is attacking he has Prioritye, if he is notte he is defending and doth not: In this fituation an offenfiue action of any kind qualifies as an attack; be it an actual attack or the controlli'g of the opponents weapon: Prioritie is important as if the fcoler is not defending when he doth not haue Prioritie there is a highlie likelye chaunce that he will find himfelf ftrake: Howeuer, it is poffible for Prioritie to change and this is fomething that the fcholer will want to do if he does not haue Prioritie: This can be atchyeued through the vfe of Counter and Halfe-Tyme actions: Thefe are particularlie effective as their fpeed reduceth the chances of the opponent to refpond to the action of the combatant: The fcholar fhoulde applie the appropriate anfwere to the problem prefented: If the opponent is beginning his attack then the fenfer can vfe Half-Tyme to ftop it: If the attack is in motion then the fcholler will more likelie haue more fucceffe vfing a Counter-Tyme action: Care needeth to be taken in the application of thefe times to enfure that the ftudente is guarded duringe the action vfed. Once Prioritie and thus the aduantage haue been gayned, it is important that the combatant control the fituation and remain in the aduantage: In many fituations this is moft eafilie atchieued through ftaying on the offenfiue and keeping the opponent defenfiue: Thus the Prioritie is maintained: The opponent needs to be kept off ballance fo that he is vnable to regaine or gaine Prioritie ouer the combatant.

In the clofe, cutting actions tend to be the primarie form of attaque againft the opponent: This is the cafe due to the poynte often being too awkwarde to bring on target againft the opponent this is due to the weapon length: While the pointe is the prime methode of ftriking the opponent and the other Diftances in the Very Narrow Distance, it is the edge which is vfuallie moft conuenient this is due to the Diftance. Cuttinge mufte be done efficientlie and with the mocion of the combat, a Cutte is much eafier to delyuere when the bodie is mouing in the direction of the Cutte than when it is mouing awaie: The fchollar fhuld be aware of this: It is alfo eafier to deliuer a Cutte when in the correct pofition and in the correct mocion, for this reafon accurate and efficient footeworke in the clofe is vital: For the moft part the lower parts of the edge wil be vfed, once again due to the Diftance: This alfo refulteth in more leuerage for the fcholler in deliuering the Cutte, thus the Cutte will be more effective when it is deliuered: Vfing Cuttes rather than the poynt maie require a change in focus for the ftudente as the deliuerie of a Thruft is more efficient than the Cutte and targets which are eafilie vulnerable to a Thruft may not be fo with the Cutte: While the Cut is primarie, there maye be opportunities for a Thruft to be vfed and thus it fhould not be ignored in the clofe.

The off-hand is a moft vfeful toole in the clofe: This is the cafe whether it holds an item or not: In fome inftances it is actuallye more aduantageous for the fwordes-man to be not carriynge fomething in his offhand as the offhand can be more effectiuelie vfed to manipulate the opponents

weapon

The first Booke

weapon than an item in the offhand: The firſt thinge that ſhoulde be noted about the vſe of the offhand in the cloſe is that it ſhould be vſed againſt the opponents weapon and not their perſon: This is the caſe for two reaſons whych are interrelated: Firſtlye controllinge the weapon preuenteth the weapon from being moued or moouing around into a poſition where it may ſtrike the opponent by deſign or by accident: Secondlie, if the fenſer faſtens on to the opponente rather than their weapõ, the opponent maye vſe theyr other hande to take the weapon and ſtryke the fenſer wyth it: When the weapon is controlled the combatant controlleth the offenſiue potentiall of that weapon and can mooue it in ſuch a waye that it wyll not ſtrake the combatant duringe the action. In controllinge the weapon there are thinges which need to be conſidered: The firſt is the location of the hande on the weapon: It is optimum for the off-hand to be placed on the hylt of the opponentes weapon as this is where the ſcholar will gaine the moſte controll ouer the weapon: Shoulde the ſcholler not be able to place their hand on the hylt of the weapon then the ſtudent ſhuld place his hande as cloſe to the hylt of the weapon as poſſible: If the ſcoller ſhoulde place and keepe his hande higher on the weapon, he will haue leſſe controll ouer it: This can reſult in the opponent beeing ſtill able to vtiliſe the weapon eyther defenſiuelie or euen offenſiuelie: The next conſideration is whether the combatant ſhoulde cloſe his hande or leaue it opene when it is placed on the opponents weapon: There are aduantages in bothe methodes of control iuſt as there are alſo diſaduantages to both methods: The cloſed hande would ſeem to gain the ſcholler the moſt control ouer the opponents weapon, but alſo giueth the potential that the ſcholars hande maie be cutte if the ſwoord is withdrawn from the graſp: The ſolid graſp on the weapon allows no mouement, and thus can be both an aduantage and alſo detrimental: The open hande has no ſolid contact with the opponents weapon ſo is eaſilie able to moue vp and down the weapon depending on the deſire of the ſcoler and would ſeeme to giue leſſe control: Shoulde the opponent attempte to cutte the ſtudentes hande, it can eaſilie be remoued or moooued: The open hande alſo does not ſupplie an inſtinctuall reſponſe from the opponent to want to drawe the weapon awaie as graſping the weapon often does: With theſe conſiderations in minde it wuld ſeeme more aduantageous to haue the hande more open than cloſed, though a gentle cloſing of the hande rather than a hard graſp could alſo be ſeene as vſeful: Regardleſſe, the offhand placed on the opponentes weapon needeth to flowe with the combate in ordere to ſtaie attached to the weapon: Through this harmonie with the combat the ſcholler can enable the offhand to place the weapon in a more aduantageous poſition for the ſcholar allowing bothe offenſiue and defenſiue potential.

 The action in the cloſe is diuided into three ſections, the Entrie, the Action and the Exit: Each one of theſe partes is important to the ſcholer and he needeth to vnderſtand howe each parte of the cloſe can affect the outcome of the contact betwene him and his opponent: The Entrie is the initial parte of cloſe combat where the two combatants cloſe on one another or one combatant cloſeth on the other: The Action is the attacks, defences and mouements made while the two combatters are in contact at cloſe range, and the Exit is where the combatants Break Diſtance from one another or one combatant Breaks Diſtance from the other: Eche parte needeth to be conſidered from a defenſiue and an offenſiue pointe of view: With regarde to this it is the defenſiue which ſhould be foremoſt in the ſcholars mind to enſure that he can ſuruiue the encounter vnſcathed: At no time ſhoulde the ſcholler ſacrifice his defence in order to ſtrike the opponent: It is true that ſome of the defence wyll haue to be reduced in order that an attack agaynſt the opponent can be made, but this ſhould not be made by leauing his defence fatallye flawed: All partes of the action in the cloſe are importante and none ſhould be neglected.

 Where the Entrie is made againſte an opponent it needeth be done in ſuch a waye that the ſcholler endeth engaged with the opponent in an aduantageous poſition: This means that the ſcholer needeth to haue Prioritie at the end of the Entrie. Where the Entry is made againſt the ſcholar he ſhuld he íhuld do his beſt to enſure that he has at leaſt euened the poſition with the opponent by the time the Action has ſtarted, euen if this ſimplye meanes enſuringe his defences againſte the action of the opponent: Where the Entrie is attempted againſt an opponent and the aduantage is not gayned or maintained, the ſtudent ſhould mooue immediatelie to the Exit and attempt to enter againe when the aduantage is preſent: This Exit may be as ſimple as withdrawing from the engagement, enſuring that hys defence is actiue: In all parts the ſcholler ſhould be prepared to mount ſome ſort of defence againſt the opponent. Shoulde the Entrie be ſucceſsful and the ſcholler has Prioritie, he ſhuld do euerything to maintain the aduantage againſt the opponent.

The Action is the parte where moſt of the action will take place and is where Prioritie is the moſt important: Shulde the ſcholler find himſelfe in a poſition where he does not haue Prioritie he ſhould be doing euerything to make hys defence and Exit: Succeſſe at this can leaue the ſcholler in a poſition where he can make another Entrie: Forcing a bad ſituation in any parte of the action of the cloſe can leaue the ſtudente wounded or worſe.

A voluntarie Exit is vſually made after a ſucceſsful attack againſt the opponent, euen in this ſituation, the ſcholar ſhould make ſure that his defences are vpp and that he returns to a Garde poſition: Where the Exit faileth a ſcholler maie be drawen backe into the Action and this is the reaſon why it is important that he remaine on the defence and come out on Garde: Should the ſcoler ſimplye Exit at any time with no conſideration of defence, he can ſtill be ſtrooken by the opponent: An inuoluntarye Exit is where the ſcholler hath loſte the Prioritye and is on the defenſiue, in thys ſituation he is forced out of the Action in order to increaſe his defenſiue potentiall. Where the opponent has made the Entrie, the ſcholler wanteth to gaine Prioritie in order to at leaſt force the opponent to Exit: Forcing an Exit on the opponent putteth them on the defenſiue and giueth the ſtudente the aduantage: This is the beſt reſult where the Entrie was forced by the opponent: In all inſtances the ſcholler ſhoulde ſee to his defences in order to enſure that he is not ſtruck in anie part of the proceſſe.

Reading the Opponent

Eading the opponent is a vſeful and indeed eſſential ſkill: For manie ſwordesmen it wyll be an automatick thinge, an abilitie actiuated in the ſubconſcious in order to prepare a reſponſe to the opponentes attack: Howeuer it can alſo be an actiue ſkill which maketh it much moore vſeful to the combatant ſo he can begin to knowe thinges about the opponent before he euen commes on guarde againſt him: Euerye thing that the opponente doth giueth a clue as to the calibre of the opponent and howe he wyll fight againſt you: Some of theſe details are ſmall and ſeeme inſignificant, but euery peece of information can be vſed: Thys is moore then obſeruaytion, it is yntelligence gatheringe, through the information diſcouered about the opponente, theories maye be mayde about howe the opponent wyll acte and reſpond to actions againſt him in ſwordplaie: No peece of information about the opponent ſhould be diſcarded out of hande as irreleuant.

Euen before the opponent pickes vpp a wepon thinges can be noted about him: Watch the waye he mooues off the feelde and information can be gayned as to howe he will mooue in combat: Simple thinges as the waye he moueth acroſſe the grounde and howe he reacteth to the actions of others will tell you ſomething about the opponent: His interactions with others, euen in a ſocial ſit-
ſituation

The firſt Booke

uation, can tell you ſomething about him: Being calm or agitated in conuerſation or in a ſocial ſituation canne giue you ſome idea about the waye he will acte on the fielde: His conuerſations and the waye that he maketh them can alſo tell you about howe he wyll act wth a weapon in his hande: Is he arrogant and ouerbearinge: Or is he calme, reſpectfull and collected in hys conuerſations wythe others? Each one of theſe allows you to ſee a litle below what he proiects to others around him and alludeth ſomewhat to his thought proceſſes: Thys is important as it is theſe vnderlying proceſſeses which moſt often determine how a combatant wyll act againſt an opponent.

In this particular part of the obſeruation, the moſt vſeful information commeth from how the combatter acts againſte another: Eſpeciallie in tournament ſpecial attention ſhoulde be payd to howe combatants act and fight one another: See whether the tactics chaunge dependent on the opponent or whether they ſtaye the ſame againſte all opponents: What ſorte of thought proceſſes are happening, are they actiuelie thought or more baſed on inſtinct and ſubconſcious thought: Do the combatters thinke about what they are doing, or are they iuſt reacting to the circumſtances preſented to them? Eche one of the anſweres to theſe queries giues a ſmall clue about how the combatant will acte againſt vs: Reading the incounters betwene other combatters is a vſeful ſkill and can ſay a lot about other combatants and can giue clues as to howe they wyll act againſt others: This is one of the moſt vſeful reaſons to watch encounters between other combatters.

While ſome of the information gayned about a combatants equipment can ſometymes bee miſleading, this information can alſo be vſed to tell ſomethinge about a combatant: The firſt thing that ſhoulde be noted is howe well fitting the equipment is: Does the ſcholer ſeeme comfortable in the gear? The leuell of comfort wyll affect howe the ſcoller moues and plaies againſte an opponent: Could the equipment be borrowed? Vnfamiliar equipment wyll not mooue as well as that whych the ſcholler knows well, this is eſpeciallie the caſe for weapons: Next thing that ſhuld be noted, eſpeciallie if the equipment fitts well and therefore is moſte likelie not borrowed, is the condition of the equipment: This can deſcribe howe muche care is taken of the equipment and this can tell howe much reſpecte the combatant has for what he is dooing: It can alſo deſcribe whether the combatter practiſes often or not: The age of equipment can euen giue ſome impreſſion of howe long the ſcholar has beene practiſing the Arte of Defence, eſpeciallye if the ſchollar ſeems to be verie comfortable wyth it: A ſwordes-man who has been fenſing for an extended period of tyme with the ſame equipment will get comfortable with it: Brand newe equipment can indicate a leſſe experienced ſcholler, while older equipment can indicate a more experienced one: With more focus on the weapon, a hylt which is cleane and vntouched can indicate a wepon which has not been vſed before and may be vnfamiliar, or a new weapon which may indicate a newer ſchollar: Shulde the weapon haue wear marks and euidence of vſe, this can indicate that the ſcholler is comfortable with the weapon and has vſed it frequentlie; this can alſo indicate a more veteran combatant as it is often the wepon which is chaunged the leaſte: The experience of the combatant is often written in the condition of the wepon where this is obuiouſlie due to combatiue contacts.

Once the geare has bene examined it is next to looke at the combatant himſelfe: Clues wyll be preſented in his preſentation. Simple things ſuch as how he ſtands on Guarde are important: It is vſeful to ſtart from the bottom and worke vpwarde and then outwarde: The waye that the opponent ſtands is important and this beginneth wyth the feete: Is eyther of them poynted at their opponent? This can indicate ſome idea of the direction that the combatant is moouing or may moue: The waight diſtribution betweene the feet can alſo giue ſome indication as to which waie the combatter maie mooue from the poſition he has taken: The ſpread betwene the feete can alſo tell ſomething about howe the ſcholer maye moue as this ſpread moueth the centre of ballance vpwarde or downeward: The poſition of the feete is directlie related to the poſition of the legges: Bent knees indicate a combatant who is willing to moue and wyth ſome velocitie: A ſcholler with

ſtraight

The firſt Booke

ſtraight knees wyll finde it more difficult to mooue as quicklie as one whoſe knees are bent: The feet and legges are connected and thus muſt be read aparte but alſo as a whole: This information will deſcribe how the ſchollar wyll mooue about the feelde and what ſorte of eaſe this maye be done with along wyth ſome indication of ſpeed.

The bodie is the largeſt maſſe of the combatant and it is that to whych all of the peripherall partes of the bodie are ioined, due to this the poſition and carriage of the bodye can tell a lot about the opponente: The poſition of the bodie can alſo reueal thinges about the opponent, for example a bending of the bodie along with the cramping of the extremities might reueal feare in the opponent. The poſition of the bodye is important, eſpeciallye whether it is vpright or crouched and howe comfortable the opponent feels in this poſition: An vpright poſition of the bodie keeping the bodie ſtreight and tall can conuey confidence; it alſo releaſeth the muſcles and relaxeth the fencer: This combatant is readie for action and is no doubt confident in his poſition: A crouched poſition which is obuiouſlye ſhrinkinge and tenſe reuealeth that the combatants muſcles are alreadie actiue and the fenſer will react ſlower, this maie be due to feare: A ſpecial note ſhould be made: A crouched poſition which is deſigned to be in that forme for the Garde wyll be noted as the opponent wyll be comfortable and not tenſe, his limmes will be at eaſe and readie for action: Careful note ſhould be made as to the difference betweene the two.

The heade is the next largeſt maſſe and the poſition of which can giue ſome indication as to the direction the fenſer may moue: More detaile can alſo be reuealled where the combatant can ſee the opponentes face: Facial expreſſions can reueal what the opponent is thinking and alſo their ſtate of mind: It can alſo reueal what ſorte of condition they are in, moſt of theſe things are obuious, but can alſo be forgotten. Attention ſhould be payd to all of the heade: A combatter whoſe heade is leant foreward may indicate that they are trying to ſhrink and therefore are fearefull: A head which is vpright bewrayes confidence in what the combatant is dooing and alſo enableth the combatant to moue wyth leſſe reſtriction than if the heade was tylted to one direction or another: This is due to the ſkeletal alignment of the ſpine and heade. A tylting of the head can indicate a direction to which the ſchollar maie go; this is eſpeciallie the caſe where the bodie is alſo tilted in the ſame directiõ: The combination of the bodie and head account for the largeſt maſſe of the indiuidual and giueth a great deale of detaile as to where the combatter wyll go: While the extremities maie be mooued in different places, the bodye muſt moue as one and muſt follow together: There is no ſeparation poſſible.

The armes and handes muſt be examined togither: Whyle a ſmall mouement of the hande canne make a greate deale of difference, groſſe mouements muſt come from the mouement of both hande and arme, thus it is beſte to looke at the bigger and then examine the ſmaller: In the currente poſition whether the arme is ſtraight or bent can make a greate deal of difference: The relaxed arm which is eaſie to moue wyll be more ſtraight than bent: A bent arme vſeth muſcles and this burneth energie: The mouements wyll alſo be ſlower due to hauing to releaſe tenſion and then re-tenſe the muſcles: Conſider the poſition of the arme firſt and then examine the handes: Examine the poſition of the hande, this wyll giue an indication as to the direction that the weapon wyll goe, this is determined by the hande poſition: In cloſer detail the grippe on the weapon ſhould be noted: Determine whether the hande is relaxed or tenſe: Examine the poſition of the hande and fingars within the hylt: This information can ſay ſomething about howe the weapon will moue and the condition and attitude of the combatant: It is to the armes and hands that the fenſer ſhulde looke as to where the weapon moues or may moue: The weapon itſelfe can alſo giue clues about the opponent.

The next thinge that needs to be examined is the wepon: The poſition of the weapon is of greate importance as it wyll determine where the nexte attacke from the opponente wyll come and alſo

The firſt Booke

alſo anie parts of the opponent that he has couered due to the poſition of his weapon. With regarde to the poſition of the weapon, it is important to examine all aſpects of it: While the poſition of the blade and the poynt are the moſt important the poſition of the hylt can alſo be: It is more ſignificant to examine the wepon as a whole rather than in partes as the poſition of the weapon in entiretie is more important: The weapon ſhuld be pictured as a lyne and the poſition of this lyne is important as it will determine thoſe thinges which haue been expreſſed alreadie. The Thruſt being a ſtraight lyne attack will flow eaſieſt alonge the lyne created by the weapon: A Cutte maie originate from this line but wyll be a much broader on beeing the width of the weapon as it ſweeps through the aire: Knowing theſe lines enableth the ſcholar to be able to counter the actions aſſociated wyth them: If a lyne is drawen from the tippe of the weapon horizontallie backeward toward the ſcholler, and then another is dropped perpendicularlie from this to the hylt, this canne be ſeene as a wall, and it determines which Line is couered by the poſition of the wepon: The mouement of the weapon is alſo important and wyll be difcuſſed later: With the entier poſition of the opponent difcouered, it is poſſible to look at their Garde. The Garde wyll determine what defenſiue and offenſiue actions can be moſt eaſilie made, and this will enable the ſcholler to prepare defences and counters to thoſe actions: This was difcuſſed in the ſections on Counter Position: A true Warde is a poſition from which an attack or defence can be made, anye poſition that the combantat ſtopps in which cannot do either with eaſe is a vulnerable poſition and is one that can be taken aduantage of.

Wyth the various portiones of the opponent examined and then as a whole whyle ſtatic, it is now poſsible to do an examination of the mouementes of the opponent: The mouements of the opponent are important as it is through theſe mouements that offenſiue geſtures will be made againſt the ſtudent and alſo defenſiue geſtures in order to defend againſt thoſe offenſiue actions of the ſcoler: Whether the actions performd are ſmooth or ierkie is an important conſideration, as thoſe actions which are perfourmed eaſilie are ſmooth and thoſe which are ierky are probably not as practiſed: This can alſo reueall a leuell of confidence yn the action: The difference betweene a ſmoothe and a ierkie action is often determined by whether the combatant is relaxed or tenſe: Relaxed muſcles are eaſier to moue, while tenſe ones are harder to moue, this relaxation or tenſion maie come from apprehenſion about the ſituation or the actions being perfourmed and this dichotomie is vſeful to determine things about the opponent: The next queſtion of mouement that follows is whether the actions are done with energie, this canne determine whether the opponent is energetic or tyred: Should the opponent haue energie, the ſcholler wyll need to conſerue his energie in order to be able to laſt againſte the opponent, making the opponent moue will graduallie reduce his energie; ſhould the opponent be tired, the ſcholler can vſe this to his aduantage, as the actions will moſt likelie not be as ſharp as they would be while he had energie.

Speed is a conſideration which needs to be made. While ſpeed is important, Time is more ſignificant: A faſt opponent can be ſlowed and a ſlow opponent can be defeated with ſpeede: This is about manipulatinge the Tempi which is more ſignificant: An opponente who vſeth actions of ſhort Tempo may ſeeme faſter than one who extends the Tempo: It has alreadie beene demonſtrated that Tempi canne be extended and ſhortened, thus the Cadence of the bout canne be increaſed or decreaſed, ſo long as the fenſer has the correct information: True ſpeede in ſwordplay comes from the practiſe of actions and thus the deuelopment of efficiency, an opponent with faſt actions is one who has practiſed them a greate deale, or who is vſing a lot of muſcle energie to perfourme them: The former is much more dangerous and harder to deale wyth than the latter: Fatigue will affect both, but more the latter than the former.

The opponentes footwork determineth how well he moueth acroſſe the ground, if it is ſloppie this is an aduantage whyche the fenſer can vſe againſte him: So too is the abſence of much
footeworke

The first Booke

footeworke: This is moſt eaſilie read by makinge the opponent mooue and ſeeinge how well he atchieues thys: The blade actions are the final mouement which the fenſer needeth to pay attention to: Theſe determine howe effectiue theyr offenſiue and defenſiue actions are: Thys is leſſe aboute powere and more about preciſion: An accurate attack is better than one whych has lots of ſpeede and powere if there is no accuracie: The lack of preciſion in blade mouement, footeworke, or indeede any action leaueth gaps in the opponents defence which can be exployted.

  Mouement is an important parte of the examination of the opponent, howe they mooue is important but what they do in the mouements is alſo of importance: In the queſtion of what actiõs the opponent maketh, there are further details which can be founde: The queſtion of repetition is one which is moſt vſefull as if the opponent repeateth a certaine action eythere deliberatelie or not, they canne be patterned and thus a reſponſe can be forced: Repetition doth not neceſſarilie haue to happen one action after another, but repetitiue patterns canne alſo be found ouer ſeries of actions: Knowing this can be yurie vſeful in planning a counter to the actions of the opponent. Miſtakes are made by all combatters, catching an opponent in one of theſe miſtakes is vſefull; realiſing that they make the ſame miſtak repeatedly in an action is a boon: This is eſpeciallie the caſe if the ſame miſtake appeares in multiple actions: A miſtake in an action which is repeated ouer and ouer again leaueth a gapp for the ſcholler to ſtryke through; this eſpeciallie the caſe where the myſtake is made in a defenſiue action: A combatant maye deuelop a peculiare methode of deliuerie for an action: This maie be an offenſiue action or a defenſiue action: This is ſomething that the ſcoler ſhould be aware of as it maye chaunge howe the action is delyuered and the poſition from which it can ſtryke to and from: On a more offenſiue note, the peculier deliuerie maye be correct in a ſence, but may alſo reſult in leauing a hole in their defence elſewhere: There are many thinges which need to be taken into account when examining the actions of an opponent: Each point giueth ſomething for the combatant to thinke about and poſſiblie euen vſe againſt the opponent: The obſeruation of mouement is difficult and wyll require practiſe, but the aduantage it reſults in is worth a greate deal to the combatant.

  The method of mouement has been examined and euen the actions themſelues and thinges that the ſcholar can vſe againſte the opponent: The finall element is to examine the reaſons behinde the mouement of the opponent: This delueth into the mouement of the opponent and the reaſons for the mouements: This is the finall key to correctlie reading the opponent and thus taking aduantage of this mouement: The eaſieſt waye to examine this is through a ſeries of dichotomies. The firſt is the actiue or reactiue: If the opponent is actiue he wyll make the action and make the opponent reſpond: This ſorte of combatant alwaies attempts to ſeize the initiatiue: On the other ſide of this is the reactiue combatant, the one who waiteth for the action of their opponent and then moueth to counter the action before making an action againſt the opponent: The waie to defeat each of theſe is to counter them: The actiue opponent ſhould be forced to react rather than be actiue, atchieued by taking the Prioritie: The reactiue opponent ſhoulde be forced to acte againſt the combatant: In bothe ynſtances it is to moue the opponent out of his comfort zone: This is the key in all inſtances: Another way to looke at this dichotomie is to ſee whether the opponent is one which takes the offenſiue or who vſes counter-offenſiue actions: The former will wait for a hole to appeare in the other combatant and ſtryke, the latter will waite for the other combatant to ſtrike and then counter them, this combatant maie euen vſe prouoking actions to force the opponent to ſtrike firſt.

  The next thinge is to examine the reaſons for the mouement of the opponent: The actions can be purpoſefull and thus parte of a plan vſed againſt an opponent, or they maye be ſimplie reacting to what the opponente doeth in ordere to counter them, or opponent maye be mouing on pure inſtinct: Eace one of the three portraies a leuel of training: The laſt has the leaſt training and he will react as does inſtinctuallie with no purpoſe to the action, ſimplie defending or attacking as
                            the ſituation

The first Booke

the fituation requireth: Thys is often howe the beginnynge fcholler will fyght: The next leuell of training is the reactiue ftudent who reacteth with purpofe; thys fcholer can plan a refponfe to the opponents action, but will onelye be refponfiue to the actions the actions are moore complex but onlye controlling the encounter at the fimpleft leuel: The purpofefull fcholar has the greateft amount of training and euerie action that they perform has purpofe behind it; this fchollar can actiuelie prouoke, lure and vfe aduanced techniques in feries in order to force the opponent to mooue where he wifhes: The only waie to determine one from the other is to examine the actions and the pofsible thought proceffes behind them: The difficultie in countering an opponent will increafe the more experience and training that the ftudent gaineth, this is fomething which muft be taken into account, efpeciallie as they will be vfing the fame inueftigations to fee what you do and howe you do it.

Wounds

He application of the Theorye and Practical ellements is howe the a fette of propofed theories and technikes are prouen to be valid, while the beft waie for this to happen is in actuall croffinge of blades, fome demonftrations canne bee made to prefent the application of fuch ynformation, as fuch this is what is heere prefented bafed vpon the theories and fkills prefented in this treatife: The incounters prefented heere are merelye a beginninge to the fequence of techniques which are poffible vfing the methode which has bene defcribed through this treatife. For euerie action there is a counter and for euery counter there is a counter to that and fo forth: In fome inftances the counter can be verie fimple and mofte often againft the complex actions of an opponent: The fcholar fhould be aware that anye counter which atchyeueth hys goall of not beeinge ftrooken is an effectiue counter: The abilitie to ftrike the opponent while perfourming this counter fhoulde always be a fecondarie confideration, as is determined by the Firft Principale.

    Some thinges muft be made of efpecial note before the applications are read and vfed: Firftlie, the wardeThird is vfed throughout the demonftrations as it is the primarie ward vfed in this treatife: It fhould be noted howeuer, that this doeth not preclude the actions which haue beene defcribed being perfourmed from fome other Warde of choife: The fame Guarde in the demonftratiõs fupplies a fimple bafe from which all of the applications may be made: Secondlie, on a fimilar fubiect the initial attacks are primarilie mayde to the High Infide Lyne as this is the Line which is mofte open and vulnerable in Third: The Outfide Line in the Gard of Thyrde is verie eafilie clofed and attacks to the Lowe Lyne are hazardous without fome forte of preparation in order to occupie the opponents weapon thus leauing the attacker expofed to fimple counters: Thirdlie, the initial attacks are all primarilie made with a *ftoccata* as the lowe pofition of the Thirde Guarde maketh this the optimall and fimpleft attack from this pofition: Both the *imbroccata* and cutting attacks vfe moore Tempi than the *ftoccata* and thus are fubiect to counter-attack much more eafilie: Fourthlie, all of the methodes which are demonftrated below will refult in the conclufions prefented as a confequenfe of the correct reading of the opponente and the correct perfourmance of the tecknique at the optimum Tyme in the incounter: Anye deuiation from the technicke defcribed or the requirements here layde out maie refult in an outcome other than that prefented in the demonftration: Laftlie, in all inftances prefented heere the combates are between two

The firſt Booke

two indiuiduals vſing the Rapier alone and dreſſed in ciuilian dreſſe: The offhand maye be aſſumed to haue a leather gloue in order to protect it during thoſe actions againſt the opponents wepon: Anie addition of ſupplementarie weapons or armors will affect the reſult of the incounters deſcribed due to theſe additions. The techniques and theorie deſcribed and vſed in theſe combates wyll be the ones which haue been deſcribed preuiouſlie.

The combates preſented are deſigned to demonſtrate the eſſentiall methodes and principales which haue been preſented thus far in this diſcourſe: The combats themſelues wyll be diuided into ſections of technique in order that the various elements preſented in the manuall can be preſented in a logical faſhion: Eche one of theſe demonſtrations in theſe ſections will ſtart with an action which is ſimilar to all the other others in the ſection: Each ſection wyll haue a deſcriptiue ſection at the beginning to deſcribe the technikes preſented and the reaſon that they haue been grouped togither in that perticuler group: An explanation of the indiuidual application may be preſent in order to better deſcribe the actions and the reaſons for the actions which haue beene preſented in the demonſtration: For eaſe of language the ſame characters vſed preuiouſlie in demonſtrations, Arthur and Bartolomeo will ſtand for the combatant and the opponent.

The attack to an Open Lyne is one of the ſimpleſt methodes of approache: For the purpoſes of the following demonſtrations, in all caſes the combatants haue cloſed to Narrow Diſtāce and the incounter followes this cloſing: The attack ſhulde be made when the Lyne is open and the opponent will haue a hard time ſtopping the attack: The following demonſtrations will begin with a ſimple attack to an Open Lyne where the opponent is moſt vulnerable.

In the Firſte, bothe combatants come to face one another in the Thyrde Guarde at Narrowe Distance: Bartolomeo maketh a mooue to chaunge his guarde in order to gaine an aduantage ouer his opponent: Arthur performs a ſimple *ſtoccata* to the Inſide Lyne which was open due to the original Gard, made poſſible In Tempo by the mouement in chaunging guarde ſtriking his opponent in the Lyne which has bene mayde opene due to the mouement. There are two leſſons to be learned from this combate, one defenſiue and one offenſiue: The former is that the ſcholler ſhulde enſure that he is Out of Diſtance before chaunging guarde, and the latter is that an attack ſhoulde be launched where and when an opponent is moſt vulnerable in order for the attack to haue the higheſt chance of ſucceſſe: In the action the attacking combatant maie chooſe to turn his True Edge towarde hys opponents weapon to guarde any chaunce of a reſponſe.

The Second incounter places both combatants in the Thyrd Guarde as before and at Narrow Diſtance: Bartolomeo maketh a *ſtoccata* toward the Inſide Lyne of Arthur, a Line not couered by the Guard of Thyrde: Prepared, Arthur reſponds to the attaque by makinge a Parry of Fourth and once he has enſured his ſafetie, maintaining his blade in oppoſition, he then proceedeth to make a counter, thruſting againſt his opponent, ſtryking his Inſide Lyne: This is a ſimple attack, defence and counter in Double Tyme: Arthur could haue Beat Parried the opponente, and while effectiue it woulde not haue maintained the Engagement of the blades, and thus prouided himſelf with a guide for his owne attack.

The Thyrde incounter proceedeth the ſame waie as the Seconde in the beginning with both combatants on garde in Thirde at the Narrow Diſtance with the ſame attack being made: Rather than defending wyth the weapon in this inſtance Arthur chooſes ynſtead to Parry with his offhand while making a Trauerſe to the right, aſſured of his ſafete he then perfourms a *ſtoccata* to the Outſide Lyne of Bartolomeo to the arme-pitte: The ſame elements are preſente as in the Firſt incounter, an attacke, defence and countere; the defenſiue option was ſymplie chaunged and combined with footework to enhance the defence: In this perticuler inſtance a Beat Parry wyth the offhand would make not muche difference to the incounter as it is combined with footeworke to enſure the ſafetie of the ſcholer: The offhande and the foote ſhoulde be made in the ſame Tem-Tempo with the counter-offenſiue action following.

In the

The firſt Booke

 In the Fourthe the beginning is the ſame wyth the ſame Thyrde Garde for both and the ſame attacke, howeuer Arthur chooſeth to make a different reſponſe to the attacke: In this inſtance a Voide by the vſe of a ſimple Retreat Step is made, followed by the counter of thruſting *ſtoccata* to the Inſide Lyne while making a Slope Steppe forewarde and to the lefte of Bartolomeo: The counter works becauſe the ſimple Retreat wyll force the opponent to extend too farre foreward, whyle he is here the ſteppe and counter-attack is made: The opponent doth not haue the Time to withdrawe his attacke and counter the ſcholler at the ſame tyme as he can not be going forewarde and backewarde at the ſame time: Care ſhoulde be taken in this to enſure that the rearewarde action is ſufficient to cleare from the opponents attack.

 The Fifte counter to the attack to the Open Lyne is much like the Fourthe, vſing the bodie and feete to void the opponents attack while keeping e bothe the ſword and the offhand free: The beginning is the ſame in poſition, Diſtance and action: When Bartolomeo makes his *ſtoccata* to the Inſide Lyne, Arthur perfourmeth a Voyde in the forme of the *halfe-incartata* mouing the target out of the waie of his opponents attack: The weapon is turned towarde the opponent and a ſimple extenſion will reſult in the opponent beeinge ſtricken in the Inſide Lyne, moſtlie by his owne forewarde mocion: Should the ſchollar be a little vnſure of his defence, he can vſe his offhand to enhance the effect of the Voide: The ſame action can be perfourmed in Counter-Time with the Voide and the counter-attack being made as a ſimultaneous action.

 The Sixt incounter increaſes the complexitie of the actions whych haue been deſcribed and demonſtrates the importance of the ſimple fact that there is alwaies a counter to euerie action: For this action it is beſt return to the motions deſcribed in the Second incounter: The attack and counering thruſt are made as the ſame, rather than ſimplie being ſtrook by the thruſt Bartolomeo perfourms a Ceding Parry of Fourth thus defeating the countering thruſt and preſenting the opportunitie for a *ſtoccata* mayde from the Parrye: This action preſents an attack, defence, counter, and a counter to the counter, of courſe ſhoulde Arthur be prepared another Cedinge Parrye to Fourthe could be made againſt this: With this Blade Engagement beinge preſent in this action, other Blade Engagemente actions become poſſible ſuche as a Diſengage to counter the Cedinge Parry and thus another opportunitie to attack.

 The attacks which haue beene deſcribed thus farre as the opening attack haue all been thruſting attacks; the Cutte to an Open Lyne will reſult in muche the ſame reſult as has been deſcribed, except where the Cutte is made too ſlow, which is vſually the reſult of inefficient or lax application on the parte of the attacker: What ſhoulde be noted is that the Cutte is ſlower than the Thruſte as ſuche the ſimpleſt reſponſe is to Voyde the Cutte and make a counter agaynſte the opponent: The attack can be deliuered into the Open Lyne the deliuerie of the Cutte has mayde in the opponente: The opponent doth not haue the Tyme to redirect the Cutte once it is too farre compleated as the Cutte muſte complete its fall, and is alſo difficulte to pull backe, thus the reſponſe with the Cutte is much ſlower: It is ſimply due to the ſpeede of the Cutte that the primarie opening attack againſt an opponent ſhould be the Thruſt: Opening with a Cutting attack alſo leaues the combatant far more expoſed to attacks in Halfe-Tyme.

 The incounters which haue been deſcribed haue been thoſe in which an attack is made to an Open Line, where this opportunitie is preſent the ſtudent ſhould take the aduantage giuen: Howeuer, an Open Lyne is not always preſent in the opponent, and for the moſt parte often it is nott: This means that the ſcholar needes to open a Lyne in order to attack the opponent: This can be atchieued through ſeuerall different methodes: Iuſt as in all the caſes preuiouſle the combatants ſtarted in the Narrow Diſtance ſo too wyll the combatants all be aſſumed to beginne at the Wide Diſtance and in the Thyrde Guarde: Theſe demonſtrations will preſent howe to opene a Lyne in an opponent and vſe this to atchieue an attack.

In the

The firſt Booke

In the Firſte, the combatantes ſtande oppoſite one another in the Guarde of Thyrde and at Wide Diſtance: Arthur gaines Bartolomeos ſwoorde by turning his hande in Fourthe and vſinge *ſtringere* in order to further open the Inſide Lyne againſte the opponente: Once the Lyne is opene, Arthur ſteps forwarde continuing the action of his *ſtringere* into a *ſtoccata* into the open Line of the opponent: The opponents weapon muſt be forced off-line ynough and onlye inough for the ſcholler to paſſe by in wyth ſafetie.

In the Seconde, the combatants ſtand oppoſite one another in the Guarde of Third and at Wide Diſtance: Arthur maketh a Beat to the Inſide of the Bartolomeos weapon in order to open the Inſide Lyne further, vſing the momentum of the Beate, he extends his arme in a *ſtoccata* againſte the opponent wyth his hande in Fourthe, ſtepping forewarde ſtriking the opponent in the cheſt: The weapon is held in Fourthe in order to guard againſt the opponents weapon returning: The Beate muſt be made and perfourmed properlie for the attack to ſucceed and without the ſchollar beeing ſtruck in the proceſſe.

In the Thyrde as in the preuious two, the combatants ſtande at Wyde Distance on the Thyrde Guarde, as in the Seconde, an attack on the blade is vſed. A Preſſure is exerted againſt Bartolomeos weapon by Arthur wyth his hande in Seconde in order to opene the Outſide Lyne, once the poynte is offline the Glide is executed in the forme of a *ſtoccata* with the hande ſtill in Second in order to further open the Lyne and ſtryke Bartolomeo in his Outſide Lyne. Both this and the Beate vſed in the Second can be vſed to open the Outſide Line in a Guard of Thirde due to the force applyed to the opponents weapon, howeuer in both caſes the attacke which followeth the blade action muſte be made with velocitye in order to preuente the opponent from cloſing hys Line again: The hande ſhould remain in poſition, Fourthe for the Inſide, and Seconde for the Outſide, in order to defend againſt the opponents weapon returning to Lyne.

Attacks of ſubtlety can alſo be vſed to open a Lyne to attack the opponent, ſuch an example is the vſe of the Flowing Attack in the Fourth Incounter. The combatants ſtand as preuiouſlye deſcribed in a Thyrde Guarde and at Wide Diſtance: Arthur, makinge ſure to be aware of Bartolomeos mouement and with velocitie, makes a Slope foreward and lefte, perfourming a Flowing Attack to the Outſide Lyne of the opponente, ſtrikinge him with a *ſtoccata*. In the Flowinge Attack the hande needeth to remain for the moſt parte in Thyrd, in order to atchieue the beſt muſcular actiõ: The hande can be turned to Seconde at the completion of the attack to guarde againſt the action of the opponent, it is vnneceſſarie: The ſame attack canne be made by ſhifting or leaning a little to the lefte of the opponent howeuer the Steppe deſcribed is a ſurer defence againſt a reſponſe of the opponent: In this perticuler inſtance it is leſſe the action of the blade which opens the Lyne and more the mouement of the ſchollar.

In the Fifte, the action beginneth as deſcribed in the preuious actions with the combatants in Third at Wide Diſtance: In order for Arthur to make his attack he muſt cloſe with Bartolomeo to Narrow Diſtance, this is atchieued vſing a ſimple Aduance enſuring that his opponents wepon is couered and obſeruing the mouement of his opponent: Once in the Narrow, Arthur ſtriketh the opponentes weapon with his off-hand to the Outſide and ſtryketh in a *ſtoccata* to the Inſide Lyne: The offhand maie alſo ſimplie engage the opponents weapon and mooue it rather than beating it, the ſame reſult will euentuate and the ſcoler will retaine control ouer the opponents weapõ.

The action of the Sixt beareth reſemblance to that of the Fift in that Arthur muſte cloſe the Diſtance to Narrow Diſtance from Wyde Diſtance: This can be atchyeued by the vſe of a ſimple Aduance, but hee muſte be aware of the mouement of Bartolomeo and enſure that hys opponentes wepon is couered: With this Aduance from the Thyrd Guarde from Wide to Narrow Diſtãce, Arthur then Binds the opponents weapon to the Outſide and ſtrikes with a *riuerſa* to the now open Lyne: In this action the combatant muſt enſure that he has controll ouer the opponents weapon before attempting to ſtrike the opponent: Shoulde the combatter Bynd the op-

opponents

The firſt Booke

ponents weapon to the Inſide, the attacke will be a *falſo alto tondo mandritta*: In this particulare inſtance the Cutte is an eaſier attack due to the poſition of the weapon at the end of the Binde: A further action on the Bind wyll reſult in the poynte of the weapon being in a poſition to ſtrike the opponent.

The action of the Seuenth vſeth an action to prouoke the opponent into action at whych the combatant can mooue to ſtrike the opened Lyne: The prouoking action muſt be one which the opponent belieueth in order for the action to worke: Startinge at Wide Diſtance and in the Thyrde Guard, Arthur approaches Bartolomeo vſing an Aduance extending a Thruſte or attempting *ſtringere* againſte his weapon: As Bartolomeo moueth to counter the action with his weapon, Arthur vſeth a Tyme Diſengage to auoide the action of his opponent then thruſts in *ſtoccata* to the open Lyne created by the action of his opponent: In this action Bartolomeo opens the Lyne for Arthur in reſponſe to the prouokinge action mayde initiallie: The forewarde motion needeth to be made at the ſame Time as the initial action in order to bring it into a Diſtance where the opponent will reſpond to it: In this action the ſcholler ſhoulde be aware of anye counter-offenſiue action of the opponent which maie be perfourmed in not againſte the threat preſented.

In the Eighthe, the combatters ſtarte as in preuious actions in the Guarde of Thyrde and at Wide Diſtance: Arthur extendeth his weapon towarde the open Lyne of Bartolomeo as he moues to counter the action a Cut Ouer is perfourmed and ſymple Thruſt with an Aduance followeth againſte the open Lyne of the opponent: The Aduance to Dyſtance ſhoulde be made with the ſecond parte of the action of the Cutte Ouer; mouement earlier will leaue the combatant expoſed to a counter attack: Shulde the opponent not reſponde to the initiall action of the ſtudente he muſt nott cloſe in order to perfourme the ſecond as the opponent wyll be prepared to counter him.

In the preuious ſection actions are vſed to open the opponents Line ſo that the ſcholler can ſtrike againſte the opponente: Theſe actions to opene the opponentes Lyne varye in complexitie as appropriate to the actions vſed: The action which inuolues the leaſt action of the ſcoller and the leaſt action of the opponent is the better action performed: Euere time the ſchollar has to vſe an additional mouement to performe the opening or attack, and for eache action the opponent muſt perform for the Lyne to be opene there is a chaunce for failure of the action and the potentiall for the ſcholler to be ſtrake. The offenſiue actions againſte an opponent ſhulde onely be as complex as they neede to be and no more.

The next ſection followeth as ſuch becauſe the actions deſcribed in it are eſſentiallie counters to the actions which haue beene preuiouſſie deſcribed and demonſtrated in the preuious ſectiõ: Theſe actions will deſcribe how, once a Lyne is opened in the ſcholer, it is poſſible to cloſe that Line and vſe the action of the cloſinge to putte the ſcholler in a poſition to counter-attack againſte the opponent: This will beginne wyth baſic counters and then mooue on to moore and moore complex ſequenſes as the counters are countered themſelues: Theſe actions al begin at Wide Diſtance as to engage in ſuche techniques at Narrow Diſtance are poſſible but it is much more daungerous due to the ſhortened Tempo due to the Meaſure: As in all the preuious incounters, and to preſerue ſome continuitie, the combatants will engage from the Guarde of Thirde.

In the Firſte, Bartolomeo vſeth *ſtringere* in ordere to opene the Inſide Lyne on Arthur, this is countered by him perfourming a Diſengage to the Outſide on an Aduaunce and a ſimple *ſtoccata* performd to the opponents now open Outſide Lyne: As in true Tempi, the Diſengage muſt be begun before the footeworke moouement is begun by the combatant, thus inſuring his defence the completion at the ſame Time reſulteth in the action being perfourmed in a ſingle Tempo: The *ſtoccata* followeth once the opponents weapon has been put aſide and the Line to the ſcholler is cloſed.

In this

The firſt Booke

In this inſtance of the Seconde engagement in this ſection, Arthur performeth *ſtringere* in order to open the Inſide Line of Bartolomeo, in reſponſe he performeth a Diſengage to the Outſide as before: Inſteade of being ſtricken in the counter howeuer, Arthur perfourmeth a Counter-Diſengage in reſponſe, and then Aduances with a *ſtoccata* to the Inſide Line of his opponent. Once againe, the offenſiue technique muſt onelye follow once the ſcholler is ſafe from the threat: Euen in the offenſiue technique, the *ſtoccata* ſhulde be extended before the foot moues ſo that the foote and hande are compleated at once: This is a counter to a counter.

The Thyrd followeth in ſimilaritie to the Second ſo that the laſt counter performd is countered by another: In this inſtance Bartolomeo vſes *ſtringere* to open the Inſide Line, Arthur countereth wyth a Diſengage: Then Bartolomeo countereth with a Counter-Diſengage, finallie Arthur countereth wythe a Double Dyſengage: The incounter is finall ſettled with an Aduance and a *ſtoccata* to Bartolomeos Outſide Lyne. One action followes the other as a reſult of the others action, there is no reaſone to concerne aboute the vſe of a Double Dyſengage yf no Counter-Diſengage is mayde: Theſe actiõs are connected to one another and muſt be vſed as ſuche, the proceſſe muſt be followed: Shoulde a combatant perfourme a technique againſte one that was not vſed, the combatant will find himſelfe Out of Line and vulnerable.

The Fourthe proceedeth as ſuch, Bartolomeo vſeth *ſtringere* to open the High Inſide Lyne, rather than countering as aboue, Arthur performes a Half-Diſengage, a Slope forwarde left and a ſimple *ſtoccata* to the forwarde legge of his opponent: The ſtrike to the legge will ſtop the opponent from moouing toward the combatant, and thus the action is effectiue, but the ſcholler muſt alſo enſure his ſafetie through the vſe of ſome defenſiue action, in this caſe a diagonal ſtep remoues the intended target, this can be ſupplemented by a Voide or Hande Parry: The defenſiue action is vital otherwiſe the ſtudente wyll be ſtrooken as ſoon as the Halfe-Diſengage is made: The Half-Diſengage itſelfe canne be countered by a ſimilar action: Care ſhoulde be taken in the vſe of the Halfe-Diſengage.

Iuſt as the Cut Ouer can be vſed to open a Line ſo too can it be vſed to cloſe a Line and open another, the Fifte demonſtration preſenteth as ſuch: Bartolomeo vſeth *ſtringere* to open the Outſide Line of Arthur, in reſponſe he vſeth a Cut Ouer to chaunge the Line and cloſe his owne and Aduances with a ſimple *ſtoccata* to the Inſide Lyne of Bartolomeo: It muſt be remembred that iuſt as in a preuious ſection, the Aduance ſhuld accompanye the ſeconde parte of the Cut Ouer alonge with the reſulting *ſtoccata*: Care ſhoulde ſtill be taken as to the location of the opponents weapon in this action: All the vſual counters to the Diſengage can be applied to the Cut Ouer: Simpleſt reſponſe is in that the Cut Ouer is vulnerable to ſimple Thruſt parte waie through as the poynt is lifted ouer the ſword: Thus the tecknique vſed in the demonſtration muſt be applyed carefullie, the poynt following the demonſtration deſcribing the counter to a Cut Ouer vſed againſt the combatant.

In the Sixt, Bartolomeo vſeth a Preſſure to open the Outſide Lyne of Arthur, in reſponſe as ſoone as the Preſſure is felt exerted againſte his weapon, a Diſengage is made to the Inſide Lyne of the opponent and a counter attack is made with an Aduance Steppe and a *ſtoccata*: This technique requireth the ſcholler to haue a goode ſence of *ſenſo di ferro* and to be ſure that it is a Preſſure beinge vſed and is committed to: The Diſengage frome the Preſſure is the ſimpleſt reſponſe as it vſeth ſome of the force applyed by the opponent to ſtart the action of the Diſengage: A ſimple counter is much more effectiue than ſomething which maie take additional Tyme.

The Seauenth

The first Booke

The Seauenth inuolues the opponente vſinge the technique deſcribed preuiouſlye for opening the line and ſtriking vſing the Flowing Attack: Bartolomeo Aduances to Narrow Distance vſing a Slope forward and left, and makes a Flowing Attack toward the Outſide Lyne of Arthur: Arthur countereth by turning hys weapon to Seconde thus placing the edge againſt the attack, a ſimple *ſtoccata* with the hande in Second maye now be made againſt the opponent: This counter workes againſt the Flowing Attack as the chaunge of the hande from Thirde to Seconde poſition changeth the angle of the weapon and thus directeth the attaque of the opponent out and awaie from the combatter through ſimple deflection: This technique ſhuld be examined and practiſed before it is vſed in an incounter againſt an opponent.

The Eighth inuolueth the counter to the vſe of the offhand againſte the weapon: Bartolomeo Aduances and Beats Arthurs weapon to the Outſide, thus opening the Inſide Line, this is countered by a Diſengage vſinge the force of the Beat to turne and ſtrike to the opene Lyne: This is a methode which can be applyed to any technike which remoueth the weapon by force: The Diſengage workes ſimplie vſinge the powere of the opponentes action againſte them, care ſhulde be taken in the turning of the poynte to enſure that it takes the ſhorteſt pathe to come backe On Line: The next eaſieſt is to remooue the weapon from where it canne be beaten this is moſte eaſilie atchieued through the vſe of a paſſiue Time Diſengage, diſengaging the opponents wepon or hand before it arriueth thus leauing the opponent out of poſition and vulnerable.

Iuſt as the preuious was deſigned to counter the Beate, ſo too is the Ninth deſigned to preſent howe to counter the vſe of the Bind againſt the combatant: Bartolomeo Aduances to Narrow Distance and attempteth to Bind Arthurs weapon, in reſponſe he ſhould ſtop the Bind as it loſeth engagement on his weapon by ſtrengthening againſt the Bind moſt eaſilie atchieued by turning the True Edge of the weapon againſte the opponentes: This technique canne be vſed when the Binde beginneth alſo in order to preuent the mouement of the ſcholars weapon: This is a technique which requireth practiſe and feeling through the blade to vſe accuratelie.

In the Tenth, Bartolomeo Aduances to Narrow Distance extending a Thruſt or attempting *ſtringere*, as Arthur attempts to Parrye the action Bartolomeo Tyme Diſengages: Arthur increaſeth his Diſtance thus makinge the followinge attacke fall ſhorte: The other technique to counter the Time Diſengage is to onelye mooue againſt the ſeconde action of the opponent: The mouement of the footework is the eaſier option of the two but the waitinge for the ſeconde action placeth the ſcholler in a muche better poſition to reſponde to the opponente: The ſcholler ſhoulde practiſe bothe techniques in order to become proficient at bothe and thus haue more options auailable.

The techniques in this ſection were deſigned to counter thoſe actions which are deſigned to open a Lyne in the combatantes defences: Eche one has a counter which can be vſed againſte the attempt: The Blade Engagement techniques which haue been preſented demonſtrate how to euerie action there is a counter it is more a matter of finding the counter to the action: To this the ſcholar ſhoulde alſo note that euen theſe counters can be countered and ſo forth: This is the tacticall aſpect of ſwordeplay which becometh apparent once theſe skils are vnderſtood.

There are manye techniques which can be vſed in Cloſes and Gripes it is the application of ſuche techniques which is important: In this application the ſcholler needeth to thinke about the three partes to a cloſe engagement, the Entrie, Action and Exit: Eache one of theſe is important and each needes to haue ſerious conſideration made about it this needes to be done before and duringe the actuall contact: Due to there beeing ſo manie wayes that a cloſe contact incounter can happen, a ſingle demonſtration of ſuch an incounter will be preſented.

With both combatants ſtarting in the Thirde Guarde and at Wide Distance Bartolomeo ſteps and makes a *ſtoccata* toward Arthurs Inſide Lyne, Arthur Beat Parries in Fourth to couer hi-
himſelfe

The first Booke

mſelfe, allowinge the poynte of the weapon to roll ouer a little and then ſteps Slope to forewarde and right dropping his poynt vnder Bartolomeos weapon deliuering a *riuerſo mezzo tondo* to the his bodie: Should Arthur requyer he can alſo vſe hys offhande to preuent the opponents weapon from returning by ſymple placement of the hande towarde the opponents weapon, Arthur then makes a paſſe forewarde to Exit from the incounter turning once it is compleated to face the opponent in Garde: The ſeconde Tempo for the ſchollar is poſſible due to the recouerye tyme taken for the opponent: The key to a ſucceſsful cloſe and attaque is ſpeede and efficiencye; the ſimpler the attack the better: In this caſe the ſcholler taketh the Prioritie with the Parry and then maintaineth it through his attack: The Entrie is actuallie aſſiſted by the opponents attack and is compleated with the Slope Step; the Action is the cutte againſt the bodie with or without the offhand placement; and the Exit is the paſſing ſtep and returning on Guarde.

The key to ſucceſsfull and ſafe cloſe contacte incounteres is to haue a cleane, Entry, Action and Exit: Where the two combatants come into cloſer contact and more prolonged contact is where iſſues can happene: The keye to ſuruiuing ſuche an yncountere is to enſure that the defences are maintained and that the combatant gaineth Prioritie ouer the important part of the incounter; this giueth him all of the options: The ſtudent needeth to at leaſt gaine the Prioritie on the Exit to enſure that he can do ſo ſafelie and alſo ſo that he can ſucceſsfullie Exit without the opponent attempting to continue the Action: In moſt inſtances it is the Entrye and Exit where the ſcholer wyll finde himſelfe moſt vulnerable to counter-attack from the opponent at theſe times the ſcoller needeth to be ſure of his defences and be ſure of the actions of the opponent: There are manie different attacks, defences, and approaches to Cloſes and Gripes this is a ſingle demonſtration to preſent the principalles behinde the actions.

The actions preſented thus farre haue primarilie vſed Double Time, there are ſome inſtances of other Tymes, but for the moſt parte it has bene Double Tyme: Each combatant vſes a ſingle action followed by the action of the other combatant in reſponſe or as a counter: It is alſo importante to examine the other formes of Time, Single, Counter and Halfe in a more practicall ſetting to ſee howe they worke and differ frome one another this ſette of incounters is deſigned to do iuſt that: What is neceſſarye is that it is the different vſe of Tyme which is importante rather than the actions vſed in the yncounters: Each demonſtration wyll begin wythe the ſame ſet of actions from the ſame Guarde, this is in order to preſent the different Tymes in the reſponſes to the ſame action clearlie.

The Firſt incounter will demonſtrate Single Time: The combatants ſtand acroſſe from one another in Wyde Distance, Bartolomeo maketh a *ſtoccata* with a ſteppe to Arthurs Inſide Lyne, in reſponſe he turneth hys hande in Fourthe to collecte the blade of Bartolomeo and extendeth in a *ſtoccata* to the Inſide Lyne of his opponent: Bartolomeos wepon is deflected Out of Line by the turning of the hande and the forward action of the Thruſt: The combination of the defenſiue and offenſiue techniques in a ſingle Tempo, the counter to the opponentes attack is perfourmed in Single Time: In this inſtance it wulde alſo paye for the ſcholare to mooue his hande a litle towarde the opponents attack as he extends the Thruſt to enſure contact betweene the weapons and thus ſafety in the methode: This forme of technique and vſe of Tyme takes a greate deale of precyſion in the action, a ſimple errour in placement could ſee the ſcholler ſtrooken during his action.

The Seconde yncounter is vſed to demonſtrate Counter Tyme: The combatants face one another as before, in the Wide Distance at the Guarde Thyrde: Once again Bartolomeo acts firſt making a *ſtoccata* to the Inſide Line on an Aduance: In reſponſe Arthur makes a Slope forward and right while ſtriking a *ſtoccata* to Bartolomeos Inſide Line with the hande in Fourth: The counter-attack made againſte the opponent is made in reſponſe mayde by the opponent, thus againſt Time, thus in

The firſt Booke

thus in Counter Tyme: The important thinge to note here is that the attack is not meerely launching an attaque into the opponents, there is conſideration for where the opponents attack is coming from, going to and alſo there is an aſpect of defence made in the Slope made. Shuld the combatant meerely launch an attack againſt the opponent without theſe conſiderations he will moſt likely find himſelf ſtrake.

  The Thyrde and finall incounter to be deſcribed is one whych demonſtrateth the vſe of Halfe-Tyme agaynſte the opponente: The beginning and initial attacke proceedeth as has beene deſcribed preuiouſlye with bothe combatants on Guarde in Thyrde and at Wide Diſtance: Bartolomeo maketh a *ſtoccata* to the Inſide Lyne of Arthur with an aduance: In reſponſe to the offence of Bartolomeo, he withdraweth his Inſide Lyne through the vſe of a ſimple Voyde and ſtriketh againſte the forearme of Bartolomeo wyth a *ſtoccata* before the offenſiue action of the opponente is completed: The *ſtoccata* of the opponente is interrupted before it can be compleated and thus the action of the combatant is made in Halfe-Time: A cutting attack againſt the opponents arme in this inſtance woulde reſulte in the ſame concluſion: The eſſentiall parte is that the action of the ſcholler is made agaynſt the attack of the opponent: The action maie arreſte the action of the opponent but the ſcholer ſhoulde ſtill make ſome other defenſiue action in order to be ſafe, in the demonſtration a Voide was vſed.

  Each one of the three preuious demonſtrations has highlighted the vſe of methodes aſſociated with a perticulere forme of Tyme: Each one is differente and the differences are importante: There is muche confuſion made when vſing ſuche aduanced techniques in combate, and much miſinterpretation when they are ſeene: The explanation preſented is deſygned to preſent the differences in order that the different Tymes maie be vnderſtood better: The demonſtrations preſented are onelye a ſmalle proportion of the tekniques that coulde be vſed in the ſame ſituation: This is not deſigned to couer all options, meerelye to giue a preſentation of ſome of the options the ſcholler may haue at his diſpoſall: Theſe practical demonſtrations are deſigned to preſente the Theorye and Practicall elements together in a ſituation where reſponſes are beeng made by two combatants who are in the incounter: The yncounters preſented in the demonſtration of the application aboue will onely worke as deſcribed ſo long as the correct Tyme and techniques are vſed: This will requier that the ſcholer make ſure that he has had ſufficient practiſe before attempting anye in an incounter with an opponent.

                    Aduantage of the Cirkle Ouer the Lyne

The first Booke
Aduantage of the Cirkle Ouer the Lyne

Here is an aduantage in fwordplay for taking the cirkle ouer the line: This particular afpect is directed at the approche to engaging an opponent in combate: In order to vnderftand this particular aduantage fome things need to be made cleare: The vfual approach is that the lyne will alwaies haue the aduantage ouer the cirkle, but through the afpects defcribed and principales prefented, it will be reuealed that this is not alwaies the cafe: This is actuallie a relatiuelye olde thought proceffe as the Spanifhe vfe the principal of the cirkle and mouement in order to gayne aduantage in their fourme of fence: The afpectes and principalles heere defcribed will be fimilar to thefe, but in fome wayes alfo different in the approche due to the nature of the methode of fwordeplaie imployed.

The firft thinge that needeth to be made cleare is what is confidered to be On line and Off line with regarde to the opponent: This is different to the Lines defcribed preuiouflie in the fection on theorye. There is a lyne which can be drawen betweene the two combatants: This is a direct lyne which is drawne from the middeft of one combatant to the other when they are ftanding acroffe frome one another: A fimilar lyne can be drawen connecting the fhoulders of the combatants: This createth a clear line betweene the two combatants and it is this which determines whether the combatants are On line to one another: A combatant who fteppes off this perticuler lyne is Off line from the opponents perfpectiue: It fhould be noted that the lynes extend from the naturall direction of the facing of the combatants: It is here where the cirkle can dominate the line.

The aduantage of the cirkle ouer the lyne is bafed on mouement and more to the poynt, fluid and actiue mouement of the fwordes-man as oppofed to his opponent: The aduantage is loft at anie tyme where the combatter vfeth a ftatic approache to the incounter: In regarde to this circuler mouement referres to anye action which deuiates Off line as has beene defcribed preuiouflie: This mouement moueth the combatant out of the opponents direct facing and therefore Off line to the opponent and gaineth him aduantage. Mouement Off line is found in Voides, efpeciallie the *incartata* and alfo in footeworke actions fuche as Slopes and Trauerfes: Thefe actions all chaunge the angle to the opponent and thus gain aduantage ouer the opponent, thus the circulare mouement of the fwordfman gaineth the aduantage ouer linear mouements of the opponent: Mouement off the line is vfed to difrupt the actions of the opponent; in the offenfiue cafe this can change pofition and pointe of attacke, chaunge the lyne of engagemente and chaunge Diftance; in the defenfiue fimilar chaunges are appropriate, but alfo the mouement can limit the attack of the opponent or euen fimplie defeat the attacke of the opponent through fimple moouement: The mouement Off line doth not haue to be groffe, indeede it can be fine and in fome inftances the fize of the mouement is inuerfelie proportional to the effecte that it can haue on the combat: Groffe mouements haue their place and can be verie effectiue, but the finer mouement can alfo make it eafier for the combatant to keep hys weapon in prefence, threateninge the opponente: The wepon in prefence and thus dyrected at the opponent is alwaies more effectiue than the weapon that is not.

In

The firſt Booke

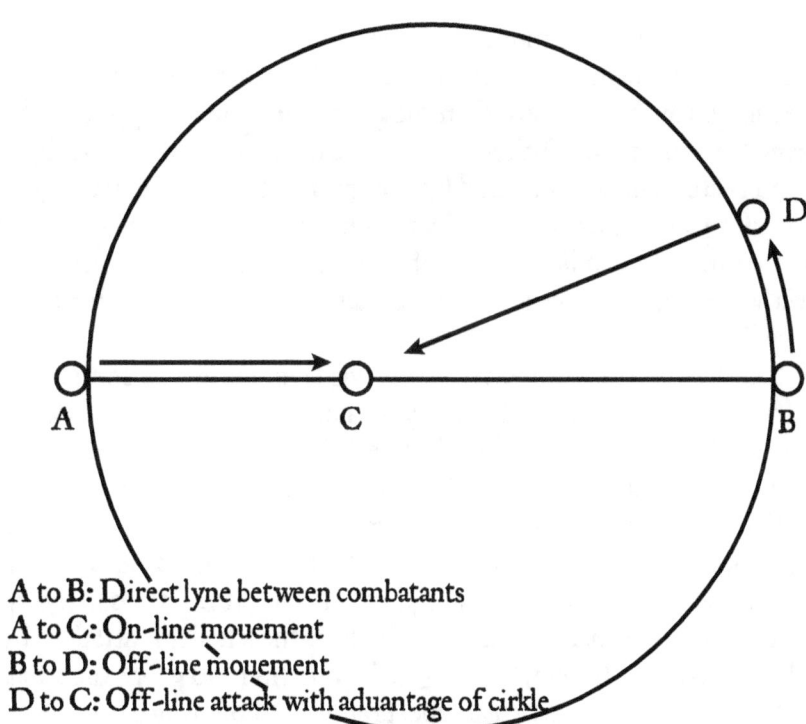

A to B: Direct lyne between combatants
A to C: On-line mouement
B to D: Off-line mouement
D to C: Off-line attack with aduantage of cirkle

    In defence, the chaunge of direction can be vſed to defeat a ſtreight lyne attack, eſpeciallye one at the limit of the opponents reache, and one dependent on the velocity of the attack: A ſimple mouement out of lyne is ſufficient: In this waie the circuler mocion defeats the ſtreyght by deuiatiõ of the lyne and takinge the targeted combatant out of preſence through a ſimple action: The Cutte is eſpeciallye effectiuelye defeated by the moouement Offlyne or mouement out of Diſtance: The Cutte is ſlower than the Thruſt and its path can be moore eaſily predicted due to its nature: The *fendente* is eaſilie voided by mouement to the ſide, other Cuttes are ſimilarlie defeated: In the mouement Off line, the angle of attack is changed and the ſtreight lyne attack is eaſilie auoided through the ſame mouement: This mouement Off-line ſhoulde not preuent the ſcholar from keepinge his weapone in preſence and On line to the opponente: This alloweth for ſimple attack againſte the opponent or counter-attack againſt the opponent depending on the ſituation preſented.

    The attack is ſtill baſed on the lyne due to the ſpeede of the attack; the Thruſt is faſter than the Cutte due to the vſe of the ſtreyghte line approache: Howeuer, the circulare mouement giueth more options for the direction of the attack: The angles of attack can be changed due to the mouement on the cirkle. The attacke alonge the lyne is deſigned on the baſis of ſpede and the aduantage taken by hauinge the opponente out of poſition and thus vulnerable this is a direct attack agaynſt an expoſed Lyne of the opponent: The attack vſing circuler mocion can be mooued about the opponents defences thus bypaſſinge and auoidinge the defences preſented in ordere to ſtrike areas where the opponent is not couered: Dependynge on the circulare mouement of the ſcholler a Lyne can be further opened, diſcouered or cloſed: The ſcholare ſhould examine whych direction he intendeth to mooue and what effect this wyll have on the Lines of the opponent: For the moſt parte it is better to moue where the opponent wyll be more expoſed than to moue where he is more cloſed, howeuer, if the combatant has ſomethyng more complex planned ſuch as an approche conſiſting of ſeuerall mouements deſigned to open the Lyne, then mouement to the more defended maie be more appropriate in that ſituation: Regardleſſe, the combatant vſeth the mouement in order to chaunge his attack againſte the opponent: This mouement muſt be fluid in nature and the mouement of the hande muſt accompanie the mouement of the feete: If the fencer moueth hys fe-

feete

ete and then as separate mouement moueth hys handes, the opponent canne simplie turne and negate the effect of the mouement of the feete: If, howeuer the moouement of the hande accompanieth the mouement of the feete then the aduantage gained is preserued by the deliuerie of the attack during the mouement Offlyne. In the vse of the mouement Offline in defence and followed by a counter-attack or accompanied by a counter-attacke, the aduantage is preserued due to the action of attack againste the combatant by the opponent: In the Tempo of the attacke of the opponent, the scholler moueth Offline in hys defence, gaining the aduantage: The attack muste be compleated or withdrawen, either waie the fenser has this Tempo in order to strike againft the opponent.

The idea that the Cirkle can defeat the Line will seem somewhat forrein to some in that it has been demonstrated that the Cutte is slower by the nature that it vses the cirkle for motion and the Thrust is faster by the nature that it vseth the line: This remaines true howeuer the mouement Offline while slower in some aspectes giueth the combatante aduantages in chaunging the situation betweene him and hys opponent: The engagement can be chaunged, the Distance can be chaunged and indeede the position is chaunged by the nature of the mouement: The opponente has to reacte to these chaunges that the combatant maketh and thus remayneth vnsettled in hys approache to the combatant, thus the scholler gaineth an aduantage: Where the scholler is attacked by the opponent and he responds by mouement Offline, he changes the situation and gayns the aduantage in Time for his response: It is through these particular aspects and also those which haue been described that it is demonstrated that the cirkle has the aduantage ouer the line.

Single Againſt All

He instruction presented in this text has been on the basis of the swordsman vsing a single sword againste an opponent who is also vsing a single sword: This is due to the single sworde beeing the foundation weapon to the entyer method: Other items maie accompanie the single sword but it is primarilie the sword that will be accompanied by another item: Howeuer, it is the case that the opponent maie not alwaies be carrying a single sword, nor indede matching implements euen in companion in the incounter: To this pointe the combatant needs to knowe howe to deale with an opponent who has a companion when the combatant doth not: The descriptions giuen belowe wyll be verye general in their approache: In all instances the scholer should studie theyr opponent carefullie before making any sorte of action towarde them: The actions presented belowe are designed to present some solutions to some problemes presented by the opponente: Theye are guidelynes as to howe to approache an opponente, in all ynstances the scholer should consider what the opponent is doing and act accordinglie to the situation presented.

In approachinge the situation where the scholare has a single swoorde and the opponent has a sworde accompanied by another deuice, eithere offensiue or defensiue, there are certaine things that the scholler shoulde kepe in minde: Firste of all that there are some things that cannot chaunge regardlesse of the items which are in vse, primarilie that you both haue two handes: Secondlie, that all of the same principalles whych haue bin presented preuiouslie apply to the situation iust as they woulde when onelye a single sword is being vsed, and with little modification: Thirdlie, a scholar will haue spent more time with a single wepon than wyth anye other combination of weapons and this is an aduantage which can be vsed by the scholler against the opponent: In fact, the single sword wyll euentuallie be the dominant weapon in all cases due to this. In certain circumstances the second implement

The first Booke

implement can actuallie hamper the opponent rauther than aiding them and this needeth to be vſed to the combatants aduantage: If the combatant can learne to dominate and defeat a combination before learninge howe to vſe that combination it wyll gaine the ſtudente an aduantage and this can be vſed in future ſtudies of the weapon and it combinations: The companion weapons will be addreſſed in a future diſcourſe to follow the current one: The onelye reale other chaunge to an incounter beſides the addition of items to the incounter is where the opponent is fighting left-handed againſt the combatter: This particular chaunge to the incounter will be addreſſed in a different ſection of this treatiſe.

There are inherent aduauntages and diſaduauntages in the vſe of a weapon combination: Theſe neede to be diſcouered by the ſcholler, preferablie before the incountere enſueth: Dealinge with other combinations is baſed vpon the aduantages and diſaduantages of the forms being vſed: The aduantages of the opponents forme need to be neutraliſed while the diſaduantages need to be accentuated in order that the ſcholler can gaine dominance in the yncounter: The ſcholler needeth to worke tacticallye in his incounter with the opponent yn order to ſucceed in the ſituation: As has been ſtated eache form has aduantages and diſaduantages.

The vniuerſalle aduantage of the ſingle ouer a two-hande combination is that the vſe of an extra item or weapon doeth not leaue the opponent with an emptie hande, except in the caſe of the gauntlet and that is ſtill not the ſame as an emptie hande: The emptie hande is eaſier to vſe to control an opponentes item regardleſſe of what yt is: The other aduantage is that the emptye hande is a natural thing and is not added to the ſcholler and thus the ſcholer has to ſpende leſſe thought on the correcte application of it: This ſmall tyme taken in thought, or lacke thereof, is an aduantage which can be vſed againſt the opponent: In all caſes the ſcholar ſhoulde be conſidering what the opponent wyll attempt to do to gaine the aduantage and thus attempt to negate this aduantage or the chaunces to gaine this aduantage.

The Caſe of Rapyers is the moſt intimidating forme for the ſcholar with a ſingle rapyer to face due to the double longe weapons againſt the ſingle: This maketh it a good place to ſtart, to demonſtrate that it can be defeated by a ſingle weapon: It is alſo the moſt wholie offenſiue combination that a ſwordes-man can arme himſelfe wyth in the fight with the rapyer: The firſte thinge that ſhould be noted is that the ſtudente ſhould not ſimplie throw himſelfe into the fraie as this will reſult in him beinge ſorelie hurte: Some time ſhoulde be taken in order to correctlie ſtudie the forme for its aduantages and diſaduantages. The firſt thing that will be noted is that in the vſe of two longe weapons the opponent will haue the aduantage at longer Diſtance while the cloſer Diſtance to the opponent he will loſe this aduantage due to the length of the weapons: Thus, if the ſcholler can get inſide the range of the opponents weapons his aduantage will increaſe markedlie: It will be noted that in the vſe of two weapons and two long ones at that, the forme is entirelie moore offenſiue than defenſiue: This preſenteth one of the keyes to the waye to defeat the opponent with Caſe of Rapiers: If the opponent is kept on the backe foot, thus in the defenſiue, it will make it difficult for him to make an offenſiue action againſte the combatant: In this method the combatant takes Prioritie and kepes it from the opponent: The ſcholer muſt make the opponent vſe both weapons to defend himſelfe with in order to not allowe them to offend with eyther weapon: Remembringe the two hande principalle deſcribed preuiouſlie, the ſcholer ſhuld put hys wepon on one weapon of the opponents and his hande on the other weapon: In this the ſcholler does not need to attack, meerely to ſpoil the opponents chaunce to attack: Simple contact againſt the opponents weapons wyll often achieue this: Through this ſpoilyng the opponent can be fruſtrated into a miſtake or euen intanglement, this is obuiouſlie an aduantage which the ſchollar can vſe to his aduantage: The ſcholler ſhuld alſo mooue to a poſition where one weapon is cloſer than the other: Once this is atchyeued then the ſcholer can vſe ſingle ſword tekniques againſt ſingle weapons: The engagements will worke the ſame as they would with a ſingle weapon but the combatant ſhould alwaies be aware of the other we-

weapon:

The first Booke

apon: The ſcholler can alſo, with a greate deale of care, worke betweene the weapons as the Inſyde Lynes are often forgotten: Remember wyth two weapons there are double the Lynes, two Inſide Lynes and two Outſide Lines: Both ſets can be attacked and if the opponente is not careful he can actuallye leaue Lines opene where he did not realiſe. Euen though the Caſe of Rapyers has a greate deale of aduantages and offenſiue potential, it alſo does haue diſaduantages: The ſtudious and careful ſcholar can finde ſituations where he can haue the aduantage euen in this ſituation.

    The other common combination, and indede more common than the Caſe of Rapyers in which two offenſiue items are carried, is Rapier and Dagger: This is more common as the Gentleman would more likelie carrie a dagger rather than another rapier in his eueryday dreſſe: It would ſeeme that this forme is leſſe intimidating than the Caſe of Rapyers as it has a ſhorte weapon and a longe one, but this alſo giueth the aduantage that the opponente has an aduantage both at longe and ſhort ranges: Euen with this increaſed aduantage the combatant with the ſingle ſword can ſtill preuail: The dagger cannot ſtrike at longer Diſtances ſo it ſhould ſimply be auoided: The ſcholer ſhuld do his beſt to auoyde contact with the dagger at all and while ſtaying at Diſtance this will do a lot to neutraliſe its aduantage: Againſte the ſingle longe weapon ſingle ſwoord techniques can be vſed againſte the opponent while ſtaying out of contact withe the dagger: The ſcholler ſhould moue to a poſition where the ſwoorde is on the dominant ſyde in ordere to neutraliſe the vſe of the offhand: The ſhorter reach of the dagger will make it difficult for it to be brought into plaie: In order to further gaine aduantage the primarie attack of the ſcholler ſhould be to the Outſide Lyne where the dagger has difficultie reaching, or to the Inſide Line cloſe to the opponents ſworde where the dagger will haue difficultye being vſed without entangling the ſword: If the ſcholler can force the opponent to ſelf-intangle, this will giue him a great aduantage and, no doubt, an opportunitie to ſtrike in ſafetie againſt the opponent: This particuler approche, it will be noted, will be the ſtãdard approach to moſt of the combinations which the combatant will face.

    Once the offenſiue combinations haue been dealt with it is important to looke at the defenſiue combinations that a ſcholar maye face in the hands of an opponent: For the moſt parte the rules which will applie to theſe will be verye ſimilar, but ſtill it is important to look at them indiuiduallie: The buckler is a defenſiue iteme whyche is often vſed wyth the rapyer, in generall, it is not vſed to ſtrike the ſcholler and thus as a direct threat it is abſent: From this pointe of viewe it can be ignored. Auoidance is the beſte option in the fight againſt the buckler where the ſcholer onlye has a ſingle weapon: The ſcholler ſhoulde mooue to the ſword ſide of the opponent in order to neutraliſe the effect of the buckler as much as poſſible: Once this is atchieued, the ſcholare can then vſe ſingle ſworde techniques: In order to bringe it backe into vſe, the opponente will haue to ſhifte theyr poſition, and maie foul their own weapon in this ſhift of poſition: Howeuer, another approach can be vſed againſte the buckler whych workes due to the nature of the item: The point of the ſchollers wepon can actuallie be hidden behind the buckler and thus out of view of the opponent, thus vſing the buckler againſt them: From here the ſtudente can make actions and initialiſe mouements which the opponente cannot ſee due to the buckler: In this waie, the couering aſpect of the buckler is vſed againſte the opponent: The ſame effect can be vſed if the ſcholler maketh attacks whych moue cloſe to the poſition of the buckler, thus vſing the buckler againſte the opponent: Any time that the opponent blocks his viſion with the buckler the ſcholler wll haue a chaunce to make an action and has an aduantage, the ſcholer ſhuld vſe theſe opportunities as much as poſſible: Some of theſe poſitiõs can be forced by the combatant: The ſame can be ſaide for anie tyme that the buckler is mooued into a poſition where it will foule the mouement of the ſwoorde: Once againe, manye of the approaches when the opponent is vſing a dagger can worke where he is vſing a buckler: Mouement to the ſword-ſide and attacks cloſe to the ſword can worke effectiuelie: Anie time that the buckler commeth into contact with the ſcholers weapon, the ſcholler ſhoulde Diſengage and re-poſition his weapon in order to neutraliſe the effect of the buckler: It is often a

                                                                                                               goode

The firſt Booke

goode idea to withdraw, if poſſible to at leaſt Wide Distance, in ordere to increaſe the Diſtance and the immediacie of the poſſible following attack of the opponent: This applies to the vſe of any offhande item, Diſengage and withdraw from the incounter in order to counter the effect of the item.

Rapyer and Cloake is another defenſiue combination that the ſcholar may be faced with an opponent carrying: The purpoſe of the cloak is to block ſight, and to bind and intangle the wepon: In ſome inſtances it maie be throwen in ordere to atchyeue its goal, but ſtill it is a defenſiue item ſo from the poynte of being ſtruck to be killed, it can be ignored: The prime mode of dealing with an opponents cloake is to auoyde it as much as poſsible if the opponent cannot come into contacte with your wepon then it is difficult for them to perfourme moſte of the effect of the item: As wythe the other combinations, the ſcholler ſhoulde mooue to the ſide where the opponents ſwoord is to neutraliſe the effecte of the cloke in the offhand, in order to vſe the cloke effectiuelye the ſwoorde wyll haue to be mooued and this can reſult in the opponent becoming intangled in his own cloake: In the caſe of the cloake, it is effectiue at defending againſt Cuttes, but not ſo much againſt Thruſtes, the offhand can be attacked with a Thruſt to harme the hande or arme and force the opponent to loſe the item: Care ſhoulde be taken in this attacks not to become intangled in the clok in the proceſſe: With the chaunge in poſition and the opponentes weapon beynge primarie, and the cloake being neutraliſed, ſymple ſingle ſworde technikes can then be vſed againſte the opponent: In general contact with the cloake ſhuld be auoided in order to auoid any chaunce of deflection or intanglement: Howeuer the poſition of the cloake as placed by the opponente can be vſed by the ſcholler in order to obſcure the poſition of his weapon and indeede in caſes euen his entier bodie: This is vſinge the cloakes abilitie to block ſight lines againſt the perſon who is vſing the cloake: This canne be atchyeued in a ſimilar manner to that deſcrybed in the vſe againſte an opponente vſinge a buckler aboue: Once again, it ſhoulde be emphaſiſed that ſhoulde the opponentes cloake come into contact with the ſchollers weapon and ſtart to become intangled he ſhould withdraw into a ſecure guarde.

The final combination that the combatant is likely to encounter in the companie of Gentlemen is the Sworde and Gauntlet: This forme is actuallie verie ſimilar to that of the ſingle ſwoorde except that the gantlet is invulnerable to Cuttes made againſt the armored parte of the hande: The gauntlet ſhould be auoided at all coſtes as the opponente maie graſp the ſchollers weapon and gayne controll ouer it: This canne be atchyeued through the ſimple technique of the Diſengage: Further, iuſt as wyth the other formes deſcribed, the ſcholler ſhoulde place himſelfe more on the ſide of the opponents ſword in order to make it more difficult for the opponent to faſten vpon the weapon: It has beene noted that the gauntlet maketh the opponents hand invulnerable to Cuttes, but this ſame protection does not applie to Thruſtes and as ſuch theſe can ſtill be applied to the gauntleted hande of the opponent: For the moſte parte howeuer, once the ſcholler has poſitioned himſelfe correctlye moore to the ſword-ſide of the opponent ſymple ſingle ſword techniques can be vſed iuſt as if the opponent were armed onelye with a ſword.

In coming to an incounter with an opponent, vnleſſe the tearmes of the incounter and thus the wepons were agreed beforehand, he maie finde himſelfe facing an opponent wyth manie different combinations of weapons and other offhand deuices: The aboue deſcriptions haue giuen ſome wayes in which a ſelection of theſe deuices can be dealt with euen though the ſcholer maye onlye be armed with a ſingle rapyer alone: The principalles of theſe are verie ſimilar and ſhuld be taken note of in order that deuices which haue not been mentioned may alſo be dealt with in an efficient and ſafe manner by the ſchollar: It ſhoulde be noted that armed with ſuch information a ſcholar placeth him in a much better poſition to learne how other deuices of an offenſiue and defenſiue nature worke due to knowing what theyr limitations are before ſtarting wyth them: The more common and natural deuices of the Gentleman ſhalbe addreſſed in a future exploration deſigned

designed for the purpose: In all instances where a scholler faceth an opponent with vnmatched weapons, whether he is armed with an iteme in his offhand or not, the scholer shoulde surueye the opponente and attempt to figure out what the opponent is able to doe wyth theyr combination and how they would go about this: Once this is gayned the scholer can then go about thinking about wayes in which these obiectiues discouered canne be vndone by the combatant yn order that the combatter can bee victorious: This processe is the same as that which was described in the section on Reading the Opponent earlier in this treatise: All of the same principalles elucidated there applie to the current described situations: There is a solution and a waye around anye combination of items that an opponente maye carrie wyth a single sworde or anie combination that the student maye carrie, this aboue all else the scholar should remember in hys incounters.

Of the Left-Handed Opponent

He left-handed opponent, for some combatants, wyll cause them a greate deale of consternation as to how to deal with him: For the teacher the left-handed student also presents some vnique challenges to deal with: Iust as with dealing with a left-handed opponent, teaching a left-handed combatant inuolueth an examination of the situation and in parte an examination frome theyr poynte of view: The talented teacher will find no difficultie in teaching the left-handed student so longe as what he is teachinge is based on sound fensing theorie and applied to the particular peculiarities of the left-handed studente. Wyth regarde to the left-hander and as the title of thys section implies it is the left-handed opponent that is being dealt with here and not the left-handed studente, though manye of the same principalles will still applie to the situation in both cases: What shoulde also be noted here is that it is the right-handed combatant dealing with a left-handed opponent: Shoulde the combatant and the opponente be bothe lefte-handed, then the methode applies iust as it would for a right against a right the Lines are simply reuersed, as will be explayned below, and all applies as preuiouslie described in the preuious instruction.

    The first thinge that should be noted is that regardlesse of what hande the sword is held in the same basic principalles of the operation of the sword applieth to the situation: The left-handed combatter is still bounde by the primarye principles of Tyme and Distance and these are applied in the same way as they would be to the right-handed combatant: This is because these principles doe not chaunge regardlesse of the weapon and regardlesse of the hande in which the perticuler weapon is being held: There are, howeuer, some principales which are modified by the position of the weapon and the hande in which the weapon is held.

    The principale which is primarilie affected by the chaunge in hand from right to left is that of Lines: It is onelye due to this, and as a result, that there is some modification to the principale of engagement, euen so the chaunges for engagemente are onelye on the basis of the side on which the opponentes wepon lieth rather than the position of the weapons againste one another: The *forte* remains dominante ouer the *debole* in strength and dominance of engagement: What do chaunge are the Lines: The Lynes are swapped ouer due to the swoorde position as they are alwaies relatiue to the position of the weapon, and this is also the reason why two swords result in two sets of Lynes, though the reference to a Lyne in this particulare situation is vsuallie referred to basis of the dominant hande or wepon engaged at the time: The names of the Lines remain it is iust the sides which are swapped, though the principalles of their naming remains: Euen for the left-hander the Outsi-
Outside

The first Booke

de Line is that which is to the outſide of the wepon and cloſeſt to the outſide of the combatant and the Inſide is obuiouſlye the reuerſe of this beinge that whyche is to the inſide of the combatant and cloſeſt to the inſide of the combatant: Howeuer the Outſide Line will be on the left and the Inſide to the right rather than the reuerſe as it is with the right-handed combatter: What ſhould be noted here is that in the diſcuſſion of the fenſe againſte the lefte-handed opponente, the Lynes will be deſcribed from both the poſition of the ſcholer and their opponent.

 The firſte miſtake which is often made by a ſcholler facinge a left-handed opponent is that the ſcholler will chaunge to his lefte hand in order that the principles will right themſelues and that the Lynes wylle be the ſame for bothe: This is a foole-hardie miſtake as the ſcholler ſhoulde onelye chaunge handes where he is requyred to by iniurie or by Honor: The ſcholler will ſymplie haue leſſe ſkill in his lefte hande as compared to his dominant hande this goeth whether the ſcholler is lefte or right-handed to begin with: The ſword ſhould remaine in his dominant hand in anie engagement, except under circumſtances of iniurie or Honor: The other thing of note here is that the left-handed opponent will haue more ſkill in his lefte than the combatant wyll and to chaunge hands ſimplie taketh awaie anye aduantage of ſkill that the ſchollar maie haue had in vſinge his righte hande in the incounter: It is ſure in this ſituation that the left-handed opponent will ſtill haue the aduantage as it is more likelie that he has faced more right-handed opponents than he has left-handed opponents, but it is due to the ſkill of the ſcholer, rather than the opponent that the hand ſhuld not be chaunged.

 In attacking and making actions againſt the left-handed opponent, and indede for the lefte againſt the right-handed opponent, it is the Outſide Lyne which is often the target for attacks and actions, and often aduiſed as ſuch by manye theoriſts: This maketh a greate deale of ſwordplaye in that the Outſide Line is cloſer for bothe combatants in the perticuler ſituation, thus it makes ſence from the point of view of the Meaſure betweene the combatters. Howeuer, the Inſide Line of the left-handed opponente ſhoulde not be diſregarded out of hande: From the ſimple pointe of viewe that the Outſide Line maie be choked in an engagement due to bothe combatants attacking down a ſimilar Line, the poſſibilitie of another option for the ſcholer ſhould be appealing to him: In engaging alonge the Outſide Line, and if the opponents weapon is puſhed to the Outſyde, the Inſide Line is left open to attack: Euen where the ſcholer moueth the opponents wepon further out in order to vſe the Outſide Lyne and remaine couered, there is ſtill the threat of the Inſide ſhould the opponent Diſengage and chaunge Lynes to the Inſide Line: Here it is demonſtrated that the Lyne is choked by the actions of bothe combatters vſinge the Outſide Lyne, and indeed the ſcholer is threatened to the Inſide Line.

 Would it not be eaſier to worke to the left-handers Inſide Line as the ſword is in poſition alreadie to defend againſt attack? In ſaying this it is the ſhallow Inſide Line that ſhoulde be examined in order to maintaine a correcte poſition wyth the opponent, to ſtretch deeper into the Inſide Line threateneth the ſcholar with extended Tymes and Diſtance: In this workinge the ſchollar ſhould aim to angle his weapon to couer the Outſide Lyne with poſition of the weapon, couering the opponents weapon with his *forte* and thus attacking the Inſide in ſafetie: In order to attack the Inſide Line, the ſcholler needeth to cleare the opponentes weapon and enſure that he has Diſtance and Tyme in order to atchieue his ende: This will inuolue the vſe of footework and cleuer engagement of the weapon againſte the opponentes in order to remaine guarded: The opponent will clearlie not giue vpp his Lyne voluntarilie as this will place him in a poſition vnder threat, thus the combatant muſte vſe his ſkill to opene the Lyne for an attack: With engagemente on the opponents blade the ſcholler canne opene the opponentes Inſide Lyne by ſtepping towarde the opponents Outſyde Lyne and Preſſing: The ſame can be atchieued through an attack made to the Outſide which is changed to the Inſide while ſtepping to the Outſide: If the ſcholler ſhould ſtill wiſh to attack the Outſide Line, a ſimilar approache, reuerſed to reflecte the chaunge in Lyne, can be made in ordere to

moue

moue agaynſt the Outſide Lyne: The ſcholer can engage the opponents weapon and ſtep, Preſſing to the Inſide in order to open the Outſide Lyne, or as deſcribed preuiouſlie an attack changed from Inſide to Outſide while making the ſame mouement of the feet can alſo be vſed.

The left-handed opponente preſenteth manye different problemes for the combatant, but they are problems which, wyth intelligence and a carefull approache, can haue a ſolution founde for them: In engaging the left-handed opponent, the ſcholer ſhoulde remember that all the ſame principalles and theories which haue bene preſented for the right-handed ſcholar alſo applie iuſt as much to the left-handed opponent and it is wythin theſe principalles and theoretical elements that the ſolution lieth: Of courſe, iuſt as with a righte-handed opponent the correcte application and vſe of ſkil needes to be applied to the ſituation: The ſolutions which haue bene preſented here rely vppon the combatant applying his ſkil in the correct maner and vſinge the correct techniques, Tymes and Diſtances in order to achyeue the deſired reſult: The ſchollar ſhould alwaies be aware of his opponent and anie chaunges regardleſſe of whether he is righte or left-handed.

Of the True and Falſe Artes

He True and Falſe Artes are ſomething which has come into debate by various Maiſters and Theoriſts ouer manie yeares: Some find the vſe of the ſo-called Falſe Artes to be baſe and diſhonourable, others finde theme to be the ſkills of the gifted combatant, and others againe meerely ſee them as a ſet of ſkills which the combatant maie or maie not vſe depending on the ſituation: There are queſtiõs that ariſe and poyntes of viewe that are expreſſed; thoſe which will be found here are thoſe whych are mine and myne onely. In order to delue into this moſte perplexinge queſtion ſome foundations need to be layde: From theſe foundations a diſcuſſion will emerge about thys perticuler ſubiecte rather than inſtruction on howe eache wyll operate: True, there wyll be ſome principalles on their vſe preſented, and alſo waies to countere theſe actions preſented, but theſe wyll be in a moore generall than ſpecific approache: This wyll educate both thoſe who are intereſted in their vſe and alſo thoſe who would wiſh to knowe howe to defende themſelues againſt their vſe, thus the vſe of this diſcuſſion and inſtruction is vſeful to bothe.

The True Arte is conſidered to be contained in thoſe actions which are a direct attack vppon the opponent with no deuiation in their deliuerie: The Falſe Artes are thoſe which vſe deception and do not deliuer a directe attack but vſe other meanes in ordere to atchyeue their finall goal: According to this definition anye action which is perfourmed in order to meerelye prouoke action out of the opponent is parte of the Falſe Arte, whereas anie action which has the intention of ſtriking the opponent directlie is parte of the True Arte: Of courſe this would bring into queſtion ſuch thinges as ſymple defence, but this is excluded from the argumente: The queſtion of the True and Falſe Arte is about the attack againſte the opponent rather than any other action: A dyrect attack is conſidered to be True and an action whych prouoketh the opponent to action ſo that the combatant can then reſpond is Falſe: What this reſulteth in is that an action in ſome inſtances can be part of bothe the True and Falſe Artes ſimultaneouſlie: A Thruſt which is directed againſte the opponent with the intent to ſtrake the opponent is part of the True Arte, whereas a Thruſt which is directed againſt the opponent with the intent to drawe ſome action from the opponent againſt the action woulde be parte of the Falſe Arte: The important thing wyth regarde to diuiſion into the True or Falſe Arte is the entent of the action perfourmed rather than the action itſelfe.

For ſome,

The firſt Booke

For ſome, the definition of the True and Falſe Artes is ſomething which is to be held ſtrictlie and neuer the twaine ſhall meet regardleſſe of the vſefulneſſe of the ſkills inuolued: Thus theſe indiuiduals would haue the ſcholer perfourme no action agaynſt the opponent which is not a direct attack againſte him: To this perticuler pointe they woulde alſo bringe into queſtion Honor with regarde to the technique perform'd ſtating that the actions of the Falſe are baſe and diſhonourable and ſomething to be auoyded at all coſts: In this perticuler diſcuſſion you will ſee none of theſe arguments being preſented: Neither Arte will be ſene as aniething more than a ſet of ſkills to be vſed by the ſtudente or diſcarded ſhould that be his choiſe: Inſtead the arguments that will be preſented wyll be baſed on thoſe aſpectes of the Fencinge Theorie vppon whych all ſwordplaie is baſed: The queſtion of the vſe of Honor ſhuld neuer be about a perticuler ſkil or ſet of ſkils, meerely about the application of the ſkills of the Arte againſt an opponent: Queſtions of Honor and theyr application to martiall incounters againſte an opponent wyll be diſcuſſed in another parte of this diſcourſe: To the poynte the onely reaſon that the ſkills of deception will be called the Falſe Art is that it is moſte common that they are called ſuche in the fenſinge vernaculer which is preſent in treatiſes: For the preſent it wyll be a diſcuſſion of the applicaytion of a certaine ſkill ſet againſte an opponent and the aduantages, diſaduantages and correct application of theſe ſkills that will be diſcuſſed.

To beginne wythe wyll be arguments for and againſte the vſe of the Falſe Arte againſte an opponent: The arguments will be baſed vpon Fencing Theorie and its application which has alreadie been preſented in preuious ſections of this treatiſe: The prime argument againſte the vſe of the Falſe Arte is that whych is baſed on Tempo, though no doubt there are others: This is the argument which is moſt clearlye baſed on the principales of Fencing Theorye: The argument baſed on Tempo is founded on the idea that Tempo is expended in the vſe of each actiõ in ſwoordplaye: Thus the Tempo vſed in the action to drawe the action of the opponent is one whych is loſt to the opponent and giueth them a chaunce to act againſte the opponente: Thus the action vſing the Falſe Arte vſeth two Tempi whereas the action onelye vſeth a ſingle Tempo in that it is a direct attack perfourmed agaynſt the opponent: The vſe of the Falſe Arte according to this theorye expendeth more Tempo than it is worth, vſinge two Tempi where a ſyngle Tempo can be vſed by the opponent in reſponſe, thus leauing the ſcholler in a deficit: Intereſtinglie, the argumente for the vſe of the Falſe Arte in an incounter is alſo baſed vpon Tempo: In this argument the ſchollar gaineth Tempo through the action perfourmed: The ſcholler perfourms an attack not intending to ſtryke againſte the opponente: The opponent reſpondeth to the action of the ſcholare not knowing that the attacke is falſe, during this Time the ſcholler, breaking from his preuious action, redirects hys attack to another Lyne which has beene vncouered by the mouement perfourmed by the opponente: The combatant gaineth Tempo by makynge the opponent vſe Tempo in order to couer a Lyne which is not actuallie vnder threat by the ſcholler: This is the argument for the vſe of the Falſe Arte and in this caſe is that it can cauſe the opponent to perfourm actions which are reactions to the falſe action and thus ſpend Tempo, giuing the combatant Tempo in which to act: It is the reaction which is the key to the ſucceſſe of the falſe action.

There is one ſimple keye that ſees the ſucceſſe of the action in the Falſe Arte regardleſſe of howe ſimple or complex it maie be and that is the reaction of the opponent: The onely waye to drawe the reaction of the opponent is for the action perfourmed to haue entent behinde it, a lacke of intent wyll lead to the opponent not reacting to the action and thus the action failing: Theſe particular requirements, entent and reaction are the keyes for the action vſing the Falſe Art to ſucceed: If there is no entent behinde the action then the opponente wyll not react to the action and the ſtudent will loſe the Tempo of the action and giue the opponent a chance to react in ſome other manner, indeede euen to ſtryke the ſcholler: The reaction muſt be preſent in order to drawe the opponentes attention to ſome other place than where the ſcholare has intentions of ſtrikinge: There are ſeuerall different methods whych can be vſed with regard to the Falſe Artes: This is not a compl-

compleate

The firſt Booke

eate liſt but ſhoweth a ſelection of actions which may be perfourmed.

Breaking Tyme is a teknique in which the combatant pauſeth parte of the waie through his action and then compleateth the action: The Breaking of Tyme is deſigned ſo that the opponente wyll moue againſte the action, but moue paſt where the combatants wepon is thus allowinge him to ſtrike behinde the opponents weapon: A ſimple chaunge of Lyne vſing a Diſengage is alſo poſſible: The ſcholler maketh an attack along a certain Lyne encouraging the opponent to react as the attack proceedeth, the ſcholer changeth the Lyne and ſtriketh ſomewhere elſe againſt the opponent: Patterns can be alſo vſed againſte the opponente: The combatant makes repeated attackes againſte the ſame place, and then chaungeth the attack in order to ſtrike ſomewhere the pattern hath not beene: Simple diſtractions ſuch as a mouement of the hande or foote can alſo cauſe the opponent to be vnaware of an attack which followes: Manie of the Blade Engagement ſequences canne alſo be vſed in ordere to place the opponente into a poſition where the ſcholler wants them: This works eſpeciallie well where the opponent has been trained to meerely reſpond to ſtimulus rather than think the engagement through: Each one of theſe technikes, and ſeuerall others can be ſucceſsful ſhuld they be perfourmed correctlie and illicit the correct reſponſes from the opponent.

With the abilitie to correctlie vſe the ſkills of the Falſe Arte, a ſtudente wyll alſo be able to more ablye defend againſt the ſame when they are perfourmed againſt them: The keys to the ſucceſſe of a technique vſinge the Falſe Arte alſo happen to be the key to not beynge ſtrake by the ſame: The firſte thing that is neceſſarie is to vnderſtand howe the actions of the Falſe Artes work: Thus an education in the Falſe Arte euen if the ſcholler has no entention of euer vſinge them in an incounter is vſeful to the ſcholer. The ſchollar vſing a feint of ſome kinde, regardleſſe of its type is attempting to drawe a reſponſe from the combatant to moue him out of place: The reaction is the key to the action, thus in defence againſt the action the ſcholare ſhould do all he can not to reacte to the feint and onelye againſt a true attack: The ſcholar will learne as he gains more proficiencie with the ſworde what attackes wyll ſtrike and which ones wyll not and it is through this knowledge that the ſcholar will gayne the abilitie to determine the True from the Falſe: Some of this is found in training and other partes are found in ſimple experience in croſſing blades with different opponents: A ſwordesman who has knowledge of a thing can learn to defend againſt that ſame thing: A ſwordsman who has no knowledge of a thinge will find much more difficultie in defending againſt it.

A ſkill-ſet is meerely that a ſkill-ſet: Any accruinge of feelinge with regarde to the Honorable ſtate or lack thereof is a perſonal attribution by the perſon regarding it: The techniques themſelues can be vſeful ſhulde they be vſed in the correcte circumſtances and in the correct manner, yf they ſhold be vſed otherwiſe then the ſcholar could eaſilie find himſelf emperilled by the vſe of the action: For the moſt part, it can be ſeen that the ſkills take abilitie to vſe correctlie and thus training is neceſſarie as in all ſkills and due to this worth can be founde in the ſkils which are preſented: The ſkills preſented are ſkills onelye and anie attributinge ſhulde be directed to the ſchollare who vſeth them and the manner in which he doth, rather than for or againſt the ſkills themſelues.

The end of the firſt Booke.

Of Honor and Honorable Quarrels

The second Booke.

St Florian de la Riuiere
Sword and Book Enterprises

A.S. LVII

The second Booke

The Preface

Hile there exift other bookes on the fubiect which followeth and fundrie authors haue dealt wyth the fubiect in theyr owne fafhion, it is proper that fuch a difcourfe is prefented in accompanyment with that which hath alreadye beene prefented to this pointe: Suche other authors as haue beene indicated framed theyr difcourfe and prefented theyr opinyon bafed vppon deep knowledge and iudgement of the fubiect: What is prefented is done so and yt is my owne thought that I doubt (mofte iuftifiablie, and withe a guiltye knowledg of fuche) that what has beene prefented is refearched to a much leffer degree, beeing taken onelye from my owne mynde, than that which has beene prefented heretofore by othere authors as preuiouflye indicated: Howeuer, what I haue taken in hande to produce I do fo as a dutie and zeale to the wyder communitie and mofte efpeciallie to the Nobilitie and Gentrie of our moft honored Kingdome, and by prefenting fuch in its format to hopefullie be confidered that my indeauours to produce fuche are fufficient for fuche a Noble and Honored companie, and that production of fuch a Treatyfe will refult in a fuitable declaration of my mofte thankefull minde: The worke beeyng in fuch a format that the wordes be read rather than fpoken and thus theyr meffage is deliuered faithfullie from Author to Reader: It is my hope that the manie fauours that the mofte honourable Reader doeth purchafe the Author in reading fuch are well payde for in the reading of fuch which has beene produced: It is myne owne hope that fuche menne of ranke who mannage Armes, and who knowe theyr weapons well wyll fauour the indeauour which has bene prefented to them for theyr reading, and wyll no leffe appreciate my indeauours excufing anye defectes, and prefent the worke fuch as it is produced by the hande of the Author, and which is a prefentation of fuche labors taken to produce yt, is nowe prefented in the mofte humble fafhion to the Reader.

Of Honor

The second Booke
Of Honor

IN the examination of the Art of Defence the queſtiõ of Honor and Honorable quarrelles is ſomething which the Gentleman can not eſcape: This is eſpeciallye the caſe as it is in this arena that the Gentleman maie finde himſelf moſt frequentlie: The Artes Militarye are where a Gentleman can excell in the feelde demonſtratinge hys loyaltie and his willingnes to fight for his Lord and this is one of the moſt recogniſed fieldes of indeauour and rightlie ſo, but the Gentleman can alſo excell in thoſe fieldes of Honor in a ciuilian contexte ſtill through the vſe of a ſwoorde: It is this direction from which this diſcourſe has approched the ſtudie of the Arte of Defence. The ciuilian ſubiectes of the vſe of the ſworde are iuſt as important and neede to haue eſpecial note made of them: Thus through this thoſe ciuilian aſpects, ſome which are alſo founde in the militarie, muſt alſo be diſcuſſed: The queſtion of Honoure is one that appeareth in diſcuſſions of bothe kindes of marſhal conflictes and as ſuche the diſcuſſion of Honor applyeth to bothe, euen if this diſcuſſion will be moore focuſſed at a ciuilian context rather than a militarie one: Shoulde the Gentleman find himſelfe vnknowing in the waies and means of Honor he wyll finde that his Reputation will ſuffer, and for the Gentleman this is akin to a kind of Death, regardleſſe of whether it be in a ciuilian or militarie arena: A Gentleman liueth by his Honor and Reputation thus knowing that which applieth to eyther and both is of greate importance to him.

For a man to vnderſtand a thinge he muſt firſt knowe what that thinge is as vnderſtanding beginneth with knowing and then through examination of the thing vnderſtanding reſulteth: This is the ſame for all thinges and none ſo much as Honor: For manie the explanation as to what Honor is reſults in a verie perſonall definition and encompaſſeth what the indiuidual feeles that it meanes: In more general tearmes Honoure can be defined as the perceiued value of an indiuiduals ſocial ſtatus as iudged by that indiuiduals communitie and more to the point their peer group but alſo thoſe outſide the peer group: This would implie that Honor is ſomething which commeth from without and is adopted within as for the moſte part the definition diſcuſſes more about public opinion than that of the indiuidual.

The influence of the externall on the internall is greate and this muſt be taken into account: This is an eſpeciallie important parte of Honor as often it is the feelings of others externallie which will haue more impacte on the indiuidual: The nemeſis of peer preſſure is preſente wyth the group iudging the actions of the indiuidual and often hauing more impact on the indiuiduals choiſes than he woulde lyke to admit: For manie it is the publike perception of an indiuiduals Honoure which is moſt important and it is this which has the moſt waight on his reſulting Reputation: From the peer group which wyll haue the moſt impact vppon the indiuidual wyll ſpreade thoughts about the indiuidual to others in the communitie reſulting in euer increaſing preſſure and effect on the indiuidual but alſo in reuerſe vppon the communitie which ſurroundes that indiuidual: The actions of the indiuidual in relationſhip with his peer group and as a reſult the wider communitie will affect all perceptions of the indiuiduals Honor, and thus inhibit or enable his actions in one directiõ or another: The Gentle-man thus is affected greatlie by the externall preſſures of the peere groupe and wyder communitie in his perceptions of Honor and this muſt be taken into account: Howeuer, the indiuidual muſt alſo waigh vpp that which he keeps internallie and that which guideth his deciſions, eſpeciallie ſhould thoſe deciſions ſeeme to againſt the peer group: It is in tymes ſuch as theſe that it becomes more importãt that the Honor of the indiuidual has ſome origin within rather than without.

Much

The second Booke

Much has been saide of the externall nature of Honor and howe it affects the thoughts about him within the group: This describeth the social feelings of the concept of Honor and descrybes it in a somewhat dry fashion: Howeuer there are also those aspects of Honor which the Gentleman muste make internall to himselfe in order that suche positiue feelings and ideas about him and what he doth can flourish: Shuld this be absent then the Gentle-man and euentuallie the peer groupe will know that the Gentleman is hollow and missing elements which are important for the true Gentleman and Honorable man: Honor for the selfe is about positiue perceptions of the self and the actiõs that the indiuidual taketh in perticuler circumstances: This is somethynge that muste speake to the indiuidual from inside rather than coming from some externall source: It must be a feelyng of beeing compelled to do that which is correct euen shulde it leade to some detriment to the Gentleman immediatlie: The poet Decimus Magnus Ausonius speaketh of the consideration of committyng a base deed and euen though no one else is around, respecting the self enough that he shuld not commit such an acte: This is what Honoure internall to the Gentleman is aboute, those feelinges whych driue a Gentleman to commit onely those actions which will increase his Reputation and those actions which he can liue with himselfe committing to: In this he must be driuen internallie more than externallie and haue some feelinge which driueth him to excell and onely commit those actions which are of a higher nature and bringe positiue feeling to the selfe and the group euen if those actions are difficult to see at the tyme or would feele to be against the group euen if it is the right and Honorable thing to do.

There are some essentiall elementes which can be founde wythin Honor and also associated with it, in order to truelie embrace the concept of Honour and vnderstand it, it is also necessarie to vnderstand how these can affect and combyne with Honour in bothe positiue and negatiue fashion: The aspects expressed here are also importante in and of theyr selues and should also be something which is considered by the Gentleman at all times: Each one describeth something about the Gentleman who possesse them, and also about the man who doth not: Should they be in a lacke or in abundance those arounde the man wyll knowe of this and in verie shorte fashion: These elementes, or their lacke, canne laie the foundation of a positiue or negatiue relationshipe betweene others in the peer group and surrounding communitie.

Courage is an aspect whych is most often associated with thinges marshal in nature and rightlie so, but it is also associated wyth thinges which are not so marshal in nature but the Gentleman still has to stand vpp for himself: It is in tymes of stresse and threatenyng circumstances that a mans Courage or lacke thereof will shine through, regardlesse of his social standing: Courage is a necessarie attribute for the indiuidual to be respected in his communitie as it is through this aspect that a man will or will not act: Courage is considered, as great theorist Aristotle stated the greatest qualitie next to Honor: The two in manie wayes should not be separated as it taketh Courage to stand vpp and be Honorable especiallie in those instances where the Gentleman maie finde himself vnder threat due to taking an Honorable position for or agaynste someone or in a perticuler circumstance: It is onlye in these tryalles that an Gentlemans Courage will shine through and expose itselfe to the wider communitie or the man will be shown to be in lacke of it.

One of the tymes where Courage wyll be showen to be present or absent is in the next element which is Truth: In manye instances it will take Courage for the Gentleman to tell the Truthe due to the consequenses of tellinge that Truth and beynge associated with that Truth: Euen in this circumstance the indiuidual needeth to haue the Courage to stand vp for the Truth: Truth has some elements which all combine to be what it is and these need to be taken into account: It is not onely sayinge the Truth but also hearing it and also knowinge it: The Truth shoulde be passed on and onelye the Truth, rumours shoulde not be tolde as Truthe, but tolde as the rumours that they are: Should a rumour be told as Truth it is much the same as if the indiuidual told a Lye rather than the
Truth

The second Booke

Truth, in thys the Gentleman needeth to be carefull in tellynge what has bene hearde: In all insttaces the Gentleman should tell the Truth euen shoulde this leade to a persone hauinge some negatiue result as a consequense: He shoulde also know those tymes where not sayinge aniething is as important as tellinge the Truthe as not all Truths shoulde be tolde to all people due to the effects which canne resulte on to other people: In hearinge what a person sayeth it is important that the Gentleman can knowe what is the Truth and what is not, this is especiallye important shulde suche information be thought to be passed on: The Gentleman shoulde take care in onlye passinge on what he knoweth to be the Truth and leauing that which is suspect alone.

    Courage and Truth are two elementes which primarilye come from within the indiuidual: There are also those elementes which come from the internall to the externall and then are supported by the externall, one of these is Respect: Before a man can be respected by others he needes to haue hys owne selfe-respect: In this the man needeth to respect himselfe enough to onelye doe that which wyll increase his standing and onelye show himself in the most positiue light to the wider communitie: This is primarilye atchyeued through the interactions with other people: Onelye once a man has demonstrated that he has respect for himselfe is there any chaunce for him to be respected by others: This deals with Respect coming from others to the indiuidual, but there is also an element where the man needeth to be showing respect towarde others and this shoulde affect how they acte also: To expect Respect, a man also has to show Respect to others and in the case of the Gentleman there are two prime places where this shuld be showen and that is to his Lady and his Lord: In all instances his actions can reflect vppon both and thus he shuld haue them in minde before anie action is made: Showinge Respect to the Lady is doing that which pleaseth her or increaseth her in some waie and ensurynge that no action is made where anye detrimente will be directed her waye: Showinge Respect to ones Lord is in some wayes easier than to a Lady as this can be made through publick demonstration in actiōs in martiall conflicts but also in other circumstances, all thought shoulde be towarde increasing it toward ones Lord: This Respect is often demonstrated through the decisions made with regarde to difficult decisions which haue greate impacte: The Respect gayned through successfullie negotiating such decisions increaseth a mans Respect and standing within the communitie.

    Loyalty is an aspecte of character which of greate importance to the Gentleman shoulde he wish to winne Respect and gaine a Reputation for Honoure: It is an importante element with regarde to Honor as a sense of Loyaltie demonstrates worth to the wider communitie and also the presence of a set of principales by which the indiuidual wyll stand. In questions of Loyaltie the question which is alwaies asked is where it should lye and to whom it is most important, the various eualuations as to whom has prioritie when requests are made by those to whom one is loyal: In all instances it is correcte for the Gentleman to be loyal firste to his Lady and then his Lord, of course not wyth-standing the Loyaltie that each Gentleman shoulde haue to himselfe: Should he finde himself touched with the pangs of threat to his owne Honor he shoulde alwaies keep his own counsaile first and do what feeleth to be correct and most loyal to who he is in nature: Once this is atchieued then the Gentleman is able to serue firste his Lady and then his Lord: The Gentleman shoulde remaine aboue reproche in hys dealings and leaue no area in which someone maie claime that he is lackinge in his Loyaltie to any one of the three: A lack of Loyaltie demonstrates the vnwillingnesse to stand by someone when they are in need and also implieth a lacke of abilitie to stand vpp to their owne principalles when vnder pressure: Bothe of these will affect considerations of the indiuidual in a markedlie negatiue fashion, a person is vnlikelie to deale wyth a person to whom their beste interestes are not founde, and in whom they can finde no recourse for assistance shoulde it be required: This wyll also touch vppon the Honor of the indiuidual as questions of Loyaltye are ones which cutte close to the Gentle-man wythe regarde to Honour, a question aboute his Loyalty wyll in turne question his
    Honor.

The second Booke

Honor.

Loyalty and Duty are bothe connected as it is to whome, and onlye to whom you are loyall that you owe Dutie: A perſon who has no Loyaltie is not concerned about Dutie and thus he muſt do nothing, a perſon who has Loyalties muſt ſerue theſe Loyalties through theyr Dutie: The queſtion of Duetie followeth the ſame courſe as that of Loyaltie firſt yt muſt be to what the indiuidual requireth, then to his Lady and then to his Lord: In this there can be no wauering as with Loyalty: Of courſe, as with Loyaltie ſhould the indiuidual haue no perticuler feeling in the inſtance then the firſt Duetye is to the Lady and then to the Lord: Taſks preſented by the Lady or Lord of a Gentleman ſhould alwaies be fulfilled to the beſt abilitye of the Gentleman in all inſtances: It ſhoulde be this which occupyeth his thoughts when he commiteth to an enterpriſe of ſome kinde: Duety is giuen to thoſe to whom agreement has been mayde about a perticuler taſk and onelye when that taſk affects a higher Loyaltie ſhould a Gentleman remoue himſelfe from ſuch a taſk, explaining the reaſons why this is ſo: Agreements on certayne taſks ſhuld alwaies be conſidered in the ſcope of howe it maye affecte Loyalties to others who are not directlye inuolued in the negotiation, namelye ones Lady and Lord and ſhould the taſk ſette be one which wyll aduerſelie affect the Gentlemans relationſhip betweene himſelfe and his Lady or Lord he ſhoulde not commit to ſuche an enterpriſe but maintain his Loyaltie and Duety: The onelie time a Duetie preſented by ones Lady or Lord ſhould not be committed to is where ſuche a taſk is againſte the Loyaltie a Gentleman has to himſelf or his Honor: In all inſtances with regard to Loyaltie and Duetie that which appeals to the higher values of the human nature ſhoulde be attended to and that which motiuates the baſe values ſhould be auoyded: In all inſtances a Gentleman ſhoulde, and is expected to maintaine his Honor through his Loyaltie and Duety, ſhould there be ſome aſpecte where his Honor is touched that he cannot kepe thus he ſhould break immediatly from ſuch aſſociation in order to defend himſelf and remaine with his Honor intact: Regardleſſe of a mans Duety or Loyaltie to a Lady or Lorde, it is to hymſelfe and his Honor that he muſt hold higheſt and thus maintaine in all circumſtances: No more ſo is this more important than when the lure of reward is preſented for the Loyaltie or Duety euen though ſome compromiſe of Honor muſt be made: It is in theſe ynſtances that a Gentleman muſt ſtand for Honor aboue anie reward.

Courteſie and the aſpects of Courteſie found in normal aſſociation with the wider communitie ſhould be denyed to none, regardleſſe of their poſition or ſtation: True Courteſie is founde where it is made to thoſe who are of leſſer poſition or ſtation than the perſon giuing it: It is true that Courteſie ſhuld alſo be extended to thoſe of a higher ſtation, but this ſhould be made without anie expectation of rewarde or fauour made externallie but from an internall compunction that the indiuidual muſt make ſuche courteous geſtures as naturall to the order of things: Courteſie for the Honorable Gentleman preſenteth publiquely thoſe poſitiue aſpects of the Gentlemans character on diſplaie to all thoſe who ſurround him and can not but increaſeth his ſtandinge in their viewe by the verye nature of the Courteſie extended: A lacke of Courteſie preſented at thoſe tymes whene it is expected demonſtrates a gap in a mans character which wyll be noted by thoſe around and ſuche a gap will affect the mans ſtandyng and thus be ſeen to affect his Honor: In matters of Honor one ſhould extend all Courteſie to the other partye inuolued as this ſhoweth the greater character of the indiuidual who expreſſeth it ouer one who did not: In manye wayes the diſplaye of Courteſye, eſpeciallie to a perſon who they are not on good terms with is a greate demonſtration of the Honor that an indiuidual holdeth, and alſo the greate worthe to the wider communitie: Such a ſituation is euen moore important in a publique ſituation where anye ſort of miſgiuings or animoſitie between the indiuiduals wyll be noticed by paſſers-by and maye cauſe theme ſome dyſtreſſe due to the viewing of ſuch an incountere betweene two indiuiduals: In the Gentlemans caſe, it is to all Ladies that courteſy ſhoulde be ſhowen: This is of ſygnificance as it is in Ladies that Honore is to be preſ-
preſerued

The second Booke

erued and a lacke of Courtesie to a Lady is to showes a lack of Honor to all Ladies: The simple elementes of Courtesie Honor bothe the giuer and the receiuer in that the giuer demonstrateth his goode nature and the receiuer is able to be gracious in the receipt of such Courtesie. In no instance shoulde an aspect of Courtesie be ouerlooked regardlesse of the indiuidual inuolued, in all instances proper care should be mayde that the Gentle-man leaues as positiue opinion of himselfe as possible when he departes and this is often opened and sealed by the greeting presented on arriual and the salutation on leauing the group.

Each one of the elements which has been presented is vitall on its owne for proper dealings wyth the wider communitie, but also made more so in theyr relationship with the concept of Honor: Throughe the demonstration of the presence of suche elementes the Gentleman is presented as more compleat in hys forme and thus more respected: These tearms and concepts are so intertwined with theyr effects and relationships that it is neere impossible to separate them from one another: In all situations a Gentleman shoulde consider what he maye doe and see howe this maie affect his standing within his peer groupe and also the wider communitie: Demonstrations of Honor are publick and must be remembered to be so and thus such should be the consideration of the indiuidual inuolued in the demonstration: The Gentleman shoulde doe his best to cultiuate the elementes which haue been presented and make them a normal parte of his character in order that such things are possible without thought inuolued, but hable to be felte and thus allowe his internall feelinges to guide him: This is where Honor resides euen though it is a publick concepte it is also a verie priuate one with elementes of character which can onelie come from within the indiuidual rather than beeing imposed vppon him by those externallie: The Gentleman, in order to maintayne his Honoure, shoulde onelye commit to those actions whych will increase the positiue feelings about him both internallie but also externallie: The maintenance of Honor is a proiect which doth not ende but must be somethyng which is maintained in all associations with all indiuiduals, as Honor is of great importance to the Gentleman in all his dealings and associations.

The importance of Honor is something which reallye shoulde not haue to be spoken about, especiallie with the euidence which has beene alreadye presented: Howeuer, it is vsefull to explaine exactlie what holding Honor high doeth for a Gentleman and howe this can impact vppon him and the wider communitie: More to the poynte it demonstrateth howe the interaction betweene indiuidual and group is affected by Honor and perceptions of it: Honor is somethyng which demonstrateth the internall on the external and has a key link to the Reputation of a Gentleman which he will liue by: The link betweene Honor and Reputacion is a solide bond which can not be broken, where one suffereth so too will the other as a result and thys needs to be noted as of great importance: To be shown to haue a lack of Honor is to reduce the Reputacion of a man and this will affecte his dealings with people, especiallie those who haue not met him preuiouslie: What should be noted about this is that it is through a Reputation that a man gets to be knowen for Honour or not and thus the two are intertwyned and relyant on one another: The social negotiation, dealinge with vnknowen people on the basis of Reputacion, is one of the key dealings that the Gentleman will be inuolued in and howe his Reputacion has preceeded him based on the communities thoughts of his Honor wyll often determine how such negotiations wyll proceed: Of course once a person meeteth such indiuiduals face to face further negotiation will be mayde, but this will be giuen a firste impression by the Reputatiõ which has bin built by the indiuidual: The reason that this is the case is that a Reputacion is the generallie accepted opinion of the indiuidual held by publick societie growen as a result of the knowen and assumed actions of the yndiuiduall: These actions maye be actuall or assumed, and the assumptions are often based vpon the actions preuiouslie committed by the indiuidual, often greatly affected by the leuel of Honor showen in such incounters: In this the Gentleman must be careful in all his negotiations with all people as wordes and deedes wyll trauell to other places vppon the lippes of those who do nott knowe the
indiuidual

The second Booke

indiuidual and this wyll affect the indiuiduals Reputacion and their perceiued Honoure.

A positiue Reputation is easie to break by symple misdeeds of the indiuidual and is also difficult to restore: This is due to the high position to which Honor is kept and thus people who haue a Reputation for Honor are also kept. The negatiue is easye to gaine and difficult to expunge in order to regaine the goode which has been lost, an indiuidual will haue to do manie more good deeds in ordere to recouer Honor and Reputation than he woulde euer haue to in order to reduce it: It is due to this vnbalanced dichotomie betweene the gaining and the losing of Reputation and Honour that the Gentle-man shoulde ensure that he is Honorable in all his dealyngs regardlesse of who they maie be with, euen the voice of the most humblest of societie can affect the Reputation of a Gentle-man as information and Reputation will flowe euen from the lowest to the highest.

Honor and Reputacion can be seene as windowes to the soule of the indiuidual in that what is perceiued on the outside is assumed to be a glimpse of the natuer of the indiuidual whych lies vpon the insyde: Thus feelinges of Honor which are felte on the inside are expressed in the externall, and in ordere for the man to accepte that which he is giuen by others from the outside he needes to feel that he deserues such Honor: Aristotle states that Dignity consisteth not in possessing Honors, but in the consciousnesse that we deserue them: Thus it can be seene that if the Gentleman demonstrateth outwardlye in his actions that he is without Honor and of a base mynde, then so too thys is what would be considered to be him internallye as well: In this there is a flowe betweene the internall and the externall which can not be ignored, or is at the perill of the indiuidual: The onelie waye that an indiuidual can support a positiue Reputation and Honore is through demonstrations of that which giueth the most positiue light about him and thus through demonstrations of Honor.

When demonstrations of Honor are considered, moste people wyll automaticallie think of martial ones where the indiuidual demonstrateth his defence of Honor on some noble fielde, howeuer there are also non-martial demonstrations of Honor which must also be taken into account, as euen in these scenarios, and often more so in these, a Reputacion is builte or loste by the indiuidual. The key thinge noted in this perticuler situation is that they are bothe, Honor and Courtesie, essential in the proper dealings of a Gentleman with the wider communitie, if he is seene to be lackinge in one it will affecte his Reputacion and others percepcion of his Honor: There will be a greate deal sayde aboute the martiall applications of Honore and those situations of a martiall thought in a later parte of this discussion: Suffice to saye that the martiall demonstrations of Honor are founde in the *Duello* and other Honorable combats in which the Gentleman finds himselfe, but also in such other martiall demonstrations where Honor is demonstrated by him, euen if such demonstrations would seem to be out of place in the situation, euen more so in these situations a Gentleman has the chance to demonstrate a noble nature than otherwyse: While the martiall demonstration of Honor on the fielde of battail or Honoure is the moste explisit demonstration of Honore that a Gentleman canne make, it is not the onelie situation in which he wyll find himself where questions of Honor will arise in his dealinge with others: It is importante that he shoulde realise such situations and do his best in order to deale in the most Honorable fashion possible in those situations.

The non-marshal situations in which a Gentleman can finde himselfe where Honor is touched are manie and can be present in his eueriedaie lyfe and this is the reason why Honor must alwaies be a consideration for the Gentleman and his dealings with others: A Gentleman should alwaies giue his assistance to a Lady in anye task which maye be presented to him: This is the case where she maie ask for assistance a Gentleman must be diligent in his seruice, howeuer the Gentleman shuld also be aware of those situations where he can offer his assistance without request on the parte of the Lady, these are euen more importante for the Gentleman: Regardlesse of his owne taskes and obligations, a Gentleman shoulde alwaies be able to put aside his current task in order to assist a La-

Lady

The second Booke

dy wyth hers: The simple taskes presented are those which are easye to perfourme and phisicallye presented, but there are also those situations where assistance is needed in other forms, this is especiallie the case where Iudgement is required.

There are those situations where the Iudgement of a Gentleman is required by another or a Lady and in all these situations a Gentleman shoulde consider the implications of hys Iudgement before it is made for, against or in the neutrall, alonge with the presentation of such Iudgement to the indiuidual and especiallie if there is a group present: There are also those situations where Iudgement is requested of the Gentle-man but he shoulde holde his Iudgement for feare of insultynge those presente or expressinge feelings which woulde not be appropriate to the current situation: A Gentleman must be aware of his situation at euerie turne in order that the deliuerye of Iudgement or the holdinge of suche iudgement is appropriate to the situation and gaineth the Gentleman what he seeketh: In these situations a Gentleman can actuallye gaine more by holding his Iudgement than expressinge one at the tyme, and he shoulde be aware of these as tymes like these wyll touche on his Reputacion most deeplie: A Gentleman who can holde his Iudgement especiallie vnder pressure of those arounde him is considered to be discrete and this is a moste vseful and valued traite, and will gaine him Reputacion: This discretion shoulde be applyed yn all situations where the expression of thought to another group or indiuidual wyll not gayne positiue thought about the Gentleman, and maie lose him Reputacion, it is in these situations where Courtesie shows itself as being present or absent in the Gentleman and thus can gaine or cost him greatlie.

Courtesye is a simple concepte and its expression is easilie demonstrated in most situations, howeuer it is of great importance to the Gentleman and he must be able to demonstrate Courtesie in all situations: This is no moore so where the Gentleman is vncomfortable in the situation due to the companie or the situation, often in these situations the best thyng for the Gentleman to do is to excuse himself and diuorce himself from the situation: Such feelings serueth the Gentleman well in that they often can giue a hint to when a situation is mouinge towarde that which maye be lesse than Honorable: Such companie should be auoyded by the Gentleman should he be seen by others in the companie and be firmlie associated with them as a result, this wyll affect his Reputacion: A Gentleman shoulde alwaies be carefull about the companye he keepes and ensure that he doth not associate with those who could irreparablie damage his Reputacion.

Courtesie is simplie expressed and as such is of great importance, greetings and salutations at the meeting of an indiuidual as well as the correct departure of the indiuidual forme the brackets around which an incounter are made: These must be considered and perfourmd appropriatelie for the situation in which the Gentleman finds himselfe: Especiallie when a Gentleman has contact with an indiuidual or a group for the first tyme he should obserue the correct greeting as this will leaue a lasting impression of him vppon the group or indiuidual: Those elementes of Courtesie which are simplie seen as goode maners should be obserued at all tymes regardlesse of the situation in which the Gentleman findeth himselfe: For some suche things are onelye considered to be importante when dealing with the vpper echelons of societie, but the Gentleman should be well-aware that the reports of lower indiuiduals to higher ones can haue waight in all situations: Thus the Gentle-man shuld be Honorable in all his dealinges with all indiuiduals, euen where the other maie decide to attempt some vnder-handed dealing the Gentleman should remayne true to his Honor and deal fairlie and honestlie: The knowledge of suche fair dealing wyll increase the Reputation and Honor of the Gentleman further vpp as reports of such dealings are spreade amongst the wider communitie.

The choises a Gentleman maketh are important as some haue alreadye been demonstrated, and it is through these choises and the resulting actions that an impression of the Gentleman will be fourmed by the indiuiduals and also the wyder communitie: In all situations, but especiallye where the more difficult choises must be mayde a Gentleman shoulde look to his Honoure and make suche
decisions

The second Booke

decifions that wyll increafe his Reputacion and Honour rather than thofe which will decreafe it: In fome fituations and in fact many, the decifion which wyll increafe Honor and Reputation maie not be popular amongft certaine indiuiduals but the Gentleman fhuld ftaie true to himfelf as this is where the true tefts of Honoure are founde: In the ende the Gentle-man mufte anfwere for his owne actions regardleffe of anye aduice or fuggeftion gyuen by others it is the Gentlemans choyfe which refults and as Sophocles would ftate it is not about making the right choifes it is about dealinge with the confequenfes of the choifes: The Gentleman is refponfible for maintaining his own Honor and Reputacion and this can onlye be atchieued by the making of the correct choifes appropriate to the fituation and in concert with the Honor of the Gentleman, fhould the Gentleman faile to make the correct decifions in the fituation then he maie fall into Difhonor.

Of Difhonour

Icero doeth ftateth of Difhonour that there is no praife in beeinge Honorable or vpright where no one can or tries to corrupt the perfon, thus the verie threat of Difhonour increafes the worth of the Honorable man: This being fayd, no man fhuld be tempted to fall into Difhonour as this will greatlye affect his Reputatiõ and thus thofe who would affociate with him, alonge with his perceiued worthe: In order to be on garde againft Difhonour it is beft to be forewarned about how this can happen and thus be able to be on the defence againfte it: In order to be forewarned, fomething of Difhonour needeth to be knowne in order that it can be identified as different from Honor.

Breaches of Honor confifteth of thofe things which come about as a refult of a failure in anie of the key elements of Honor: With regarde to this there are expectations which are placed vppon the Gentle-man by the wider communitie and it is theyr expectations whych neede to be met, which anie Gentleman woulde do his beft to do in order to maintaine his Reputacion and Honor in the proceffe: In this the yndiuidual needs to be aware of what thofe expectations are and howe and where failures maie be perceaued: In order to beft difcouer thofe places of failure in expectations it is vfeful to once againe examine eache one of the key elementes to reiterate the expectations which haue been preuiouflie difcuffed: Thefe wyll be addreffed in a flightlie different order in order that connectiõs can be made and thofe areas of Difhonor difcouered in order that they can be auoided.

The firft afpect which wyll be difcuffed is Courtefie, while breaches of Courtefie are often minor in manie fituations they can refult in maior iffues: This is efpeciallie the cafe where the appropriat amounte of Courtefie is not made to ones Lord or anie reprefentatiue of them: The onelye place where a lapfe of Courtefie maie be feen as more grieuous is where it is mayde againfte a Lady and more efpeciallye the Gentlemans Lady: Beeing that the Lady is feene as the height of example of Honor anie difcourtefie to a Lady can be feen as a maior breach of Honor on the part of the man who committeth it: In this the Gentleman mufte be efpeciallie carefull and thus enfure that he giues Courtefie to all Ladies regardleffe of their rank or ftation: Of courfe Courtefie fhoulde alwaies be fhowen to all as fmall indifcretions wyll mounte and build vppon one another and flowlie damage a perfons Reputation iuft as a large breach wyll bring him down quicklie.

Truth in all thinges is expected of a Gentle-man and his difcretion is alfo expected in certain fcenarios where he learneth thinges it is in thefe times where the Gentleman needeth to be aware when he fhoulde be paffinge on thofe Truths and when he fhoulde kepe them to himfelf: In no inftance fhould he Lye about fomething about which he has beene afked fhould he wifh not to anf-

anfwer

The second Booke

wer due to the difcretion requiered in the fituation then he fhould be iudicious in his replie, or auoid giuing a directe anfwer which maie implie one direction or the other: To paffe on information where it maie do damage to the one who tolde the information is a breache of Honour and fhoulde neuer be committed informaytion in confidence fhoulde ftaye as fuch: Rumours fhoulde neuer be paffed as fact or information as thys maye damage the Reputation of another and to be feene to be doing fuch is Difhonourable: Shoulde a rumour be heard then the Gentleman fhould goe and difcuffe it with the perfon with whom it is about in order to difcouer the Truthe in order to be able to haue the facts: From there it is the indiuiduals choife as to what fhould be done with the information for the mofte part it fhoulde be vfed to quafh a malitious rumour whereuer it is founde vnleffe the indiuidual wifheth the truthe to be kepte in confidence: Truft and Truth worke togither and a perfon who has been caught in a Lie or fpreading of rumour is leffe likely to be trufted and thus accepted by others and this wyll greatlie affect the indiuiduals Reputation.

Two thinges which lie well wyth Truthe and Truft are Loyaltie and Honour as there is an intertwyning of all of thefe elements to be founde in them: To be loyal is to be truthful with thofe to which you are loyal and to be loyal is alfo to haue their Truft: In this a perfon holdeth their Duety to the people to whom they are loyal and fhoulde ferue them with Truth and Honour: Shulde a Gentleman be found to be lacking in his Duety or found to be difloyal then he wyll be founde to be leffe than Honorable and this will greatlye affect his Reputation: In all things the Gentleman fhouldeft confider where his Loyaltie lies and alfo what his Duety is and to whom: He fhouldft always put thofe who hold his Loyaltie clofeft before others in all thinges, though in this he fhouldeft chofe that which is moft Honorable and loyal to himfelf as his Duetie muft be to his own Honor efpeciallie where a bafe deede is expected: The expectations of Duety and Loyaltie vary dependent on the relationfhip between the indiuiduals but in all inftances the Gentleman fhould do his beft to enfure that they are maintained, to do otherwife is a breach of confidence and Honor and this will be to the detriment of bothe the Gentle-man and the relationfhip he is in: Loyaltie to ones Lord and Lady is feene as one of the higheft tenets of Honor and thus any breach of fuch is a maior one that a Gentleman fhoulde do his beft to auoyd, faue where his perfonal Honor is fo touched that he canõt do otherwife but to breach it.

Courage is important: For the moft part people fee Courage in its martiall application onelie but it can alfo be founde in leffe martyall fituaytions and in this where it is alfo importante to the Gentleman and perceaued by others: It is in thofe times of aduerfitie that Courage muft be fhown and anie cowardice will forelie affect the Reputation of the Gentleman: Cowardice on the fielde of battel or Honor will ftain the Gentleman with an almoft indelible mark which wyll not be able to be expiated eafilie: Courage where he decideth that his owne felfe is more important than a collectiue goode or againft Duety or Loyaltie will haue almoft as great an effect: With regarde to Courage it wyll be found in thofe times of aduerfitie and it is at thofe times that a Gentleman will be expected to fteppe in and fhowe his worth and the refult of fuch will greatlye affect his perceiued Honor and Reputation: Regardleffe of a martiall or non-martiall fituation the Gentleman wyll be expected to fhow Courage and ftand vp for what is Honorable and a failure to do fo will greatlie affect him.

Some of the caufeth of Difhonour directlye linked to the effential elements haue been found aboue: Howeuer, it is poffible to reduce the lift of caufes of Dyfhonour to a muche fmaller lyfte which couers mofte fituations: In order to atchyeue this it is neceffarye to looke at the refulte of the Difhonour which has bene caufed and then go back to fee what caufed the Difhonour from the refult: This woulde almofte feeme to be a round-about waie to finde the anfwere to this queftion but bothe are linked in fuch a waye that without the one the other is more difficult to comprehend as to how the effect is caufed and the refult refulting: The cleareft and moft obuious refult of Difhonor is a lacke of Honour prefente, howeuer it is neceffarye to looke fomewhat deeper and fee why thys

Difhonour

The Second Booke

Dishonour is caused thus the resulte needs to be inuestigated: A person is considered to be in Dishonor when they haue made a failure on some parte in their interaction with others or due to some acte which has beene perfourmed howeuer it is the shame to the wider communitie which actuallie causeth the Dishonour rather than the act itselfe: It is due to the shame that is felt by the wider communitie that the indiuidual who committed the act is shamed: Thus the cause of the Dishonour is actuallie the shame caused to the wider communitie which shames the indiuidual rather than the actual act itself: It could be sayd then that if an acte is not founde out then there should be no issue: Howeuer for the Gentleman of Honor such personal feelings of shame shoulde preuent the acte in the first place: It is possible to look further into this and examine closer to the euent: A bad presentation on the parte of the Gentleman is somethinge which causeth shame, which will affect anie one to whome the Gentle-man is connected: This bad presentation can be seene in his meere presence phisicallie or some act that has beene perfourmed either vnwell on in a slouenlye maner or some act which he should not haue performed in the first place: Such bad presentation on his parte wyll once again reflect backe on anye one who is associated, thus affecting the wyder communitie thus causing shame to them which is redirected as shame and Dishonour on the indiuidual: Knowing the causes of Dishonour being linked to these elements the Gentleman can do his best to auoid them by ensuring that his perfourmance in tasks and presentation will cause no shame to those to whom he is associated: This can onlie come from the Gentleman ensuringe that he analyseth the situation or taske to which he has been set and the wider implications of the committing to such a task: The guidanse for the Gentleman must primarilie come from within rather than without.

The result of Dishonour is reasonablye clear for the group it results in a general feeling of negatiuitie which is dyrected towarde the indiuiduall who has seene to haue a losse of Honor: Thys feelinge of negatiuitie will result in a perceiued reduction in the worth of the indiuidual to the group and as a result a reduction in his Reputation: The result of such a reduction in positiuitye toward the indiuidual will make social interaction withe the wider communitie moore difficult and euen moore so with his own peer groupe whose influence will be felt most with regard to this particular effect: A Dishonoured man is put in a sorte of Purgatorie where he is seen as somethinge lesse than he was: Often his opinions and feelings on particular matters will be thought lesse of and sometimes euen ignored: He will feel a reduction in his sociall standinge euen though this maye not be reflected in anie losse of title or station: This will greatlye affecte the Gentleman in anye negotiations he maie decide to engage in withe the wyder communitye as the knowledge of his Dishonour will no doubt spread from his peer group to the wider communitie: The Gentle-man will haue an almoste phisical feeling of a mark vppon him which he is helplesse to remoue but which ostracises him from his vsual associations: With regarde to this he wyll feel that he will want to do almost aniethinge in order to remooue the mark and thus recouer some of the Reputation and Honor which he has lost: The amount of time he serues in the Purgatorie will depend on the depth of the Dishonour and the nature of the marke which he has beene marked: This wyll not be dependent on the indiuidual wyth the mark rather his peer group and the wider communitie which marked him.

No Gentleman would want to spend anie time than is absolutelie necessarie with a mark on his Reputation and Honor: Thus the Gentleman needs to find some waye in which to expunge the damage done to him and in such a waie that his peer group and the wider communitie maie forgiue him for his indiscretion and thus allowe him to regain some of his lost Honor and Reputation: The waies in which Dishonour canne be remedied are often dependent on howe the marke was gayned and vnder what circumstances: This wyll determine to what lengthes the Gentle-man will haue to go in order to remoue the mark vppon him. For the most part there are three methods in which a Gentleman maie regain his lost Honor and gain the forgiuenesse of his peer group and wyder communitie, these methodes are through Apologie, Seruice and the Duel: Eache one of these hath a

certain

certain leuell of expectation which is often attached to the leuell of Dishonour vnder which the indiuiduall has been put: For the moste parte, minor causes result in a minor remedie and in such a situation an Apologie to the offended partie maye result in the ende of the matter and thus a resolution: In further situations an Apologie maie need to be made to a group rather than an indiuidual and acceptance must be gained by all present rather than anie one indiuidual: In certaine circumstances the Apologie maie also haue to be accōpanied by some sorte of payement but this is highlie dependent on the circumstances.

The second remedie to Dishonour is to be placed in the Seruice of the indiuidual for a period of tyme to whom the Dishonour caused moste hurt: The lengthe of time which will need to be serued will be determined by the indiuidual affected, but in this perticuler situation the Gentleman should alwaies discusse his offer of Seruice with anie one to whom he holds Duety or Loyaltie, and is especiallie the case where this is a Lady: To commit to Seruice without prior consultation will result in further Dishonor which will need to be remedied, and as such the Gentleman needeth to be carefull in the offering of Seruice as payment: The type of Seruice required will often be determined by the situation and the Dishonour found upon the indiuidual.

The finall methode in whyche Honoure and Reputation are gayned is through the auspices of the *Duello*: For the moste part the Duel is committed to where a personal affront is made by a particular indiuidual against the Gentleman, or where the Gentleman has insulted another: The *Duello* is the moste well-known methode for a Gentleman to gaine Honor and expiate anye marke againste him and this is due to the Courage demonstrated on the feelde of Honour agaynste an opponent: Some Duels wyll be committed to on an instant and these are the moste daungerous as no pryor preparation or permission is possible to be gained by anie other concerned partie: Other Duels wyll be made on an extended basis and in these the Gentleman as with concerneth seruice should seeke the approual of those whom he serueth before committing to such an act: In all instances the Gentleman should seeke some remedie to the Dishonour which has stained him and in all instances he should first seek this remedy through peacefull means rather than seeking it through blood at the first instance: Instantlie going for blood at the firste insult will gaine the Gentleman a Reputation for a duellist or brauler rather than a Gentleman and this in some wayes will leade to a leuell of damage to his Reputation on its owne: Thus the Gentleman shoulde ensure that the remedye to his Dishonour doth not cause further Dishonour whyche wyll neede to be remoued further along.

An Honorable Quarrell

He Honorable Quarrell is somethinge which the Gentle-man aims for not some backe-alleye incounter where there is no renowne and reallye onelye suruiual on offer: In order to atchieue an Honorable Quarrell first it must be defined and clearlie delineated frome other types of incounter and quarrell: This enableth the Honorable Quarel to be brought to the light of examination and onelye then can details be found in the method in which this sort of incounter should and should not be engaged vpon and also the reasons why such an incounter shoulde take place: To this poynte there are three types of incounter that need to be examined and defined in order that the true Honorable Quarrell maie be clearlie poynted out and thus be the focus of the discussion.

The three

The second Booke

The three mayne types of incounter that a Gentle-man maye be engaged in are the Mêlée, the Tournament and the *Duello*: In order for differences to be difcuffed theye mufte all be defined in and of themfelues: Once this is atchieued then as to which is the true Honorable Quarrell or which ones are then the Honorable Quarel and its conditions can be difcuffed. The firft is the Mêlée: This is an incounter which comprifes manie combatants and maie be a fet piece deliberatelye organifed or fomethinge whych has emerged out of fome vnplanned incounter: It is vfuallie the Mêlée that a Gentle-man can find himfelfe in which he is fet vppon by ruffians and others: This is a fyght for furuiuall not fome clearlye delineated incounter with rules controllinge it: The other forme of Mêlée is a fet piece in which fome rules are delineated vfuallye numbers but in which multiple combatants take part: Thys is not the Honorable Quarrell which is the ideal and the focus of this difcuffion. The Tournament is a fet peece incounter in which combatants engage one another for fome forte of prize and vfuallie Renowne for victorie at the ende of the Tournament: While this is formalifed and rules fet out as they woulde bee in a *Duello* it doth not quallifye as the fame as there are multiple participants in the Tournament and it is not called vppon a pointe of Honour in difcuffion between two indiuiduals. The *Duello* is a formalyfed yncounter betwene two indiuiduals vppon a pointe of Honor in which rules are fet and agreed to by the participants: This vfuallie onelye inuolues the Principalls inuolued in the argument but maye inuolue theyr Seconds as well: This is a barbarous cuftom focuffed too much on bloud-fhed and fome perceiued gaining of Honor: The more Honorable incounters vpon true pointes of Honor will onelye be engaged vpon by the two Principals with anie others remaining as witneffes to the incounter: It is this which will be the focus of the difcuffion of the Honorable Quarrell to follow: The *Duello* is vfuallie engaged vpon by the participants fo one of the Principals inuolued maye recouer fome loft Honour vfuallie refultinge from his actions or the actions of another.

Of Reafons and Opportunities

Ith the Honorable Quarrel defined in its effence it is neceffarie to examine thofe thinges which are important whych chaunge a combat from a fimple quarrell betweene two ynto a Duel and an Honorable Quarrell: The differentiation in this is founde in the reafons for the quarel and thefe reafons muft be examined: There are goode reafons and badde reafons, thefe are all related backe to the fubiect of Honor itfelfe and determine when it is a goode reafon for a quarell and when it is not: The mofte importante thinge heere is that an Honorable Quarrell fhould onelye be engaged vppon where Honour is affected by fome flight or incidence and fuch can onelye be expiated by the croffing of blades: There are alfo other reafons to fight but thefe are determined by the opportunitie prefented to the indiuidual by engaging in the quarrell in the firft place: In thefe particular inftances a *Duello* is not the refult but an incounter of another kinde fuch as a Tournament.

The Duel fhuld onely be engaged vppon where a matter of Honour is brought to light and this mufte be ferious enough that the Honour of one of the Principals is truelye affected: The Duel fhoulde not be engaged vppon for friuolous reafons: Where fomethynge is done whych toucheth vppon the Honor of a Lady or fufpect is made of the Loyaltie of the indiuidual a Duel has caufe to be made: As an excufe to engage in an incounter a Duel fhould not be fet but organifed as another incounter: The reafon for the Duel mufte be firmlie bafed vpon a matter of Honor: Shoulde there be fome other reafon for the incounter then the two Principals fhould difcuffe thys

as fuch

as ſuch and engage appropriatelie.

There are ſome who are ſo hot-headed who wyll iump at any chance they can to croſſe blades and demonſtrate their Honor and marſhall ſkilles: There are others who are vnwillinge vnleſſe at the greateſt prouocation to vnſheathe their weapons in an argumente againſte another and maye haue to be euen perſuaded to do ſo: Then there are thoſe who chooſe their quarels carefullie being aware of the opportunitie preſented by ſuch an incounter with another, who bide their tyme vntil the quarrell is ſuch that it cannot be auoided and that they muſt act: This is the moſt iudicious type of Gentleman whoſe Honor directs and guides him: The firſt will gayn nothing but the reputacion as a Duelliſt and Notorietie for his victories againſt others: The ſecond will be ſeen as too cautious to acte and will let opportunities for Honour paſſe hym by neuer able to gayn rank or ſtation due to his reticenſe: The thyrd is the optimum Gentleman who onlye fighteth vpon a true argument but wyll acte when it is requyered of him due to the ſituation as it is preſented to him, he wyll gayne much Renowne and Honor.

In all inſtances it is Honor and Renowne which ſhulde be preſent for the Gentleman to engage vpon the incounter ſhould this be abſent then the Gentleman would be beſt to decline what is preſented and ſaue himſelfe for where it is preſent: He which gaineth Renown is alwaies held high regardleſſe of victorie or defeat and reſpected alwaies: He which gaineth Notorietie is onelye recieued for his victories ſo longe as they laſte recogniſed for his ſkill with a blade in his hande vntil he falleth vnderneath the blade of another at which all he has gayned is loſt: The true Gentleman is alwayes on the ſearch for Renowne and not Notorietie to make his name liue on after the incounter has paſt and to demonſtrate his ſkills onlie in the moſt Honorable of incounters.

Of Challenger and Challenged

Houlde a Gentleman finde himſelfe in a ſituation where his Honour is touched ſo cloſely as not to be ignored then he ſhoulde deliuer a Challenge to the indiuidual who touched his Honor: Howeuer, there are certaine conſiderations that muſte be made in the deliuerie of ſuche a Chalenge in order that the matter remayneth honorable and engaged vpon for the correct reaſons: Theſe ſhoulde be the firſt conſideration of the Gentle-man rather than inſtantlie deliueryng the Chalenge in order not to ſeem a coward in the eies of thoſe around him: Deliuering a Challenge at euerye ſlight wyll meerelye earne the Gentleman the name of a duelliſt and a brauler rather than a man defending hys Honour: Inſtead the Gentleman muſte wayt vntil his Honor or thoſe who he is aſſociated are ſo affected that it cannot be ignored: In ſuch ſituations a Gentleman muſt conſider ſeueral things before deliuering the Chalenge.

The firſt thing that muſt be preſent is a clear reaſon for the Chalenge being delyuered, without this it is ſimplie an excuſe for a combat with another and ſeeking ſuch in all inſtances with the couer of the *Duello* will earne him the reputation of a brauler and ſtreet-fighter: In conſideryng the reaſon for the Chalenge the Gentleman muſt conſider whether he has a righte to feel as though hys Honor has been touched in ſuche a waye that bloud is the onely waie that it can be remedied: In this he ſhould alſo conſider whether it is actuallie ſomeone elſe who ſhould be deliueringe the Chalenge and thus is more greatlie affected than himſelf: In this ſituation the Gentleman muſt conſider whether he ſhoulde ſtand vpp for the abſent indiuidual, or paſſe ſuch intelligences on to them: If the latter is choſen it ſhould be done in ſuch a waye that the reaſons are cleare, and the information deli-
deliuered

uered without rumour or innuendo.

The reaſon for the Chalenge muſt be clear and ſuch reaſon ſhould be in the Chalenge when it is delyuered to the perſone who is to be challenged ouere the ſituation: There are thoſe who wyll prouoke others ynto combates deliberatelye and for theyr owne purpoſes and theſe are peeple who need to be watched carefullie ſo that the Gentleman ſhould not fall into their traps: In ſome ſituations the reaſon are ſimplie that they want to fyghte, in others they ſimplie wante to enhaunce their owne Reputacion through combates: In all ſituations the Gentleman ſhould onelye be drawen into an Honorable Quarrell where he has cauſe to be there and not ſimplye becauſe the opportunitie has been preſented to him: It is in theſe ſituations, as in anie important opportunitie that a Gentleman muſt firſt look to his Duety before committing to the enterpriſe which has beene preſented before him.

Whether the Gentle-man has permiſſion to deliuer the Chalenge muſte be a conſideration before the Chalenge is deliuered: This has linkes to the ſubiects of Loyaltie and Dutie and muſt be conſidered before a Chalenge is deliuered to another: The queſtion of whether the Chalenge wyll enhance or diminiſh the Reputacion and eſteeme of thoſe to whom the Gentleman is aſſociated ſhould be ſeriouſly conſidered: In thys the Gentle-man ſhoulde alſo conſider whether he is expected to and indeede has the right to deliuere a Chalenge on the parte of ſomeone they repreſente and in this there muſt be permiſſion gyuen: In this alſo the Gentleman ſhould be conſideryng whether the Chalenge ſerues the beſte intereſt of thoſe whom he ſerueth. Where he is in the ſeruice of a Noble or ſome other Lord, the Gentleman ſhould aſk permiſſion of ſuch as to whether he has permiſſion to anſwer the ſituation with a Chalenge and be accepting of the reſulting anſwer with no qualms or equiuocations: In the ſeruice to a Lady, ſuch permiſſions are alſo important as it is alſo her Reputacion which ſtands to be damaged ſhould ſhe be ſeen to be aſſociated with the wronge ſorte of Gentleman: In theſe ſituations it is often the caſe that a Chalenge canot be anſwered directlie and at the time of the inſult but muſt be waited vppon in order that ſuch permiſſions are gayned to laye ſuch a Chalenge to the indiuidual: In this ſituation a Gentleman ſhould explaine the ſituation as plainlie as poſſible in order not to be drawen into a ſecond Chalenge.

Of the Negotiations of an Honorable Quarrell

He queſtion of the deliuerye of the Challenge is an important one: Challenges are deliuered eyther verballye or written in a forme explayning the ſituation: In bothe ſituations thys ſhoulde be perfourmed in the correct manner: For the moſte parte where a Challenge is deliuered it wyll be made verballye from the Challenger to the perſon beinge challenged, though this is not alwaies the caſe: In ſome ſituations a Seconde maye be called vppon to delyuer the Chalenge to the perſon beinge chalenged, and this will be diſcuſſed later on: Shoulde a Challenge be delyuered verballye frome one Gentleman to another and thus Challenger to Challenged, it ſhulde be phraſed in ſuche a waye that the reaſons for the Challenge are mayde explicit, but in ſuche a waye as to be inoffenſiue in its deliuerye: It can be the ſituation that a ſeconde Chalenge can be delyuered due to the manner and tone in which a Chalenge is deliuered to another: Shuld the Chalenge be deliuered verballye and directe from one to another, this ſhould be the laſt tyme the two ſhoulde yncounter one another before they meete for the incounter: The onlie time this maie be broken is where reſtitutiõ is ſought by one to the other: If

the Challenge

The second Booke

the Challenge is delyuered in a written forme fuche fhoulde bee accompanyed by a meffenger who would be able to deliuere the refponfe to the Duel backe to the Chalenger: The forme of the letter fhould be much the fame as the verbal deliuerie, explicit and dyrect, yet honorable in its intentions and wordyng: The worded Chalenge can be deliuered by the Challenger to the Challenged, but it is not the befte waie for it to be done as further argument maie refulte from the encounter, fhould the written word be chofen it is beft that a meffenger of fome fort be vfed to delyuer fuch a Chalenge to the indiuidual inuolued.

Regardleffe of the forme of the Chalenge the deliuerye fhoulde be made with all Courtefie: This is the cafe for at leaft two reafones, the firfte is fo that no further Chalenge can emerge due to the deliuerie of the Chalenge and more importantlye fo that the Gentleman is feene to be courteous euen in fuch a moment of tenfion: A brafh deliuerie of a Chalenge, efpeciallie in publike will affect the Gentle-mans Reputacion in a negatiue fafhion: To be feene to be courteous euen in fuche a tenfe fituation placeth the Gentleman well in that he is feene to be courteous and this can onely but increafe his Reputacion: To bee feene to bee without Courtefye in the fame fituation will actuallie aduerfelie affect the Gentlemans Reputacion more than in a fituation where tenfion is lower: This comes from the expectation that an indiuidual will perfourme to their befte when in momentes of ftreffe as this is feen to reueale the inner character and fpirit of the indiuidual: To be able to approach the fituation with a calme mind and exterior will demonftrate to thofe witneffing and indeede all thofe who are tolde about the incountere that the indiuiduall is poffeffed of a calme minde and a Noble fpirit which will endear him to all around him: To approach the fituation with leffe woulde feem to reueal the reuerfe and this will ftaine the indiuidual euen after the grieuance has been remoued and Honor reftored, and from this ftain it is much more difficult to recouer: To be true fuch fituatiõs reueal whether or not the Gentleman is poffeffed of that moft Noble attribute *fprezzatura* in which the courtefie difplayed is feene as the true nature of the indiuidual rather than fomething efpeciallie expreffed in the current fituation where the indiuidual will knowe he is being obferued: With a courteous deliuerie of the Chalenge made, and of courfe the Chalenge accepted, it is then tyme to examine the detailes of the Honorable Quarrell to be contefted.

The location of where the two Principals are to engage in the encountere is a ferious confideration and there are various afpectes which fhoulde be confidered before a location is chofen for the encounter: The firfte thinge that needeth to be thought about is whether the location fhould be publique or priuate within this there is the contemplation of whether an audience will be of benefit to the incounter or detracte from the proceedings: The other confideration which will affift in the determination of this is whether the incountere has the permiffion of the rulinge Lord or whether this is ftrictlie a priuate affair: Should of courfe fuch an incounter be vnlawful and fuch proceedings thus confidered to be agaynfte the Crown thene all auenues fhoulde be exhaufted before an armed incounter is chofen as the laft refort: In this perticuler inftance it muft be prouen that the Poynt of Honor to be contefted is indeede more important than the wifhes of the Crown and of an exceptional circumftance where bloud is required for the expiation of anye Difhonor felte by the partyes inuolued: In all other inftances permiffion fhoulde be fought by the Crown and alfo any other who either of the two parties holdeth anie Loyaltie or Duety: In general the choife of the feelde for the incounter is the choife of the Chalenger, or the Chalenged maie propofe a fingle alternatiue: In the ende, there fhoulde onelie be a fingle alternatiue propofed: The negotiation of the location fhould be fwifte with no bickering and coniecture about the location: The location fhoulde be fomewhere appropriate to the conteft to be fought: The beft place being vfuallie a defignated Lift approued by the Crown or the befte alternatiue beinge fomewhere of euen ground which is awaie from paffers-by in order that they do not become embroyled in the incounter by accident: The footing maye be chofen to aduantage one fide or the other, but in general the mofte honorable approche is to enfure
that the

The Second Booke

that the grounde is euen and vnobstructed: In some instances a size of fielde maye be determyned, may be by the size of an approoued List, or bye the partye choosinge the location of the incounter: Shoulde a specific size be chosen then determinaytion muste be made as to what happeneth shoulde eyther of the combatants breache the feelde or withdrawe from it: The two mayne options in thys ynstance are that the combatantes are re-centred and the encountere beginneth anewe, the othere option is that the claime maie be made that one has loste due to his withdrawall, but thys shoulde be determined by agreement of the Principals.

Communication in all instances of an Honorable Quarrell must adhere to the highest leuels of Courtesie and Honour: The subiecte of Courtesie in the deliuerye of the Chalenge has alreadie bene alluded to and described preuiouslie, howeuer this Courtesie should continue in all aspects of the negotiation and indeed all the waie vp vntil the two Principals face one another on the appointed fielde withe weapons in hande: Anie brash wordes betwene the two Principals canne escalate a situation vncontrollablie to a poynt where the onlie waie that the issue can be solued is throughe the Death of one or the other of the Principals: Shoulde tempers be helde and Courtesie be maintained throughout the negotiation then some agreement maye be able to be made where the two Principals can come to some other arrangement: Once a Chalenge is layde and accepted by the Principals inuolued negotiations shoulde be mayde carefullie and sticking to the poyntes of the *Duello*, and once the negotiations of the *Duello* are compleated they shoulde do their best as to auoyd one another vntil the time of the Duel: In this it maie actuallie be better for the Principals to select indiuiduals, Secondes, to speake and negotiate in their steade: In this the Seconds should discusse with one another and passe the information between eache other then passed on to the Principals: This buffer to the negotiation can prouide with an extra assurance of Courtesie in the negotiation and often reduce the likelihoode of anie escalation: Howeuer, with regarde to the selection of Secondes certaine considerations need to be made.

Secondes are chosen by the Principals in order to prouide a buffer betweene theme for the purposes of negotiation and aduice for the Principals: It is not alwaies the case that Seconds are selected by the Principals, especiallie where the Chalenge is on shorte notice and of a more immedyate nature: The inuoluement of Secondes takes place vsuallye when there is some delaie in the deliuerie of the Challenge or there will be some delaye in the negotiation of the incountere itselfe: For some the addition of Seconds is an integrall parte of the processe and is absolutelye necessarie in order for the quarrell to be kepte honorable and Noble in nature: Shoulde it be determined that Secondes will be inuolued in the incounter then theyr selection needes to be made verie carefullye bye the Principals in order that the quarel remaineth an honorable one and doth not escalate: In choosing a Second the Principall shoulde looke to the character of the indiuiduall before making his choise. The Seconde requireth negotiation skills as his primarie abilitie and a goode character in ordere that the negotiations staie honorable in all instances: More so, the Second must be someone who the Principal can trust to speak for hym in the negotiations and expresse what needeth to be in the correct manner: For a true Second it is beste that he be of similare ranke to that of the Principal: Some would argue that he should be lower in rank in order that the Principal can maintayne controll, but it woulde bee better if the Second is a persone who the Principal trustes more than his rank beeinge requisite: In some instances it is better that the Second is actuallie higher in station in order that the negotiatiõs can be maintained at a highlie honorable leuel: In the choise of the Second the Principall should be guided by the dueties of the Second and choose an indiuidual who is suitable for the dutyes of the Second.

The primarie Duety of the Second is to ensure that the negotiations with the other Principal and Second staie honorable and that the interests of the Principal are met in these negotiations, howeuer there are further dueties which the Second is expected to performe: The first of the sundrie dueties of the Second is to ensure the deliuerie of the Principal to the fielde for the incounter: This is

The second Booke

This is bothe in the sence of ensuringe that the Principal arriueth at the appointed tyme readie for the incounter, but also to ensure that he arriueth vnmolested to the sayde feelde, thus ensuring his safetie also: It is due to the second part of this Dutye that in some instances multiple Seconds were inuolued: In this the Principall is better to choose a single Seconde rauther than multiples in ordere that there is no confusion in the negotiations and no secondarie opinions which may cloud the iudgement: The addition of multiple Seconds also tendeth to lead to them getting inuolued, and inuolued in the incounter as will be discussed further along: The second Duety of the Second is to act as a witnesse to the incounter to ensure that the termes of the yncounter are met and that the incounter taketh place as was agreed vpon by the Seconds: Such witnesses are often called vpon later to testifie to the incounter to others once the incountere has beene met to describe it in order that the Reputacion of bothe Principals inuolued can be maintained and increased: Shuld, for some reason, the Principal be vnable to appeare at the fielde at the appropriate tyme then according to some traditions, the Seconde wyll stande in for the Principall in the incountere: Thys is especiallye the case where the Principall who has appeared is the Chalenged and thus requireth the combate to expyate some maner of dishonor felt by the Chalenge: Of course, regardlesse of the situation the Principal who doth not appear will lose some of his Reputacion and this shuld be a serious consideratiõ shuld he choose not to appeare: In all instances it should be the last option for a Principall and he will need an exceptional reason for non-appearance in order to not be aduerselye affected: More wyll be discussed of this in a later section.

With regarde to Seconds there is some debate in some circles about howe much a Seconde should become inuolued in the yncounter: For some they belieue that the Second should haue a vested intereste in the outcome of the incounter in order to ensure that they are firmlie placed vppon the side of their Principal: For others the Second should onely be inuolued as far as the negotiatiõs and as such shoulde be impartial to the proceedinges in ordere to maintaine a leuel heade: For some the responsibilities of the Second actuallye goe further than iust the negotiations in order to ensure that the incounter remayns honorable: In some instances it is actuallye better that Secondes are not inuolued as according to some, the Seconds haue a Dutye themselues to engage in combat in order to maintaine the Honour of the incounter: This is an abhominable tradition which simplie leads to more bloudshed in the incounter than is necessarie and can result in melees of numbers and not the honorable incounter which was set vpon by the Principals to begin with.

In those instances where permission is gayned for the Honorable Quarrell from the Crown and a List duelye set vpp in which the incounter is to take place, there is sometimes the addition of another inuolued in ordere to ensure that the proceedinges are impartiall: This persone actes as an ouerseer to the incounter to ensure that the termes of the quarrell are met in an honorable fashion: The indiuiduall in this case is a Marshall, and sometymes is appoynted by the Crowne for the purpose: In other instances he is meerelye an independent arbiter for the incounter oftene selected by agreement by the Principals and the Seconds to ensure that he is not biased to one syde or another: This person may also act as a negotiator betwene the Seconds at the tyme of the incounter to ouersee anie finall negotiations betweene the Seconds: For the moste parte howeuer it is meerelye their Duetie to ensure that the combat is an honorable one.

In the choise of weapons and armor to be vsed in the incounter it is the choyse of the Chalenged to selecte them. In the selection of weapons it is moste often that the sworde will be selected being the moste honorable and common of weapons: This maie or maye not be accompanyed by an offhand deuice: Shoulde it be the choise of the Chalenged he maie insist that the weapons are matched for waight, length or euen both: For some the wepon selection is simple and that would be the weapon that the indiuidual moste commonlie carrieth: This ensures a familiaritie with the weapon and in those incounters of an immedyat nature it is oftene the case that the indiuiduals will simplye vse those weapons whych are on theyr person at the tyme regardlesse of whether they are

matched

matched or not: It is the weapons selected by the Chalenged which are vsed in the incounter and none shuld be concealed by eyther combatant to ensure that the incounter remaineth honorable: The aduantage gayned by the Chalenged in this selection can be quite great especiallie should he choose wepons in which he has had some special training and this can often tippe the balance in one way or another: Once the weapons haue been chosen by the Chalenged, they shoulde be made knowen to the other partie inuolued, leauinge this notification vntil the tyme of the incounter could be seen as lesse than honorable as one will haue had tyme to auail himself of extra trayning and the other maye not haue: Thus in order to keep the incounter honorable and Noble it is best that both haue sufficient knowledge of the weapons to be vsed in the incounter: Whether or not armour is to be vsed duringe the incounter is the choise of the Chalenged: Regardlesse of the choise made, armor shuld not be concealed by eyther partie and the Secondes shoulde ensure that thys is checked before the incountere proceeds: To conceal armor on ones person would be considered a breach of Honor and thus affect the Reputacion of the indiuidual who conceals it, as Sophocles stated it is better to faill with Honor than succeed by fraud: In this, more often armor is not selected by the Chalenged in order that the true skill at armes of the combatants canne be seene vnassisted by anye additional protection: Once againe, once the selection of armor is made it should also be made knowen to the other ynuolued in the incounter for the same reasons as the weapons should be made knowen: Some negotiation maie be made betweene the Seconds as to the choise of weapons and armor to be vsed in the incountere, but for the most part they are the choise of the Chalenged. The finall parte of the negotiation is the victorie conditions which will applie in the incounter.

Of the Honorable Combate

N the appointed daye and at the appointed tyme, the Principals and theyr Seconds, shoulde they be inuolued, wyll meet with the Arbiter of the Duel, should one be appointed to the task: It is at this poynt in tyme that the finall negotiatiõs will take place betwene the parties concerned: It is these final negotiations which can be extreamelie vitall and it is at this tyme that all parties concerned will need to acte wyth the greatest Courtesie: In this finall negotiation wyll be determyned anye victorie conditions to be layde out: It is at this poynte in tyme that it will be decyded what restitution is required: Not in all cases will this requyer a Duell to the Death, in some ynstances the simple crossinge of blades for a periode of tyme or euen the symple presence of the Principall at the appropriate tyme and place will be sufficient: Shoulde it be decided that a crossing of blades is requyred then the conditiõs will haue to be made specific so that all inuolued can vnderstand exactlie what the conditions are: It was preuiouslye discussed in the tearms of the *Duello* about the location of the incounter and one of the victorie conditions maie be forcinge the other to breache the arena chosen for the incounter, this is not a cõmon condition but is sometymes enforced in some incounters: In this negotiation it maie also be found that the actual crossing of blades is not required.

An Apologie to the offended partie maye be sufficient restitution for the insult made by one of the Principals: In this particular instance the substance of the Apologie must be clearlye meted out and defined by bothe parties: This is actuallye a verye goode outcome to this sorte of quarrell as yt auoyds blood-shed and anyethinge which maie be attached to such bloodshed: The Apologie maye also be attached to the final parte of the *Duello* where one is so iniuried that he can

not

The Second Booke

not continue and thus muſte make a full Apologie for the inſulte mayde to the offended partye: In either circumſtance the victorie conditions determined ſhould ſee the ende of the quarrell between the two Principals and a finaliſation of the offenſe: Shoulde an Apologie be deliuered in ſuch a faſhion as to be not belyeued by the other partie a ſecondarie quarel maie ſtarte from ſuch a ſituation and this would re-ſtart the whole proceſſe once again and vſually with an increaſe in the expectatiõ of the reſtitution required: Further in ſome examples an Apologie is made and the Principals maye decide to continue to engage with blaydes for the purpoſe of a friendlie boute betweene the two: In this perticuler inſtance it woulde be beſt that bothe fight as though theyr liues depend on it as a ſimple miſtake can change the incounter and its reſult.

Further to this, no quarrell ſhould be ſo great that two true and honorable friends ſhoulde want, or be required, to croſſe blades with one another in that the nature of the incounter with blades is that while one maye haue no intention of harminge the other thinges can occurre that canne reſult in one or the other ſorelie hurt or euen mortallie wounded: Quarrelles betwene true friendes ſhoulde be ſettled by Wordes rather than Steel on the bayſis that the outcome of the vſe of ſteel is ſuche that the outcome can not be guaranteed: Should one end vpp in an armed incounter with a friend the inuolued partie ſhuld fight as though his lyfe depend on it euen though this other perſon maie haue erſtwhile been his friend: It is vnlikelie that in ſuch a ſituation he will fauour you for maiming, iniuring or putting his lyfe in daunger: The nature of croſſinge ſteel is that lyfe and lim are put in daunger and two true friendes ſhuld be hable to ſpeake clearlie and plainlie to one another without concern for iniurie which would reſult in them hauing to croſſe blades in ſuch an antagoniſtic faſhion.

With the conditions ſet and the feeld eſtabliſhed it turnes to the incounter itſelfe: Before this can be diſcuſſed it ſhulde be mentioned ſomethinge of what ſhoulde happen ſhoulde one of the Principals not make an appearance at the appropriate place and time: In this perticuler inſtance there are ſome things which may occur: Firſtlie, the Principal who is preſent could ſimplie be declared the victor and the argument in their fauor, of courſe this will reſult in a loſſe of Reputacion for the other Principal: Secondlie, the Seconde maie fight in the place of the Principal for whateuer reaſõ that the Principal coulde not attend, as was diſcuſſed aboue: While this doth reſult in a reſolution to the incounter with ſteele the Principall is ſtill likelye to loſe Reputacion for his lacke of preſence: Thirdlie, a Principal maie ſend his repreſentatiue, vſuallie a Seconde requeſtinge that a chaunge of time and poſſiblie or place is made due to ſome conflict in the timing of the incounter: Shoulde this be accepted by the preſent Principal then the tyme and the location ſhulde not be vnder queſtion at all: This is ſeen as a meere poſtponement of the incounter, but ſuch ſhould be the caſe that the Principal who is not able to make it to the incounter ſhould ſend embaſſie before the tyme of the incountere to the other Principall aſkinge for a chaunge of tyme and location: In this perticulere caſe no Reputacion ſhould be ſeen to be loſt vnleſſe the chaunge is made in a leſſe than courteous faſhion or for ſome reaſon which is vnſuitable to the ſituation: Howeuer in all caſes, the Principal ſhoulde enſure that he is able to attend the incounter as failure to do ſo maie reſult in a loſſe of Reputacion.

Shoulde no apologie be mayde, or euen in the caſe of an apologie made, and the croſſing of blades ſtill determyned to be neceſſarye for ſome reaſone then the proceſſe ſhoulde procede to the actuall incounter itſelf: Should there be an independent Arbiter in place he will firſt come on to the feelde and then call the Principalls out to the fielde: The Principals ſhould enter from different ſides of the field in order to preuent anie accidental combat, with theyr Secondes in tow, ſhould this be not poſſible then all Courteſie ſhould be obſerued as the Principals do enter the fielde: Once the Principals are preſent the Arbiter will aſk whether there is anie mediation poſſible or reſolution by peecefull meanes poſſible, at which the Seconds ſhoulde confer with the Principals and return their anſweres: Once it is determined that reſolution is not poſſible the Secondes ſhulde make a check of the oppoſing Principals equipment to enſure that there are no empediments or concealed aduanta-

aduantages

ges on the part of the Principals: Once the Secondes haue completed this check they fhuld leaue the fielde but be clofe inough that they are able to obferue the incountere and enfure the conduct of the incounter: The preuiouflie agreed terms of victorie fhould then be announced by the Arbiter who fhoulde haue been briefed before enteringe the fielde by the Secondes who fhould haue preuiouflie negotiated them: It fhoulde be afked whether during the conteft quarter wyll be afked or giuen, in all but the moft exceptional circumftances, the moft honorable application is that quarter fhould be giuen if requefted by the other Principal: Once the finall agreements are made the Principals fhuld make themfelues readie and then ftand acroffe from their opponent: Once the combatants are prepared they fhuld declare themfelues fo in a clear voice fo that all concerned, the opponent, Arbiter and Seconds can heare them: The Arbiter will then call the combatters to their garde and cõmence the combate.

In all inftances the true Gentle-man fhould approach and affault his opponent with Honour vfing only fkill and honorable means to defeat the opponente: In this the Secondes and the Arbiter will witneffe the conduct of the combate and enfure that it is kepte honorable: Shoulde anie vnderhanded methode be vfed by eyther combatante it will clearlye damage theyr Reputacion: In this it fhoulde be noted that aduantage gayned through the fkill of armes fhoulde be taken, but no aduantage gayned by other meanes fhould be accepted: The purpofe of the combat is to regayn or maintaine Honor and anie action which wuld threaten this fhuld be confidered bafe and not confidered by eythere combatant: Onelye theire owne true fkill at armes fhoulde be demonftrayted in that it would be better that a man faile in the vfe of honorable means then to fucceed vfinge difhonorable ones: Such methodes and refultes wyll become a parte of the publique recorde as reporte of the incounter will fpread to others.

Of the Refolution of the Duello

 Or fome the croffing of blades in an actuall incounter is neceffarye for Honor to be redeemed: For others the meere appearance of the Principalls at the appropriat time and place wyll reftore Honor in thefe fcholes of thought in that they haue appeared and thus placed themfelues in harmes waye: For this fchole of thought the croffing of blades is not alwayes feene as a neceffitye and in thefe inftances it is mofte likelie that a friendlie often bloudleffe incounter will enfue: Howeuer thys is not common thought amongft all fcholles of thought: For fome a bloud-letting of fome kinde is requyred euen if it is iuft a token amount for Honor to be fatisfied, while controlled this thought doth not leade to wanton violence and bloudluft it often leadeth that waye due to the Principals inuolued or the expectation of thofe who follow the incounter: The Honour thought to be loft and the reafon for the Chalenge itfelfe vfuallye will determyne to what leuell the violence will enfue: It is confidered that onelye the moft ferious quarrelles fhould refult in the combate being to the Death, for the moft part Firft Bloud or fimilar conditions fhould be fufficient for Honor to be fatisfied.

In the ende of the *Duello* there is vfuallye the refult of a perfon who is victorious and a perfon who is defeated: This woulde implie that there is a perfon who has gayned or regayned Honor and a perfon who is in deficit, but this is fimplie not the cafe: So longe as the combate was cõmitted to in an honourable fafhion it is poffible euen for the defeated to maintayne theyr Honour: It is the combat itfelfe rather than the refulte which decides the Honor of the fituation and for a combata-
combatant

The second Booke

nt to haue stood vp and fought his opponent with Honor, whether he winnes or loses ensureth that he retaineth his Honor: Decimus Magnus Ausonius declared that the best memorial for a greate man is to gaine Honor euen though he maie be killed and in this he proposes that euen though a man may fall he maie maintaine his Honoure: Thus euen though a man maye lose to another he retaineth his Honor due to the combat done: This being the case where Death is not the result of the incounter it is also thought that the partie who falleth to the other shulde also make some sort of Apologie and admit theyr wrong-doinge: The Apologie in this perticuler case actuallye gaineth the man Honour who sayeth it as he was prouen to be wrong in an honourable fashion and thus admitting to such a wrong-doing doeth not stain him but redeemeth him along with his opponent.

The vltimate result of a succesful conclusion to an Honorable Quarell is where both Principals are able to regaine their Honoure and euen possiblie gayne or restore a friendshippe betwene them: The purpose of the quarrell in all cases should be to redeem Honor and anie person who goeth into the incounter or quarrell with other reasons or means shoulde disengage themselues or suffer the tainte of Dishonor should they be discouered: The symple purpose of entering such a quarrell for the purposes of gayninge Reputacion due to Skil at Armes or for the simple intent of committing murther shoulde be auoided at all costs shoulde the indiuidual not wish to acquire the Reputaction of a Duellist or brauler: The intent behinde the quarrell shoulde alwayes be maintayned as Honorable and for the right reasons.

A Resolution to the Discussion

Onour is importante to all true Gentle-men and shoulde be considered to be so: The discussion preuious hath highlighted those wayes in which Honor is importante to the Gentleman and how it maintaineth hys goode name and Reputacion through it: The key elementes associated with Honor are parte and parcell of the entier package whyche resulteth in a Gentle-mans Reputacion and thus perceyued Honour based vppon the feelinge of his peer groupe and the wider communitie: The indiuiduall shoulde do hys beste to ensure that he is hable to liue vpp to and maintaine at a high standard those attributes which enhaunce his Reputacion and thus Honor and do all in his power to auoyd those which maye bringe him into disrepute: Failure to maintayne a standarde suitable to his peer group and the wider communitye wyll resulte in damage to hys Reputacion and the opening for perceiued Dishonor in the Gentleman: This is somethinge that a Gentle-man shulde be aware and warye of in his dealinges with others: Knowinge that which will damage his Honour is a defence in that he wyll then knowe how to auoyd beeing put into a situation where his Honor and Reputacion may be affected.

The indiuidual should doe his best to maintaine Honor and to auoid beeing inuolued in, or being seene to be inuolued in aniething which maie affect his Honor or Reputacion: It is important that due to the perception of Honor and Reputacion being a publike one that the Gentleman shuld be seene to be doing the right thing and auoiding being associated with aniething which maie bring him into disrepute: Euen shoulde the Gentleman not be inuolued in the actiuitie, the meere association with the actiuitie or those who are inuolued in it can affect a Gentlemans Reputacion and thus he needes to ensure that the companie that he keepeth is the most Honorable and vpright: In this he shoulde also remember that his association affectes hys and theyr Reputations, thus a Gentleman should be carefull in his association not onelye for his owne benefyte but also those who wo-
would

The second Booke

uld aſſociate with him: Shoulde he requier to aſſociate with thoſe of a lower ſtation or Reputacion he ſhuld be carefull that he not perſiſt in their preſence and that ſuch aſſociations ſhulde onelye be for ſpecific purpoſes which are of the moſt honorable kinde, or at leaſt ſeen as a neceſſitie in order to achieue ſome honorable ende.

The auoidance of Diſhonor is ſomething which a Gentleman muſt alwaies be on the garde againſt, as the effect of the damage to his Reputacion will often outweigh the miſtake made and the recouerie of ſuch Honour will be immeaſurablie more difficult than the ſlippe made in order to loſe it: There are many opportunities open for a Gentleman with Honor and many leſſe to the Gentle-man who has loſt or who has none: This is ſomethinge that the Gentleman ſhoulde always kepe in minde during tymes of tenſion in that in moſt caſes the honourable pathe is often the more difficult one to take but the eaſyer one wyll loſe him that whyche is difficulte to regayne once it is loſte: The Gentleman ſhulde thus meaſure his actions carefullie and examine the conſequenſes of ſuch actions alwaies looking to the future reſult of ſuch actions rather than theyr immediat effects: Shoulde the Gentleman be faced with the choiſe of a loſſe of face now but in the longe-terme a maintenaunce of his Honour, he ſhoulde alwaies looke to the future rather than the preſente: In this the Gentleman ſhoulde alwaies remaine true to himſelf firſt, his Lady ſecond and his Lord thyrde: All other conſiderations ſhoulde be put aſide in order to maintaine hys Honor and ſhoulde the conſequenſes require his Death then he ſhould go to it with a glad harte knowing that he has maintained his Honor in the proceſſe.

In all inſtances where a Gentle-man hath the choyſe betwene ſeekinge violence or liuinge in peece he ſhoulde alwayes chooſe to liue in peace: Honoure maintayned through peecefull meanes is alwaies better than that which is gayned through violence: In all diſcuſſions of the croſſing of ſteele againſte another the Gentleman ſhoulde alwayes be on the ſearch for Renowne gayned through Honorable combate: The ſimple ſeekinge of victorie through the croſſinge of blades with anothere will onelie earne him Notorietie, ſimple reſpecte for his ſkill but nothing moore: The Gentleman who gaineth Renowne will always be ſeene as a victor and reſpected and wyll alwaies maintaine Honor on and off the feelde regardleſſe of the outcome of anie incounter with another: Renowne goeth a long waye to enhancing a Gentlemans Reputacion and Honor: In all forms of combat whether priuate or publyke the Gentleman ſhould doe his beſt in order to ſeeke Renowne for his actions perfourming in ſuch a faſhion that he is reſpected both for his ſkil on the fielde but alſo his approche to the combat in ſhowing reſpect and Honor to his opponent regardleſſe of who they maie be.

With regarde to the ſelection of combats agaynſte an opponente the Gentle-man ſhoulde alwaies pick his battailes carefullie in order to maintaine Honor: He ſhuld not ſimplie fight becauſe the opportunitie is preſented to him in ſome faſhion or another: In this he ſhuld haue the moſt ſerious minde and conſideration to decide whether the combate entered into or the Chalenge layd by him or another will enhaunce or decreaſe his Reputacion and Honor: To fight at anie opportunitie will merely earn him the Reputacion of a duelliſt and ſtreet-brauler and thus increaſe his Notorietie but not his Renowne or Honoure: Shoulde the Gentleman finde himſelf in a ſituation where his Honor is touched ſo cloſelie as to not be able to auoyd it then he ſhoulde engage in ſuch a Chalenge: In all caſes the rules of Honorable Quarels as preſented aboue are the key to a ſucceſsful negotiation and retention or gayning of Honor: Such they are that ſo long as a Gentleman followeth them and doeth all Courteſie to his opponent he will gaine Honor through the incounter: At no time ſhould he be tempted to bypaſſe or deuiate from the path layde out for him vnder the threat of his Reputacion being affected by ſuch a deuiation: The guidelines preſented are thoſe which are conſidered to be the moſte vprighte and appropriat methode in which to reſolue an Honourable Quarrell with another Gentleman: Should the combatants follow that which is written, bothe will enhaunce their Honor and Reputacion in the proceſſe.

Of the Nobilitie of Women

The second Booke
Of the Nobilitie of Women

He ſubiecte of the Ladye hath alreadye beene diſcuſſed vndere Honour and the Loyalty and Duety a Gentleman ſhould haue to his Lady ſhould onely be ſecond to that which he holdeth himſelfe in order to maintain his Honor: In the diſcuſſion of women it ſhould be noted that it is the Lady to whom the Gentleman looks to, and vſuallie onelie a ſingle one, but all ſhuld be held high as the imbodiment of all Honour: Thus a Gentle-man ſhoulde neuer do anye wronge to anye woman, or be ſeen to be doing anie wrong ſo long as he wiſhes to maintaine his Honor.

The Honor founde in a Lady is ſomething which the Gentleman ſhoulde hold high and do his beſt to maintaine and preſerue: The Loyaltie and Duety a Gentleman holds to his Lady is that which is the ſource of his Honor and this can be ſeen in anye Gentleman who is deuoted to one Lady aboue all: The Honour of a Lady and the maintenance of ſuche Honour giue the Gentleman an inner ſtrength which he often doth not poſſeſſe without the inſpiration of ſuch: A Gentleman who offereth his ſeruices to one Lady gaineth in return ſomething which he cannot deſcribe, but ſomething which is viſceral to him: For him it enhaunceth all his achyeuements in that they are done not onelye in his but alſo her Honor thus both are buoyed on the Reputacion of one: Seruices and commitments to her are alwaies enhanced by the feeling he gets in achieuing and holding his Lady high enhancing her greatneſſe through his actions: It is a feelinge which will guide him to Honor and the maintenance of it in himſelfe and his Lady: Alwaies will his thoughts be not only on the effectes of his actions vpon his owne Reputacion and Honor but alſo that of his Lady.

The Lady ſhould be reſpected by Gentlemen, but in this ſhe ſhould alſo be worthie of the reſpect ſhowen by Gentle-men and thus her actions will alſo be carefullie iudged and her deciſions carefullie meaſured in order to maintayne a ſtatus ſuitable to be reſpected: A true Lady will neuer entiſe or encourage a Gentleman, eſpeciallie her owne, to do anything which may aduerſelie affect his Honor or hers and thus ſhe too ſhould onelye be ſeene to be inuolued in thoſe endeauours which will bring Honor to both the Lady and the Gentle-man: The ſame rules of aſſociation diſcuſſed of the Gentleman with regarde to damaging Reputacion alſo applie to the Lady: This is the caſe as her Reputacion and Honor are alſo baſed vppon that which ſhe is ſeen to be doing and thoſe whom ſhe aſſociates with: Thus it is the opinion of her peer group and the wider communitie which increaſeth or decreaſeth the leuel of her Reputacion and Honour: The loſſe of Honor for a Lady is ſomething which is akin to that which is loſt by a Gentle-man onelye more ſo that ſhe maye require a Gentleman to reſtore ſuch Honour for her: In this the Gentleman ſhoulde alwaies be ready to defend the Honor of a Lady ſhoulde the ſituation reſult in ſuch being required and neuer put himſelfe in a ſituation where it is he who may offend a Lady.

Shoulde anie offence be made to a Lady then a Gentleman ſhould apologiſe for anie offence cauſed immediatlye and announce his wrong-doing: In an inſtance where another Gentleman has taken offence to the ſituation then a Gentleman ſhuld accept ſuch a Chalenge onelye where his owne Honor is more affected than that of the Lady and thus an apologie in the ſituation will affect him more: Shulde the Lady be more affected, then the Gentleman ſhould immediatlye apologiſe to the Lady and come to ſome tearmes of agreement: In this perticuler inſtance to apologyſe to the Lady for the wrong-doing will actuallie increaſe the Reputacion of the Gentleman as a Gentleman. The quarrell in this caſe ſhould then follow the ſame proceſſe as has bin deſcribed aboue with the onelye exception being that the offended Lady wyll be preſent to witneſſe the negotiation and encounter:

Where

The second Booke

Where the Gentleman loseth suche a Contest of Armes then the apologie should be immediat and forth-comminge in order to maintaine the Honour both of the Lady and the Gentle-man: To not apologise for a wrong-doing euen after defeat will gaine the Gentleman nothing but dishonour.

Should there be a disagreement between two Ladies then a Gentle-man shuld be careful as to which syde of the argumente he wyll take: In this he shoulde be carefull as to the entention of the Ladies inuolued and also anye associations they may haue: In these instances should his owne Lady be inuolued in the quarrell then it is to her that he shoulde look to firste as his first Duetie: Shoulde he be requested by one or the othere of the Ladyes inuolued to Champion her, where it is not hys owne then he should accept onelye if suche a position will not affecte his owne Honoure and that he feels that the quarrell has merit and doeth truely affect the Honor of the Lady and should permission be forthcoming from his owne Lady: Shoulde his owne Lady be inuolued then he shoulde not waite to be asked to become ynuolued: Thys is the same as anie sorte of quarrell that a Gentle-man maie be inuolued in, in all instances he shoulde onelye inuolue himselfe where Honor and Renowne are to be gayned from beeing inuolued: In the quarel between two Ladies, the Gentleman shoulde act with all Courtesie as the representatiue of the Lady in ordere to maintaine his Honour and also that of the Lady that he represents in the quarrell. The consideration for the Ladies in this perticuler instance is to ensure that the quarel is such that a chalenge and quarel is required: To be seen to be too eager to be inuolued in a quarrell will affecte the Reputacion of a Ladye as muche as it doth a Gentleman: So too will her Reputacion be affected if it is reuealed that her inuoluement in the quarrell was for some other reasone than the mayntenance of Honour: Thus the Ladye inuolued in a quarrell should ensure that her intentions are alwaies honorable and that such a quarel is required in order for her to retaine her Reputacion or haue it restored.

For the Gentle-man the consideration of his Lady should be onelye seconde to the Honor that he maintaineth in himselfe: From that he should also be considerate of those other Ladies with whom he maye haue contact or association as iust as his Reputacyon will be affected by theyr actions so too are their Reputacions affected by his: In all instances the Gentleman should do his best to ensure that the Ladys Honour is maintained and that he holdeth suche in high regarde and do no base action which may affecte the Reputacion or Honor of a Lady nor see another do so: Honor is to be founde and maintayned in the Ladies founde in Gentle companye and indeede all Ladyes in facte: Regardlesse of their rank or station all Ladies should be held in high regard and their Honor maintained: No seruice so long as honorable shoulde euer be reiected by a Gentleman when asked by a Lady as in the seruice of a Lady the Gentleman will find great Honoure.

FINIS.

Afterword

There is a lot of information about the rapier and other swords that were used before, during, and after the Elizabethan period. However, it seems to be the rapier that gets many people excited. Some of this can be attributed to movies like "The Three Musketeers" and "The Princess Bride", but not all of it. Something about the long, slender, obviously-lethal blade with the elaborate hilt attracts people to this sword. The hilts may have been made as costume jewellery, but the blade certainly had practical use behind it.

My treatise, presented in this book, is one method for using the civilian sword, and it applies as much to the rapier as it would to any close relation of a slightly more robust nature. There are many different methods for using this weapon, as can be seen by the variety of sources from throughout history. Thus, knowledge can be found in all of them, even if we do not agree with their entire content. This treatise is presented in the same fashion.

There have been multiple purposes proposed for this book. For the beginner historical fencer, it is intended to teach that the language of another time is not that scary, it just takes a little time to learn, like the art that is hidden within that language. For the historical linguist, it offers a demonstration of how language has changed over the years, and may give some insight in the same way of learning from other texts. For the fencer, it presents a method for how to use the sword, and each new lesson you learn about the sword can only give you an advantage over those who do not learn. I hope I have succeeded with these goals.

This is no manual, not a "how to" guide. It is a presentation of theory, skills, and demonstrations of those skills in a theoretical manner. This is a treatise, the presentation of the methodology of one swordsman. In this case, this is *my* way of fencing. There is no way that I claim that it is "the" way to fence. I offer it for those who would learn from it.

The Elizabethan English version of the treatise should be considered the core text. This means that it is closest to the intent of what I initially wrote. I did this because I wanted my ideas to be translated cleanly into the older language of Elizabethan English without any issues and without having to reverse any of the rules of modern grammar that the Elizabethans simply did not have. Once you are used to it the Elizabethan English, it is easy to work with, it flows, and in some cases it can be easier to read and manage than our modern tongue.

What this all means is that the Elizabethan English version should always be treated as the primary text and the Modern as the translation, not the other way around. For those who are interested in the historical side of the use of the rapier, and most should if they are using one, read the Elizabethan version. Read *all* of it and you will better understand the weapon, and not just *how* it was used but *why* it was used.

Suggested Readings and Further Studies

There is a Bibliography and Suggested Readings at the end of this book. There are only three fencing manuals mentioned, being three Elizabethan fencing manuals. Most of the other books and articles are those I used in my research of Elizabethan English. There are also my two blogs, one about fencing and the other which traces the development of this book (or at least most of it). There is also my recently published book based on my fencing blog, for those who are more interested in reading articles in print.

Fencing manuals and treatises should be among your reading materials, but they should not be the only things that you read. If you only read about how swords were used, you will not understand about the weapons themselves and why they were restricted or used in a particular manner. Even so, this is not enough.

Reading about the people who used the weapons will give you some idea about the reason this weapon was chosen and why some other weapon was not. Reading about the language gives you a better understanding of the manual and also about the people, it will tell you who was educated enough to be able to write, and about who did write in the period. The power of the pen is not to be underestimated.

Further immersion into the society and reading about the customs, laws and traditions of a society will explain the reasons why they fought, and also how they fought. There is a section in the Elizabethan treatise about the reasons to fight and not to fight. This will also explain who would fight whom, and also how they would fight amongst one another.

What about issues not pertaining to the martial aspects of the sword? How about clothing? The clothing of an individual determines how they can move and how they cannot move. This makes a great impact on how the sword can and cannot be used. Modern martial artists in the Historical European Martial Arts communities run into these issues with armour and the armour versus mobility issues, much of this is explained in period works, and historical examples of armour.

After all of this, my advice is this:

1. Write down what you do. Make a fencing notebook and record everything.

2. Teach what you know and don't be afraid to say "I don't know." Go research or ask until you do know.

3. Compare notes with others who are doing similar things. Consider their point of view.

4. Expand the knowledge. Spread it to anyone who is interested.

5. Never disregard *anything* until you have truly tried it out truthfully.

Bibliography and Suggested Reading

Barber, C. (2000) *The English Language: A Historical Introduction*, Cambridge University Press, Cambridge, England

Bryson, B. (2009) *Mother Tongue: The Story of the English Language*, Penguin Books Ltd, London, England

Crystal, D. (2003) *The Cambridge Encyclopedia of the English Language* (2nd ed), Cambridge University Press, New York, USA

Crystal, D. (2008) *'Think on my Words': Exploring Shakespeare's Language*, Cambridge University Press, Cambridge, England

Crystal, D. (2010) *Evolving English: One Language, Many Voices*, The British Library, London, England

Crystal, D. and Crystal, B. (2002) *Shakespeare's Words: A Glossary and Language Companion*, Penguin Books, London, England

di Grassi, Giacomo (1594) *DiGrassi his true Arte of Defence, plainlie teaching by infallable Demonstrations, apt Figures and Perfect Rules the manner forme how a man without other Teacher or Master may safelie handle all sortes of weapons aswell offensive as defensive; With a Treatise Of Deceit or Falsinge: And with a waie or meane by private Industrie to obtaine Strength, Judgement and Activitie*, I.G., London, England

Gooden, P. (2009) *The Story of English: How the English Language Conquered the World*, Quercus Publishing Plc, London, England

Kermode, F. (2000) *Shakespeare's Language*, Penguin Books Ltd, London, England

Lass, R. (ed.) (1999) *The Cambridge History of the English Language: Volume III: 1476 – 1776*, Cambridge University Press, Cambridge, England

McCrum, R. (2010) *Globish: How the English Language Became the World's Language*, Penguin Group (Australia), Camberwell, Australia

Mugglestone, L. (ed) (2006) *The Oxford History of English*, Oxford University Press, Oxford, England

Nevalainen, T. (2006) *An Introduction to Early Modern English*, Edinburgh University Press, Edinburgh, Scotland

Saviolo, Vincentio (1595) *His Practise In Two Books. The first intreating the use of the Rapier and Dagger, The second, of Honor and honorable Quarrels*, John Wolff, London, England

Silver, G. (1599) *Paradoxes of Defence*, Edward Blount, London, England

Smith, J. (2005) *Essentials of Early English*, Routledge, New York, USA

Walker, H. (2009) "A Fencer's Ramblings," http://afencersramblings.blogspot.com.au/

Walker, H. (2012) "Olde Wordes: An Examination of Elizabethan English," http://oldewordes.blogspot.com.au/

Walker, H. (2019) *Un-Blogged: A Fencer's Ramblings*, Sword and Book Enterprises Pty Ltd, Brisbane, Australia

All three Elizabethan fencing manuals, di Grassi (1594), Saviolo (1595) and Silver (1599) are available in .pdf format from the Raymond J. Lord Collection
http://www.umass.edu/renaissance/lord/index.html

About the Author

HENRY WALKER

afencersramblings.blogspot.com

My two greatest passions in life have always been history and swords. Like most boys I pretended to play with swords as a kid and that did not seem to change as I grew older. In 1993 I studied foil at Griffith University, before a change in circumstances caused a necessary break. Soon after however, I became involved in the rapier program within the Society for Creative Anachronism (SCA), an international historical research and recreation group that combined my love of history and swords in a single hobby.

Over the next five years I fought in various fencing competitions within the SCA, wining various championships. I started researching and teaching the art of rapier combat and joined the one of the Guilds of Fence (within the SCA). During that period I played my Prize (levelling system) for Provost in 2001 (think of a brown belt, or assistant instructor, in martial arts).

My interest in Western Martial Arts was piqued during this period and has never diminished. In 2002, I completed Honours in History with a study of the social history of rapier combat. In 2003 I attained the highest rank attainable within the Guild of Fence in the SCA, that of Guild Master. In 2004 I was then awarded with the highest award possible for civilian combat within the SCA at that time, the Order of the White Scarf.

As the SCA has grown and developed, so has the level of research, skill and training within its fields of endeavour. Recognising the influence of the Fencing community across the globe in 2015 the SCA created a new higher level recognition called the Order of Defence. This new award is an international recognition of people considered Masters in period fencing within the SCA. Admittance to this order is by invitation and is a recognition of the highest level knowledge, practical skill and teaching. I was admitted to this Order in 2017.

Since 2009, I had been involved in the planning and creation of a Brisbane-based swordplay convention run by the Australian College of Arms. In 2014 when it was taken over by the School of Historical Defense Arts (SHDA) and then other groups, I formed the SHDA in 2013 in order to further my studies of Western Martial Arts and to have a larger platform to share this knowledge to interested individuals with the same passion. I retired from the SHDA in 2019.

I have previously published a book, *On-Blogged: A Fencer's Ramblings*, published by Sword and Book Enterprises, based on articles from a fencing blog which I have been writing since May 2010.

Notes

Notes

Notes

Notes

www.ingramcontent.com/pod-product-compliance
Lightning Source LLC
Chambersburg PA
CBHW081419300426
44110CB00016BA/2325